George Bullard
HMB
1984

W9-CCX-901

The City,
A Dictionary of
Quotable Thought
on Cities and Urban Life

The City,
A Dictionary of
Quotable Thought
on Cities and Urban Life

James A. Clapp

Published in the United States by the Center for Urban Policy Research, Rutgers University,
New Brunswick, New Jersey 08903.
Manufactured in the United States of America.

Library of Congress Cataloging in Publication Data

Clapp, James A.
   The city, a dictionary of quotable thought on cities and urban life.

   Includes index.

   1. Cities and towns—Quotations, maxims, etc.—Dictionaries. I. Rutgers University.
Center for Urban Policy Research. II. Title.
HT111.C576   1984   307.7′64   83-19006
ISBN 0-88285-095-4

For Laura and Lisa, city-born, city-bred, and city-bound.

CONTENTS

Publisher's Note

There are few new urban warts—or new encomiums under the sun—as Professor Clapp has discovered—and as the reader will observe. Whether in praise or despair they all have precedent—and all provide insight into our own age. It is a privilege, therefore, to present Professor Clapp's splendid collection on the city.

We were fortunate in being able to employ Ms. René Kammeyer to provide the accompanying illustrations and jacket design. Edward Duensing, Librarian at the Center for Urban Policy Research, served as project coordinator and struggled manfully with the problems of provenance and communications across the continent. Last, but far from least, we had the services of an extremely skillful and conscientious typesetter in the person of Lee Quinn of Lee D. Quinn, Typography.

The range of reference and source is very wide. Despite all of our efforts there are many attributions, and indeed varying formats of expression which are open to question. We look forward to hearing from our readers and incorporating their suggestions into subsequent editions.

George Sternlieb

PREFACE

This dictionary of quotable thought on cities and urban life, containing epigrams, epithets, verses, proverbs, scriptural references, witticisms, lyrics, literary references, historical observations, etc. on cities (specific and general) and urban life from antiquity to the present day, is designed for use by writers on, and students and scholars of, cities and urbanism. Quotations are drawn from the written and spoken words of over a thousand writers, speakers, poets, songwriters, politicians, philosophers, scientists, religious leaders, historians, social scientists, humorists, architects, journalists, travellers and others; some famous, others less so.

The choice exercised in the selection of quotations in this book is, needless to say, subjective. What may be a memorable or significant statement to one person may not be to another. Some security has been obtained by checking with several collections of quotations, such as *Bartlett's* and the *Oxford Dictionary of Quotations*, for both guidance and source material; but the vast majority of selections in this book have been obtained from reading the voluminous literature of cities and urban life over my several years as a student and professor of, and writer on, urban affairs and city planning.

In general, I have applied three areas of focus: first, a concentration upon statements on cities and urban life in general, such as definitions, descriptive statements, and comparisons and contrasts with, say, country life or different historical periods. Second, for quotations on specific cities, particularly those of greatness and historical significance, I have surveyed numerous books and other sources on or about cities, such as New York, Paris, Rome, London and many other major cities throughout the world. Third, I have worked from an extensive list of famous writers, scientists, political figures, artists and others, whose works I have consulted to determine what, if anything, they have to say about cities and city life, in general or of specific cities. Beyond this, it should be noted, I have extensively surveyed influential and rich sources, such as the Bible and the works of Shakespeare.

While the key word for the vast majority of quotations in this book is "the city" or "cities," a variety of synonymous terms which denote the city also appear and are indexed where appropriate. Thus, terms, such as "town," "village," "metropolis," "megalopolis," "conurbation," "urban area," "urban place," "metropolitan areas" and others, are frequently employed interchangeably by authors with the term, "city," to convey large or small size, or other characteristics of urban settlements. Less common terms, such as "technopolis," "ecumenopolis," "cosmopolis," "world city," and "necropolis" have also been indexed. In addition, since this collection treats quotations on the characteristics of the city and urban life, key words, such as "urban," "urban process," "urbanization," etc., are also indexed. With reference to quotes of greater specificity, topics, such as "urban politics," "urban economics," "suburbs and suburbia," "slums," "ghettos," "planning," "transportation," etc., have been included.

Generally, I have tried to select citations which I regard as insightful, cogent, belletristic, clever, humorous, witty, and otherwise unusual and/or interesting.

This dictionary has been prepared with a variety of users in mind. The primary users will probably be "urbanists"—students and professors of urban studies, city planning, urban history, urban sociology, urban economics, urban geography, architects and urban designers, and historians. It is anticipated that this book will be most useful in the preparation of general research on cities and urban life, research on specific cities, and for documentation and epigrammatic citations. It should be useful to the thousands of mayors, councilmen, legislators and other public officials who prepare a vast number of papers and public addresses each week on specific cities, urban problems and related subjects. I also had in mind journalists (both print and electronic media) and feature writers and correspondents for the growing number of "city" magazines, as well as travel writers, authors of guide books, and documentary script writers who might find such a reference source useful. A large number of books, articles, speeches and programs begin with and include definitions of the city and related terms, literary references, and other quotations from famous works and writers about specific cities and urban life in general. Thus, the triple indexing system of this work allows a writer or researcher to apply to a specific author (e.g., Twain, Emerson, Spengler, etc.) or to a specific topic ("pollution," "the city versus the country," "suburbia," etc.) or to a specific city (New York, Paris, Tokyo, Lima, etc.).

The American writer and editor, Clifton Fadiman, once remarked "writing about American cities is a little like writing a biography of Chester A. Arthur. It can be done, but is it worth it?" A large number of writers would seem to think it is worth it, as much has been written about American cities and cities in general, much of it by writers of renown, and much more has been written about cities than about Chester A. Arthur. If so many men and women of letters have been inspired by cities and urban life to choose them as the subjects of their poems, novels, plays, essays, and witticisms, it can be hoped that this collection of their words will inspire, enlighten and entertain its readers.

Over the several years this book has been in preparation, I have been blessed by the assistance of several people. A number of friends, students and colleagues were kind enough to write down citations and quotes which they came across in their readings. The most welcome help came from those who typed the thousands of index cards on which the quotations were recorded. Without the help of Shauna Stokes, Lisa Clapp, Eunice Farris and, especially, Merrie Appleman, who served as typist and research assistant, this project would still be little more than an idea. George Sternlieb and Ed Duensing of the Center for Urban Policy Research also provided valuable insights on the layout of the book. As in all my endeavors, the encouragement and patience of my wife, Patricia, were of inestimable support in the completion of this project.

J.A.C. 1983

INTRODUCTION

THE CITY AND URBAN LIFE: A QUOTATIONAL PERSPECTIVE

Writing reputedly began in the ancient cities of the Mesopotamian River Valley some nine millenia ago, and it has been speculated that the first purpose of this specifically human activity was record-keeping, perhaps to chronicle the periodic flooding of the rivers that naturally irrigated the land or to maintain records of supplies in city granaries. Whatever the original purposes of writing may have been, literate people soon turned to setting down their opinions about cities themselves, and the features of life within them. They have been doing so ever since.

In the broad sweep of commentary on cities and urban life, the city has been characterized in virtually every conceivable way: It has been loved and loathed, praised and scorned, called the home of the gods and the spawning place of evil spirits, seen as ennobling and demeaning, regarded as the place or occasion of freedom and enslavement, called beautiful and ugly, created in some a sense of fear, in others security, considered both natural and unnatural to human existence and purpose, and posed as humankind's greatest invention and expression of its highest purposes, and the "zoo" in which humankind has entrapped itself and which will ultimately bring on the extinction of the species.

The purposes of this essay are not to treat these antinomies in any specific way. Rather, the immediate intent is to orient the reader to a limited selection of broad categories around which some of the quotations in the main body of this work coalesce. In so doing, I will, of course, draw heavily and liberally upon the written and spoken words of those more eloquent.

*   *   *

"What is a city but the people?" Shakespeare wrote in *Coriolanus*. It's an economical, yet profound, definition, so far as it goes; but like most verbal equations, it can break down. What is a nation—any social unit, for that matter—but the people? Certainly the people, but such a reduction then affords little basis upon which to make distinctions among different forms of social organization.

The city both invites and resists definition. There is an abundance of definitions and descriptions of the city, many with common attributes, but many markedly different, in terms of the essences, fundamentals and characteristics which they stress. For Jean-Jacques Rousseau, " . . . citizens make the city." The distinction from Shakespeare's "people" appears minor; but while all citizens are people, not all people are citizens. Rousseau was interested in political theory and it is that interest, bias or perspective that influences his view of the city.

Others have emphasized the "people." Nicias, in his speech to his army after his defeat by the Syracusians in 413 B.C., claimed "It is men who make a city, not walls or ships without crews," a point of view which has also been attributable to Thucydides. Modifying slightly, Thomas Fuller said " 'Tis the men, not the houses, that make the city." Alcaeus, speaking in the 5th Century B.C., added another distinction: "Not houses finely roofed, nay nor canals and dockyards, make the city, but men able to use their opportunity." One might wonder whether "men" instead of

*   *   *

Cowper is generally credited with the statement "God made the country and man made the town," although it is probably of Roman origin. It is an apt summary of an attitude, which might be classified as "anti-urban" and which reaches back into antiquity. St. Augustine, in his *City of God*, portrayed the genesis of the "city of man" (earthly cities) as opposed to the "city of God" (heaven) and stressed that " . . . the city of man was founded by a fratricide who was moved by envy to kill his brother . . .". Augustine's theme has since been replayed in a variety of maledictions against urbanism, such as J.H. Ingraham's "Adam and Eve were created and placed in a garden. Cities are the results of the fall."

Religious sentiments may be the strongest current in the voluminous record of anti-urban sentiment, but cities and urban life have been faulted from a number of directions. While urbanites certainly have no monopoly on bellicosity—in fact, several Roman writers argued that the most reliable soldiers came from farms and rural areas—cities have often been put down for their relationship to warfare. Aristotle only alluded to this phenomenon when he coined the adage "Men come together in cities for security; only stay together for the good life." Elizabeth Peabody placed a different stress on the matter: "What absurdity can be imagined greater than the institution of great cities. Cities originated not in love but in war. It was war that drove men together in multitudes and compelled them to stand so close and build walls around them." Warfare on or between cities may, in some measure, have resulted from the wealth which they generated or contained. Consider the gloating of King Assurbanipal of Assyria over an urban prize in 663 B.C.:

> I conquered the whole city . . . Silver, gold, precious stones, all the treasures of the palace, colourful robes, linen, marvelous horses, male and female slaves, two large obelisks of shining bronze, even the gates of the temple I carried away and brought to Assyria. A tremendous booty of immeasurable value did I take with me.

The historical position of cities as engines of economic, political and military power does not require any repetition here. Historically, imperial power has always resided in cities, and conquest and subjugation of any one power by another have necessitated the *coup de grace* of urban annihilation. The power of cities and urbanized nations is no less demonstrable today than in earlier times, and part of the misgivings that urban man may have about cities may well be an anxiety derived from the enormity of urban power. Otto von Bismarck may well have been referring to such a concern when he declared to the Prussian Lower House, in 1852, "Great cities must be obliterated from the earth."

Although it appears that the weight of opinion falls to those who find cities at fault for their breaching of relationships with dieties, their warmongering, their offenses against nature and the countryside, and other crimes, cities do not lack for those who find much to praise. The Roman orator, Cicero, once declared:

> The city, the City! Devote yourself to her and live in her incomparable light. As a young man I came to a conclusion from which I have never since wa-

vered. Absenting oneself in any circumstance spells eclipse and discredit for any of us who have the capacity to add to Rome's glory by our labours.

Cicero's particular fondness was for Rome, however; he once wrote from Athens, "I cannot describe how ardently I long for town. How hard I find it to bear the stupidity of life here." In contrast to Augustine and other founding fathers of his church, Thomas Aquinas claimed "the city is, in fact, the most important thing constituted by human reason."

Like other categories of commentary on cities and urban life, encomiums on cities stress a variety of perspectives. Not uncommon is the position of William Robson:

> There is much to love and to admire in the great city. It is the home of the highest achievements of man in art, literature and science: the source from which the forces of freedom and emancipation have sprung. It is the place where the spirit of humanism and of democracy have grown and flourished, where man's quest for knowledge and justice has been pursued most constantly, and truth revealed most faithfully and fearlessly.

Others have seen fit to portray the city's vitality and energy, as exemplified by Theodore Von Laue:

> There is no greater sight in all humanity than men's social labor throbbing in the life of a great metropolis, say New York or London or any of the sprawling metropoles of the West or even their counterparts throughout the world. At dawn the human beehive, laid out flat over plains and hills, spanning rivers and estuaries as far as the eye can see (on a rare clear day), stirs to send its millions to work.

For some, the very crowdedness and what Milton called "the busy hum of men" which the city's detractors often find oppressive are turned to virtues, as in the lines of Lucy Larcom:

> Farewell! thou busy city,
>   Amid whose changing throng
> I've passed a pleasant sojourn,
>   Though wearisome and long.
> My soul is sad at leaving
>   The dear ones, not a few,
> I've met within thy mazes,
>   So noble and so true.

The anonymity which others have seen as a "lonely crowd" can, for some, become one of the city's most compelling and desired attributes. "The experience of strolling by one's self through the vast multitudes of a strange city is one of the most wonderful in life. I suppose there is nothing like it this side of heaven" was Gamaliel Bradford's point of view on the matter.

In response to those who have portrayed cities as engines of war and enemies of nature, we have the rhetorical answer of Charles Kingsley in the mid-nineteenth century:

> Yes—were I asked to sum up in one sentence the good of great cities, I would point first to Bristol, and then to the United States, and say, That is what great cities can do. By concentrating in one place, and upon one subject, men, genius, information, and wealth, they can conquer new-found lands by arts instead of arms: they can beget new nations; and replenish and subdue the earth from pole to pole . . .

For Kingsley, it was not the city itself to which is owed praise or blame, but the moral state of its inhabitants.

Cities abound with symbolism; their very names are often instantly evocative of illustrious times, historical events, good and evil, and human physical forms and personality attributes. As John Burchard litanized the range of semiotic attributes of cities:

> There are symbols of sin, at the high level of Babylon, Tyre, Sidon, Sodom, Gomorrah, or the low level of Las Vegas. There are symbols of Power such as Rome, Thebes, Berlin, Moscow. There are symbols of Holiness or Faith: Banaras, Jerusalem, Mecca, Lourdes. There are symbols of Pleasure: Paris, Vienna; of Decadence: Byzantium. There are symbols of products: Damascus, Toledo, Sheffield, Milwaukee, Hollywood. There are symbolic cities that merely suggest the exotic and the faraway: Samarkand or Timbuktu. There are cities that bear the cross of the symbolic association with one bad man or one unhappy event: Chicago, Ferrara, Dallas. There are cities with heavy symbolic significance because of a single such repeated reference: Samarra of the appointments. Symbolism pours from cities which never existed at all: Atlantis, Xanadu, The City of Brass, Anaurot, The City of Dis.

Cities, in general, have been suggestive of or likened to trees, bacteria, power stations, machines, the Bible and a host of other metaphorical referents. It is, however, at the level of the particular that cities, as Burchard illustrates, have acquired "personality." Here we find the most common images, associations, metaphors and symbols expressed in terms of human qualities and traits, both physical and mental. Mark Twain once observed that "We take stock of a city like we take stock of a man. The clothes and appearance are the externals by which we judge. We next take stock of the mind, the intellect . . . the sum of both is the man or the city."

It is noteworthy that Twain employed the term, "man," (although gender may not have been essential to his point) since, if there appears to be an overreaching master symbol for cities, it is feminine. The Greek "metropolis" (metro = uterus) and the Latin "urbs," for example, are, in denotation or gender, feminine terms (although, in the Slavic and old Germanic languages, the word, "city," is masculine in gender). C.G. Jung and Lewis Mumford view the city as a maternal symbol. Mumford employs the metaphor of the "container," noting that the woman, who carries her children inside herself, is not only an analogue for the city but, also, probably developed the first "container" crafts of pottery and basketry which were requisites for the storage and preservation of the surplus food supplies of neolithic villages. This feminine linquistic referent has carried forward in such wide ranging respects as the mythical foundation of Rome (the suckling of Romulus and Remus by a "she-wolf") to the commonplace as well as poetic reference to specific cities in feminine terms.

To be sure, there are cities which appear to resist any association with the feminine gender. Chicago, for example, seems to suggest almost exclusively male characteristics. Carl Sandburg's powerful evocation of the city's brawny masculinity may well have set the symbolic tone for subsequent writers:

> Hog Butcher for the World,
> Tool Maker, Stacker of Wheat,
> Player with Railroads and the Nation's
>   Freight Handler;
> Stormy, husky, brawling,
> City of the Big Shoulders.

Studs Terkel, perhaps that city's best known journalist and celebrant, pursues a similar line: "To some, Chicago with its lack of sophistication and its muscularity is comical, archaic in this cool era, somewhat like an old punch-drunk fighter, swinging wild roundhouse wallops to the laughter of the wisenheimers at the ringside. But when it connects—oh, baby!"

Masculine associations need not be restricted to youthful, brawling toilers in the city's abattoirs. Albert Osborne's characterization of the quaint Flemish city of Bruges employs a senescent masculinity befitting a city which lives today much upon its memories. Bruges, he writes:

> Is an easy city to get acquainted with. Its personality is not complex, awakening many and different emotions. It expresses itself simply and frankly. It is like a beautiful person who is now old and withdrawn from the activities of life, though still full of kindly interest in the world about him—a ruddy-faced old man, who wears a ready smile, and is full of wisdom and peace, whose presence is a benediction; for at Bruges you are happy and at rest.

But most cities, it seems, like ships, are characterized in feminine terms. "The city," John Lancaster Spalding writes, "is the paradise of adventurers and speculators, and there is the great matrimonial exchange which calls into play all the fine and subtle powers of a woman." The emperor, Claudian, referred to Rome as the "Mother of arms and of law...". The maternal reference has also been applied to other cities. Joseph Wechsberg writes: "Prague is called *Praha* in Czech, after *Prah*, 'the threshold.' The 'a' at the end of the word denotes a woman's name: Prague is a feminine city. Not a glamorous young woman, like Paris, but *maticka* (little mother) to her troubadours."

Other cities are characterized as young maidens. Vicuna MacKenna paints Lima as a

> Nymph of idleness, asleep on the banks of the flowering Rimac, softly resting on the very spot that its masters first designated for it, surrounded by green fields, crowned with rustic diadems, lifting its voluptuous forehead to the

caresses of a cloudless sky, she whose climate consists of light breezes without rainfall and a light that wears the impress of an eternal calm.

In the view of at least one observer, a city, in the course of its history, may undergo
a change of descriptive gender. Herbert Sass wrote that "Charleston today has so
much feminine grace and charm that the masculine power and drive which preceded
and created this beauty are overlooked."

If Chicago brings forth an exclusive masculine imagery, Paris appears to produce
the opposite result. "Paris is a beautiful woman," writes Irwin Shaw, "but so surpassingly so, so vital and self-renewing, that nothing—not the passage of years, not
drink or drugs, not bad investments or unworthy loves, not neglect or debauchery—
can ruin her." More particularly, she is, to some, a seductress. "Paris . . . takes hold of
you, grabs you by the balls, you might say, like some lovesick bitch who'd rather die
than let you out of her hands," was Henry Miller's relationship with her. Thomas
Noland found the city an unfaithful lover: "Paris is a whore—she is loved by all and
loves no one." And Robert McAlman " . . . knew all too well that Paris is a bitch and
that one shouldn't become infatuated with bitches; particularly when they have wit,
imagination, experience and tradition." Richard Le Gallienne found her to be " . . .
half Angel, half Grisette, / I would that I were with thee yet." London, he claimed,
" . . . waits me like a wife, / . . . the love of my whole life." By way of contrast, there is
Henry James' impression of London:

> London is so clumsy and so brutal, and has gathered together so many of the
> darkest sides of life, that it is almost ridiculous to talk of her as a lover talks of
> his mistress, and almost frivolous to appear to ignore her disfigurement and
> cruelties. She is like a mighty ogress who devours human flesh; but to me it is
> a mitigating circumstance that the ogress herself is not human.

Whether they are experienced and portrayed as madonnas, whores, mistresses or
ogresses, even the great ladies of urbanism may be seen as subject to the scourges
and infirmities which afflict their inhabitants. In contrast to the typical characterization of New York as the vibrant, powerful, dominant and energetic metropolis—
Christopher Morley called it "The Nation's great thyroid gland"—to John Lardner,
she " . . . moves in the forefront of today's great trend of great cities toward neurosis.
She is confused, self-pitying, helpless and dependent!"

*   *   *

Cities, in general and specific, have been the source of numerous proverbs, adages,
and witticisms. Some proverbs are relatively well-known and frequently cited; most
are of unknown authorship. "Rome was not built in a day" has come to refer to endeavors beyond city-building itself; "Stadt luft macht frei" (City air makes man
free), a medieval proverb referring to the right of a serf to become a freeman after a
year and a day in a city, has lost its meaning in the modern era, particularly to those
who today regard the city itself as a "prison" or a "human zoo." The old testament
proverb, "Except the Lord keep the city, the watchman waketh but in vain" was
adopted by the city of Edinburgh as its motto.

Some proverbs express civic pride and chauvinism, for example the Hebrew boast,

"Ten measures of beauty came into the world; Jerusalem received nine measures, and the rest of the world one"; or "He who has not seen Seville has seen nothing." Others are mildly derisive—"He who has never been to Odessa has never seen dust." Rome, a city that has spawned more than its share of satirists, has been a rich source of pejorative sayings. A medieval Latin proverb claims "the nearer to Rome, the worse the Christian"; another, "He who goes to Rome returns a beast." Still other proverbs offer insights into cities in general. An Estonian proverb observes "the town is new every day"; a Roman adage claims "A strong city can be built with brother helping brother." As with the words "city gates stand open to the bad as well as the good," many of these observations have a contemporary relevance. Such utterances become proverbs if they pass the test of time. The staying power of "the city of brotherly shove" (New York), and "Detroit with grapefruits" (Los Angeles) is yet to be determined.

Many writers have borrowed the prestige or imagery of one city to characterize another. Bangkok, for example, has been called the Paris of the Orient; Beirut, the Paris of the Mediterranean; Prague, the "Rome of the North". Leningrad and Amsterdam are both known as "the Venice of the North" (sometimes pridefully reversed to Venice as the Leningrad or Amsterdam of the South). Most often such comparisons or associations are positive, frequently with the intent of trading on the prestige, reputation or visual imagery of a more renowned city. Less often, but also significantly, writers and speakers evoke negative imagery, describing New York, London, Paris, or Berlin as a "modern Babylon" or some other city of poor repute.

With books, newspapers, TV and movies so full of commentary on their problems, cities would seem, of human institutions, to rank low as a source of humor. But, as with other human foibles and problems, there are those who have found jocularity as a means of coping or striking back at crime, pollution, slums and other urban problems. Like humor in general, witty commentary on the city ranges widely, from the bitterly satirical to good-natured fun-poking. And, as with humor in general, there is often an underlying veracity, a pricking of absurdities, vanities, peculiarities and faults. Mark Twain once stated that "the coldest winter [he] ever spent was a Summer in San Francisco." Twain's economical phrase-making could often capture salient characteristics of individual cities: "In Boston they ask, How much does he know. In New York, How much is he worth? In Philadelphia, Who were his parents?"

Another dimension of urban humor derives from rivalries between small towns and big cities. Joey Adams wrote a number of one-liners about "hick towns," among them his definition of such places as "Where everybody knows whose check is good and whose wife isn't." From the other side we have the folksy satire of Will Rogers:

> Hardly a day goes by, you know, that some innocent bystander ain't shot in New York City. All you got to do is be innocent and stand by and they're gonna shoot you. The other day, there was four people shot in one day—four innocent people—in New York City. Amazing. It's kind of hard to *find* four innocent people in New York. That's why a policeman don't have to aim. He just shoots anywhere. Whoever he hits, that's the right one.

Suburbs also provide an ample target for both sides; anonymous wags have defined suburbia as "A place where the crab grass grows greenest," and "A womb with a view."

At least one quip about the city has proved not only to have staying power but has spun-off others. One of Gertrude Stein's many memorable phrases is not about Paris, with which she is generally associated, but her native city of Oakland. She much preferred the City of Lights because "the trouble with Oakland," as she saw it, " . . . is there is no there there." The satirical phrase invited a parody by San Francisco newspaper columnist Herb Caen, "The trouble with Oakland is that when you get there it's there!" Oaklanders have been vexed by these put-downs for years, finally prompting the retort among the city's prouder residents that "there is a *here* here."

Some quips have a bitter, deprecating, tone to them. Mayor Kenneth Gibson of Newark, New Jersey, a city frequently cited as an example of the difficulties of America's older cities, is reported to have said, "Wherever the central cities are going, Newark is going to get there first." There was also an occasion when impressionist-comedian Rich Little quipped: "Mr. President, how do you keep the Russians from invading Poland? . . . Change its name to Cleveland." The city demanded, and received, an apology.

*   *   *

"The perfect place for a writer is in the hideous roar of a city, with men making a new road under his window in competition with a barrel organ, and on the mat a man waiting for the rent." Henry Vollum Morton was expressing the attitude of the writer who finds the city, the dramas in its history and the biographies of its residents as a rich mine of inspiration. Henry Miller declared that "One needs no artificial stimulation, in Paris, to write, the atmosphere is charged with creation."

This attitude ought not to be confused with the personal experience of writers about cities, in general, or specific cities, which appears to reflect the ambivalence towards them characteristic of people, in general.

The Roman poet, Horace, once penned that "The chorus of writers, one and entire / Detests the town and yearns for the sacred grove." He may have been taking a cue from the satirist, Juvenal, who, in regretting the swelling of Rome by immigrants from its empire, moaned:

> Every crime is here, and every lust, as they have been
> Since the day, long since, when Roman poverty perished.
> Over our seven hills, from that day on, they came pouring,
> The rabble and rout of the West, Sybaris, Rhodes, Miletus,
> Yes, and Tarentum too, garlanded, drunken, shameless.

All the bustle and social variation of cities may have their allure and inspirational value, although some may prefer more placid environments to ply their craft. Henrik Ibsen, for example, complained: "To think that I should live cooped up in a great city, just to be pestered and plagued by people!" Still, many writers sought out cities, more often those with illustrious pasts and vibrant presents—Hemingway, Miller, Pound and Stein to Paris; Twain, Henry James and Crane to London; Byron, Shelley and Mann to Venice—as places to write in or about, or in which to consort with kindred artists. Chaim Potok writes:

> Different cities boil within each of us. There is so much we hate—the dirt, the

poverty, the prejudice; there is so much we love—the one or two friendships that somehow crossed boundaries, the libraries where we joined ourselves to the dreams of others, the places where we composed dreams of our own, the museums where we learned how to defeat time, certain streets, alleys stair-cases, apartment-house roofs, certain radio stations we would listen to deep into the night, certain newspapers we read as if they were a testament to the ages. We remember the terrors and joys of our early urban wanderings. We write, and continue the journey.

But though writers may write from their memories of cities, some cities may fail to memorialize their literary luminaries. As Alfred Kazin, who has written extensively about his native city, put it:

> No New York streets are named after Herman Melville, Henry James, Walt Whitman, or Edith Wharton. New York does not remember its own: it barely remembers Poe in Fordham, Mark Twain on lower Fifth Avenue, William Dean Howells on West Fifty-seventh Street, Stephen Crane in Chelsea, Dreiser and O'Neill in Washington Square, Willa Cather on Bank Street, Thomas Wolfe and Marianne Moore in far-off Brooklyn, Hart Crane on Co-lumbia Heights, Allen Tate in the Village, Cummings in Patchin Place, Auden in St. Mark's Place, Lorca at Columbia. It will not remember Ellison and Bellow on Riverside Drive, Mailer in Columbia Heights, Capote in the U.N. Plaza, Singer on West Eighty-sixth Street any more than it remembers hav-ing given shelter to European exiles from Tom Paine to John Butler Yeats, Gorky to Nabokov.

Still, we find cities haunted by the writers whose works and lives immortalize them. Of London, John Updike writes:

> The city overwhelmed our expectation. The Kiplingesque grandeur of Waterloo Station, the Eliotic despondency of the brick row in Chelsea ... the Dickensian nightmare of the fog and sweating pavement and besmirched cornices ... We wheeled past mansions by Galsworthy and parks by A.A. Milne; we glimpsed a cobbled eighteenth century alley, complete with hanging tavern boards, where Dr. Johnson might have reeled and gasped the night he laughed so hard ...

While much more could be said of the writer's encounter with cities, it might, nevertheless, come to underscore Ralph Waldo Emerson's adage "If a man loves the city so will his writings love the city ..."

Quotations
on City
and Urban Life

A

ABBOTT, Lyman (1835-1922)

A1 — What shall we do with our great cities? What will our great cities do with us? These are the two problems which confront every thoughtful American. For the question involved in these two questions does not concern the city alone. The whole country is affected if, indeed, its character and history are not determined, by the condition of its great cities....

The city is not all bad nor all good. It is humanity compressed, the best and the worst combined, in a strangely composite community. *Darkness and Daylight*

ABOUREZK, James (1931-) .

A2 — In a free society — and ours is relatively free — the normal assumption would be that people live in metropolitan areas because they want to. But the public-opinion polls do not support that assumption.... If [people] want higher wages and decent social services, they have to take the urban crush, the smog, the ugliness and the depersonalization of life that is characteristic of city life. *Washington Post, April 15, 1975*

ABRAMS, Charles (1902-1970)

A3 — The American attitude toward cities contrasts sharply with attitudes in the Old World. For thousands of years, man had built cities and idealized them. Aristotle could find the common life for the noble end only in Athens, and Socrates would never leave it for the trees. Voltaire could see the London of his time as the rival of ancient Athens. Europe's culture and progress continue to this day to be reflected in its Paris, Rome, Geneva, Amsterdam, and Vienna. Urbanity was always associated with urban life, while suburban and suburbanity were contemptuous slams at the inferior ways of the provinces. But the flight to suburbia in America has taken on the semblance of a flight from scourge. *The City is the Frontier*

A4 — A city has values as well as slums, excitement as well as conflict; it has a personality that has not yet been obliterated by its highways and gas stations; it has a spirit as well as a set of arteries and a voice that speaks the hopes as well as the disappointments of its people. *Ibid.*

A5 — The diseases of housing rival those in pathology. They include irritations over spatial, physical, and financial limitations. They are involved with neighborhood tensions, the shortcomings of neighborhood schools, transportation, and police protection; lack of proper playgrounds, parks, and open spaces; noise, smoke, smells, smog, drafts, dirt, insects, and vermin. The personal vexations of the housing problem are not only multiple and complex but they defy categorization. *Ibid.*

A6 — Every industrializing nation must go through a period of slum formation, and the United States is no exception. Every nation with a pride in its environment has been moved to renew its cities, and the United States faces the prospect for the first time in its history. *Ibid.*

A7 — The history of civilization from Memphis, Egypt, to Memphis, Tennessee, is recorded in the rise or demise of cities. It is the story of Rome and its million people in the first century reduced to a city of 17,000 in the fourteenth; of scourges and famines of Paris and the renaissance that made it the intellectual capital of Europe; of the heap of ruins that was London fifty years after the Roman evacuation, its rise under mercantilism, its desolation by war, and its resurgence to the London of today. *Ibid.*

A8 — If the city's chaos is part of its planlessness, its contrasts and variety still offer relief from the sameness of suburbia. . . . People still seek escape to the metropolises, crave contrast, look for occasional anonymity, and want to see more people without being seen. . . . If the nation was just one sprawling network of suburbias, it would be a bore. *Ibid.*

A9 — The main virtue of the American system has been that it has been able to adjust itself to political and economic change. But while it has taken the industrial revolution in stride, it has not yet coped with the urban revolution that came in its wake. Only when it has done so can it demonstrate that democracy can be as valid a faith, as sound a political system, and as practical a way of life in our new urban society as it was in the society that has passed. *Ibid.*

A10 — From earliest history, the city has been linked with man's freedoms — a refuge in the days of Cain and Joshua, the hub of a vigorous political life in Greece, the impetus to law in Rome. When man's mind roamed free in Utopian dreams, it was the city that was so often closest to his conception of heaven — the 'Celestial City,' the 'Heavenly City,' the 'New Jerusalem,' the 'Holy City,' and the 'City of God.' Moreover, it was the city of trade, commerce, and property that helped undermine serfdom and that ushered in other freedoms in the process. . . . For despite its changes and challenges, the city still contains the raw ingredients of freedom. . . . It is still the marketplace for goods and ideas, the locus of a contractual society, the mirror for emulation, the meeting place for diversities, the center of culture. *Man's Struggle for Shelter in an Urbanizing World*

A11 — The Ideal City, wherever it may exist, the New Deal City conditioned by experimentation and make-work, or the Ordeal City of the atomic age whose life span is set by the whim of men who control the atoms, must all be measured by the rates of depreciation assigned to them. Each

rate ultimately will be set by forces beyond the power of the planner or the philosopher. *Quoted in The Metropolis and Modern Life, E.M. Fisher, Ed.*

ADAMS, Abigail (1744-1818)

A12 — If I was agreeably disappointed in London, I am as much disappointed in Paris. It is the very dirtiest place I ever saw. There are some buildings and some squares, which are tolerable; but in general the streets are narrow, the shops, the houses, inelegant and dirty, the streets full of lumber and stone, with which they build. Boston cannot boast so elegant public buildings; but, in every other respect, it is as much superior in my eyes to Paris, as London is to Boston. . . . *Letter to Miss Lucy Cranch, September 5, 1784*

ADAMS, Francis (New York Police Commissioner)

A13 — Before this hot August Sunday is over one of us in this city will have been murdered. Another of us will have died as the result of criminal negligence. Twenty-seven of our people will have been feloniously assaulted. Three women will have been raped. One hundred and forty of our homes and businesses will have been burglarized. Forty of us will have had our cars stolen. Thirty-one of us will have been held up and robbed on the streets of this city. Sixty-nine grand larcenies will have taken place before this day is over. And there will have been fifteen other miscellaneous felonies — such as frauds, possession of dangerous weapons and sex offenses other than rape and the like. The property which will be stolen from New Yorkers on this day will amount to more than one hundred forty thousand dollars — enough to pay the salaries of twenty-eight policemen for a year. Even in the brief half hour in which I will talk to you, seventeen crimes will be committed in the city of New York — more than one every two minutes. This then is an average day in this city — far from quiet, far from peaceful. *News Report*

ADAMS, Franklin Pierce (1881-1960)

A14 — Then here's to the City of Boston / The town of the cries and the groans, /

Where the Cabots can't see the Kabotschniks / And the Lowells won't speak to the Cohns.

A15 — The rich man has his motor car, / His country and his town estate. / He smokes a fifty-cent cigar / And jeers at Fate. *The Rich Man*

ADAMS, Henry (1838-1918)

A16 — He did notice one peculiarity about it worth remembering. London was still London. A certain style dignified its grime; heavy, clumsy, arrogant, purse-proud, but not cheap; insular but large; barely tolerant of an outside world, and absolutely self-confident.

ADAMS, Joey (1911-   )

A17 — Better known as Lost Wages, Nevada. [of Las Vegas] *Joey Adams's Encyclopedia of Humor*

A18 — A place where there's nothing doing every minute. [hick towns] *Ibid.*

A19 — Where everybody knows whose check is good and whose wife isn't. [hick towns] *Ibid.*

A20 — Where people go to church to see who didn't. [hick towns] *Ibid.*

A21 — Where the odds are you won't get even. [of Las Vegas] *Ibid.*

A22 — Where they buy a newspaper to verify what they heard earlier on the telephone. [hick towns] *Ibid.*

ADDAMS, Jane (1860-1935)

A23 — A very little familiarity with the poor districts of any city is sufficient to show how primitive and frontier-like are the neighborly relations. There is the greatest willingness to lend or borrow anything, and each resident of a given tenement house knows the most intimate family affairs of all the others. The fact that the economic condition of all alike is on a most precarious level makes the ready outflow of sympathy and material assistance the most natural thing in the world. *Atlantic Monthly, April-June 1899*

A24 — The classical city promoted play with careful solicitude, building the theater and stadium as it built the market place and the temple . . . Only in the modern city have men concluded that it is no longer necessary for the municipality to provide for the insatiable desire for play. *The Spirit of Youth and the City Streets*

A25 — Never before in civilization have such numbers of young girls been suddenly released from the protection of the home and permitted to walk unattended upon city streets and to work under alien roofs; for the first time they are being prized more for their labor power than for their innocence, their tender beauty, their ephemeral gaiety. *Ibid.*

A26 — One of the most pathetic sights in the public dance halls of Chicago is the number of young men, obviously honest young fellows from the country, who stand about vainly hoping to make the acquaintance of some 'nice girl.' They look eagerly up and down the rows of girls, many of whom are drawn to the hall by the same keen desire for pleasure and social intercourse which the lonely young men themselves feel. *Ibid.*

A27 — In every neighborhood where poorer people live, because rents are supposed to be cheaper there, is an element which, although uncertain in the individual, in the aggregate can be counted upon. It is composed of people of former education and opportunity who have cherished ambitions and prospects, but who are caricatures of what they meant to be — 'hollow ghosts which blame the living men.' *Twenty Years at Hull House*

A28 — Internationalism engendered in the immigrant quarters of American cities might be recognized as an effective instrument in the cause of peace. *Ibid.*

A29 — Private beneficence is totally inadequate to deal with the vast numbers of the city's disinherited. *Ibid.*

A30 — A city is in many respects a great business corporation, but in other respects it is enlarged housekeeping . . . May we not say that city housekeeping has failed partly because women, the traditional housekeepers, have not been consulted as to

A54 — A place where people from Iowa mistake each other for movie stars. [of Hollywood]

A55 — The American arrives in Paris with a few French phrases he has culled from a conversational guide or picked up from a friend who owns a beret. He speaks the sort of French that is really understood by another American who also has just arrived in Paris. *Introduction to Paris After Dark, Art Buchwald*

ALLEN, Frederick Lewis (1890-1954)

A56 — In our modern civilization, the metropolis is an almost irresistible magnet. For generations there has been a continuing drift of men and women from the countryside to the cities, and especially to the biggest ones. For the metropolis is where, by and large, the big money, the big decisions, and the big reputations are made. It is the nucleus of power. *The Big Change in Suburbia*

ALLEN, Robert S. (1901-1981)

A57 — There is not a city in the country, large or small, where business is not the primary stultifying, corrupting, and anti-democratic influence. The worst-managed, bedraggled, and backward communities are those dominated by business interests. *Our Fair City*

A58 — Boston has a world-famed symphony orchestra, and one of the most venal and noisome city governments in the world. Philadelphia has a multi-million-dollar art museum, and tap water so nauseous it cannot be drunk. Miami has more than three hundred hotels and superb Biscayne Boulevard, and, also, gambler rule and foul and barbarous Negro slums. Birmingham has inexhaustible iron resources, and doesn't own its own soul. It is ruled by absentee overlords residing in other states more than one thousand miles distant.

ALLEN, Woody (1935-   )

A59 — I don't want to live in a city where the only cultural advantage is you can make a right turn on a red light. [of Los Angeles] *Annie Hall*

ALLIUEVA, Svetlana

A60 — Moscow, breathing fire like a human volcano with its smoldering lava of passion, ambition and politics, its hurly-burly of meetings and entertainment . . . Moscow seethes and bubbles and gasps for air. It's always thirsting for something new, the newest events, the latest sensation. Everyone wants to be the first to know. It's the rhythm of life today.

AMBROSE, (Saint)

A61 — If you are at Rome live in the Roman style; if you are elsewhere live as they live elsewhere. *Quoted in Ductor Dubitantium, Jeremy Taylor*

AMICIS, Edmondo de (1846-1908)

A62 — Behold Constantinople! sublime, superb / Constantinople, glory to creation and man! / I had never dreamed of such beauty! /

ANDERSON, Edgar

A63 — Nature watching is quite as easy in the city as in the country; all one has to do is accept Man as a part of Nature. *Landscape*

ANDERSON, Sherwood (1876-1941)

A64 — Do you remember when you, now for so long a city man, your hair graying, were a small town boy and what the railroad meant to you? Did you dream of some day being a railroad engineer? Now the new streamline trains go whirling through the towns at eighty, ninety, a hundred miles an hour. There is the soft purr of a mail plane far overhead, cars from many states go dashing through.

All over America, in the towns, we speak the English language but the stream of English blood in us grows thinner and thinner. It has been growing thinner ever since the Revolutionary War. *Home Town*

A65 — The life in the town is a test of man's ability to adjust himself. It tells the story of his skill in living with others, his ability to go out to others and to let others be a part of his own life. You have to go on living with your neighbors. If they are sometimes queer it may be that they also think of you as queer. Without quite knowing it, you may yourself be one of the 'characters of your town.' *Ibid.*

A66 — I think you know that when an American stays away from New York too long something happens to him. Perhaps he becomes a little provincial, a little dead and afraid. *Letters of Sherwood Anderson*

A67 — There is such a lack of conversational opportunities here. It is the real limitation to country town life. *Ibid.*

ANDERSON, William

A68 — Christian literature contains many references to the city as embodying some of the highest ideals of the good life for men. We read of the city foursquare, the Heavenly City, and the City of God. Contributions to the Old Testament reveal an even earlier interest in the construction and adornment of cities. So do the monuments and records of various ancient civilizations. Greek writers of the golden age extolled the city-state as the highest form of political community, and as the sign and guaranty of the best in civilization. *Political Influences of the Metropolis*

ANONYMOUS

A69 — Alone with nature — will not ye / Who all her beauties daily see, / Beneath you native, 'house-hold tree,' / Enjoy them for the roving stranger! / I can not relish half her sweets / Till taught by bustling, crowded streets, / To sigh for nature's calm retreats, / Then task them for the city-ranger. / *The Operatives Magazine, June 1841*

A70 — America is not yet dominated by its great cities. Control of its destinies still remains in the smaller communities and rural regions, with their traditional conservatism and solid virtues . . . . Main street is still the principal thoroughfare of the nation.

A71 — Amsterdam was built on herring bones.

A72 — Any city gets what it admires, will pay for, and, ultimately, deserves: Even when we had Penn Station, we couldn't afford to keep it clean. We want and deserve

tin-can architecture in a tin-horn culture. And we will probably be judged not by the monuments we build but by those we have destroyed. *The New York Times, October 30, 1963*

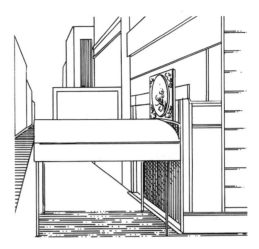

A73 — At Rome, Paris, and Venice, no one wonders at anything. *(Medieval proverb)*

A74 — Augustus at Rome was for building renowned / And of marble he left what brick he had found; / But is not our Nash, too, a very great master, / He finds us all brick and leaves us all plaster. [of London]

A75 — But when his friends did understand / His fond and foolish mind, / They sent him up to fair London, / An apprentice for to bind. *The Bailiff's Daughter of Islington*

A76 — Chicago . . . . a city of everlasting pine, shingles, shams, veneers, stucco and putty. *Chicago Tribune, 1875*

A77 — Chicago, for its size, is more given to suburbs than any other city in the world. In fact, it is doubtful if any city, of any size, can boast of an equal number of suburban appendages. *Sunday Times (Chicago), May 4, 1873*

A78 — Child-centered communities where everyone is an amateur psychologist or sociologist. [of suburbia]

A79 — City attractions and fashionable displays feed the fancy. But, admitting that a city life does afford peculiar gratification which appears congenial to man in his present condition, from the fact that so many are striving to make their destiny there; yet that is not to be relied upon as sufficient proof of its superiority, for almost every pernicious vice or snare allure their unwary victims into a vortex of ruin. *The Prairie Farmer, December 1950*

A80 — A city cannot be both great and regimented. Blessed with culture, history and size, Moscow, Shanghai and Peking ought to be great cities, but they are not. They all lack the most important element: spontaneity of free human exchange. Without that, a city is as sterile as Aristophanes' Nephelococcygia, which was to be suspended between heaven and earth — and ruled by the birds. *Time, November 14, 1969*

A81 — City gates stand open to the bad as well as the good. *(proverb)*

A82 — The city is the flower of civilization. It gives to men the means to make their lives expressive. It offers a field of battle, and it could be made a livable place if its sons would stay and fight for it, instead of running away. *Times and Tendencies, Agnes Repplier*

A83 — The city of brotherly shove. [of New York City]

A84 — A crazy-quilt of discontinuities. [of suburbia]

A85 — Detroit with grapefruits. [of Los Angeles]

A86 — Do not dwell in a city where a horse does not neigh nor a dog bark. . . . If we would be safe from danger, we must not dwell in a city where there is neither horse against an enemy, nor dogs against thieves. *(Hebrew proverb)*

A87 — Do not dwell in a city whose governor is a physician. *(Hebrew proverb)*

A88 — Due to the large quantity of business transacted by the city council, we most respectfully request that anyone wishing to insult the council please limit himself to 15 minutes or to 15 insults, whichever is shorter. *(Sign in office of Mayor Travis LaRue, Austin, Texas)*

A89 — Edmonton is as big as Chicago, but it isn't all built up yet.

A90 — The emperor is a lovely man / His home is in Berlin. / And if 'twere not so far from here, / I'd love to live therein./ *(German school song)*

A91 — Europe shall mourn her ancient fame declined, And Philadelphia be the Athens of mankind . . . . *(poet's prophecy)*

A92 — . . . the fairest, best buildid, quikkest and most populous toun of all Lancashire. [of Manchester]

A93 — The first white man to settle at Chickagou (Chicago) was a Negro. *(attributed to saying of Pottawattomie Indians)*

A94 — Forgive us when we deplore violence in our cities if we live in suburbs, where lawns are clipped and churches enlarge, or in green villages where there are too many steeples. *(Litany for Holy Communion in United Presbyterian Church)*

A95 — A fun place for the rich to visit, but a poor place to stay. [of slums]

A96 — God made the country, man the city, but the devil the little town.

A97 — A great city, a great loneliness. *(A Latin proverb taken from the Greek)*

A98 — Great is Newark's vitality. It is the red blood in its veins — this basic strength that is going to carry it over whatever hurdles it may encounter, enable it to recover from whatever losses it may suffer and battle its way to still higher achievement industrially and financially, making it eventually perhaps the greatest industrial center in the world. *(Newark businessman)*

A99 — The Half-Way House to Rome, Oxford. *Punch*

A100 — He who goes to Rome a beast returns a beast. *(Italian proverb)*

A101 — He who has never been to Odessa has never seen dust. *(Russian proverb)*

A102 — He who has not seen Seville has seen nothing. *(Spanish proverb)*

A103 — He who hath not seen Cairo hath not seen the world. / Her soil is gold. / Her Nile is a marvel, / Her women are the bright-eyed houris of Paradise, / Her houses are palaces, and her air is soft, with an odour above / aloes, refreshing the heart; / And how should Cairo be otherwise, when she is the Mother of the World?/

A104 — How many miles to Babylon? / Three score miles and ten. / Can I get there by candlelight? / Yes — and back again./ *(Nursery Rhyme)*

A105 — I am in Paris, in this royal city, where the abundance of nature's gifts not only captivates those who live there but invites and attracts those who are far away. Even as the moon surpasses the stars in brightness, so does this city, the seat of royalty, exalt her proud head above all other cities.

A106 — I sit on my stoop on Seventh Avenue and gaze at the sun-kissed folks strolling up and down and think that surely Mississippi is here in New York, in Harlem, yes, right on Seventh Avenue. *The Messenger*

A107 — If it were possible to place . . . Rome, Milan, Padua and Florence together with four other cities, they would not . . . contain the wealth and population of the half of Cairo.

A108 — If you hear an owl hoot: 'To whom' instead of 'To who' you can make your mind up he was born and educated in Boston.

A109 — If you live in Rome, don't quarrel with the Pope. *(French proverb)*

A110 — If you throw a stone in Prague, you throw a bit of history. *(Czech proverb)*

A111 — In Dublin's fair city / Where the girls are so pretty / I first set my eyes on sweet Mollie Malone / *A Terrible Beauty, Uris*

A112 — In Los Angeles people think of space in terms of time, time in terms of routes . . . and of automobiles as natural and essential extensions of themselves. . . . Los Angeles has no weather. It rains during February but when it is not raining it is warm and sunny and the palm trees silhouette against the smoggy heat haze sky. *International Times, March 14, 1969*

A113 — In my own city my name, in a strange city my clothes procure me respect. *(Hebrew proverb)*

A114 — In Paris life passes like a dream. *(French proverb)*

A115 — It is better to be the head of a village than be the tail of a city. *(Corsican proverb)*

A116 — It is 'not every man who has the luck to go to Corinth,' still less is it every man who is able to describe it when he has been there. *Times, Literary Supplement, November 24, 1911*

A117 — It is quite unnecessary to go to Europe in order to see a genuine Jewish ghetto. There is one, a large one, the largest in the New World in fact, right here in New York . . . . *The New York Times, November 14, 1897*

A118 — Kingswear was a market town / When Dartmouth was a furzy down. / [of Devon] *London Times, February 4, 1926*

A119 — LA has beautiful (if man-made) sunsets. *International Times, March 14, 1969*

A120 — A lay version of Army post life. [of suburbia]

A121 — Lima, paradise for women, purgatory for men and hell for *borricos* [donkeys]. *(Peruvian proverb)*

A122 — The lion and the unicorn / Were fighting for the crown; / The lion beat the unicorn / All round the town. / Some gave them white bread, / And some gave them brown; / Some gave them plum cake, / And sent them out of town. / *The Lion and the Unicorn*

A123 — London Bridge is falling down, / My fair lady. / *London Bridge*

A124 — Londoner-like ask as much more as you will take. *(English proverb)*

A125 — The 'luxuries' and 'polished society' and 'city investments,' which are indeed the 'poetry of city life,' and which will truly prove so, neither more or less, to the young man from the country, seem to outweigh, in his judgement, all the charms of a country life. *The Prairie Farmer, January 1859*

A126 — Many suburbs in search of a city. [of Los Angeles]

A127 — Men only feel their consequences and they can only act in a collective capacity and with vigour and effect after they have been condensed into masses and collected into cities. *Edinburgh Review*

A128 — The nearer Rome, the worse Christian. *(Medieval Latin proverb)*

A129 — A neighborhood is where, when you go out of it, you get beat up.

A130 — New York is notoriously the largest and least-loved of any of our great cities. Why should it be loved as a city? It is never the same city for a dozen years altogether. A man born in New York forty years ago finds nothing, absolutely nothing, of the New York he knew. If he chances to stumble upon a few old houses not yet leveled, he is fortunate. But the landmarks, the objects which marked the city to him, as a city, are gone. *Harper's Monthly, June 1856*

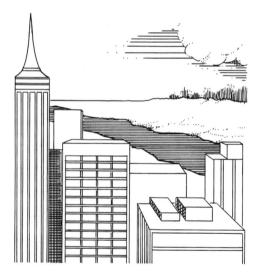

A131 — New York may be taken as a symbol, or it may be taken as a fact. As a symbol it is a symbol of America; its noisy, exuberant, incalculable towers rise out of the water like a man's aspirations to freedom. As a symbol it is the Gateway, the promise, the materialization of the New World . . . . But taken as a fact, New York is less Dantesque. To most Americans the fact is that 'New York is not America.' It is

un-American in lots of ways. The concentration of power that exists among those spires is itself un-American; so are the tumultuous, vowel-twisting inhabitants who throng the sidewalks. *Fortune Magazine*

A132 — O Father Nanna, that city into ruins was made . . . / Its people, not potsherds, filled its sides; / Its walls were breached; the people groan. / In its lofty gates, where they were wont to promenade, / dead bodies were lying about; / In its boulevards, where the feasts were celebrated, / scattered they lay. . . . / In all its streets, where they were wont to promenade, / dead bodies were lying about; / In its places, where the festivities of the land took / place, the people lay in heaps . . . / O Nanna, Ur has been destroyed; its people have been dispersed. /

A133 — Oh, the farmer comes to town / With his wagon broken down, / But the farmer is the man who feeds them all. / If you'll only look and see, / I think you will agree, / That the farmer is the man who feeds them all. /

A134 — Once there was a waltz; once there was a Vienna. *(Viennese popular song)*

A135 — One day the blow that thou hast deserved, O proud-necked Rome, shall fall on thee from Heaven. *Sibylline Oracles, VIII, 37*

A136 — One New York cabbie, or two California realtors, or three Philadelphia lawyers are a match for the devil.

A137 — The only real advantage of New York is that all its inhabitants ascend to heaven right after their deaths, having served their full term in hell right on Manhattan Island. *Barnard Bulletin*

A138 — A place so big that no one counts. [definition of a city]

A139 — A place where the crab-grass grows greenest. [of suburbia]

A140 — A projection of dormitory life into adulthood. [of suburbia]

A141 — Pussy cat, pussy cat, where have you been? / I've been up to London to look at the queen. / Pussy cat, pussy cat, what did you there? / I frightened a little mouse under the chair. / *(Song for the nursery)*

A142 — Quebec, as a city, has nothing to attract the attention of a visitor familiar with any of the large cities of Europe. *(British)*

A143 — Rome, the mother of men. *(Latin proverb)*

A144 — Rome was not built in a (one) day.

A145 — San Diego: The odds-on favorite 'most livable city.' *Ladies Home Journal*

A146 — She hath been at London to call a strea a 'straw,' and a waw a 'wall.' *(English proverb)*

A147 — She was poor but she was honest, / And her parents were the same, / Till she met a city feller, / And she lost her honest name. / *(War song, 1914-1918)*

A148 — So I said, 'Old man, for whom digg'st thou this grave / In the heart of London town?' / And the deep-toned voice of the digger replied—/ 'We're laying a gas-pipe down!' / *From the Sublime to the Ridiculous*

A149 — Sorority home communities with kids. [of suburbia]

A150 — *Stadt luft macht frei.* [City air makes man free; medieval adage referring to the right of a serf to become a freeman after one year and one day in a city.]

A151 — A strong city can be built with brother helping brother *(Roman proverb)*

A152 — The suburban husband and father is almost entirely a Sunday institution. *Harper's Bazaar, December 1900*

A153 — Sutton for mutton, Tamworth for beef, / Walsall for bandy legs, and Brummagen for a thief./ [of Birmingham] *Higson's Mss.*

A154 — Ten measures of beauty came into the world; Jerusalem received nine measures, and the rest of the world one. *(Hebrew proverb)*

A155 — That city is in a bad case, whose physician hath the gout. *(Hebrew proverb)*

A156 — There is a large class — I was about

to say a majority — of the population of New York and Brooklyn, who just live, and to whom the rearing of two or more children means inevitably a boy for the penitentiary, and a girl for the brothel. *(New York Supreme Court Judge)*

A157 — There is a tavern in the town, / And there my true love sits him down, / And drinks his wine with laughter and with glee, / And never, never thinks of me. / *There is a Tavern in the Town*

A158 — There is here here. [of Oakland]

A159 — A thoroughfare that begins in a graveyard and ends in a river. [of Wall Street]

A160 — Those who go to the city without a lucrative occupation, or the qualification necessary to gain their subsistence, need not expect success — those who leave the country to shun the rugged labor to which they may suppose themselves exposed, will also meet with disappointment; and those that go there to lounge their time away at places of dissipation or on the streets will be brought to disgrace, and probably to ruin if they persist in this degrading career. *The Prairie Farmer, December 1850*

A161 — Three wise men of Gotham / Went to sea in a bowl / If the bowl had been stronger / My tale would have been longer. / [of Gotham] *(Nursery rhyme)*

A162 — To carry coals to Newcastle.

A163 — The town is new every day. *(Estonian proverb)*

A164 — Twenty years ago the site of the metropolis of Victoria was a forest, ten years ago it was covered with a straggling village, today it has assumed the aspect of a city of magnitude and importance; and who shall define the limits of its future dignity and splendour? The prophetic eye beholds its wide and spacious thoroughfares fringed with edifices worthy of the wealth of its citizens and corresponding in architectural pretensions with the greatness of the commercial transactions of their occupants. [of Melbourne] *Australian Home Guardian, November 8, 1856*

A165 — The two moments when New York seems most desirable, when the splendor falls all around and the city like a girl with leaves in her hair, are just as you are leaving and must say good-bye, and just as you return and can say hello. *The New Yorker, January 11, 1955*

A166 — The value of any parcel of land is determined by three factors. The first is location. The second is location. And the third is location.

A167 — Verily all my birds and winged creatures have flown away— / 'Alas! for my city' I will say. / My daughters and my sons have been carried off— / 'Alas! for my men,' I will say. / O my city which exists no longer, my city attacked without cause, / O my city attacked and destroyed! / *(Lamentation for the Destruction of Ancient Ur)*

A168 — Waset (Thebes) is the pattern for every city. / Both the flood and the earth were in her from the beginning of time. / The sands came to delimit her soil, / To create her ground upon the mound when earth came into being. / Then mankind came into being within her, / To found every city in her true name (The City), / Since all are called 'city' / After the example of Waset. /

A169 — We Berliners know that we cannot defend Berlin with sweat and printer's ink alone. But we are proud of our right of freedom of speech, today above all when tyrants in this same city wish to strangle us into silence. *Berliner Illustrirte*

A170 — We will never bring disgrace to this our city by any act of dishonesty or cowardice, nor ever desert our suffering comrades in the ranks. We will fight for the ideals and sacred things of the city, both alone and with many; we will revere and obey the city's laws and do our best to incite a like respect and reverence in those above us who are prone to annul or set them at naught; we will strive unceasingly to quicken the public's sense of civic duty. Thus in all ways we will transmit this city not only not less but greater, better and more beautiful than it was transmitted to us. *Oath of the Young Men of Athens*

A171 — We will strive for the ideals and sacred things of the city, both alone and with many; we will inceasingly seek to quicken the sense of public duty; we will revere and obey the city's law—; we will

transmit this city not only not less, but greater, better and more beautiful than it was transmitted to us. *Oath of the Athenian City-State*

A172 — Whatever else it may possess or lack, a great city cannot be dull. It must have a sense of place and a feeling all its own, and its citizens must be different from and more vital than those who live elsewhere. The difference does not even have to be in their favor. The native Parisian, for instance, is born with an ineradicable hauteur that others define as rudeness, and the native New Yorker knows the meaning of avarice before he can spell the word. *Time, November 14, 1969*

A173 — When captains courageous, whom death could not daunt, / Did march to the siege of the city of Gaunt, / They mustered their soldiers by two and by three, / And the foremost in battle was Mary Ambree. / *Mary Ambree*

A174 — Where late the savage, hid in ambush lay / Or roamed the uncultured valleys for his prey, / Her hardy gifts rough industry extends, / The groves bow down, the lofty forest bends, / And see the spires of towns and cities rise, / And domes and temples swell unto the skies. /

A175 — Where the Pope is, Rome is. *(Italian proverb)*

A176 — Where you find both good and evil, there you find a city. *(Hindu proverb)*

A177 — Who has not seen Seville, has missed a miracle. *(Spanish verse)*

A178 — The wickedness and piety of Chicago are in their way marvelous. *Scribner's Magazine*

A179 — With enough ifs we could put Paris into a bottle. *(French proverb)*

A180 — With progress in roads came more cars, more roads for the cars, and more cars for the roads that had been built to accommodate more cars. *Time, October 6, 1961*

A181 — A womb with a view. [of suburbia]

A182 — Workers in urban state enterprises

are paid several tens of yuan or several hundreds .... We peasants are paid only ten, twenty or thirty yuan a year. Many workers in towns live in blocks of flats .... we are exposed to wind and rain. Just what attitude do dogs of officials responsible in the towns have towards the peasants? *(Red Guard Poster)*

A183 — York was, London is, and Edinburgh will be the biggest of the three. *(Scottish proverb)*

A184 — You must go into the country to hear what news of London. *(English proverb)*

ANTONINUS, Marcus Aurelius (121-180)

A185 — The poet says, Dear City of Cecrops; and wilt not thou say, Dear City of Zeus?

ANTONIONI, Michelangelo

A186 — I have never felt salvation in nature. I love cities above all.

APPELTON, Thomas

A187 — Good Americans, when they die, go to Paris. [also attributed to Oscar Wilde.] *Quoted in Aristocrat of the Breakfast Table, O.W. Holmes*

AQUINAS, (Saint) Thomas (1225?-1274)

A188 — The city is, in fact, the most important thing constituted by human reason. *Commentary on the Politics of Aristotle*

ARANGO, Jorge (1916-   )

A189 — Planning cities requires understanding life as the most perfect interrelation of space and time we know. Life, nature, and man are one: no meaningful interpretation of the history of man is possible without understanding life and nature, and no conception of man's future is possible without interpreting nature's past. In the planning of cities time is as important as space. *The Urbanization of the Earth*

ARBUTHNOT, John (1667-1735)

A190 — The air of cities is unfriendly to

infants and children. Every animal is adapted to the use of fresh, natural and free air; the tolerance of artificial air (as that of cities) is the effect of habit, which young animals have not yet acquir'd. *The Effect of Air on Human Bodies*

ARDAGH, John

A191 — Cosmopolitan metropolis? — or, as it is often called, 'The biggest village in Germany'? — Stuttgart is both, and knows it is both. *A Tale of Five Cities*

A192 — The sudden urbanisation of France, such as Britain knew in the previous century; the transfer from an agricultural to an industry-based economy; the resulting conflicts between tradition and modernism, sharper in France than in most countries; the enduring feud between Paris and the rest of the nation; the current anxieties about industry and youth employment — Toulouse, as much as any French town, exemplifies all of this and more. *Ibid.*

ARDREY, Robert (1908-   )

A193 — Any consideration of the problems of human space must begin and end nowhere if we deny the territorial propensities of man. If man is infinitely malleable, as so many would have us believe, then urban concentration should offer no dismay. We can adapt to anything, even to the crawling masses of insect life. . . .Urbanization is deterritorialization in the classic sense of denial of land. But perhaps there may be conceptual substitutes or symbolic channels that will preserve our biological sanity. We may be sure, however, that we must somehow preserve NO TRESPASSING signs. *The Social Contract*

A194 — We face in the urban concentration something new under the sun, something unanticipated except by the biologically, genetically directed termitary: but we lack the insect's genetic directives as we lack an evolutionary common ground. While we may live in our cities like ants in an ant-hill, as vertebrates we are genetically unprepared for such contingency. *Ibid.*

ARGAN, Giulio, C.

A195 — The ideal city was,in fact, an artistic and political invention of its time, since it was founded on the principle that the perfect architectural and urban form of the city corresponded to the perfection of its political and social arrangements, conceived and carried out by the wisdom of the prince in the same way that the geometry of the plan and the beauty of the buildings were conceived and carried out by the skill of the architect. *The Renaissance City*

ARISTEIDES, Aelius (c. 2nd c. A.D.)

A196 — Rome is not content with the extent of its built-up area, vast though this is. . . . Rome carries a whole pile of additional Romes, of equal extent, which it has hoisted up one above another. . . . If the city were to be spread out flat, so that the Romes which are now up aloft would be deposited on ground level side by side with each other, I reckon that the remnant of Italy that is not already covered by Rome would be completely filled up. There would then be one continuous city extending (from the Tyrrhene Sea) to the Adriatic. *In Romam*

ARISTIDES

A197 — To you there come from all lands and seas what the seasons bring forth and what the climates produce, what rivers and lakes and the handicraft of Hellene or barbarian make. Whoever, therefore, wishes to view all this, must either journey through the whole world or stay in this city. For the work and toil of other folks is ever here at hand, and in excess. *Laudation of Rome*

A198 — Not houses finely roofed or the stones of walls well-builded, nay nor canals and dockyards, make the city, but men able to use their opportunity. *Rhodian Oration*

ARISTOPHANES (448?-380? B.C.)

A199 — 'Tis not that we hate it [the city]; we recognize it to be great and rich, likewise that everyone has the right to ruin himself; but the crickets only chirrup among the fig trees for a month or two, whereas the Athenians spend their whole lives in chanting forth judgments from their law-courts. *The Birds*

ARISTOTLE (384-322 B.C.)

A200 — Men come together in cities for security; they stay together for the good life.

A201 — The result which the legislator has produced is the reverse of beneficial; for he has made his city poor, and his citizens greedy. *Poetics*

A202 — A city is a collective body of persons sufficient in themselves for all the purposes of life. *Politics*

A203 — A city is a perfect and absolute assembly or communion of many towns or streets in one. *Ibid.*

A204 — A city, too, like an individual, has a work to do; and that city which is best adapted to the fulfillment of its work is to be deemed greatest. *Ibid.*

A205 — A city which fronts the east and receives the winds which blow from thence is esteemed most healthful. *Ibid.*

A206 — Experience shows that a very populous city can seldom, if ever, be properly governed; all well-governed cities have a limited population. *Ibid.*

A207 — A great city is not to be confounded with a populous one. *Ibid.*

A208 — Hippodamus, son of Euryphon, a native of Miletus, invented the art of planning and laid out the street plan of Piraeus.... He planned a city with a population of 10,000 divided into three parts, one of the skilled workers, one of farmers, and one to defend the state. The land was divided into three parts: sacred, public, and private supporting in turn the worship of the gods, the defense of the state, and the farm owners . . . *Ibid.*

ARMSTRONG, John (1709-1779)

A209 — Fly the rank city, shun its turbid air: / Breathe not the chaos of eternal smoke / And volatile corruption. / . . . and tho' the lungs abhor / To drink the dun fuliginous abyss / Did not the acid vigor of the mine, / Roll'd from so many thundring chimneys, tame / The putrid salts that overswarm the sky; / This caustic venom would perhaps corrode / Those tender cells that draw the vital air . . . / While yet you breathe, away! the rural wilds / Invite. / *The Art of Preserving Health*

A210 — Of right and wrong he taught / Truths as refin'd as ever Athens heard; / And (strange to tell!) he practis'd what he preach'd / *Ibid.*

ARNALL, Ellis (1907-   )

A211 — Boston — a festering mud puddle.

ARNOLD, Matthew (1822-1888)

A212 — We are all of us included in some religious organisation or other; we all call ourselves . . . *children of God*. Children of God; — it is an immense pretension! — and how are we to justify it? By the works which we do, and the words which we speak. And the work which we collective children of God do, our grand centre of life, our *city* which we have builded for us to dwell in, is London! London, with its unutterable external hideousness, and with its internal canker of *publice egestas, privatim opulentia,*

— to use the words which Sallust puts into Cato's mouth about Rome, — unequalled in the world! . . . . *Culture and Anarchy*

A213 — Home of lost causes, and forsaken beliefs, and unpopular names, and impossible loyalties! [of Oxford] *Essays in Criticism*

A214 — One last look at the white-wall'd town, / And the little grey church on the windy shore. *The Forsaken Merman*

A215 — Quebec is the most interesting by much that I have seen on this Continent, and I think that I would sooner be a poor priest in Quebec than a rich hog-merchant in Chicago. *(Letter to Walter Arnold)*

A216 — Calm Soul of all things! make it mine / To feel, amid the city's jar, / That there abides a peace of thine, / Man did not make, and can not mar. / *Lines Written in Kensington Gardens*

A217 — Ye fill up the gaps in our files, / Strengthen the wavering line, / Stablish, continue our march, / On, to the bound of the waste, / On, to the city of God. / *Rugby Chapel*

A218 — And that sweet City with her dreaming spires, / She needs not June for beauty heightening. *Thyrsis*

ASHBURY, Herbert

A219 — Curiously enough, during the decade in which Chicago was overrun by gangsters and was a synonym for crime and corruption everywhere in the world, the population of the city increased by nearly seven hundred thousand. *Gem of the Prairie: An Informal History of the Chicago Underworld*

ASIMOV, Isaac (1920-   )

A220 — The twenty-first century will see man burrowing underground. A hundred years from today, most of mankind will still be living above ground, but every city will already have its underground portion. The underground city will have as its chief advantage an utter freedom from weather vicissitudes or day-night changes . . . . Nor will the underground dweller be deprived of the touch of nature. Quite the contrary.

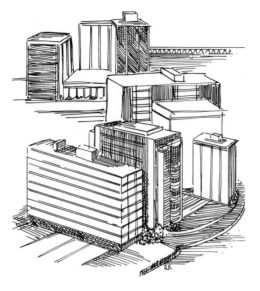

Where the modern city dweller may have to travel twenty miles to get 'in the country' the underground dweller will merely have to rise a few hundred feet in an elevator, for once a city is completely underground, the area above can be made into parkland. *Quoted in Worlds in the Making, Dunstan and Garlan*

ASSURBANIPAL (King of Assyria) (669-626 B.C.)

A221 — I conquered the whole city. . . . Silver, gold, precious stones, all the treasures of the palace, colourful robes, linen, marvellous horses, male and female slaves, two large obelisks of shining bronze, even the gates of the temple I carried away and brought to Assyria. A tremendous booty of immeasurable value did I take with me.

ASTOLPHE, Le Marquis de Custine

A222 — A Greek city improvised for the Tartars as a theater set — a decor, magnificent though without taste, to serve as the scene of a real and terrible drama — this is what one perceives at first glance in St. Petersburg.

ATKINSON, Brooks (1894-   )

A223 — All cities are superb at night because their hideous corners are devoured in darkness. *The New York Times, March 17, 1964*

ATTOE, Wayne

A224 — A variety of activities, ritual and casual, are associated with skylines. People gaze at skylines. They climb skylines and celebrate within them. Messages are sent via skylines, and skylines are manipulated and molded into preferred shapes. *Skylines*

AUDEN, W.H. (1907-1973)

A225 — Across the plains, / Between two hills, two villages, two trees, two friends, / The barbed wire runs which neither argues nor explains / But where it likes a place, a path, a railroad ends, / The humor, the cuisine, the rites, the taste, / The pattern of the City, are erased. / *Barbed Wire*

A226 — When I was a child the streets of any city were full of street vendors and street entertainers of every kind, and of the latter the Italian organ-grinder with his money was one of the most endearing. Today, officialdom seems to have banished them all, and the only persons who still earn their living on the streets are prostitutes and dope peddlers. *A Certain World*

A227 — Urban society is, like the desert, a place without limits. The city walls of tradition, mythos and cultus have crumbled. There is no direction in which Ishmael is forbidden or forcibly prevented from moving. The only outside 'necessitites' are the random winds of fashion or the lifeless chains of a meaningless job, which, so long as he remains an individual, he can and will reject. *The Enchanted Flood*

A228 — Certainly our city — with the byres of poverty down to / The river's edge, the cathedral, the engines, the dogs; / Here is the cosmopolitan cooking / And the light allows and the glass. / Built by the conscious-stricken, the weapon-making. / By us. / *Look, Stranger!*

A229 — Even now, in this night / Among the ruins of the Post-Vergilian City / Where our past is a chaos of graves and the barbed-wire stretches ahead / Into our future till it is lost to sight, / Our grief is not Greek: As we bury our dead / We know without knowing there is reason for what we bear. / *Memorial for the City*

A230 — The future which confronts us has / No likeness to that age when, as / Rome's huggermugger unity / Was slowly knocked to pieces by / The uncoordinated blows / Of artless and barbaric foes, / The stressed and rhyming measures rose; / The cities we abandon fall / To nothing primitive at all . . . / *New Year Letter*

A231 — More even than in Europe, here / The choice of patterns is made clear / With the machine imposes, what / Is possible and what is not, / To what conditions we must bow / In building the Just City now. / *Ibid.*

A232 — To build the City where / The will of love is done / And brought to its full flower / The dignity of man. / *On the Frontier*

AUGUSTINE, (Saint) (354-430)

A233 — The earthly city is generally divided against itself by litigation, by wars, by battles, the pursuit of victories that bring death with them or are at best doomed to death. *The City of God*

A234 — Now, the city of man was first founded by a fratricide who was moved by envy to kill his brother, a man who, in his pilgrimage on earth, was a citizen of the City of God. It need not surprise us, then, that long afterwards, in the founding of that city which was to dominate so many peoples and become the capital of that earthly city with which I am dealing, the copy, so to speak, corresponded to the original — to what the Greeks call the archetype. For, in both cases, we have the same crime. As one of the poets puts it: 'With brother's blood the earliest walls were wet.' For Rome began, as Roman history records, when Remus was killed by Romulus, his brother. *Ibid.*

A235 — Now, the first man born of the two parents of the human race was Cain. He belonged to the city of man. The next born was Abel, and he was of the City of God. *Ibid.*

A236 — The two cities, of God and of the Devil, are to reach their appointed ends when the sentences of destiny and doom are passed by our Lord Jesus Christ, the Judge of the living and the dead. *Ibid.*

A237 — Just as a universal Empire, made up of many cities, is known as the community of Rome; so many nations go to make up the City of which it is written: Glorious things are spoken of thee, O City of God. *Cons. Evangelii*

A238 — Rome has spoken; the case is concluded. *Sermons*

AUROUSSEAU, M.

A239 — The dense clusters of folk, who have no immediate interest in the production of the materials for their food and clothing or general comfort, but are engaged in the transporting, manufacturing, buying and selling them, or in educating the people, or in managing the affairs of the State, or in merely 'living in town,' become the urban section. *Geographical Review, XI (1921)*

AUSONIUS (4th c. A.D.)

A240 — First among cities, home of the gods. [of Rome]

AUSTEN, Jane (1775-1817)

A241 — One has no great hopes from Birmingham. I always say there is something direful in the sound. *Emma*

AUSTIN, Alfred (1835-1913)

A242 — Towns can be trusted to corrupt themselves. *Fortunatus the Pessimist*

A243 — Lo, where huge London, huger day by day, / O'er six fair counties spreads its hideous sway. / *The Golden Age*

AYALA, Perez de (1881-1962)

A244 — Cities that once were, heroic, courageous, active, and flourishing, now have only an imaginary and sleepy existence. *La Caida de los Limones*

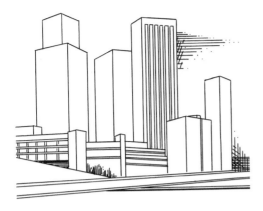

B

BABITZ, Eve (1943-)

B1 — Culturally, Los Angeles has always been a humid jungle alive with seething L.A. projects that I guess people from other places can't see . . It takes a certain kind of innocence to like L.A., anyway . . . . When people are not happy, they fight against L.A. and say it's a 'wasteland,' and other helpful descriptions. *Eve's Hollywood*

BACON, Edmund (1910-)

B2 — The building of cities is one of man's greatest achievements. The form of his city always has been and always will be a pitiless indicator of the state of his civilization. This form is determined by the multiplicity of decisions made by the people who live in it. In urban circumstances these decisions have interacted to produce a force of such clarity and form that a noble city has been born. *Design of Cities*

B3 — The idea of new towns which are self-contained entities is the pursuit of an illusion. These are suburban extensions of metropolitan areas.

B4 — Many planners, when they see scattered blight, want to tear it all down and build anew. This is comparable to cutting off your finger if you have a sore on it. It is a totally false approach. We cannot revitalize cities on this basis. We need to renew structures which are still in reasonably good condition.

B5 — If American cities are to change into something worth having, there must be a

clear image clearly conceived of what that city should be, and this image must be injected into and mature within the processes which actually dictate the form the city will take. If the image exists but does not make contact with the form-determining processes, the city will fail to achieve the humane character we seek for it. *The City Image*

B6 — In the United States we are almost devoid of a generally accepted, constructive, tangible urban image. It can safely be said that the overwhelming majority of the American people operate on the basis of the suburban way of life as the only acceptable goal for all right-minded people. *Ibid.*

BACON, (Sir) Francis (1561-1626)

B7 — Caesar, when he went first into Gaul, made no scruple to profess 'That he had rather be first in a village than second at Rome.' *Advancement of Learning*

B8 — In a great town friends are scattered; so that there is not that fellowship, for the most part, which is in less neighborhoods. *Of Friendship, Essays*

BAILEY, Pearl (1918-)

B9 — I ride home from the theatre at night, remembering what New York was when I was a girl, and it makes me cry. The politicians have milked this city dry, and the people have given up . . . . It's not just New York. Look at Philadelphia, Cleveland, Los Angeles — every city in this U.S. is based on the pride of its citizens. *Quoted in The San Francisco Examiner Chronicle, December 28, 1975*

BAKER, Russell (1925-)

B10 — The New Yorker . . . has to fit life into spaces too small for it. What he calls home would look like a couple of closets to most Americans, yet the New Yorker manages not only to live there but also to grow trees and cockroaches right on the premises . . . Trying to fit life into spaces too small for it takes a toll on civilization. Blood pressure among New Yorkers is probably always high. One goes through life most days with a temperature just one degree below the boiling point. It takes very little to push it into the danger zone. *So This Is Depravity*

B11 — Watergate left Washington a city ravaged by honesty. *Ibid.*

BAKER, Sheldon S.

B12 — The city has many attractions, / But think of the vices and sins, / When once in the vortex of fashion, / How soon the course downward begins. / To one having little or nothing to lose / A city life might have a charm . . . / BUT A FARMER SHOULD STICK TO HIS FARM. *Marmondale and Other Poems*

BAKUNIN, Mikhail (1814-1876)

B13 — Berlin is a fine town, excellent music, cheap living, very passable theater, plenty of newspapers in the cafés . . . . In a word, splendid, quite splendid — if only the Germans weren't so frightfully bourgeois.

BALDWIN, James (1924-   )

B14 — Every day in the city, on the contrary — and I grew up in the city — involves a subtle divorce from reality. There is something a little terrifying about being forty stories in the air and looking around you, and you see nothing but walls, other skyscrapers, and you don't dare look down. And if you are on the ground, if you want to see the sky, you must make an effort of the will and look up. And if you do that, you are likely to be carried off to Bellevue — but that is another story. *The Language of the Streets*

B15 — No one in the city, except your immediate family — not always they — says good morning. *Ibid.*

B16 — A ghetto can be improved in one way only: out of existence. *Nobody Knows My Name*

B17 — Whenever I think of New Orleans, I also helplessly think of Sodom and Gomorrah. *Notes of A Native Son*

BALLARD, J.G.

B18 — Ninetyfive percent of the population was permanently trapped in vast urban conurbations . . . . The countryside, as such, no longer existed. Every single square foot of ground sprouted a crop of one type or another. The one-time fields and meadows of the world were, in effect, factory floors. *Billenium*

BALLARD, Willis Todhunter

B19 — You can take a boy out of Brooklyn but you can never get Brooklyn out of the boy. *Say Yes to Murder*

BALZAC, Honore de (1799-1850)

B20 — But ah, Paris! He who has not stopped in admiration of your dark passageways, before your glimpses of light, in your blind alleys deep and silent, he who has not heard your murmur between midnight and two in the morning, does not know your true poetry not your strange and vast antitheses.

B21 — A city where great ideas perish, done to death by a witticism. [of Paris]

B22 — A veritable ocean. Take as many soundings in it as you will, you will never know its depth. [of Paris] *Pere Goriot*

BANFIELD, Edward C. (1916-   )

B23 — At worst, the American city's ugliness — or, more, its lack of spendor or charm — occasions loss of visual pleasure. This loss is an important one (it is surely much larger than most people realize), but it cannot lead to any kind of disaster either for the individual or for the society. *The Unheavenly City*

B24 — If some real disaster impends in the city, it is not because parking spaces are hard to find, because architecture is bad, because department store sales are declining, or even because taxes are rising. If there is a genuine crisis, it has to do with the essential welfare of individuals or with the good health of the society, not merely with comfort, convenience, amenity, and business advantage, important as these are. *Ibid.*

B25 — Most of the 'problems' that are generally supposed to constitute 'the urban crisis' could not conceivably lead to disaster. They are — some of them — important in the sense that a bad cold is important, but they are not serious in the sense that a cancer is serious. They have to do with comfort, convenience, amenity, and business advantage, all of which are important, but they do not affect either the essential welfare of individuals or what may be called the good health of the society. *Ibid.*

B26 — The plain fact is that the overwhelming majority of city dwellers live more comfortably and conveniently than ever before. They have more and better housing, and more and better schools, more and better transportation, and so on. By any conceivable measure of material welfare the present generation of urban Americans is, on the whole, better off than any other large group of people has ever been anywhere. What is more, there is every reason to expect that the general level of comfort and convenience will continue to rise at an even more rapid rate through the foreseeable future. *Ibid.*

B27 — The serious problems of cities, it should be stressed, are in most instances not caused by the conditions of urban life as such and are less characteristic of the city than of small-town and farm areas. Poverty, ignorance, and racial injustice are more widespread outside the cities than inside them. *Ibid.*

B28 — To a large extent, then, our urban problems are like the mechanical rabbit at the racetrack, which is set to keep just ahead of the dogs no matter how fast they may run. Our performance is better and better, but because we set our standards and expectations to keep ahead of performance, the problems are never any nearer to solution. Indeed, if standards and expectations rise faster than performance, the problems may get (relatively) worse as they get (absolutely) better. *Ibid.*

B29 — Within a very recent period three new factors have been suddenly developed which promise to exert a powerful influence on the problems of city and country life. These are the trolley, the bicycle, and the telephone. It is impossible to foresee at present just what their influence is to be on the question of the distribution of population; but this much is certain, that it adds from five to fifteen miles to the radius of every large town.

It is by such apparently unimportant, trifling, and inconspicuous forces that civilization is swayed and moulded in its evolutions and no man can foresee them or say whither they lead .... *Ibid*

BANHAM, Reyner (1922-   )

B30 — The Beaches are what other metropolises should envy in Los Angeles, more than any other aspect of the city. *Los Angeles*

B31 — Can such an old-world, academic, and precedent-laden concept claim to embrace so unprecedented a human phenomenon as this city of Our Lady Queen of the Angels of Porciuncula? — otherwise known as Internal Combustion City, Surfbia, Smogville, Aerospace City, Systems Land, the Dream-factory of the Western world. *Ibid.*

B32 — A city seventy miles square but rarely seventy years deep apart from a small downtown not yet two centuries old and a few other pockets of ancientry, Los Angeles is an instant townscape. *Ibid.*

B33 — Disneyland is almost the only place where East Coast town-planning snobs, determined that their cities shall never suffer the automotive 'fate' of Los Angeles, can bring their students or their city councillors to see how the alternative might work in the flesh and metal-to this blatantly commercial fun-fair in the city they hate. *Ibid.*

B34 — A domestic or sociable journey in Los Angeles does not end so much at the door of one's destination as at the off-ramp of the freeway, the mile or two of ground-level streets counts as no more than the front drive of the house. *Ibid.*

B35 — The fact that these parking-lots, freeways, drive-ins, and other facilities have not wrecked the city-form is due chiefly to the fact that Los Angeles has no urban form at all in the commonly accepted sense. *Ibid.*

B36 — The failure-rate of town planning is so high throughout the world that one can only marvel that the profession has not long since given up trying; the history of the art of planning is a giant wastebin of sumptuously forgotten paper projects. *Ibid.*

B37 — Indeed . . . . freeways seem to have fixed Los Angeles in canonical and monumental form, much as the great streets of Sixtus V fixed Baroque Rome, or the Grands Travaux of Baron Haussmann fixed the Paris of la belle epoque. Whether you regard them as crowns of thorns or chaplets of laurels, the freeways are what the tutelary deity of the City of Angels should wear upon her head instead of the mural crowns sported by civic goddesses of old. *Ibid.*

B38 — Planning in Los Angeles? In the world's eyes this is a self-cancelling concept. *Ibid.*

B39 — San Francisco was plugged into California from the sea; the Gold Rush brought its first population and their culture round Cape Horn; their prefabricated Yankee houses and New England (or European) attitudes were dumped unmodified on the Coast. *Ibid.*

BARBAULD, Anna Letitia (1743-1825)

B40 — And when midst fallen London, they survey / The stone where Alexander's ashes

lay, / Shall own with humbled pride the lesson just / By Time's slow finger written in the dust. / *Eighteen Hundred and Eleven*

BARR, Amelia (1831-1919)

B41 — Every city has some locality to which its heroic and civic memories especially cling; and this locality in the city of New York is the historic acre of the Bowling Green. With that spot it has been throughout its existence, in some way or other, unfailingly linked. *The Belle of Bowling Green*

BARR, Joseph M. (Mayor of Pittsburgh)

B42 — Any mayor who's not frustrated is not thinking. The problems are almost insurmountable . . . The main problem of any mayor of any city of any size is money . . . The legislatures are dominated by suburban and rural constituencies, and until that changes there's no hope for mayors who are trying to run their cities and run them properly. If the mayors don't get relief from the legislatures, God help them! *(Interview, June 29, 1969)*

BARRIE, James Matthew (1860-1937)

B43 — The greatest glory that has ever come to me was to be swallowed up in London, not knowing a soul, with no means of subsistence, and the fun of working till the stars went out. To have known any one would have spoilt it. I did not even quite know the language. *Courage (Rectorial Address At St. Andrew's)*

BARRY, Jack

B44 — The trouble with New York is it's so convenient to everything I can't afford. *Quoted in Reader's Digest*

BARRYMORE, John (1882-1942)

B45 — Chicago was always a great theater town. But discriminating. You couldn't give them the peasant doss we fed the torpid natives of the hinterland.

BARTENS (Seventeenth Century Calvinist)

B46 — The whore on the Y can be bought with anybody's money; / She serves Pope and heathen, Moor and Turk, / She bothers about neither God nor the dear fatherland, / She is concerned with profit alone, profit alone! Profit alone! / [of Amsterdam]

BARTHELME, Donald (1931-)

B47 — New York City is or can be regarded as a collage, as opposed to, say, a tribal village in which all the huts (or yurts, or whatever) are the same hut, duplicated. The point of collage is that unlike things are stuck together to make, in the best case, a new reality. *Quoted in Joe David Bellamy, ed., The New Fiction: Interviews With Innovative American Writers*

BARTLETT, Dana W. (1863-1936)

B48 — Ruralize the city; urbanize the country.

B49 — Ugliness has no commercial or ethical value. The crowded tenement, the rookery, a city's ill-kept streets and yards are not incentives to higher living. On the other hand, it is a fact made clear by years of experience that the fairer the city, the nearer to Nature's heart the people are brought; the more easily they are governed; there is less crime and more of the normal, spiritual, healthful life which is the product of the ripest civilization. *The Better City: A Sociological Study of a Modern City*

BARZINI, Luigi (1908-)

B50 — I came to know New York well after a while . . to know the immense, elusive, multiform metropolis — every city for everyman — in which, as in a cloud, a man could always see the shapes that pleased him most. *O America*

BARZUN, Jacques (1907-)

B51 — New York is a skyline, the most stupendous, unbelievable, man-made spectacle since the hanging gardens of Babylon. Significantly, you have to be outside the city — on a bridge or on the Jersey Turnpike — to enjoy it. *God's Country and Mine*

BASHFORD, Henry Howarth (1880-1961)

B52 — As I came down the Highgate Hill / I met the sun's bravado, / And saw below me, fold on fold, / Grey to pearl and pearl to gold, / This London like a land of old, / The land of Eldorado. / *Romances*

BATCHELLER, Tryphosa Bates (1878-1952)

B53 — It has been said that no Jew can live in Barcelona because of the shrewdness of the natives with whom he comes in contact in business. Even the relaxation of the siesta, the sturdy Catalan often denies himself, and in Barcelona the foreigner finds his German, American, or still more French ways and ideas awakening interest and acceptance. *Royal Spain of Today*

BATER, James H.

B54 — Despite the tragic disruptions of World War, Civil War, and internal upheaval, the Soviet city stands out as a remarkable example of what it is possible to achieve in the application of socialist principles to town planning. Problems exist to be sure: indeed, they are frequently just the same as in the Western city. But because the system offers potential solutions to them, the Soviet experience in planned urban development stands out as both different from, and of instruction to, Western society. *The Soviet City: Ideal and Reality*

BATES, Katharine Lee (1859-1929)

B55 — O beautiful for patriot dream / That sees beyond the years / Thine alabaster cities gleam / Undimmed by human tears! / *America the Beautiful!*

BAUDELAIRE, Charles (1821-1867)

B56 — In the sinuous windings of cities of old, / Where horror itself can be turned to delight, / I seek, as I let fateful fancy take hold, / The worn yet entrancing odd creatures of night. / *Les Fleurs du Mal*

B57 — Swarming city, full of dreams. *Les Sept Viellards*

BAUER, Catherine

B58 — As an organ of democratic society, the modern city poses the universal dilemma of our times — society versus freedom. The good city must protect minimum living standards but at the same time provide an environment favorable to creative experiment, freedom of initiative, and maximum consumer choice. *in The Metropolis and Modern Life, E.M. Fisher, Ed.*

B59 — The difference between the modern metropolis and the older town is in some ways analogous to the difference between a modern factory and a handicraft operation. In the latter, it was possible to proceed without a set of exact drawings — whether the general purpose was a shoe or a cathedral — because the final product was gradually built up out a number of skilled individual decisions. In the factory, however, you have to know ahead exactly what you propose to make and how. Without plans, the machinery will not produce parts that fit together. *Ibid.*

BAYH, Birch (Senator) (1928-   )

B60 — If we can put footsteps on the moon, we should be able to put a new face on down-town U.S.A.

BEACH, Joseph Warren (1880-1957)

B61 — Cities represent the ideal commonwealth, and their builders are to be honored. They are places of learning. The ideal is not fully realized and cities become starving and unhappy; they become dilapidated and need rebuilding. It is natural for their sorrowing denizens to dream of islands where there is dancing and greenness; they imagine lovely gods who come from islands and invite you to return with them across the water; there are always pilgrims describing these places of dreams . . . . The thing to do is not dream of islands but rebuild the city, restore the social ideal. *Obsessive Images: Symbolism in Poetry of the 1930's and 1940's*

BEAME, Abraham D. (Mayor of New York) (1906-   )

B62 — We [the city of New York] confront an economic paradox: When we lay off workers, our welfare and social costs increase. When we raise taxes, we drive corporate and individual taxpayers from our borders. When we cut programs and reduce services, we jeopardize the quality of life in our city. *(State of the City Address, January 22, 1976)*

B63 — I'm delighted to be here [in Groton, Conn.] for this historic launching of the nuclear submarine *New York City*. The submarine is supposed to go under. The city never will. *Quoted in The New York Times, June 18, 1977*

B64 — Whatever fate awaits New York, our country's tragedy would be greatly compounded if our national leadership deludes itself into thinking that sacrificing our city will some how exorcize the demons plaguing all of urban America. The real problems and economic pressures affecting New York should be the subject of constructive concern — and not derision. Subjecting America's largest city to humiliation and impoverishment does not enhance either the economy or the moral fiber of our nation. *Quoted in The New York Times, November 6, 1975*

BEATON, Cecil (1904-   )

B65 — After 20 annual visits, I am still surprised each time I return to see this giant asparagus bed of alabaster and rose and green skyscrapers. [of New York] *It Gives Me Great Pleasure*

BEEBE, Lucius (1902-1966)

B66 — In Reno, Nevada, a community variously celebrated as one of the last outposts of the Old West (which it is), and as the divorce capital of the universe (which it isn't), there is an element known as the see-our-schools-and-churches-group. These worthy folk deplore Reno's fame for its glittering night life and social nip-ups and make a practice of button-holing visiting firemen, especially writers, with entreaties to depict Reno as a normal, wholesome, American community. *Reno*

BEECHER, Henry Ward (1813-1887)

B67 — Nothing marks the change from the city to the country so much as the absence of grinding noises. The country is never silent. But its sounds are separate, distinct, and, as it were, articulate. *Eyes and Ears*

BEER, Thomas (1889-1940)

B68 — New York, the hussy, was taken in sin again! *The Mauve Decade*

BEERBOHM, Max (1872-1956)

B69 — A quiet city is a contradiction in terms. It is a thing uncanny, spectral. *Mainly on the Air*

BEHAN, Brendan (1923-1964)

B70 — Montreal is the only place where a good French accent isn't a social asset. *The Wit of Brendan Behan*

BEIMAN, Irving

B71 — Exploited by absentee landlords and real-estate opportunists, the city has failed to develop a real community spirit. There is no civic symphony orchestra, there are few buildings of distinguished architectural note, and a Little Theatre movement was permitted to die. Even the zoo . . . was sold, without a single protest. *Birmingham: Steel Giant with a Glass Jaw*

BELLOC, Hilaire (1870-1953)

B72 — Aix is the town of Charlemagne. His presence overshadows the place; he is buried in the heart of it; he is the influence, or the ghost, or the god of the city. [Aix-La-Chapelle] *Towns of Destiny*

B73 — Cadiz is always of its nature a city on an island and also a city more entirely of the sea in its traditions and changing fates than any other — more even than Venice; for even when it was the last refuge of national government in the resistance to Napoleon it has never attempted to govern the mainland; it has lived wholly by its harbour. Its alternate wealth and decline have gone with nothing but the alternate growth and lessening of its ships. *Ibid.*

B74 — Now there is in Spain one town where, above all others, this spirit of kingship remains as a sort of inhabiting soul, always alive, built into the very stones of the place and haunting the mind of one who dwells in it and surveys the past and the future. That town is Segovia. *Ibid.*

B75 — Of the towns in Europe which, by the sound of their names and by the connotation of them, coupled with their remoteness, carry glamour, Salamanca is one. *Ibid.*

B76 — There are very many places in the world no doubt, where something of this emotion [of nothingness] is called up and something of this wonder that such great human things can utterly vanish; but nowhere do I find that lesson impressed as it is impressed upon the site of Carthage; upon that hillside above the sea where Carthage once was. *Ibid.*

B77 — Things only are because they are one, and a city is most a city when it is sharply defined by a wall. *Ibid.*

BELLOW, Saul (1915-)

B78 — What is barely hinted in other American cities is condensed and enlarged in New York.

B79 — The air, the very air, is thought-nourishing in Jerusalem, the sages themselves said so. I am prepared to believe it. I know that it must have special properties. *To Jerusalem and Back*

BELY, Andrei (1880-1934)

B80 — Our Russian Empire consists of a great number of cities — capital cities, governmental cities, district cities, provincial cities . . . and, in addition, of a venerable old residence, and of the mother of all Russian cities. The venerable old residential city is Moscow, and the mother of all Russian cities is Kiev. *Petersburg*

BENET, William Rose (1886-1950)

B81 — The gods returned to earth when Venice broke / Like Venus from the dawn-encircled sea / Wide laughed the skies with light when Venice woke / Crowned of antiquity / *Gaspara Stampa*

BENTHAM, Jeremy (1748-1832)

B82 — The community is a fictitious body, composed of the individual persons who are considered as constituting, as it were, its members. The interest of the community, then, is what? The sum of the interests of the several members who compose it. [of Community] *The Principles of Morals and Legislation*

BERGEL, Ergon Ernest (1894-)

B83 — We shall call a city any settlement where the majority of occupants are engaged in other than agricultural activities. *Urban Sociology*

BERGER, Meyer (1898-1959)

B84 — Each man reads his own meaning into New York. *The Empire City*

BERNARD of Cluny

B85 — Jerusalem the golden, / With milk and honey blest, / Beneath they contemplation / Sink heart and voice oppressed. / *Hora Novissima: Urbs Syon Aurea*

BERNHARDT, Sara (1844-1923)

B86 — Chicago has the best bifstiks. *(Newspaper Item)*

BERRY, Adrian (1937-)

B87 — Cities on Earth are afflicted with countless difficulties that their founding fathers, being ignorant of the effects of modern industry, could never have foreseen. It is no answer to build more big cities on Earth, which would merely rob other people of their open spaces. The only ideal answer will be to build new and limitless cities in the almost limitless vastness of interplanetary space. *The Next Ten Thousand Years*

BERSTON, Hyman Maxwell

B88 — An impenetrable line of defense from the sickness of the core city. [of suburbia]

B89 — A place peopled with home-owning Republicans who were once city dwelling renting Democrats. [of suburbia]

BETTELHEIM, Bruno (1903-)

B90 — The child's present urban experience, and with it his future one, depends on whether those close to him — most of all his parents — experience urban life as uniquely enriching, or as severely depriving; whether to them the streets of the city are friendly expanses, and what goes on in the city is a source of rewarding experiences and ever new and fascinating challenges to their own growth; or whether, to the contrary, these persons impress him overtly or covertly with their anxious conviction that the city is horrid, its streets murderous jungles where dog eats dog, and that whatever meaningful activities may go on in the city are closed to them, and hence will be also to him. *The Child's Perception of the City*

BIBLE, Old Testament

B91 — Against a small city with few men in it advanced a mighty king, who surrounded it and threw up great seigeworks about it. But in the city lived a man who, though poor, was wise, and he delivered it through his wisdom. Yet no one remembered this poor man. *Ecclesiastes 9:14-15*

B92 — The land is full of bloody crimes, and the city is full of violence. *Ezekiel 7:23*

B93 — Thy borders are in the midst of the seas, thy builders have perfected thy beauty. [of Tyre] *Ezekiel 27:4-5*

B94 — Abraham drew near and said, Will you destroy the good with the wicked? If there be fifty just men in the city, will you then destroy the place and not spare it for the fifty just men within it? . . . And the Lord said, 'If I find that there are fifty just men in the city, I will spare the whole place for their sake.' *Genesis 18:23, 24, 26*

B95 — Cain was the founder of a city which he named after his son Henoch. *Genesis 4:17*

B96 — The sun had risen on the earth when Lot entered Segor. The Lord poured down on Sodom and Gomorrah sulphur and fire from the Lord out of heaven. He overthrew those cities and the whole region, all the inhabitants of the cities and the plants of the soil. *Genesis 19:23-25*

B97 — Then they said, 'Let us build ourselves a city and a tower with its top in the heavens; let us make a name for ourselves lest we be scattered all over the earth.' The Lord came down to see the city and the tower which men had built. And the Lord said, 'Truly, they are one people and they all have the same language. This is the beginning of what they will do. Hereafter they will not be restrained from anything which they determine to do. Let us go down, and there confuse their language so that they will not understand one another's speech.' So the Lord scattered them from that place all over the earth; and they stopped building the city. [of Babylon] *Genesis 11:4-8*

B98 — When the morning came, the angels urged Lot on, saying, 'Come, take your wife and daughters here, lest you perish in the punishment of the city.' *Genesis 19:15*

B99 — Arise, put on they strength, O Sion, put on the garments of thy glory, O Jerusalem, the city of the Holy One, for hence forth the uncircumcised, and unclean shall not more pass through thee. *Isaiah 52:1*

B100 — For they shall see eye to eye, when the Lord shall bring again Zion. / Break forth into joy, sing together, ye waste places of Jerusalem: for the Lord hath comforted his people, he hath redeemed Jerusalem. / *Isaiah 3:8*

B101 — In the middle of the city grows the Tree of Life and the gates of it shall never be shut. *Isaiah 60:11*

B102 — They shall rebuild the ancient ruins, the former wastes they shall raise up and restore the ruined cities, desolate now for generations. *Isaiah 61:4*

B103 — Jerusalem ... and Babylon shall become heaps. *Jeremiah 51:37*

B104 — The wide ramparts of Babylon will be razed to the ground, and her high gates will be burnt down. / Thus the labouring of the peoples comes to nothing the toiling of the nations ends in fire. / *Jeremiah 51:58*

B105 — You have as many gods as you have towns, O Judah. / You have built as many incense altars to Baal as Jerusalem has streets. / *Jeremiah 11:13*

B106 — And it came to pass, when the people heard the sound of the trumpet, and the people shouted with a great shout, that the wall fell down flat, so that the people went up into the city. *Joshua 7:20*

B107 — On that occasion Joshua imposed the oath: Cursed before the Lord be the man who attempts to rebuild this city, Jericho. He shall lose his firstborn when he lays its foundation, and he shall lose his youngest son when he sets up its gates. *Joshua 6:26*

B108 — Arrogant men set the city ablaze, but wise men calm the fury. *Proverbs 29:8*

B109 — A Brother is a better defense than a strong city, and a friend is like the bars of a castle. *Proverbs 18:19*

B110 — By the blessing of the upright the city is exalted, but it is overthrown by the mouth of the wicked. *Proverbs 11:11*

B111 — He that is slow to anger is better than the mighty; and he that ruleth his spirit than he that taketh a city. *Proverbs 14:32*

B112 — Like an open city with no defenses is the man with no check on his feelings. *Proverbs 25:28*

B113 — Beautiful for situation, the joy of the whole earth, is Mount Zion, . . . the city of the great King. *Psalms 48:2*

B114 — By the waters of Babylon we sat down and wept: when we remembered thee, O Sion. / As for our harps, we hanged them up: upon the trees that are therein. / For they that led us away captive required of us then a song, and melody, in our heaviness: Sing us one of the songs of Sion. / How shall we sing the Lord's song in a strange land? / If I forget thee, O Jerusalem: let my tongue cleave to the roof of my mouth: yea, if I prefer not Jerusalem in my mirth. / *Psalms 137:1*

B115 — Glorious things are spoken of thee, O city of God. *Psalms 87:3*

B116 — Her foundations are upon the holy hills: the Lord loveth the gates of Sion more than all the dwellings of Jacob. / Very excellent things are spoken of thee: thou city of God. / *Psalms 87:1*

B117 — The hills stand about Jerusalem: even so standeth the Lord round about his people, from this time forth for evermore. For the rod of the ungodly cometh not into the lot of the righteous: lest the righteous put their hand unto wickedness. *Psalms 125:2*

B118 — Hungry and thirsty: their soul fainted in them. / So they cried unto the Lord in their trouble: and he delivered them from their distress. / He led them forth by the right way: that they might go to the city where they dwelt. / *Psalms 105:5*

B119 — If I forget thee, O Jerusalem, let my right hand forget her cunning. *Psalms 137:5*

B120 — The sacrifice of God is a troubled spirit: a broken and contrite heart, O God, shalt thou not despise. O be favourable and gracious unto Sion: build thou The Walls of Jerusalem. *Psalms 49:16*

B121 — Thanks be to the Lord: for he hath shewed me marvellous great kindness in a strong city. *Psalms 31:23*

B122 — Unless the Lord keepeth the city, the watchman waketh but in vain. [Motto of the City of Edinburgh] *Psalms 127:1*

B123 — Who will lead me into the strong city: who will bring me into Edom? *Psalms 60:6*

B124 — He also built Upper-Beth-horon and Lower-Beth-horon as fortified cities with walls and barred gates, and Baalath as well as all his store-cities, and all the towns where he quartered his chariots and horses; and he carried out all his cherished plans for building in Jerusalem, in the Lebanon, and throughout his whole dominion. *Second Chronicles 8:6*

B125 — You can see how pleasantly our city is situated, but the water is polluted and the country is troubled with

miscarriages. *Second Kings 2:19*

B126 — His hands are as gold rings set with the beryl: his belly is as bright ivory overlaid with sapphires. / His legs are as pillars of marble, set upon sockets of fine gold: his countenance is as Lebanon, excellent as the cedars. / His mouth is most sweet: yea, he is altogether lovely. This is my beloved, and this is my friend, O daughters of Jerusalem. / *Song of Solomon 5:14*

B127 — The watchmen that went about the city found me, they smote me, they wounded me; the keepers of the walls took away my veil from me. / I charge you, O daughters of Jerusalem, if ye find my beloved, that ye tell him, that I am sick of love. / What is thy beloved more than another beloved, O thou fairest among women? / *Song of Solomon 5:7*

B128 — Thus saith the Lord of hosts: I am returned to Sion, and I will dwell in the midst of Jerusalem; and Jerusalem shall be called the city of truth, and the mountain of the Lord of hosts, The sanctified mountain. *Zechariah 8:3*

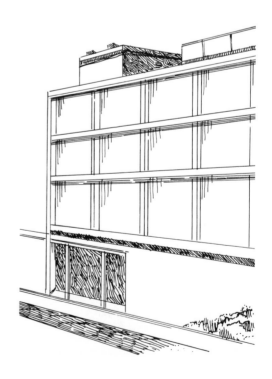

BIBLE, New Testament

B129 — Brought up in this city at the feet of Gamaliel. *Acts 22:3*

B130 — I go bound in the spirit unto Jerusalem. *Acts 20:22*

B131 — Parthians, and Medes, and Elamites, and the dwellers In Mesopotamia, and in Judaea, and Cappadocia, in Pontus, and Asia. / Phrygia and Pamphylia, in Egypt, and in the parts of Libya about Cyrene, and strangers of Rome, Jews and proselytes, / Cretes and Arabians, we do hear them speak in our tongues the wonderful works of God. / *Acts 2:9*

B132 — Paul said, I am a man which am a Jew of Tarsus, a city in Cilicia, a citizen of no mean city. *Acts 39:75*

B133 — Paul said to Barnabas, 'Let us return and visit the brethren in all the cities where we have preached the word of the Lord, to see how they are doing.' *Acts 15:36*

B134 — Ye men of Athens, I perceive that in all things ye are too superstitious. / For as I passed by, and beheld your devotions, I found an altar with this inscription, TO THE UNKNOWN GOD. Whom therefore ye ignorantly worship, him declare I unto you. / *Acts 17:22*

B135 — In perils in the city, in perils in the wilderness, in perils in the sea, in perils among false brethren. *II Corinthians 11:26*

B136 — For he looked for a city that hath foundations; whose builder and maker is God. [of Abraham] *Hebrews 11:10*

B137 — For here we have no continuing city, but we seek one to come. *Hebrews 12:14*

B138 — Can there any good thing come out of Nazareth? *John 1:46*

B139 — And whatever town you enter, and they receive you, eat what is set before you and cure the sick who are there, and say to them, 'The kingdom of God is at hand for you.' But whatever town you enter, and they do not receive you — go out into the streets and say, 'Even the dust from your town that cleaves to us we shake off against you; yet know this, that the kingdom of God is at hand.' I say to you, that it will be more tolerable for Sodom in that day than for that town. *Luke 10:8-12*

B140 — Have thou authority over ten cities. *Luke 19:17*

B141 — When ye go out of that city, shake off the very dust from your feet for a testimony against them. *Luke 9:5*

B142 — A city that is set on a hill cannot be hid. *Matthew 5:14*

B143 — Then he began to reproach the cities in which most of his miracles were worked, because they had not repented. *Matthew 11:20*

B144 — O Jerusalem, Jerusalem, thou that killest the prophets and stonest them which are sent unto thee, how often would I have gathered thy children together, even as a hen gathereth her chickens under her wings, and ye would not! *Matthew 23:37*

B145 — And a strong angel took up a stone, as it were a great millstone, and cast it into the sea, saying, 'With this violence will Babylon, the great city, be overthrown, and will not be found anymore.' *Revelation 18:21*

B146 — And another angel followed, saying, 'She has fallen, Babylon the great, who of the wine of the wrath of her immorality, has given all the nations to drink.' *Revelation 14:8*

B147 — And I John saw the holy city, new Jerusalem, coming down from God out of heaven, prepared as a bride adorned for her husband. *Revelation 21:1*

B148 — And the city had no need of the sun, neither of the moon, to shine in it: for the glory of God did lighten it, and the Lamb is the light thereof. *Revelation 21:19*

B149 — And the city stands foursquare, and its length is as great as its breadth; and he measured the city with the reed, to twelve thousand stadia: the length and the breadth and the height of it are equal. ['Foursquare' denotes perfect symmetry, and signifies the grandeur of the 'heavenly Jerusalem' of which John is writing.] *Revelation 21:16*

B150 — And the street of the city was pure gold, as it were transparent glass. [of the 'heavenly Jerusalem'] *Revelation 21:21*

B151 — And the woman whom thou sawest is the great city which has kingship over the kings of the earth. *Revelation 17:18*

B152 — Babylon the great, the mother of harlots and abominations of the earth. *Revelation 27:5*

B153 — God shall take away his part out of the book of life, and out of the holy city, and from the things which are written in this book. *Revelation 22:19*

B154 — Woe, woe, the great city, which was clothed in fine linen and purple and scarlet, and gilded in gold and precious stone, and pearls; for in one hour riches so great were laid waste! [of Babylon] *Revelation 18:16-17*

BIRD, Caroline (1915-)

B155 — New York City probably has more nubile women running around loose than any other spot on earth. There were, to be exact, 68,366 more single females than males aged 20 to 34 at the Census of 1960, when there was still a comfortable surplus of single men of marriageable age in the country as a whole. You don't have to go to the library to prove that there were more single girls in 1968, when the deficit of eligible males has become national: You can see them any fine day, striding along in their interesting clothes on the streets of the girl ghetto on the Upper East Side. *The Single Girls of the City: Why They Don't Want to Be Wives*

BIRMINGHAM, Stephen (1932-)

B156 — A great many people go after success simply for the shiny prizes it brings . . . . More men pursue it than women. And nowhere is it pursued more ardently than in the city of New York. *Holiday Magazine, March, 1961*

BISHOP, Jim (1907-)

B157 — New York, the Jerusalem of Journalism.

BISMARCK, Otto Von (1815-1898)

B158 — Great cities must be obliterated from the earth. *(Speech in the Prussian Lower House)*

B159 — I wish I could go to America if only to see that Chicago. *(1870 German Newspaper report)*

BISSELL, Richard (1913-)

B160 — A big dirty city is better than a technicolor sunrise out in the sticks, no matter how many songbirds are tweeting. In the city you may feel lost, but you also figure you're not missing anything. *A Stretch on the River*

BLACK, W. (1841-1898)

B161 — Oxford is half-way to Rome.

BLAKE, James W. (1862-1935)

B162 — East side, west side, all around the town, / The tots sang Ring-a-Rosie, London bridge is falling down. / Boys and girls together, me and Mamie O'Rourke, / Tripped the light fantastic on the sidewalks of New York. / *The Sidewalks of New York*

BLAKE, Peter (1920-)

B163 — Miami Beach — the gleamingest place south of the polar icecap. Alas, its gleam can hardly be said to be 'undimmed by human tears.' For here, in this glittering collection of our most astonishing architectural acrobatics, the affluent society has finally gone berserk! This is the ultimate junkpile — that mysterious place our television stars must mean when they talk of 'Videoland.' Here the vulgarians have outdone themselves: if Miami Beach did not exist, the enemies of America would have to invent it. *God's Own Junkyard*

B164 — With a very, very few exceptions, our cities seem to be headed for a grim future indeed — unless we determine to make some radical changes. That future looks something like this: first our cities will be inhabited solely by the very poor (generally colored) and the very rich (generally white) — plus a few division of police to protect the latter from the former. Second, they will become *primarily* places to work in — places for office buildings and for light industry. Third, they will become totally ghettofied — not merely in terms of racial segregation, but also in terms of usage: there will be office ghettos, industrial ghettos, apartment ghettos, amusement or culture ghettos ... bureaucratic ghettos, shopping ghettos, medical-center ghettos. *Ibid.*

B165 — With a very, very few exceptions, the buildings constructed in our cities are built without the slightest regard to matters of urban design. They are built, solely, for the purpose of making a fast buck faster. The laws and codes and commissions that exist for the avowed purpose of helping create better cities are utterly ineffectual, and they are seemingly intended to be so; the policies that govern taxation and financing actually encourage and handsomely reward the builders of bad buildings and penalize the builders of good ones.
   This indictment of the forces that shape our cities is no mere rhetoric. It is based on cold fact. *Ibid.*

BLAKE, William (1757-1827)

B166 — Great things are done when men and mountains meet; This is not done by jostling in the street. *Gnomic Verses*

B167 — And now the time returns again: / Our souls exult, and London's towers / Receive the Lamb of God to dwell / In England's green and pleasant bowers. / *Jerusalem*

B168 — England! awake! awake! awake! / Jerusalem thy sister calls! / Why wilt thou sleep the sleep of death, / And close her from thy ancient walls? / *Ibid.*

B169 — I will not cease from mental strife / Nor shall my sword sleep in my hand / Till we have built Jerusalem / In England's green and pleasant land / *Ibid.*

B170 — Let every Christian, as much as in him lies, engage himself openly and publicly, before all the World, in some mental pursuit for the Building up of Jerusalem. *Ibid.*

B171 — I wander through each charter'd street, / Near where the charter'd Thames does flow, / And mark in every face I meet / Marks of weakness, marks of woe. / In every cry of every Man, / In every Infant's cry of

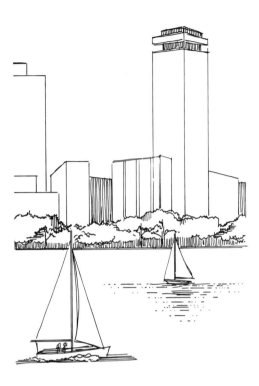

fear, / In every voice, in every ban, / The mind-forg'd manacles I hear. / *London*

BLOFELD, John (1913-)

B172 — Long before Bangkok was saddled with the irreverent soubriquet 'Paris of the East', it boasted another misleading guide-book title — the 'Venice of the East', given the many Klongs that have been filled in, the only time Bangkok remotely resembles Venice is when floods are created by the combination of abnormal rainfall in the northern mountains at the source of the Chao Phya River, and high tides that force their way upriver from the sea. *Bangkok*

BLUCHER, Gebhard Leberecht von (1742-1819)

B173 — A place to plunder! [of London]

BLUM, Barbara

B174 — The talents and energies of environmentalism must be mobilized to help cities to once again become the magnet and the stage for all that is best about being human ... Urban people need desperately to gain control over their destiny. They have had enough of other people planning for them. *(Before Sierra Club board of directors, Berkeley, California, May 6, 1978)*

BLUMENFELD, Hans (1892-   )

B175 — In the long run the development of the metropolis is likely to be influenced most powerfully by improvements in transportation and communication and by the increase in leisure time. The first may lead to an expansion of the metropolis that will embrace a whole region. The second, depending on future developments in mankind's social structure and culture, may lead to *panem et circenses* ('bread and circuses') or to *otium cum dignitate* ('leisure with dignity') Both are possible in the metropolis.

B176 — To listen to our urban developers, there is something sinful in this trend toward decentralization that threatens the city's land values and tax base; it should be reversed! It is time for these modern King Canutes to understand that this trend will never be reversed and that anyone who tries to do so is bound to come to grief. The densely crowded agglomeration of the nineteenth century with its concomittant, the fantastic skyrocketing of urban land values was a short-lived passing phenomenon caused by the time lag between the modernization of interurban traffic; once this time lag was overcome, it was bound to disappear forever; and few will regret its passing. *The Modern Metropolis*

BLUNDEN, Edmund (1896-1974)

B177 — These were men of pith and thew, / Whom the city never called; / Scarce could read or hold a quill, / Built the barn, the forge, the mill. / *Forefathers*

BOCCACCIO, Giovanni (1313-1375)

B178 — Rome, which, as much as it once was the head of the world, has now become its tail.

B179 — The ancient city which is perhaps as agreeable as, or even more agreeable than, any other city in Italy. [Naples] *Decameron*

BOGDANOVIC, Bogdah

B180 — In urban symbology the master symbol simply covers the meaning of the world 'city,' or its literary and visual transcriptions. Where there is a lack of understanding of the master symbol, the symbological morphology of the lower order symbols also lose their essential meaning. In other words a city, our own city, can sometimes be emotio-intuitively transferred into an irrational vision of 'the city' in general. *Symbols in the City and the City as Symbol*

B181 — A modern city is a 'sphynx without a secret.' *Ibid.*

B182 — Modern man is nowhere near as conscious of the identity of his city as was ancient, medieval or Renaissance man. Although at first glance it may seem odd, the loss of a relationship between the archetypal essence of a city makes many notions of the individual characteristics of cities pointless. One universal all-embracing mythical image of 'the city' in no way hindered the individaul cities from expressing their essence in very varied 'figures.' *Ibid.*

BOILEAU-DESPREAUX, Nicholas (1636-1711)

B183 — A hero may be dragged in a romance / Through ten long volumes by the laws of France. / Hence every year our books in torrents run. / And Paris counts an author in each son. / *Satire 9*

BOISTE, Pierre Claude Victoire (1765-1824)

B184 — There is no solitude more dreadful for a stranger, an isolated man, than a great city. So many thousands of men, and not one friend.

BOLITHO, William (1890-1930)

B185 — All great industrial cities have surroundings stranger than anything in the moon. *Camera Obscura*

BONE, James (1872-1962)

B186 — The City of Dreadful Height. [New York]

B187 — It was in London that Whistler discovered the nocturne. *The London Perambulator*

B188 — 'London!' It has the sound of distant thunder. *Ibid.*

BOOKCHIN, Murray (1921-)

B189 — All cities constitute an antithesis to the land. They are a break in the solidity of agrarian conditions, a germ of negation in the agrarian community. *The Limits of the City*

B190 — Contemporary city planning, insofar as it hypostatizes the design or logistical aspects of urbanism at the expense of its human and communitarian goals, becomes truly atavistic. If the priests of the ancient monumental cities were city planners who imposed a cosmological design on urbanized areas to glorify the power of deified monarchies, the modern city planners have become priests whose urban designs are crassly institutional and utilitarian. Both are architects of the mythic in that they subserve the city — its human scale and its communitarian dimension — to suprahuman and nonhuman ends. *Ibid.*

B191 — The megalopolis is an active force in social dissociation and psychic dissolution. It is the negation of the city as an arena of close human proximity and palpable cultural tradition, and as a means of collecting creative human energies. *Ibid.*

BOONE, James Shergold (1799-1859)

B192 — Cities are the centres and theatres of human ambition, human cupidity, human pleasure. On the one side, the appetites, the passions, the carnal corruptions of man are forced, as in a hot-bed, into a rank and foul luxuriance, and countless evils, which would have elsewhere a feeble and difficult existence, are struck out into activity and warmth, by their mere contact with each other. On the other side, many restraints and safeguards are weakened, or even withdrawn. Amidst these teeming multitudes, a man is too often led to persuade himself that he can live with impunity according to the worst 'devices of his own evil heart:' ... *The Need of Christianity to Cities: A Sermon*

B193 — The proof is in both ways abundant, that the atmosphere of cities is essentially a worldly atmosphere; that the life of cities is essentially a worldly life ... there is much in all cities which must be uncongenial with a vital and pure Christianity. *Ibid.*

BOORSTIN, Daniel, J. (1914-)

B194 — The American businessman — a product (and a maker) of the upstart cities of the American West between the Revolution and the Civil War — was not an American version of the enterprising European city banker or merchant or manufacturer. Not an American Fugger or Medici or Rothschild or Arkwright, he was something quite different. His career and his ideals are an allegory of an American idea of community, for he was born and bred in the dynamic American urbanism in the period of our greatest growth. *The Americans: The National Experience*

B195 — American western cities were the rare examples of a dynamic urban environment where almost nothing had been pre-empted by history. Cities were proverbially the centers of institutions, where records were kept and the past was chronicled, hallowed, and enshrined. They were sites of palaces, cathedrals, libraries, archives, and great monuments of all kinds ... The American upstart city, by contrast, had no past. At its beginning, it was free of vested interests, monopolies, guilds, skills, and 'No Trespassing' signs. *Ibid.*

B196 — An easy way to prove that one's 'city' was destined to be a great metropolis was to provide it as quickly as possible with all the metropolitan hallmarks, which included not only a newspaper and a hotel, but an institution of higher learning. [of early American cities] *Ibid.*

B197 — In the Old World a city might grow or decline, prosper or languish, depending on its transportation, among other facilities. But [in the U.S.], without transportation, there was no city at all. *Ibid.*

B198 — In the rapidly growing American West ... every settlement, real or imaginary, large or small, permanent or temporary, claimed the name of 'city.' Every place that claimed the honors of a city set about justifying itself by seeking to conjure up suitably metropolitan institutions. As early as 1747, a European settling in Burlington, New Jersey, noted that the place was called a 'City' 'tho' but a village of 170 houses.' *Ibid.*

BOOTH, Charles (1840-1916)

B199 — It is in the town and not in the country, that 'terra incognita' needs to be written on our social maps. In the country the machinery of human life is plainly to be seen and easily recognized; personal relations bind the whole together. The equipoise on which existing order rests, whether satisfactorily or not, is palpable and evident. It is far otherwise with cities, where as to these questions we live in darkness, with doubting hearts and ignorant unnecessary fears . . .

B200 — London seems the natural home of barristers, solicitors, and law clerks, and the majority are London born.

B201 — In all other departments of life the methods of transit have, during the nineteenth century, been quickened nearly tenfold and increased a hundred-fold. But in cities . . . the past hangs around us, and has made progress very slow. Let anyone now design a place of residence for four or five million inhabitants, and how greatly it would differ in plan and structure from London! *Life and Labour of the People in London*

BORSODI, Ralph (1888-1977)

B202 — Today the farm on which that happy man once lived is cut up into city streets and covered with city buildings. The men and women of Hartford no longer produce their own food, clothing, and shelter. They work for them in stores and offices and factories. And in that same city, descendants of that pioneer farmer are probably walking the streets, not knowing what to do in order to be able to secure food, clothing and shelter. *Flight from the City*

BOSSIDY, John Collins (1860-1928)

B203 — And this is good old Boston, / The home of the bean and the cod, / Where the Lowells talk to the Cabots, / And the Cabots talk only to God. / *On the Aristocracy of Harvard*

BOSWELL, James (1740-1795)

B204 — London is undoubtedly a place where men and manners may be seen to the greatest advantage. The liberty and whim that reigns there occasions a variety of perfect and curious characters. Then the immense crowd and hurry and bustle of business and diversion, the great number of public places of entertainment, the noble churches and the superb buildings of different kinds, agitate, amuse, and elevate the mind. Besides, the satisfaction of pursuing whatever plan is most agreeable, without being known or looked at, is very great. Here a young man of curiosity and observation may have a sufficient fund of present entertainment, and may lay up ideas to employ his mind in age. *London Journal, 1762-1763, ed. by Frederick A. Pottle*

B205 — The noise, the crowd, the glare of shops and signs agreeably confused me. I was rather more wildly struck than when I first came to London. *Ibid.*

BOTERO, Giovanni (1543?-1617)

B206 — A city is said to be an assembly of people, a congregation drawn together, to the end they may thereby the better live at their ease in wealth and plenty. And the greatness of a city is said to be not the largeness of the site or the circuit of the walls, but the multitude and number of inhabitants and their power. Now men are drawn together upon sundry causes and occasions thereunto them moving some by authority, some by force, some by pleasure and some by profit. Let no man think that a city may go on in increase without ceasing. Some answer, the cause hereof is the plague, the wars, the dearths — some others say, it is because God the governor of all things does so dispose. I say that the augmentation of cities proceeds partly out of the virtues generative of men, and partly out of the virtues nutritive of the cities. *Treatise Concerning the Causes of the Magnificence and Greatness of Cities*

B207 — It now only resteth, having brought our city to that dignity and greatness, which the condition of the State and other circumstances afford unto it: That we labor to conserve, to maintain and uphold the dignity and greatness of the same. *Ibid.*

BOULDING, Kenneth (1910-   )

B208 — Civilization, it is clear from the Latin meaning of the word, is what goes on in cities — conversely, a city is a peculiar product of the state of man . . . . Even in civilized man, however, there is a deep ambivalence about the city. The city is not only Zion, the city of God; it is Babylon, the scarlet woman. *The Death of the City: A Frightened Look at Postcivilization*

B209 — The inevitable pattern of a defense city is the pattern of rise and fall. Jerusalem, Nineveh, Babylon, Carthage, and Rome all followed the same grim rhythm. *Ibid.*

B210 — We can almost say that the city is destroyed by its own success. The paradox here is that by the time ninety per cent of the population are urban, the city has really ceased to have any meaning in itself. *Ibid.*

BOWEN, Elizabeth (1899-1973)

B211 — The silence of a shut park does not sound like the country silence: it is tense and confined. *The Death of the Heart*

BOWLES, Samuel (1826-1878)

B212 — All the people west of the Rocky Mountains feel a peculiar personal pride in San Francisco, and, if they would confess it, look forward to no greater indulgence in life, no greater reward in death, than to come hither. *Our New West*

B213 — London and New York and Boston can furnish men of more philosophies and theories, — men who have studied business as a science as well as practiced it as a trade, — but here in San Francisco are the men of acuter intuitions and more daring natures; who cannot tell you why they do so and so, but who will do it with a force that commands success. *Ibid.*

BRACE, Charles Loring (1826-1890)

B214 — Let but Law lift its hand from them for a season, or let the civilizing influences of American life fail to reach them, and, if the opportunity offered, we should see an explosion from this class [of criminals] which might leave this city in ashes and blood. *The Dangerous Classes of New York and Twenty Years' Work among Them*

B215 — One of the remarkable and hopeful things about New York, to a close observer of its 'dangerous classes,' is . . . that they do not tend to become fixed and inherited, as in European cities. *Ibid.*

BRADDON, Mary Elizabeth (1837-1915)

B216 — Paris is a mighty schoolmaster, a grand enlightener of the provincial intellect. *The Cloven Foot*

BRADFORD, Gamaliel (1863-1932)

B217 — The experience of strolling by one's self through the vast multitudes of a strange city is one of the most wonderful in life. I suppose there is nothing quite like it this side of heaven. *The Letters of Gamaliel Bradford*

B218 — There is a lot of provincialism about New York or Chicago or London, at least about the typical inhabitant of those cities. When one is holding entirely aloof, coolly and calmly looking on from a distance, one sometimes catches the spirit of the great, hurrying, whirling throng better than if one is driven tumultuously in the midst of it. *Ibid.*

BRADLEY, Tom (Mayor of Los Angeles) (1917-   )

B219 — If the Federal government can maintain the U.S. commitments to foreign defense budgets, then it can maintain a national commitment to social progress in our cities . . . Just as billions of dollars in post-war economic aid for Europe were spent following World War II, the same sort of investment should be made at home. The goal of such an ambitious program should be to recapture the attractive, healthy lifestyle which made this country thrive. To this end, urban recovery should become a high national priority. *Los Angeles Herald-Examiner, December 2, 1975*

BRATHWAITE, Richard (1588?-1673)

B220 — I came to Gotham, where many, if not all, I saw were fools. *Barbabae Itinerarium*

BRECHT, Bertolt (1898-1956)

B221 — All that will be left of these cities will be the wind that blew through [their streets]. *Vom Armen B.B.*

B222 — The asphalt cities are my home. *Ibid.*

B223 — The great cities stretch their joints . . . over the landscape. *Ibid.*

BREMER, Frederika (Swedish Writer) (1801-1865)

B224 — Chicago is one of the most miserable and ugly cities I have seen in America . . . very little deserving of its name, 'Queen of the Lake' . . . . rather a huckstress than a queen . . . the city seems for the most part to consist of shops . . . it seems as if . . . people come here to trade, to make money.

BRIDENBAUGH, Carl (1903-   )

B225 — Cities rise and flourish in proportion as their natural advantages correspond with the demands of a particular age. This correspondence may be either accidental or the result of preconceived purpose, but history provides many instances of towns which, lacking this harmony between physical and economic environment, have despite artificial efforts

of founders or promoters remained condemned to comparative unimportance, outdistanced by more fortunate rivals. *Cities in the Wilderness*

BRIDGEMAN, H.A.

B226 — The ideal suburbanite is yet in a process of evolution. When he emerges he will blend the best traits of the pure city man and the pure country man. He will be like his grandfather, who kept a store in Ruralville in his simplicity, integrity and industry. He will be like his father, the great city merchant . . . . But he will be better than either his father or his grandfather. *The Independent*

B227 — So long as the rush to the cities continues, the movement into the suburbs to escape the turmoil of city life can only defeat its own end. *Ibid.*

B228 — The suburbanite is a recent growth, because cheap and rapid transportation is a modern affair. In other days the choice of residence lay between the purely country and the purely city environment. The Roman noble could have his home either within the city walls or out at Tivoli, but he would hardly think of including the two localities in his daily itinerary. Fancy Maecenas hurrying to catch the eight-six train for the Forum Romanus. *Ibid.*

B229 — To be a good city man, to be a Seth Low or a Bishop Potter in New York, a Samuel B. Capen or an Edwin D. Mead in Boston, or a Philip Garrett or a Robert Welsh in Philadelphia, or a Charles J. Bonaparate in Baltimore, to love the city of one's birth or of one's adoption, or to hold in reverence its heroes, to conserve its best traditions, to be ever striving to make it a more beautiful and a more holy city — that is an ambition which any man, young or old, may well cherish as he would his own honor. *Ibid.*

BRIDGES, Robert (1858-1941)

B230 — The City's roar is rising from the street; / The old, bedraggled 'types' are shuffling through the strife; / They plod and push, and elbow as they meet, / And glare and grin, and sadly call it 'life.' / *Bramble Brae*

B231 — When men were all asleep the snow came flying, / in large white flakes falling on the city brown, / Stealthily and perpetually settling and loosely lying. / *London Snow*

BROGAN, Denis William (1900-1974)

B232 — Any well-established village in New England or the northern Middle West could afford a town drunkard, a town atheist, and a few Democrats. *The American Character*

B233 — The Englishman is interested in contemporary America. It evokes no response to tell him that Boston is like an English town. He has seen quite enough English towns and would rather hear about New York or Chicago, which are not like English towns. *The English People*

BROOKE, Rupert (1887-1915)

B234 — Every other city in Canada despises Toronto, and yet wants to be like it.

B235 — Cities, like cats, will reveal themselves at night. *Letters from America*

B236 — It is impossible to give it anything but commendation. It is not squalid like Birmingham, or cramped like Canton, or scattered like Edmonton, or sham like Berlin, or hellish like New York, or tiresome like Nice. It is all right. The only depressing thing is that it will always be what it is, only larger, and that no Canadian city can ever be anything better or different. If they are good they become Toronto. [of Toronto] *Ibid.*

B237 — The outcome of it all was a vague general impression that Montreal consists of banks and churches. The people in this city spend much of their time laying up their riches in this world or the next. *Ibid.*

B238 — Cambridge people rarely smile, / Being urban squad, and packed with guile. / *The Old Vicarage, Grantchester*

B239 — A wary eavesdropper can always surprise the secret of a city, through chance scraps of conversation, or by spying from a window, or by coming suddenly round corners. *Rupert Brooke: A Reappraisal and Selection*

BROOKS, Phillips (1835-1893)

B240 — The Bible shows how the world progresses. It belongs with a garden, but ends with a holy city. *Life & Letters of Phillips Brooks (Allen, A.V.G.)*

B241 — O little town of Bethlehem! / How still we see thee lie; / Above thy deep and dreamless sleep / The silent stars go by; / Yet in thy dark streets shineth / The everlasting Light; / The hopes and fears of all the years / Are met in thee tonight. / *O Little Town of Bethlehem*

BROUN, Heywood

B242 — A double Newark. [of Chicago]

B243 — Any fool can stand upon a hill in the country and be aware that grass is up and trees have begun to bud; but in the city spring is served a la carte rather than in heaping portions. Back on my farm lie heavy woods, yet none of these trees appeals to me so deeply as a scrubby sapling which grew in the back yard of my house in New York — when a tree digs its roots down among water pipes and gas mains and thrusts its way up through dust and cinders, that's something. I sometimes think that never blooms a tulip quite so red as that which shows its head in a Park Avenue flower bed betwen the traffic. We

Manhattan nature lovers love her best because we know so little about her. *Quoted in Reader's Digest*

BROWN, Claude (1937-)

B244 — For a long time, Negroes migrating from rural areas into urban communities chose New York, but this is not especially true today. Most Negro immigrants arriving in New York City no longer go to Harlem. . . . It seems the Negro migrants have been told that the Promised Land has been moved from Manhattan to Brooklyn. But actually, the only thing that awaits them in Brooklyn is exploitation. . . . It would be a great thing if we could get somebody or some government agency to inform the would-be migrants where the opportunities exist. They would be given realistic alternatives to going to New York, where they become victims of a hoax and have to resort to illegal means of earning a living. *What 'Ghetto' Means to the Poor*

BROWN, Edmund G., Jr. (1938-)

B245 — Corporate America depends on the regulatory power of Washington, and if that regulatory power was used not just for profit and to prop up existing privilege but to renew the cities of America, they'd be renewed; and they won't be renewed until power is used for that purpose . . . *Before National Urban League, Los Angeles, August 8, 1978*

BROWN, John Mason (1900-1969)

B246 — The more I observed Washington, the more frequently I visited it, and the more people I interviewed there, the more I understood how prophetic L'Enfant was when he laid it out as a city that goes around in circles. *Through These Men*

BROWNE, J. Ross (1821-1875)

B247 — Frame shanties, pitched together as if by accident; tents of canvas, of blankets, of brush, or potato-sacks and old shirts, with empty whisky barrels for chimneys; smoky hovels of mud and stone; coyote holes in the mountain side forcibly seized and held by men; pits and shafts with smoke issuing from every crevice; piles of goods and rubbish on craggy points, in the hollows, on the rocks, in the mud, in the snow, everywhere, scattered broadcast in pell-mell confusion, as if the clouds had suddenly burst overhead and rained down the dregs of all the flimsy, rickety, filthy little hovels and rubbish of merchandise that had ever undergone the process of evaporation from the earth since the days of Noah. [of Virginia City]

BROWNE, (Sir) Thomas (1605-1682)

B248 — All things began in order, so shall they end, and so shall they begin again; according to the ordainer of order and mystical mathematics of the city's heaven. *The Garden of Cyrus*

B249 — A man may be in as just possession of truth as of a city, and yet be forced to surrender. *Religio Medici*

BROWNELL, Baker (1887-1965)

B250 — Some may say that small communities are dull, monotonous. They do indeed lack the artificial coloration of New York. They lack the shocks, the feverish discontinuity and delirium, the displays, the fictions of significance and attention-getting, that make so much in the city that is called interesting. They express more often the continuities of living, the lifelong drama with its beginning, its middle, and its end, and the deep stability and balance of movement that human life sometimes can attain. *The Human Community: Its Philosophy and Practice for a Time of Crisis*

BROWNING, Elizabeth Barrett (1806-1861)

B251 — Fair, fantastic Paris. *Aurora Leigh*

BROWNING, Robert (1812-1889)

B252 — A hole. [of Boston]

B253 — Of all the places in the world, the one which from its literary societies sends me the most intelligent and thoughtful criticism upon my poetry. [of Chicago]

B254 — A world of men for me.[cities in general]

B255 — Four great walls in the New Jerusalem, / Meted on each side by the angel's reed, / For Leonard, Rafael, Agnolo and me / To cover. / *Andrea del Sarto*

B256 — Lo, the moon's self! / Here in London, yonder late in Florence, / Still we find her face, the thrice-transfigured. / Curving on a sky imbrued with colour, / Drifted over Fiesole by twilight, / Came she, our new crescent of a hair's-breadth. / Full she flared it, lamping Samminiato, / Rounder 'twixt the cypresses and rounder, / Perfect till the nightingales applauded. / *One Word More*

B257 — Everyone soon or late comes round by Rome. *The Ring and the Book*

BRUCKBERGER, Raymond L. (1907-)

B258 — One always feels that Americans do not feel entirely at home on their own soil, and that they are still on it as guests . . . The first time I walked up Fifth Avenue I still thought that all the people had come from the country for the day. I had the same impression in all American cities. *One Sky to Share*

BRUSH, Katherine (1902-1952)

B259 — New Yorkers are nice about giving you street directions; in fact they seem quite proud of knowing where they are themselves.

BRUSSEL, Eugene E.

B260 — A sewer for all the activities the suburbanite does not wish to support. [definition of the city]

BRYAN, William Jennings (1860-1925)

B261 — You come to tell us that the great cities are in favor of the gold standard; we reply that the great cities rest upon our broad and fertile prairies. Burn down your cities and leave our farms, and your cities will spring up again as if by magic; but destroy our farms and the grass will grow in the streets of every city in the country. *Cross of Gold Speech*

BRYANT, William Cullen (1794-1878)

B262 — How fast the flitting figures come! / The mild, the fierce,the stony face; / Some bright with thoughtless smiles, and some / Where secret tears have left their trace. / These struggling tides of life that seem / In wayward, aimless course to tend / Are

eddies of the mighty stream / That rolls to its appointed end. / *The Crowded Street*

B263 — And when the hour of rest / Comes, like a clam upon the mid-sea brine, / Hushing its billowy breast — / The quiet of that moment too is thine; / It breathes of Him who keeps / The vast and helpless city while it sleeps. / *Hymn of the City*

BRYCE, (Lord) James (1838-1922)

B264 — Any European student of politics who wishes to understand the problem of government in the United States, whether of city government or any other form of it, must first of all transfer himself, if he can, to a point of view precisely the opposite of that which is natural to him. *The American Commonwealth*

B265 — A European city, but of no particular country. [of New York]

B266 — For many years, Americans applied to cities the theories which they had successfully embodied in the government of their States. It is only as some of these theories have broken down, when applied to cities, that Americans have begun to realize that they have on their hands a problem, new for them, which must be solved, so to speak, by rules of its own. *The American Commonwealth*

B267 — In great cities the forces that attack and pervert democratic government are exceptionally numerous, the defensive forces that protect it exceptionally ill-placed for resistance. Satan has turned his heaviest batteries on the weakest part of the ramparts. *Ibid.*

B268 — In many of the cities of the United States, indeed, in almost all of them, the population not only is thus largely untrained in the art of self-government but it is not even homogeneous. So that an American city is confronted not only with the necessity of instructing large and rapidly growing bodies of people in the art of government, but it is compelled at the same time to assimilate strangly different component parts into an American community. It will be apparent to the student that either one of these functions by itself would be difficult enough. *Ibid.*

B269 — It may be claimed for American institutions even in cities, that they lend themselves with wonderfully little friction to growth and development and to the peaceful assimilation of new and strange populations. *Ibid.*

B270 — It may justly be said, therefore, that the American city, if open to serious blame, is also deserving of much praise. Every one understands that universal suffrage has its drawbacks, and in cities these defects become especially evident. It would be uncandid to deny that many of the problems of American cities spring from this factor, especially because the voting population is continually swollen by foreign immigrants whom time alone can educate into an intelligent harmony with the American system. In this Americanizing of the large immigration into the United States, the American cities, through their public-school system, are doing their full share and are doing it rapidly and well. *Ibid.*

B271 — Now the Spoils system, with the party machinery which it keeps oiled and greased and always working at high pressure, is far more potent and pernicious in great cities than in country districts. For in great cities we find an ignorant multitude, largely composed of recent immigrants, untrained in self-government . . . . *Ibid.*

B272 — One particular in which the American city may be thought to have come short of what might have been expected, may be described in general terms as a lack of foresight . . . The improvement of cities seems everywhere to have been made by tearing down and replacing at great cost, rather than by a far-sighted provision for the demands and opportunities of the future. *Ibid.*

B273 — The population of American cities is much more heterogeneous than the population of these European cities; yet the American cities are free from soldiers, and although they have a smaller police force than corresponding European cities, public order is just as well preserved. The fact is that in American cities the people keep themselves in order, because they feel the city is theirs. Manhood suffrage in American cities, as everywhere else in the United States, wakes the people up and develops a population of great average capacity. *Ibid.*

B274 — The story of municipal reform in the United States is everywhere a story of the effort, by constitutional amendment, to limit the power of the State legislature to interfere with the details of city government. *Ibid.*

B275 — Taxes are usually so much higher in the larger cities than in the country districts or smaller municipalities, that there is a strong tendency for rich men to migrate from the city to its suburbs in order to escape the city collector. Perhaps the city overtakes them, extending its limits and incorporating its suburbs; perhaps they fly farther afield by the railway and make the prosperity of country towns twenty or thirty miles away. The unfortunate consequence follows, not only that the taxes are heavier for those who remain in the city, but that the philanthropic and political work of the city loses the participation of those who ought to have shared in it. *Ibid.*

B276 — There is no denying that the government of cities is the one conspicuous failure of the United States . . . . The faults of the State governments are insignificant compared with the extravagance, corruption, and mismanagement which have marked the administrations of most of the great cities. For these evils are not confined to one or two cities. The commonest mistake of Europeans who talk about America has been to assume that the political vices which became notorious in New York are found everywhere. The next most common is to suppose that they are found nowhere else. *Ibid.*

B277 — Two tests of practical efficiency may be applied to the government of a city: What does it provide for the people, and What does it cost the people? *Ibid.*

B278 — What Dante said of his own city may be said of the cities of America: they are like the sick man who finds no rest upon his bed, but seeks to ease his pain by turning from side to side. Every now and then the patient finds some relief in a drastic remedy, such as the enactment of a new charter and the expulsion at an election of a gang of knaves. *Ibid.*

B279 — Why is it, then, that Americans are less proud of their institutions, as illustrated in city government, than anywhere else? *Ibid.*

B280 — Great cities are liable to become great dangers in a political sense, because the more men are crowded in great masses, the more easily they become excited, the more they are swept away by words, and the more they form what might be called a revolutionary temper. *The Menace of Great Cities*

B281 — It is a great evil in the city that people are cut off from nature and communion with nature, so that they who would like to enjoy the sights and scenes and blessings of nature can do so only on rare occasions and by taking a journey. *Ibid.*

B282 — Life in the great city tends to stimulate and increase beyond measure that which is the menace of the American city — intensification of nervous strain and nervous excitability. *Ibid.*

B283 — What you want [in Washington] is to have a city which every one who comes from Maine, Texas, Florida, Arkansas, or Oregon can admire as being something finer and more beautiful than he had ever dreamed of before; something which makes him even more proud to be an American. *The Nation's Capital*

BUCHAN, John (1875-1940)

B284 — London at the turn of the century had not yet lost her Georgian air. Her ruling society was aristocratic till Queen Victoria's death and preserved the modes and rites of aristocracy .... In the summer she was a true city of pleasure, every window box gay with flowers, her streets full of splendid equipages, the Park a show ground for fine horses and handsome men and women .... Looking back, that time seems to me unbelievably secure and self-satisfied ... The world was friendly and well-bred as I remember it, without the vulgarity and the worship of wealth which appeared with the new century. *Memory Hold the Door*

BUCHWALD, Art (1925-)

B285 — Any sportsman will tell you that the only three things to see in the Louvre are the 'Winged Victory of Samothrace,' the 'Venus de Milo' and the 'Mona Lisa.' The rest of the sculpture and paintings are just so much window dressing for the Big Three, and one hates to waste time in the Louvre when there is so much else to see in Paris. *Down the Seine and up the Potomac*

B286 — Every person who comes to Venice is influenced in some way by one of the great writers who have written about the city. Hemingway has probably influenced me more than anyone, and without *Across the River and into the Trees*, I doubt if I'd even have enjoyed being there. *Ibid.*

B287 — This city, which has now become the PX to the world, has a population of 3,239,548 people, of whom 3,239,546 earn their living as tailors. The making of suits in Hong Kong is the most important industry in the country, and in the struggle for the backs of men, this British crown colony looks like Gimbels basement on a Saturday afternoon before Father's Day. *Ibid.*

B288 — Today there isn't a town in Italy that doesn't have several first-class *Far Rumore* [to make noise] teams. While refinements have been added, the objective of the sport is still the same — to keep tourists from sleeping. In some cities, motor scooters and Ferraris have replaced the pigs and donkey carts, and the automobile horn is as important to the Far Rumore player as the cape is to the matador. *Ibid.*

BUCKMASTER (Lord)

B289 — Nor can you without the influence of the law enable a mere group of sheds to become a great city throbbing with life. *Address to the Canadian Bar Association*

BUDER, Stanley

B290 — The motivating vision in the development of the American suburbs has been, and to an extent remains, that of the family preoccupied with achieving a private environment, and extending the family's personal space both within and without the house. Family territoriality, rather than general use or public has been the primary concern. *The Future of the American Suburbs*

BUNYAN, John (1628-1688)

B291 — It beareth the name of Vanity Fair, because the town where 'tis kept is lighter than vanity. *Pilgrim's Progress*

BURCHARD, John Ely (1898-1975)

B292 — Symbolic suggestions [are] implied in the very names of some cities. There are symbols of sin, at the high level of Babylon, Tyre, Sidon, Sodom, Gomorrah, or the low level of Las Vegas. There are symbols of Power such as Rome, Thebes, Berlin, Moscow. There are symbols of Holiness or Faith: Banaras, Jerusalem, Mecca, Lourdes. There are symbols of Pleasure: Paris, Vienna; of Decadence: Byzantium. There are symbols of products: Damascus, Toledo, Sheffield, Milwaukee, Hollywood. There are symbolic cities that merely suggest the exotic and the faraway: Samarkand or Timbuktu. There are cities that bear the cross of the symbolic association with one bad man or one unhappy event: Chicago, Ferrara, Dallas. There are cities with heavy symbolic significance because of a single such repeated reference: Samarra of the appointments. Symbolism pours from cities which never existed at all: Atlantis, Xanadu, The City of Brass, Anaurot, the City of Dis. *The City as Symbol*

B293 — The big metropolis can make all the greater joys possible. That is because it presents the statistical probability that within its boundaries there are enough potential customers for each experience which may be caviar to the general. We have to remember that most experiences are caviar, even professional football. The Green Bay Packers could not stay in business on the Green Bay audience, enthusiastic and chauvinistic as it is. *The Limitations of Utilitarianism as a Basis for Determining Urban Joy*

B294 — The essence of the ideal city is that a wide variety of individuals living in it have a clear chance to live a richly individualistic life *if they want to*; and I project this still further to include in the essence the stipulation that the humane city shall itself have individuality. *Ibid.*

B295 — The city is the only place where true diversity can thrive and where specialization can reach its apogee. *Quoted in The Metropolis and Modern Life, E.M. Fisher, Ed.*

B296 — We must remind ourselves that a city must be free to be ideal. Paris was not ideal in 1793 or in 1940. No city is ideal where the citizens hide in corners, tremble before the fear of the anonymous denouncer, or look at each other in suspicion. All the other desirable qualities might reside in Buenos Aires, Madrid, Moscow or Prague. Yet suspicion residing there destroys the ideal. This could also happen in New York. *Ibid.*

BURGESS, Anthony (1917-   )

B297 — But why not write somewhere else? In Manchester, England, where I was born, or London, or Toronto? The answer is, I think, that in many of our great industrial cities, writing, making poetry, music, statues, or churches is not really approved of. It is not part of the day's work. The day's work is making bread and mending shoes and building machines.
   In Rome, however, art is part of daily life. One makes one's statues or poems or books as one makes bread or mends shoes. Art is part of Rome's business. And Rome itself is a work of art as well as a living breathing being, which is what all cities should be. *Quoted in Cities, John McGreevy*

B298 — Despite the traditions, Rome is not in fact a holy city. The Romans are not a holy people; they are pagans. *Ibid.*

B299 — Rome is a mother. Rome is a whore. Rome can be domineering, imperious, corrupt, vicious. But Rome can never be ungenerous. Rome gives all of her sensual pleasures, without stint. *Ibid.*

BURGON, (Rev.) John William (1813-1888)

B300 — A rose-red city — 'half as old as Time'![of Petra] *Petra*

BURNABY, Andrew (1732-1812)

B301 — Can the mind have a greater pleasure than in contemplating the rise and progress of cities and kingdoms? *Burnaby's Travels through North America*

B302 — Philadelphia, if we consider that not eighty years ago the place where it now stands was a wild and uncultivated desert, inhabited by nothing but ravenous beasts, and a savage people, must certainly be the object of every one's wonder and admiration. *Ibid.*

BURNEY, Charles (1726-1814)

B303 — The streets of Vienna are rendered doubly dark and dirty by the extreme height of the houses; but as these are chiefly of white stone [stucco] and in a uniform, elegant style of architecture, in which the Italian taste prevails, as well as in music, there is something grand and majestic in their appearance, which is very striking; and even many of those houses which have shops on the groundfloor, seem palaces above. Indeed, the whole town, and its suburbs, appear, at first glance, to be composed of palaces, rather than of common habitations.

B304 — Vienna is so rich in composers and encloses within its walls such a number of musicians of superior merit, that it is but just to allow it to be, among German cities, the imperial seat of music, as well as of power.

BURNHAM, Daniel (1846-1912)

B305 — Make no little plans, they have no magic to stir men's blood.

B306 — Chicago, on becoming a city, chose for its motto Urbs in horto — a city set in a garden. *The Plan of Chicago, 1909*

B307 — The city, is constantly drawing from the country the young men and women of ambition and self-reliance, who are lured thither by the great prizes which in a democracy are open to the competition of all. *Ibid.*

B308 — City planning, in the sense of regarding the city as an organic whole and of developing its various units with reference to their relations one to another, had its origin in Paris during the Bourbon period. *Ibid.*

B309 — Each city differs from every other city in its physical characteristics and in the nature of its opportunities, so that the development of every city must be along individual lines. This very fact allows full scope for the development of that peculiar charm which, wherever discovered and developed irresistibly draws to that city people of discrimination and taste, and at the same time begets a spirit of loyalty and satisfaction on the part of the citizens. *Ibid.*

B310 — The experience of other cities both ancient and modern, both abroad and at home, teaches Chicago that the way to true greatness and continued prosperity lies in making the city convenient and healthful for the ever-increasing numbers of its citizens; that civic beauty satisfies a craving of human nature so deep and so compelling that people will travel far to find and enjoy it; that the orderly arrangement of fine buildings and monuments brings fame and wealth to the city; and that the cities which truly exercise dominion rule by reason of their appeal to the higher emotions of the human mind. *Ibid.*

B311 — The growth of the city has been so rapid that it has been impossible to plan for the economical disposition of the great influx of people, surging like a human tide to spread itself wherever opportunity for profitable labor offered place. Thoughtful people are appalled at the results of progress; at the waste in time, strength, and money which congestion in city streets begets; at the toll of lives taken by disease when sanitary precautions are neglected; and at the frequent outbreaks against law and order which result from narrow and pleasureless lives. So that while the keynote of the nineteenth century was expansion, we of the twentieth century find that our dominant idea is conservation. *Ibid.*

B312 — Paris is the international capital because in its planning the universal mind recognizes that complete articulation which satisfies the craving for good order and symmetry in every part. *Ibid.*

B313 — The rapidly increasing use of the automobile promises to carry on the good work begun by the bicycle in the days of its popularity in promoting good roads and reviving the roadside inn as a place of rest and refreshment. With the perfection of this machine, and the extension of its use, out-of-door life is promoted, and the pleasures of suburban life are brought within the reach of multitudes of people who formerly were condemned to pass their entire time in the city. *Ibid.*

B314 — The tendency of mankind to congregate in cities is a marked characteristic of modern times. This movement is confined to no one country, but is world-wide. Each year Rome, and the cities of the Orient, as well as Berlin, New York, and Chicago, are adding to their population at an unprecedented rate. Coincident with this urban development there has been a widespread increase in wealth, and also an enlarged participation on the part of the people in the work of government. As a natural result of these causes has come the desire to better the conditions of living. *Ibid.*

BURTON, Robert (1577-1640)

B315 — The commonwealth of Venice in their armoury have this inscription: 'Happy is that city which in time of peace thinks of war.' *Anatomy of Melancholy*

B316 — Isocrates adviseth Demonicus, when he came to a strange city, to worship by all means the gods of the place. [of Rome] *Ibid.*

BUTLER, Samuel (1835-1902)

B317 — Stowed away in a Montreal lumber room / The Discobolus standeth and turneth his face to the wall; / Dusty, cobweb-covered, maimed, and set at naught, / Beauty crieth in an attic and no man regardeth: O God! O Montreal! / *A Psalm of Montreal*

BUTWIN, David

B318 — If you can imagine San Francisco without hills or Palm Springs without desert, then you can picture San Diego without water. Water is a part of every San Diegan's life and it quickly seeps into the experience of every outsider who happens by. *Saturday Review*

BUTZ, Earl L. (Secretary of Agriculture) (1909-   )

B319 — One of the problems that has been created in inner cities has been the exodus of rural people to downtown Baltimore, Philadelphia, Detroit, St. Louis and New York, without the skills to be a productive citizen, without the cultural background to live there. They constitute a breeding ground for crime and delinquency, and cause welfare rolls to skyrocket. We should have kept them in the country. We could keep them much cheaper out there, much more productive out there than we have them in the ghettos of the inner cities. *The New York Times Magazine, April 16, 1972*

BYRON, (Lord) George Gordon (1788-1824)

B320 — Lone mother of dead empires. [of Rome]

B321 — There was a sound of revelry by night. / And Belgium's capital had gathered then / Her beauty and her chivalry, and bright / The lamps shone o'er fair women and brave men. / [of Brussels]

B322 — Alas! the lofty city! and, alas / The trebly hundred triumphs! and the day / When Brutus made the dagger's edge surpass / The Conqueror's sword in bearing fame away! / Alas, for Tully's voice, and Vergil's lay, / And Livy's pictured page! — but these shall be / Her resurrection; all beside — decay. / Alas, for Earth, for never shall we see / That brightness in her eye she bore when Rome was Free! / *Childe Harold's Pilgrimage*

B323 — Ancient of days! august Athena! where, / Where are thy men of might? thy grand in soul? / Gone — glimmering through the dream of things that were: / First in the race that led to Glory's goal, / They won, and pass'd away — is this the whole? / [of Athens] *Ibid.*

B324 — The Goth, the Christian, Time, War, Flood, and Fire, / Have dealt upon the seven-hill'd city's pride; / She saw her glories star by star expire, / And up the steep barbarian monarchs ride, / Where the car climb'd the Capitol. / [of Rome] *Ibid.*

B325 — I live not in myself, but I become / Portion of that around me: and to me / High mountains are a feeling, but the hum / Of human cities torture. / *Ibid.*

B326 — I stood in Venice, on the Bridge of Sighs / A palace and a prison on each hand. / *Ibid.*

B327 — O Rome! my country! city of the soul! *Ibid.*

B328 — While stands the Coliseum, Rome shall stand; / When falls the Coliseum, Rome shall fall; / And when Rome falls — the World. / *Ibid.*

B329 — Much hath been done, but more remains to do — / Their galleys blaze — why not their city too? / *The Corsair*

B330 — I've stood upon Achilles' tomb, / And heard Troy doubted; time will doubt of Rome. / *Don Juan*

B331 — A mighty mass of brick, and smoke, and shipping, / Dirty and dusty, but as wide as eye / Could reach, with here and there a sail just skipping / In sight, then lost amidst the forestry / Of masts; a wilderness of steeples peeping / On tiptoe through their sea-coal canopy; / A huge dun cupola, like a foolscap crown / On a fool's head — and there is London Town. / *Ibid.*

B332 — Thou art in London — in that pleasant place, / Where every kind of mischief's daily brewing. / *Ibid.*

B333 — Troy owes to Homer what whist owes to Hoyle. *Ibid.*

B334 — Bologna is celebrated for producing popes, painters, and sausages. *Letter to John Murray*

B335 — Maid of Athens, ere we part, / Give, oh give me back my heart! / Or, since that has left my breast, / Keep it now, and take the rest! / *Maid of Athens*

B336 — And Freedom hallows with her tread / The silent cities of the dead. / *On the Star of The Legion of Honor*

C

CABLE, Mary (1920-   )

C1 — All cities impose on nature, but it might be said that New Orleans doesn't just impose, it defies. Common sense had little to do with its founding, the swampy shores of the lower Mississippi being a most unwise choice as a city site. *Lost New Orleans*

CADY, Lyman V.

C2 — We are lonely even in the milling crowds of a city, where we may only be recognized as customers for goods and services. Our personalities are weakened and starved by the impersonal life in a city. That is why there is so much wreckage in a city. Our families answer this need to some degree, but not completely. And so, in the last analysis, it is only God who can give us the comfort of utter understanding.

CAEN, Herb (1916-   )

C3 — The trouble with Oakland is that when you get there it's there!

CAESAR, Julius (100-45 B.C.)

C4 — After January 1 next no one shall drive a wagon along the streets of Rome . . . after sunrise or before the tenth hour of the day.

CAHILL, William T. (Governor, New Jersey) (1912-   )

C5 — The Federal government can no longer avoid its responsibility to the Newarks of this country. Housing, health, education and the myriad problems of urban America cannot wait much longer . . . Newark is a sign of the times — the end result of a series of mistakes throughout the years . . . . *The New York Times, December 24, 1970*

CAKE, Lu B.

C6 — In a great, Christian city, died friendless, of hunger! / Starved to death, where there's many a bright banquet hall! / In a city of hospitals, died in a prison! / Homeless died in a land that boasts free homes for all! / In a city of millionaires, died without money! / *Devil's Tea Table and Other Poems*

CALDWELL, Erskine (1903-   )

C7 — Urban living, I think, is an anti-civilized thing. You put people in the slums of the city and lock them up in those high-rises and complexes with no outlet whatsoever for their lives. There are bound to be problems. *The Washington Post, January 29, 1976*

CALDWELL, Taylor (1900-   )

C8 — Once power is concentrated in Washington — admittedly not an immediate prospect — America will take her place as an empire and calculate and instigate wars, for the advantage of all concerned. We all know, from long experience, that progress depends on war. *Captains and the Kings*

CALVINO, Italo (1923-   )

C9 — With cities, it is as with dreams: everything imaginable can be dreamed, but even the most unexpected dream is a rebus that conceals a desire or, its reverse, a fear. Cities, like dreams, are made of desires and fears, even if the thread of their discourse is secret, their rules are absurd, their perspectives deceitful, and everything conceals something else. *Invisible Cities*

CAMERON, Donald

C10 — Tawdry and romantic, bourgeois and

raunchy at once, Vancouver is where the small ambitions flourish and the large dreams move furtively. *Weekend, April 19, 1975*

CAMERON, James

C11 — It is as though London stretched unbroken from St. Albans to Southend in a tangle of ten-lane four-deck super parkways, hamburger stands, banks, topless drugstores, hippie hide-outs, Hiltons, drive-in mortuaries, temples of obscure and extraordinary religions, sinless joy and joyless sin, restaurants built to resemble bowler hats, insurance offices built to resemble Babylon, all shrouded below the famous blanket of acrid and corroding smog. [of Los Angeles] *Evening Standard (London), September 9, 1968*

CAMUS, Albert (1913-1960)

C12 — The cities Europe offers us are too full of the din of the past. A practised ear can make out the flapping of wings, a fluttering of souls. The giddy whirl of centuries, of revolutions, of fame can be felt there. There one cannot forget that the Occident was forged in a series of uproars. All that does not make for enough silence. *The Myths of Sisyphus*

C13 — It is impossible to know what stone is without coming to Oran. In that dustiest of cities, the pebble is king. *Ibid.*

C14 — The loves we share with a city are often secret loves. Old walled towns like Paris, Prague, and even Florence are closed in on themselves and hence limit the world that belongs to them. But Algiers (together with certain other privileged places such as cities on the sea) opens to the sky like a mouth or a wound. In Algiers one loves the commonplace: the sea at the end of every street, a certain volume of sunlight, the beauty of the race. And, as always, in that unashamed offering there is a secret fragrance. *Ibid.*

C15 — Salzburg would be peaceful without Mozart. *Ibid.*

C16 — There are no more deserts. There are no more islands. Yet there is a need for them. In order to understand the world, one has to turn away from it on occasion; in

order to serve men better, one has to hold them at a distance for a time. But where can one find the solitude necessary to vigour, the deep breath in which the mind collects itself and courage gauges its strength? There remain big cities. *Ibid.*

C17 — As a remedy to life in society, I would suggest the big city. Nowadays, it is the only desert within our means. *Notebooks, 1935-42*

CANNING, George (1770-1827)

C18 — Pitt is to Addington / As London is to Paddington. / *The Oracle*

CAPOTE, Truman (1924-)

C19 — Venice is like eating an entire box of chocolate liqueurs in one go. *(news summary), November 26, 1981*

C20 — New York is the only real city-city. *Writers at Work*

CAREY, Hugh L. (Governor, New York) (1919-)

C21 — The suggestion that New York redeem its honor by imposing new taxes fails to recognize that New York is the highest-taxed state in the nation, and New York city the highest-taxed locality in the world. We tax everything that moves and breathes. *The New York Times, October 11, 1975*

CARLETON, Will (1845-1912)

C22 — The rich and voluptuous city, / The beautiful thronged, mansion decked city, / Gay Queen of the North and the West . . . / [of Chicago]

CARLYLE, Jane Welsh (1801-1866)

C23 — Some new neighbors, that came a month or two ago, brought with them an accumulation of all the things to be guarded against in a London neighborhood, viz., a pianoforte, a lap-dog, and a parrot. *(Letter to Mrs. Carlyle)*

CARLYLE, Thomas (1795-1881)

C24 — How men are hurried here; how they are hunted and terrifically chased into double-quick speed; so that in self-defence they *must not* stay to look at one another! [of London]

C25 — A huge immeasurable spirit of a thought, embodied in brick, in iron, smoke dust, palaces, parliaments . . . Not a brick was made but some man had to think of the making of that brick. [of London]

C26 — Ever toiling Manchester, its smoke and soot all burnt, ought it not, among so many world-wide conquests, to have a hundred acres or so of free greenfield, with trees on it, conquered, for its little children to disport in; for its all-conquering workers to take a breath of twilight air in? *Past and Present*

CARMAN, Bliss (1861-1929)

C27 — Tyre and Sidon, —where are they? / Where is the trade of Carthage now? / Here in Vancouver on English Bay / With tomorrow's light on her brow! / *Vancouver*

CARMAN, Harry J. (1884-1964) and Richard TUGWELL

C28 — Somewhere in our agricultural past there lie the roots of Americanism. What we are in body and spirit is not to be discovered growing embryonically in any early city; its beginnings are to be found on the homestead or in the village, and only there. *Agricultural History*

CARVER, Humphrey

C29 — Everyone likes to live in the suburbs. Everyone pokes fun at the suburbs. That's fair enough. Everyone respects those who made the suburbs. Everyone despises the suburbs. Everyone's friends live in the suburbs. Everyone hates the kind of people who live in the suburbs. Everyone wants bigger and better suburbs. Everyone thinks there is just too much suburbs. The You and I live in the suburbs — its lovely to have a home in the suburbs. The whole idea of the suburbs fills us with dismay, alarm, and frustration. Almost everyone's business is dedicated to making life in the suburbs more and more and more enjoyable. The suburbs are a crashing bore and desolating disappointment. The suburbs are exactly what we asked for. The suburbs are exactly what we've got. *Cities in the Suburbs*

CASANOVA, Giovanni Jacopo (1725-1798)

C30 — I knew that Rome was the only city where anybody coming from nowhere could become somebody.

CASSERLY, J.V. Langmead (1909-)

C31 — The best and the worst things happen in cities. The metropolis is a center of culture as well as a home of uncultured masses whose debased standards present a constant threat to our culture. It is the source of law and order and the headquarters of crime; a religious and ecclesiastical center and a place of indifference and piety. The great city lives in a perpetual state of paradox. In the Bible, side by side we find images like Sodom, Gomorrah, and Babylon on the one hand and Zion and the New Jerusalem on the other. *The Children of God in the City of Man*

C32 — Urban loneliness is quite distinct from the solitude of the rural worker. It is a loneliness which a man experiences only among a large number of his fellow men in the knowledge that he is not related to any of them on a genuinely personal level. In fact, urban loneliness is not really solitude at all. It is the experience of being outside of rather than away from a group. *Ibid.*

CASWALL, (Rev.) Edward (1814-1878)

C33 — Earth has many a noble city; / Bethlehem, thou dost all excel. / *Earth Has Many a Noble City*

CATHER, Willa (1873?-1947)

C34 — Freedom so often means that one isn't needed anywhere. Here you are an individual, you have a background of your own, you would be missed. But off there in the cities there are thousands of rolling stones like me. We are alike; we have no ties, we know nobody, we own nothing. When one of us dies, they scarcely know where to bury him. Our landlady and the delicatessen man are our mourners, and we leave nothing behind us but a frock-coat and a fiddle, or an easel, or typewriter, or whatever tool we got our living by . . . . We have no house, no place, no people of our own. We live in the streets, in the parks, in the theatres. We sit in restaurants and concert halls and look about at the hundreds of our own kind and shudder. *O Pioneers!*

CATHERINE the Great (1729-1796)

C35 — I do not like Moscow at all . . . . Moscow is the seat of idleness . . . there [in Moscow] is a collection of riff-raff of every kind, who are always ready to oppose law and order, who since time immemorial turn into a riotous mob at the least trifle, who even cherish the tales of those riots and feed their minds upon them . . . . In Petersburg the people are more submissive, more polite, less superstitious, more accustomed to foreigners. *Notes*

CATHERWOOD, Mary (1847-1902)

C36 — The world of city-maddened people who swarmed to this lake for their annual immersion in nature . . . *The Cursed Patois*

CATO, Marcus (234-149 B.C.)

C37 — Carthage must be destroyed.

CAVANAGH, Jerome P. (Mayor, Detroit) (1928-1979)

C38 — I know it's trite to say money is the answer. I know that some academics now find it stylish to deny that there is an urban crisis at all, let alone one that money can solve. But once — just once — I'd like to try money. *The New York Times, May 22, 1970*

CAVOUR, Camillo (1810-1861)

C39 — Rome must be the capital of Italy, because without Rome Italy cannot be constituted. *(Speech)*

CENDRARS, Blaise (1887-1961)

C40 — It's raining electric lightbulbs / Montrouge Gare de l'Est subway North-South river boats world / Everything is halo / Profundity / In the Rue de Buci they're hawking *l'Intransigeant* and *Paris-Sports* / The airdome of the sky is on fire, a painting by Cimabue. / [of Paris]

CERVANTES, Miguel de (1547-1616)

C41 — And although the things that happened to me there were not very pleasant, if not actually wearisome still I bore them without a grudge just for the pleasure of having seen the place. [of Barcelona] *Don Quixote de La Mancha*

C42 — To Rome for everything. *Ibid.*

CHALMERS, Thomas (1780-1847)

C43 — We believe the difference, in point of moral and religious habit, between a town and country population, to be more due to the difference, in point of adequacy, between the established provision of instruction, for the one and the other, than to any other cause . . . The doctrine of a celestial influence . . . calls for a terrestial mechanism, to guide and extend the distribution of it; and it is under the want of the latter, that a mass of heathenism has deepened, and accumulated, and attained to such a magnitude and density in our large towns. *The Christian and Civic Economy of Large Towns*

CHAMBERLAIN, Joseph (1836-1914)

C44 — The clearing-house of the world. [of London] *(Speech, Guildhall, London)*

CHAMBERLIN, Everett

C45 — What built Chicago? Let us answer, a junction of Eastern means and Western opportunity. The East had an excess of enterprise and capital which as naturally pushed West, on lines of latitude, as water runs down hill . . . . But what made the opportunity? We answer, the simple fact that the district of country within two hundred and fifty miles of Chicago filled up with settlers. *Chicago and Its Suburbs*

CHAMBERS, Robert (1802-1871)

C46 — Manchester streets may be irregular, and its trading inscriptions pretentious, its smoke may be dense, and its mud ultra-muddy, but not any or all of these things can prevent the image of a great city rising before us as the very symbol of civilization, foremost in the march of improvement, a grand incarnation of progress. *Chambers' Edinburgh Journal*

C47 — Musselbrogh [Musselburgh in Midlothian] was brogh When Edinbrogh was nane; And Musselbrogh 'ill be a brogh, When Edinbrogh is gane. *Popular Rhymes of Scotland*

CHAMFORT, Nicolas (1741-1794)

C48 — Had anyone told Adam, on the day following the death of Abel, that some centuries later there would be places where, in an enclosure of twelve square miles, seven or eight hundred thousand people would be concentrated, piled upon one another, do you imagine he would have believed it possible that such multitudes could ever live together? Would he not have conceived an idea of the crimes and monstrosities that would be committed under such conditions much more terrible than the reality has proved? This is a point we ought to bear in mind, as a consolation for the drawbacks of these extraordinary assemblages of human beings.

C49 — Paris is a city of gaieties and pleasures, where four-fifths of the inhabitants die of grief.

CHANCELLOR, Richard (?-1556)

C50 — Moscow itself is great; I take the whole town to be greater than London with the suburbs; but it is very rude and standeth without all order.

CHANDLER, Raymond (1888-1959)

C51 — [Los Angeles] a city no worse than others, a city rich and vigorous and full of pride, a city lost and beaten and full of emptiness.

CHAPIN, Edwin H. (1814-1880)

C52 — The city is an epitome of the social world. All the belts of civilization intersect along its avenues. It contains the products of every moral zone and is cosmopolitan, not only in a national, but in a moral and spiritual sense.

C53 — A city life is a great school for principle, because it affords a keen trial for principle. The man who passes through its temptations, and yet holds on, unyielding, to the right will be proved as if by fire. *Christianity, The Perfection of True Manliness*

C54 — I observe that the first lesson of the street is in the illustration which it affords us of the diversities of human conditions. The most superficial eye recognizes this. A city is, in one respect, like a high mountain; the latter is an epitome of the physical globe; for its sides are belted by products of every zone, from the tropical luxuriance that clusters around its base, to its arctic summit far up in the sky. So is the city an epitome of the social world. All the belts of civilization intersect along its avenues. It contains the products of every moral zone. It is cosmopolitan not only in a national, but in a spiritual sense. Here you may find not only the finest Saxon culture, but the grossest barbaric degradation. *Humanity in the City*

C55 — The city — in this instance, as in many others, representing the world at large — is essentially a race-course, or battle-field, in which, through forms of ambitious effort, and cunning method, and plodding labor, and ostentation, the aspirations of thousands appear and carry on a *Strife for Precedence. Ibid.*

CHAPLIN, Charlie (1889-1977)

C56 — San Francisco, the gateway to the Orient, was a city of good food and cheap prices; the first to introduce me to frog's legs a la Provencale, strawberry shortcake and avocado pears. Everything was new and bright, including my small hotel. Los Angeles, on the other hand, was an ugly city, hot and oppressive, and the people looked sallow and anemic. Nature has endowed the North of California with resources that will endure and flourish when Hollywood has disappeared into the prehistoric tarpits of Wilshire Boulevard . . . . *My Autobiography*

CHARLES II (of England) (1630-1685)

C57 — You will have heard of our taking of New Amsterdam . . . 'Tis a place of great importance to trade. It did belong to England heretofor, but the Dutch by degrees drove our people out and built a very good town, but we have got the better of it, and 'tis now called New York. *(Letter)*

CHATEAUBRIAND, Francois Rene de (1768-1848)

C58 — . . .the celestial Jerusalem. [of Prague]

CHAUCER, Geoffrey (1345-1400)

C59 — All roads lead to Rome. *Astrolabe*

C60 — Ful wel she song the service divyne, / Entuned in hir nose ful semely; / And Frensh she spak ful faire and fetisly, / After the scole of Stratford atte Bowe / For Frensh of Paris was to hir unknowe. / *Canterbury Tales*

C61 — She was a worthy womman al hir lyve, / Housbondes at chirche-dore she hadde fyve, / Withouten other companye in youthe; / But therof nedeth nat to speke as nouthe. / And thryes hadde she been at Jerusalem; / She hadde passed many a straunge streem; / At Rome she hadde been, and at Boloigne, / In Galice at seint Jame, and at Coloigne. / *Ibid.*

CHESTERFIELD, Lord (1694-1773)

C62 — Everything is best at capitals; the best masters, the best companions, and the best manners. Many other places are worth seeing, but capitals only are worth residing at. *(Letter to his son)*

C63 — Paris is the place in the world where, if you please, you may best unite the *utile* and the *dulce*. *(Letter)*

CHESTERTON, Gilbert Keith (1874-1936)

C64 — Lord Lilac thought it rather rotten / That Shakespeare should be quite forgotten, / And therefore got on a Committee / With several chaps out of the city. / *The Shakespeare Memorial*

CHEVALIER, Louis (1911-)

C65 — The growth of cities generally brings about a heightening of living standards and progress in moral and material civilization. But considering that urbanization also causes an apparent decline in fertility of the urban population, it seems to endanger the very standards of living and civilization it sustains. *Urban Communities and Social Evolution in Nations*

CHRISTIE, Agatha (1891-1976)

C66 — A detective city. [of New York City]

CHRYSOSTOM (345?-407)

C67 — The dweller in the country has a higher enjoyment than the rich inhabitant of the city. To him belong the beauty of the heavens, the splendors of the light, the purity of the air, the sweetness of quiet sleep. You shall find in this life true contentment and security, good name and health, and the fewest dangers to the soul. This people dwells in peace, leading a modest and venerable life.

CHURCH, Frank (Senator) (1924-)

C68 — If during the past demented decade the Federal government had spent a tenth as much salvaging our own biggest city as we squandered on Saigon, New York City would not now be teetering on the brink of bankruptcy. *Los Angeles Times, October 21, 1975*

CHURCH, Richard (1893-1972)

C69 — Places, especially man-made places, possess character as obviously as do human beings. Some are definitely evil, some banal, some spiritual, others supple and vigorous. We can think of Rome and London, New York and Florence, Venice and Edinburgh and at once there springs to our minds a composite image of each of these great cities as firmly outlined as the face of any man or woman whom we know. How to command that outline, to reproduce it with the full significance of character, and still more of personality, which it reveals, is a task to put the artist on his mettle. *A Portrait of Canterbury*

CHURCHILL, (Sir) Winston (1874-1965)

C70 — We shall defend every village, every town and every city. The vast mass of London itself, fought street by street could easily devour an entire hostile army; and we would rather see London laid in ruins and ashes than that it should be tamely and abjectly enslaved. *(Radio Broadcast)*

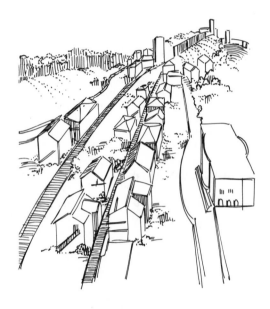

C71 — We shape our buildings; thereafter they shape us. *Quoted in Time*

CICERO, Marcus Tullius (106-43 B.C.)

C72 — The city, the City! Devote yourself to her and live in her incomparable light. As a young man I came to a conclusion from which I have never since wavered. Absenting oneself in any circumstance spells eclipse and discredit for any of us who have the capacity to add to Rome's glory by our labours. *Ad Familiares*

C73 — To fly from the town to the country as though from chains. *De Oratore*

C74 — I cannot describe how ardently I long for town, how hard I find it to bear the stupidity of life here. [Written from Athens] *Letters to Atticus*

C75 — The site of the city — a matter which calls for the most careful consideration of a founder who wishes to set up a state that will long endure — was chosen by Romulus with almost unbelievable foresight — I believe, Romulus foresaw that this city would provide a visiting place and a home for a world empire: for certainly no city placed in any other part of Italy could more readily have wielded such great authority as Rome. *On the Republic*

C76 — I am a Roman citizen. (Civis Romanus sum.) *In Verrem*

CLARK, (Sir) George

C77 — The early Christian monks who retired to the Syrian and Libyan deserts were not merely seeking solitude. They were consciously repudiating the tradition of city life. This aversion might be traced back to the beginning of towns. It is epitomized by the escape of Lot from the cities of the plain. *Ideal Cities of the Past and Present*

C78 — Little as we know about the conditions which made cities possible, we know even less about the motives, hopes and fears which actuated their builders. If written evidence were available, it would probably indicate that every side of human nature was active in creating the first cities, including those aspects which are called idealistic. But no writings exist, for the urban revolution was prehistoric. *Ibid.*

CLARK, Irving Jr.

C79 — Seattle has few rich, few poor, no eccentrics, and no bohemians . . . We have a large, prosperous middle class. Indeed, we are the most nearly classless community in the country. We are strikingly friendly to outlanders. We are everlastingly healthy. *Life, December 24, 1965*

CLARK, Joseph S. (1901-   )

C80 — As the former Mayor of a large American city — and one with a reasonably successful and far-reaching urban renewal program — I believe that unless the Federal Government comes to the rescue, our cities, and all they stand for in our civilization, are doomed. *The New York Times Magazine, April 30, 1961*

CLARK, Neil M. (1890-   )

C81 — After dozing . . . for centuries, this little Spanish town awoke to become captive of the Atomic Age. Now in delayed adolescence it gets bigger every time screaming jets roar over Central Avenue. [of Albuquerque] *Saturday Evening Post*

CLARKE, John (?-1658)

C82 — London Bridge was made for wise men to go over and fools to go under. *Paraemiologia*

CLAUDIAN (4th c. A.D.)

C83 — A city greater than any upon earth, whose amplitude no eye can measure, whose beauty no imagination can picture. [of Rome]

C84 — Mother of arms and of law, who extends her sway over all the earth and was the earliest cradle of justice. [of Rome]

C85 — [Rome] has given a single name to the human race . . . we are all one people. *De Consulatu Stilichonis*

CLAY, Grady (1916-   )

C86 — I . . . regard cities and their urbanizing regions as consisting of time as well as materials, and forever changing. This is the real continuity. There is no universal and everlasting right way for cities to present themselves to us. Each reflects the ideas, traditions, and energies available to its citizens in past centuries, as well as at this moment. Each landscape and townscape is an intricately organized expression of causes and effects, of challenges and responses, of continuity and, therefore, of coherence. It all hangs together, makes sense, fits one way or another — for good or for bad, loosely or tightly. It has sequences, successions, climaxes. It reveals patterns and relationships forming and re-forming. *Close Up*

C87 — No true secrets are lurking in the landscape, but only undisclosed evidence, waiting for us. No true chaos is in the urban scene, but only patterns and clues waiting to be organized. *Ibid.*

C88 — There is hardly any real country left, especially east of the Mississippi if one defines 'country' as territory devoid of urban influences; and the so-called edge of the city has become a complex zone of contention extending in some instances for hundreds of miles. The rightful place of nature in this scene is endlessly debated and remarkably subject to disruption by expanding urban energies. *Ibid.*

C89 — The typical downtown big-city American building side, I would estimate, has been re-used at least four times since 1800, but dependable records of such shiftings are hard to come by. Most American cities are so grossly under-studied, most urban scenes so short-lived, that every person's own memory becomes a historic record, especially west of the Mississippi and in mushrooming suburbias. *Ibid.*

CLEMENT, Clara Erskine (1834-1916)

C90 — The history of no city exceeds that of Constantinople in dramatic interest, and no other can boast of so commanding a position, or one so well suited to the splendid capital of a proud and powerful empire. *Constantinople, the City of the Sultans*

CLEVELAND, Grover (1837-1908)

C91 — The abiding place of wealth and luxury. [Cities in general]

CLEVELAND, Harland (1918-   )

C92 — There isn't anything we don't know about the modern city — its demography, its water table, its engineering design, its art, its slums, its economics, its politics. We just don't seem to know how to make it beautiful, accessible, solvent, safe and clean. *The National Observer, August 16, 1975*

CLINTON, DeWitt (1769-1828)

C93 — New York City . . . will in course of time become the granary of the world, the emporium of commerce, the seat of manufactures, the focus of great moneyed operations, and the concentrating point of vast, disposable, and accumulating capitals, which will stimulate, enliven, extend, and reward the exertions of human labour and ingenuity, in all their processes and exhibitions. *A View of the Grand Canal*

CLIVE, Robert (1725-1774)

C94 — The most wicked place in the universe. [of Calcutta]

CLOSE, Frederick J. (1905-   )

C95 — Most of our difficulties stem from the fact that more and more Americans are living closer and closer together, clustered in our great urban complexes — their daily lives increasingly dependent on each other. So all of the problems and pressures of our society converge to hit and hurt us where we live: in our cities. *(Before Assoc. of Western Advertisers)*

CLOUGH, Arthur Hugh (1819-1861)

C96 — Rome, believe me, my friend, is like its own Monte Testaceo, / Merely a marvellous mass of broken and castaway wine-pots. / *Amours de Voyage*

CLUGSTON, W.G. (1899-   )

C97 — Cities, like human beings, are what they are because of their antecedents and backgrounds. From the day it came into existence as a place where there was just one saloon and one store, Kansas City was bent to business and profits more than to any other possble goal for existence. And this dominant lust of its founders has never ceased to be the ruling motif of their successors. *Kansas City, Gateway to What?*

C98 — Greed for gain set Kansas City in motion and has been chiefly responsible for everything that has been done to make it big and bustling — and in some ways beautiful. *Ibid.*

C99 — When historians of the future appraise the influence that daring, ruthless, and selfish businessmen have had on American cultural development, they will have to give more than a passing attention to Kansas City. *Ibid.*

COHAN, George M. (1878-1942)

C100 — After you leave New York, every town is Bridgeport.

C101 — Give my regards to Broadway, / Remember me to Herald Square, / Tell all the gang at Forty-second Street / That I will soon be there. / *Give My Regards to Broadway*

COKE, (Sir) Edward (1552-1634)

C102 — So the earth hath He appointed as the suburbs of heaven to be the habitation of man. *First Institute*

COLBERT, Elias

C103 — Chicago . . . another Pompeii in luxury if not in licentiousness. *Chicago Tribune*

COLBY, Frank Moore (1865-1925)

C104 — If a large city can, after intense intellectual efforts, choose for its mayor a man who merely will not steal from it, we consider it a triumph of the suffrage. *The Colby Essays*

COLEMAN, William T. Jr. (1920-   )

C105 — The city that is not accessible cannot serve its people. The city that lacks mobility is a poor host, a harsh landlord. *U.S. News & World Report, August 16, 1976*

COLERIDGE, Samuel Taylor (1772-1834)

C106 — In Köhln, a town of monks and bones, / And pavements fang'd with murderous stones / And rags and hags, and hideous wenches; / I counted two and seventy stenches, / All well defined, and several stinks! / Ye Nymphs that reign o'er sewers and sinks, / The river Rhine, it is well known, / Doth wash your city of Cologne; / But tell me, nymphs, what power divine / Shall henceforth wash the river Rhine? / *Cologne*

C107 — I was rear'd / In the great city, pent mid cloisters dim, / And saw naught lovely but the sky and stars. / *Frost at Midnight*

C108 — 'Tis sweet to him who all the week / Through city-crowds must push his way, / To stroll alone through fields and woods, / And hallow thus the Sabbath-day. / *Home Sick*

COLLINS, Emily

C109 — We breathe a freer, if not a purer, atmosphere here among the mountains than do the dwellers in cities, — have more indeed, are less subject to the despotism of fashion, and are less absorbed with dress and amusements. *(Letter to Sarah C. Owen)*

COLLINS, John F.

C110 — Suburbanites come into the city every day, make their living, then go back to a couple acres of land, drink a couple of martinis and chuckle over urban problems.

C111 — If we look at our urban environment we would come to a very early conclusion that despite the technological and scientific advances that have been achieved in the conquest of space and related activities, very few have been transferred to the improvement of the environs in which 160 million Americans reside and work. *The Management of the City of the Future*

COLMAN, George (the younger) (1762-1836)

C112 — Oh, London is a fine town, / A very famous city, / Where all the streets are paved with gold, / And all the maidens pretty. / *The Heir-at-Law*

COLTON, Charles Caleb (1780?-1832)

C113 — I have found by experience, that they who have spent all their lives in cities, improve their talents, but impair their virtues; and strengthen their minds, but weaken their morals. *Lacon*

C114 — If you would be known, and not know, vegetate in a village; if you would know, and not be known, live in a city. *Ibid.*

C115 — In great cities men are more callous both to the happiness and the misery of others, than in the country; for they are constantly in the habit of seeing both extremes. *Ibid.*

COMBRAY, Richard de

C116 — In Abu Dhabi town, dazed by the heat, blinded by the sun, one gropes one's way across half-built sidewalks suddenly ending in rubble and sand and open drains. One keeps watching one's feet, like a goat, to get a grip on the solid parts. The sound of drilling and jackhammering, of welding and cement mixing fuse with the radio and cassette players tinnily hawking Arab dirges, Indian ragas and the latest Salsa rock music; even *Tits and Ass*, from an American musical, finds its way to the local radio station, bleating indecipherably into the air as women, not only veiled but masked underneath by something resembling pickerel skulls sheathed in black, bundle by. *Caravansary – Alone in Moslem Places*

C117 — In the north of Tunisia, things are different. The city of Tunis is extremely civilized. There is something blameless about Tunis, blameless, even bland. Gone is the suppressed rage of Algiers, the voracity of Casablanca. It is easier here, cleaner, gentler. Tunis is the San Francisco of North Africa. *Ibid.*

C118 — It is called simply Casa by those who know it, depriving the name of all the atmosphere the city possibly never had. Travel writers have usually avoided it; guidebooks try to give it an appropriate amount of space: Fodor tells you that its 'sights' can be seen in a morning. Tourists go there to change trains and planes, transsexuals go there to change genders, others pass through to straighten out tickets, collect mail or take a hot bath. It is almost impossible to circumvent it once you have entered Morocco, like trying to avoid the Winged Victory once inside the Louvre. [of Casablanca] *Ibid.*

COLUMELLA (1st c. A.D.)

C119 — For as those who kept within the confines of the country houses were accounted more slothful than those who tilled the ground outside, so those who spent their time idly within the walls, in the shelter of the city, were looked upon as more sluggish than those who tilled the fields ... *De Re Rustica*

COMMYNE, Phillipe de (1447?-1511)

C120 — The most triumphant city I ever set eyes on. [of Venice]

CONDON, Richard

C121 — Made by General Motors, on order from Sears Roebuck. [of American cities] *Newsweek, February 11, 1963*

CONNALLY, John B. Jr. (1917-   )

C122 — No useful purpose can be served by permitting a great national city, a great international city, to go down the drain. We can't let New York go under without it having an almost disastrous impact on all the countries of the world. Trying to hurt New York, you only hurt the nation .... [Calling for Federal aid to New York during the city's fiscal crisis] *Los Angeles Herald Examiner, October 11, 1975*

CONNOLLY, Cyril (1903-1974)

C123 — No city should be too large for a man to walk out of in a morning. *The Unquiet Grave*

C124 — Slums may well be breeding-grounds of crime, but middle-class

suburbs are incubators of apathy and delirium. *Ibid.*

CONOVER, O.M. (1825-1884)

C125 — Alone I walk in the people city, / Where each seems happy with his own; / O friends, I ask not for your pity — / I walk alone. *Via Solitaria: Reconciliation*

CONRAD, Barnaby (1922-   )

C126 — A cosmopolitan labyrinth of infinite surprises. [of San Francisco]

CONRAD, Joseph (1857-1924)

C127 — Then the vision of an enormous town presented itself, of a monstrous town more populous than some continents and in its man-made might as if indifferent to heaven's frowns and smiles; a cruel devourer of the world's light. There was room enough there to place any story, depth enough there for any passion, variety enough there for any setting, darkness enough to bury five millions of lives. *The Secret Agent*

CONSTANTINE (288?-337)

C128 — Oh, Christ, ruler and master of the world. To you now I dedicate this subject city, and these scepters and the might of Rome. Protect her; save her from all harm. [of Constantinople]

COOKE, Alistair (1908-   )

C129 — Babylon in the desert ... it is Everyman's cut-rate Babylon. [of Las Vegas] *America*

C130 — The mass of city dwellers do not seem willing to trust either the authority of Washington or the power of their own municipal governments. In the past twenty years millions of them have abandoned the city and its afflictions altogether and gone to new suburbs in open country. These too have quickly taken on the city's monotonous order and copied its addiction to drugs and its random violence. *Ibid.*

COOPER, James Fenimore (1789-1851)

C131 — I expected to see a capital in New

York, Grace, and in this I have been grievously disappointed. Instead of finding the tastes, tone, conveniences, architecture, streets, churches, shops, and society of a capital, I found a huge expansion of commonplace things, a commercial town, and the most mixed and the least regulated society that I had ever met with. Expecting so much, where so little was found, disappointment was natural. But in Albany, although a political capital, I knew the nature of the government too well to expect more than a provincial town; and in this respect I have found one much above the level of similar places in other parts of the world. *Home as Found*

C132 — It has long been a subject of investigation among moralists, whether the existence of towns like those of London, Paris, New York, etc., is or is not favorable to the development of the better qualities of the human character. As for ourselves, we do not believe any more in the superior innocence and virtue of a rural population than in that of the largest capitals ... If there be incentives to wrong-doing in the crowded population of a capital town, there are many incentives to refinement, public virtue, and even piety, that are not to be met with elsewhere. *New York*

COOPER, Thomas (1759-1839)

C133 — America is a large place; and between the different states, there are strong shades of difference; nor does a large town furnish the same answer to your queries as the country. *Some Information Respecting America*

COPPA, Frank J. (1937-)

C134 — Suburbs, the outer part of a continuously build-up city and not separated from it by intervening land, have been in existence for thousands of years. Such regions were to be found about the ancient city-states of Sumeria and Greece and about Imperial Rome. Medieval Florence and Venice spawned suburbs as did London by the sixteenth century. *Cities and Suburbs in Europe and the United States*

C135 — The systematic study of cities in the United States was initiated by individuals who were in the main born and raised in

nonurban environments. Small wonder that so many of them found the cities chaotic. *Ibid.*

CORTÉS, Hernando (1485-1547)

C136 — We saw a multitude of boats upon the great lake, some coming with provision, some going off loaded with merchandise ... and in these towns we saw temples and oratories shaped like towers and bastions, all shining white, a wonderful thing to behold. And we saw the terraced houses, and along the causeways other towers and chapels that looked like fortresses. So, having gazed at all this and reflected upon it, we turned our eyes to the great market-place and the host of people down there who were buying and selling: the hum and the murmur of their voices could have been heard for more than a league. And among us were soldiers who had been in many parts of the world, at Constantinople, all over Italy and at Rome; and they all said they had never seen a market so well ordered, so large and so crowded with people. [of Tenochtitlán]

COTTERELL, Geoffrey (1919-)

C137 — A marvelous city. No wonder there are songs about it. It is full of ghosts and full of a tantalizing conflict of doubts and hopes. [of Amsterdam] *Amsterdam*

COULANGES, Fustel de (1830-1889)

C138 — Sentiments and manners, as well as politics, were ... changed [by Christianity]. The ideas which men had of the duties of the citizen were modified. The first duty no longer consisted in giving one's time, one's strength, one's life to the state. Politics and war were no longer the whole of man; all the virtues were no longer comprised in patriotism, for the soul no longer had a country. Man felt that he had other obligations besides that of living and dying for the city. Christianity distinguished the private from the public virtues. By giving less honor to the latter it elevated the former; it placed God, the family, the human individual above country, the neighbor above the city. *The Ancient City*

C139 — We should now lose sight of the fact that the ancients never represented God to themselves as a unique being exercising his action upon the universe. Each of their innumerable gods had his little domain; to one a family belonged, to another a tribe, to a third a city... Thus religion was entirely local, entirely civic, taking this word in the ancient sense — that is to say, special to each city. *Ibid.*

COUSTEAU, Jacques-Yves (1910-   )

C140 — Psychologists today believe that people in cities behave like captives. The pattern of frustration, desperation, suicides now observed with captive animals is observed in city life. *The Washington Post, January 4, 1975*

COWARD, Noel (1899-1973)

C141 — In Hong Kong / They strike a gong / And fire off a noonday gun / To reprimand each inmate / Who's in late ... / *Mad Dogs and Englishmen*

COWEN, Joseph (1831-1900)

C142 — The gathering of men into crowds has some drawbacks. It has, in the past, not contributed to the public health, and there are those who maintain that it has dwarfed and enervated our race. But the application of science to the wants of common life has minimized the evils complained of. London, the largest city in Europe, is now one of the healthiest. The concentration of citizens, like the concentration of soldiers, is a source of strength. *The Life and Speeches of Joseph Cowen, M.P.*

C143 — Our towns are the backbone of the nation. They give it strength, cohesion, vitality. Scattered populations are usually ignorant, and oppression is always most easily established over them. The power conferred by concentration may be abused, has been abused, but when regulated by vigilantly supervised representative institutions there is no fear either for the liberty of the individual or the community. *Ibid.*

COWLEY, Abraham (1618-1667)

C144 — God the first garden made, and the first city Cain. *The Garden*

C145 — Well then; I now do plainly see / This busy world and I shall ne'er agree; / The very honey of all earthly joy / Does of all meats the soonest cloy, / And they (methinks) deserve my pity, / Who for it can endure the stings, / The crowd, and buz, and murmurings / Of this great hive, the city. *The Mistress, or Love Verses*

C146 — Let but thy wicked men from out thee go, / And all the fools that crowd thee so, / Even thou, who dost thy millions boast, / A village less than Islington wilt grow, / A solitude almost. / *Of Solitude*

COWPER, William (1731-1800)

C147 — The centre of a thousand trades. [of London]

C148 — Rome shall perish — write that word / In the blood that she has spilt. / *Boadicea*

C149 — John Gilpin was a citizen / Of credit and renown, / A train-band captain eke was he / Of famous London town. / John Gilpin's spouse said to her dear — / Though wedded we have been / These twice ten tedious years, yet we / No holiday have seen. / *John Gilpin*

C150 — From cities humming with a restless crowd, / Sordid as active, ignorant as loud, / Whose highest praise is that they live in vain, / The dupes of pleasure or the slaves of gain; / Where works of man are clustered close around, / And works of God are hardly to be found. / *Retirement*

C151 — . . . Cities then / Attract us, and neglected Nature pines / Abandon'd, as unworthy of our love. / *The Task*

C152 — God made the country, and man made the town. *Ibid.*

C153 — In cities foul example on most minds / Begets its likeness. Rank abundance breeds / In gross and pamper'd cities sloth and lust, / And wantonness and gluttonous excess. / In cities, vice is hidden with most ease, / Or seen with least reproach; and virtue taught / By frequent lapse, can hope no triumph there / Beyond the achievement of successful flight. / *Ibid.*

C154 — O thou, resort and mart of all the earth, / Chequer'd with all complexions of mankind, / And spotted with all crimes; in which I see / Much that I love, and more that I admire, / And all that I abhor; thou freckl'd fair, / That pleaseth and yet shock'st me. / [of London] *Ibid.*

C155 — There is in souls a sympathy with sounds; / And as the mind is pitch'd the ear is pleased / With melting airs or martial, brisk or grave; / Some chord in unison with what we hear / Is touch'd within us, and the heart replies. / How soft the music of those village bells / Falling at intervals upon the ear / In cadence sweet! / *Ibid.*

C156 — The town has tinged the country. And the stain / Appears a spot upon a vestal's robe, / The worse for what it soils. The fashion runs / Down into scenes still rural, but alas! / Scenes rarely graced with rural manners now. / *Ibid.*

C157 — . . . Where has commerce such a mart, / So rich, so throng'd, so drain'd, and so supplied / As London, opulent, enlarged, and still / Increasing London? Babylon of old / Not more the glory of the earth, than she / A more accomplish'd world's chief glory now. / *Ibid.*

C158 — Greece, sound thy Homer's, Rome thy Virgil's name, / But England's Milton equals both in fame. / *To John Milton*

COX, Harvey (1929-)

C159 — The contemporary urban region represents an ingenious device for vastly enlarging the range of human communication and widening the scope of individual choice. Urbanization thus contributes to the freedom of man. *The Secular City*

C160 — If the Greeks perceived the cosmos as an immensely expanded polis, and medieval man saw it as the feudal manor enlarged to infinity, we experience the universe as the city of man. It is a field of human exploration and endeavor from which the gods have fled. The world has become man's task and man's responsibility. *Ibid.*

C161 — Our modern metropolis became possible only after technical advances had solved some of the problems which had heretofore placed iron limits on the size of cities; but the technical metropolis in a sense simply actualized the steel and glass, in pace and personality, what had already been present embryonically in Athens and Alexandria. *Ibid.*

C162 — The polis appeared when bellicose clans and rival houses met here and there to form a new type of community, loyalty to whose laws and gods replaced the more elemental kinship ties which had previously held force. *Ibid.*

C163 — The real illness of the American city today, and especially of the deprived groups within it, is voicelessness. *Ibid.*

C164 — The rise of urban civilization and the collapse of traditional religion are the two main hallmarks of our era and are closely related movements. Urbanization constitutes a massive change in the way men live together, and became possible in its contemporary form only with the scientific and technological advances which sprang from the wreckage of religious world-views. Secularization, an equally epochal movement, marks a change in the way men grasp and understand their life together, and it occurred only when the cosmopolitan confrontations of city living exposed the relativity of the myths and traditions men once thought were unquestionable. The ways men live their common life affects mightily the ways they understand the meaning of that life, and vice versa. *Ibid.*

C165 — The storied Greek polis never realized in full the ideals of town life. It never became fully open or fully universal. It always remained partly a tribe. *Ibid.*

C166 — Urbanization means a structure of common life in which diversity and the disintegration of tradition are paramount. It means a type of impersonality in which functional relationships multiply. It means that a degree of tolerance and anonymity replace traditional moral sanctions and long-term acquaintanceships. The urban center is the place of human control of rational planning, of bureaucratic organization — and the urban center is not just in Washington, London, New York, and Peking. It is everywhere. *Ibid.*

C167 — When man changes his tools and his techniques, his ways of producing and distributing the goods of life, he also changes his gods. Tribal, town, and technopolitan existence represent first of all different forms of social, economic, and political community. As such they symbolize different religions or belief systems. *Ibid.*

C168 — The City remains our existential polity. It exists at that crucial level of life, somewhere between the circle of family and friends on the one hand and the *imperium* of mankind on the other, the level where life must be made civil as well as livable. *The Seduction of the Spirit*

C169 — Man's 'fall' in the old myth did not begin with his exceeding his limits. It began when he asked the snake to make the first decision he confronted, whether to snatch for the status of deity. His sin was not pilfering God's fire but abdicating his choice to a fork-tongued consultant, not so much pride as sloth. After that, of course, Adam panicked. He tried to become the

omnipotent all-controlling deity. Instead of imaginatively fulfilling that part of the cosmos-tending he was well equipped to do, he plotted to become the Master Programmer, the Ultimate City Planner. *Ibid.*

C170 — The religion of *homo urbanitas*, the dweller in the city, is a special kind of religion. Regardless of his or her religious past, once the city really makes its impact on the psyche, any city person's religion begins to have more in common with that of other city people than it does with the faith of people of his own tradition who still live, either physically or spiritually, in the countryside or in small towns. *Ibid.*

C171 — Religious anti-urbanism is deeply ironic. Christianity was born in a troubled provincial capital, flourished in the slums and ghettos of the ancient Mediterranean basin (Rome, Corinth, Ephesus) among an urban proletariat, spread through the settlements of Europe, spawned new cities in North and South America, and hymned its vision of destiny with the image of a New Jerusalem. *Ibid.*

C172 — Someone once wrote that the best literary descriptions of the Catholic Church are not written by 'born Catholics' but by people who have either been converted to it or left it. One thinks for example of Graham Greene the convert and James Joyce the apostate. The same is true about the city. To be able to write about it one must probably have had to come to it or to have fled it, to have felt firsthand the difference it makes.

CRAIG, Maurice James (1919-   )

C173 — The brides they will mourn / And the stones they will weep, / And the damp Logan fog / Lull the city to sleep. / It's to hell with the future, / And live in the past. / May the Lord in his mercy / Be kind to Belfast. /

CRANE, Hart (1899-1932)

C174 — Dinners, soirees, erratic millionaires, painters, translators, lobsters, absinthe, music promenades, oysters, sherry, aspirin, pictures, Sapphic heiresses, editors, books, sailors. And how! [of Paris]

C175 — The subway yawns the quickest promise home. [of the subway] *The Tunnel*

CRATES (of Thebes) 4th c. B.C.

C176 — I have not one single city, but the whole world in which to live.

CROSSING, W. (1847-1928)

C177 — When Plymouth was a vuzzy down, / Plympton was a borough town. / *Folk Rhymes of Devon*

CROW, Carl (1883-1945)

C178 — The history of the interesting and dynamic city of Flint has been worth recording because it is more than the chronical of an individual city. It epitomizes the history of America . . . America is a story of the industrial development which has brought us such a high standard of living. *The City of Flint*

CROWELL, Paul and A.H. RASKIN

C179 — If New York has a unifying characteristic, it is a spirit of urgency. It is a city in a hurry. *New York, 'Greatest City in the World'*

C180 — New York is not a city. It is a thousand cities, each with its own life and spirit, all jampacked into an area of two hundred ninety-nine square miles. It is Broadway and the Bowery; Wall Street and Union Square; Park Avenue and the lower East Side; Coney Island and the Stork Club. *Ibid.*

CROWLEY, Aleister (1857-1947)

C181 — Toronto as a city carries out the idea of Canada as a country. It is a calculated crime both against the aspirations of the soul and the affection of the heart. *The Confessions of Aleister Crowley*

CUMMINGS, e.e. (1894-1962)

C182 — . . . the city / wakes / with a song upon her / mouth having death in her eyes /

C183 — When i am in Boston, i do not speak. / and i sit in the click of ivory balls. /

C184 — Whereas . . . New York had reduced mankind to a tribe of pygmies, Paris (in each shape and gesture and avenue and cranny of her being) was continually expressing the humaneness of humanity.

C185 — Any skyscraper / bulges in the looseness of morning / but in twilight becomes / unutterably crisp / *Tulips and Chimneys*

CUNLIFFE, Barry (1939-   )

C186 — To understand the meaning of a city it is necessary to focus not so much on the buildings themselves as upon the functions they performed. A city, above all, provided a range of services for its territory. *Rome and Her Empire*

CURRIGAN, Thomas G. (Mayor, Denver) (1920-   )

C187 — I hope to heaven cities are not ungovernable, but I'll admit there are some frightening aspects that would lead one at least to think along these lines . . . Our cities were structured financially when we were a rural nation, and our structures of government are such that the mayor lacks not only the financial resources but the authority to do the job. *(Interview)*

D

DAHLBERG, Edward (1900-1977)

D1 — Can one ever go back? — to a withered amour, to a childhood friend or to one's native city? No matter how trashy our memories are, we cannot relinquish them. In some way Kansas City, Missouri, is as important to me as an El Greco painting. I don't know why, for I cannot understand what I am save that I am the result of all the streets, shanties, livery stables and gimcrack stores of this buxom, hilly town I knew in the early part of this century. Its grass, dandelions, sunflowers and stones are a song in my blood. I walk upon each olden footprint as if it were Christ's Capernaum and Bethlehem. *Return to Kansas City*

DALEY, Richard J. (Mayor, Chicago) (1902-1976)

D2 — The experts are all saying that our big cities have become ungovernable. What the hell do the experts know? *Newsweek, April 5, 1971*

DANA, Richard Henry

D3 — Two days brought us to San Pedro,

and two days more (to our no small joy), gave us our last view of that place.

D'ANNUNZIO, Gabriele (1863-1938)

D4 — 'Do you know, Perdita,' suddenly asked Stelio, — 'do you know of any other place in the world like Venice, in its power of stimulating at certain moments all the power of human life, and of exciting every desire to the point of fever? Do you know of any more terrible temptress? *The Flame of Life*

DARIDA, Clelio (Mayor, Rome, Italy)

D5 — The basic difference between New York City and Rome is that the Italian state gives us credit and Washington doesn't give New York City credit. If I had one message for Mayor Beame, it would be to get all American cities to put pressure on your central government. Cities can't survive by themselves. *Quoted in Christian Science Monitor, November 26, 1975*

DARWIN, Charles (1809-1882)

D6 — One of the most regular [cities] in the world. [of the plan of Buenos Aires] *The Voyage of the Beagle*

DASHKIN, Jerry

D7 — A city of no seasons but that of wet, wind and cold. [of San Francisco]

DAVENPORT, William E. (1862-1944)

D8 — Great is the City of a thousand streets, / The greatest city in the modern land. / Yet are the people blinded in their minds, / By teachings false, the vainest ways of life. / How many dream that money maketh rich. / How many judge that learning maketh wise. / How many cry: 'Position giveth strength.' / Yet it is false, and all the world is fooled. / *Perpetual Fire*

D9 — But of the City: there alone exists / True Beings and real Selves; Identities . . . / That come and go, and are not and yet are. / There also Powers . . . pass, abide, and brood, / And bring forth awful births. / *Visions of the City*

DAVID, Richard S.

D10 — Consider dear Old Lady Thrift. That is, the plump and smiling city of Milwaukee, which sits in complacent shabbiness on the west shore of Lake Michigan like a wealthy old lady in black alpaca taking her ease on the beach. *Milwaukee: Old Lady Thrift*

DAVIDOFF, Paul (1930-)

D11 — The ghetto is a social atrocity. It is a place where people are forced to live. It is unbelievable to me that liberal leaders can speak of 'rebuilding' ghettos. They must be destroyed. If a Negro wants to live in Harlem, great, he should have that choice. If he wants to get out, he should have that choice, too. Today, ghetto living is imposed upon him. This contributes to things like the cry for 'black power' and what is called the politics of frustration.

DAVIDSON, Abraham A. (1935-)

D12 — Until the beginning of the twentieth century the city was a subject almost completely unexplored in the art of the United States. For the American artist, and his patrons, art could be ennobling or inspiring (as were most of the landscapes), instructive (as were the history paintings), escapist (as were most of the bucolic genre scenes), even terrifying or mystifying (as were the paintings by Ryder and others of the visionary tradition). But it could never be ordinary or demeaning or depressing — the very qualities that the city, crowded with men and women going about their routine activities in typically grimy surroundings, represented. *The Story of American Painting*

DAVIES, William Henry (1871-1940)

D13 — What glorious sunsets have their birth / In Cities fouled by smoke! / This tree — whose roots are in a drain — / Becomes the greenest Oak! / *Love's Rivals*

DAVIS, Dorothy Salisbury (1916-)

D14 — There are seasons in Washington when it is even more difficult than usual to find out what is going on in the government. Possibly it is because nothing is going on, although a great many people seem to be working at it. *Old Sinners Never Die*

DAVIS, John H. (1929-)

D15 — Although the pride and dignity of La Serenissima can never be revived, the example of Venice will endure as a permanent source of inspiration for all men. That example was one of consummate heroism — the triumph of a people who turned barren mudflats into a supreme work of beauty, who turned a nightmare of devastation and defeat into a towering victory of the human spirit. *Venice – Art and Life in the Lagoon City*

DAVIS, Kingsley (1908-)

D16 — Today virtually every part of the world is more urbanized than any region was in antiquity. Urbanization is so widespread, so much a part of industrial civilization, and gaining so rapidly, that any return to rurality, even with major catastrophes, appears unlikely. On the contrary, since every city is obsolescent to some degree — more obsolescent the older it is — the massive destruction of many would probably add eventually to the impetus of urban growth. *Origin and Growth of Urbanization.*

D17 — It is worth reminding ourselves that the end of the century is not far away. About two-thirds of the people now living on earth, if mortality continues downward, will still be alive by the year 2000. The projected urban trend, should it come to pass, will therefore put a substantial proportion of present humanity into cities of a size that no human being up to now has ever come close to experiencing. *World Urbanization 1950-1970*

DE GAULLE, Charles (1890-1970)

D18 — There is and has long been . . . a special bond between New York and me . . . . How often, at difficult moments, I looked to New York, I listened to New York, to find out what you were thinking and feeling here, and always I found a comforting echo. *The New York Times, April 27, 1960*

DE JESUS, Carolina Maria (1921-)

D19 — I classify Sao Paulo this way: The Governor's Palace is the living room. The mayor's office is the dining room and the city is the garden. And the favela is the back yard where they throw the garbage. *Child of The Dark: The Diary of Carolina Maria de Jesus*

DEBO, Angie (1890-)

D20 — It is a truism to say that Tulsa is the most American of American cities. All the forces that have gone into the making of a Republic have been intensified there. The successive stages through which the country as a whole has passed during three hundred years — Indian occupation, ranching, pioneering, industrial development . . . . have been telescoped within the single lifetime of some of the older Tulsans. The result has been the quintessence of Americanism — its violence, and strength, its buoyant optimism, its uncalculating generosity, its bumptious independence. *Tulsa: From Creek Town to Oil Capital*

DEUTSCHER, ISAAC (1907-1967)

D21 — Soviet urbanization, in tempo and scale, is without parallel in history. *The Unfinished Revolution*

DE VISE, Pierre (1924-)

D22 — We no longer need very large cities. We developed these behemoths like New York, Chicago and Philadelphia on the basis of late 19th-century transportation and technology . . . . This kind of central location is no longer justified for most industries . . . . I really see little in the cards that will make the city attractive to industry. *U.S. News & World Report, April 5, 1976*

DEWING, Thomas W. (1851-1932)

D23 — Why, if you're not in New York you are camping out.

DIAZ DEL CASTILLO, Bernal (1492?-1581)

D24 — Gazing on such wonderful sights, we did not know what to say or whether what appeared before us was real, for on one side in the land were great cities and the lake itself was crowded with canoes, and in the causeway were many bridges at intervals, and in front of us stood the City of Mexico. [of Tenochtitlan]

DICK, Cotsford (1846-1911)

D25 — In mufti clad, no fashion's frown, / No bores to feed, no calls to pay — / There's nothing half so sweet as Town / When all the *beau monde* is away. / *Back in Town*

D26 — Let those who like pastoral pleasures, / Of daisies and buttercups sing; / But for me — in the town, and its treasures, / I find the delights of the Spring. / *Spring's Delights*

DICKENS, Charles (1812-1870)

D27 — A city without baths or plumbing, lighted by gas and scavanged by pigs. [of New York City]

D28 — The country round this town Toronto, being very flat, is bare of scenic interest; but the town itself is full of life and motion, bustle, business, and improvement. The streets are well paved, and lighted with gas; the houses are large and good; the shops excellent. Many of them have a display of goods in their windows, such as may be seen in thriving country towns in England; and there are some which would do no discredit to the metropolis itself. *American Notes for General Circulation and Pictures from Italy*

D29 — Indeed, it may be said of Kingston, that one half of it appears to be burnt down, and the other half not to be built up. *Ibid.*

D30 — This dismal Cairo [Illinois], an ugly sepulchre, a grave uncheered by any gleam of promise.

D31 — Lo, the city is barren, I have seen but an eel. [of London] *Bleak House*

D32 — This is a London particular . . . . A fog, miss. *Ibid.*

D33 — The rising clash and roar of the day's struggle . . . surprise and curiosity in the faces flitting past her . . . long shadows coming back upon the pavement . . . voices that were strange to her asking her where she went . . . Where to go? Still somewhere, anywhere! Still going on; but where! She thought of the only other time she had been lost in the wide wilderness of London . . . *Dombey and Son*

D34 — She often looked with compassion, at such a time, upon the stragglers who came wandering into London, by the great highway hard by, and who, footsore and weary, and gazing fearfully at the huge town before them, as if foreboding that their misery there would be but a drop of water in the sea, or as a grain of sea-sand on the shore, went shrinking on, cowering before the angry weather, and looking as if the very elements rejected them. *Ibid.*

D35 — It was a town of red brick, or of brick that would have been red if the smoke and ashes had allowed it; but as matters stood it was a town of unnatural red and black like the painted face of a savage.

It was a town of machines and tall chimneys, out of which interminable serpents of smoke trailed themselves for ever and ever, and never got uncoiled. [of Coketown] *Hard Times*

D36 — They went quietly down into the roaring streets, inseparable and blessed; and as they passed along in sunshine and in shade, the noisy and the eager and the arrogant and the froward and the vain, fretted, and chafed, and made their usual uproar. *Little Dorrit*

D37 — Close about the quays and churches, palaces and prisons: sucking at their walls, and welling up into the secret places of the town: crept the water always. Noiseless and watchful: coiled round and round it, in its many folds, like an old serpent: waiting for the time, I thought, when people should look down into its depths for any stone of the old

city that had claimed to be its mistress. Thus it floated me away, until I awoke in the old marketplace of Verona. I have, many and many a time, thought since, of this strange Dream upon the water: half-wondering if it lie there yet, and if its name be Venice. *Pictures of Italy*

D38 — The town in western Europe and North America may be defined as a compact settlement engaged primarily in non-agricultural occupations. *City, Region and Regionalism*

D39 — The very essence of urban character is the function of service for a tributary area . . . . The universally distinctive characteristic of the town arises from the mode of life and activities of its inhabitants. The town differs from the village in the occupations of its people, who are not concerned directly with farming, and who live and work in the settlement, sharing in its life and organization . . . . True town character implies some measure of community service and organization — what is sometimes called community balance . . . It is this grouping of centralized services in a clustered settlement which is the essence of a town and which, at a higher grade, is the hall-mark of a city. *Ibid.*

D40 — The city, in the widest sense, as it appears throughout all ages and in all lands, as the symbol and carrier of civilization, has certain fundamental characteristics. The first and the most important of these is that it is an institutional centre, the seat of the institutions of the society which it represents. It is a seat of religion, of culture and social contact, and of political and administrative organization. Secondly, it is a seat of production, agricultural and industrial, the latter being normally the more important . . . Thirdly, it is a seat of commerce and transport. Fourthly, the city is a pleasurable seat of residence for the rulers, the wealthy, and the retired, where they can enjoy all the amenities of civilized life that the institutions of their society have to offer. Fifthly, it is the living place of the people who work in it. *The West European City*

DIDION, Joan (1934-)

D41 — New York is full of people on this kind of leave of absence, of people with a feeling for the tangential adventure, the risk adventure, the interlude that's not likely to end in any double-ring ceremony. *Mademoiselle, February 1961*

D42 — It is often said that New York is a city only for the very rich and the very poor. It is less often said that New York is also, at least for those of us who came there from somewhere else, a city for only the very young. *Slouching Toward Bethlehem*

DIEBOLD, John (1926-   )

D43 — The real problem with most city services is they're labor-intensive at a moment in history when that's a suicidal approach. It can only mean traumatic increases in costs as people are less and less inclined to do dirty work or menial jobs. The reason most city jobs stay so labor-intensive is they're bound up in politics and there's no motivation to apply science and technology. *U.S. News & World Report, November 17, 1975*

DILLON, John F. (1831-1914)

D44 — Municipal corporations owe their origin to, and derive their powers and rights wholly from, the state legislature. It breathes into them the breath of life, and without which they cannot exist. As it creates, so it may destroy . . . . [Municipal corporations] are the mere tenants at the will of the legislature. *City of Clinton vs. The Cedar Rapids and Missouri River Railroad Co.*

DIOGENES (c.400-325 B.C.)

D45 — I would rather live on a few grains of salt at Athens than dine like a prince at Craterus's table.

DIOGENES LAERTIUS (2nd c. A.D.)

D46 — Like sending owls to Athens, as the proverb goes. *Plato*

DISRAELI, Benjamin (1804-1881)

D47 — A city of cities, an aggregation of humanity, that probably has never been equaled in any period of the history of the world, ancient or modern. [of London] *(Speech in the House of Commons)*

D48 — The key of India is in

London. *(Speech, Manchester, House of Lords)*

D49 — A roost for every bird. [of London]

D50 — A great city, whose image dwells in the memory of man, is the type of some great idea. Rome represents conquest; faith hovers over the towers of Jerusalem; and Athens embodies the pre-eminent quality of the antique world, art.

In modern ages, commerce has created London; while manners . . . have long found a supreme capital in the airy and bright-minded city of the Seine. *Coningsby, or the New Generation*

D51 — Rightly understood, Manchester is as great a human exploit as Athens. *Ibid.*

D52 — There never was such a great city with such small houses. [of London] *Endymion*

D53 — The gondola of London. [A hansom] *Lothair*

D54 — London; a nation, not a city. *Ibid.*

D55 — London is a modern Babylon. *Tancred*

DOBRINER, William M. (1922-   )

D56 — Wherever the suburban spearhead is pressing the rural village, the village has little hope of surviving unchanged, because the forces behind metropolitan expansion are irresistible. For a while the village may resist by elaborate zoning requirements or other legal barriers to invasion, but these are at best delaying actions. The tides of urbanism may be diverted for a decade or so, but what direct assault has failed to do a fifth column will accomplish. The city will seduce the young people of the village; they will go to urban colleges, take jobs in the metropolis, extend their range of contacts and eventually adopt an urban (suburban) way of life. *The Yale Review*

DODGE, L.C.

D57 — In the formation of a national education, as of a national character, the country more than the city must control. The city becomes cosmopolitan; its people, blending all nationalities, lose distinctive national characteristics, and I have sometimes thought, judging from popular manifestations, love of country as well. *Report of the Commissioner of Agriculture for the Year 1866*

D58 — It can now be seen why so much prominence is given to the rural population in our dreams of educational progress. It comprises a larger and more hopeful element of improvement than the city—an element that has more of truth and nature, more of virtue and principle. In the country will the defects of the present system be most readily remedied, and there will reforms be inaugurated most hopefully. *Ibid.*

DOHERTY, Henry L.

59 — Denver has more sunshine and sons-of-bitches than any town in the country.

DOLCE, Philip (1941-)

D60 — Suburbia, the middle ground between nature's beauty and civilization's conveniences, has been viewed as the promised land by millions of Americans over the last several generations. *Suburbia*

D61 — There are working-class suburbs, elite suburbs, black suburbs, ethnic suburbs, industrial suburbs, and planned suburbs among others. Suburbia today is a reflection of America's pluralistic and segmented society. *Ibid.*

DONALDSON, Scott (1928-)

D62 — The overwhelming majority of people who live in rows of identical little boxes brought a . . . limited dream with them from the city: a little open country, a little fresh air, at a price they could afford. It is a dream they think they have realized. Whose duty is it to disillusion them? [of Suburbia] *The Suburban Myth*

DONALDSON, William A.

D63 — What's happened in city government is that you have 18 or 20 different governments — the water department feuds with the sewer department, and the sewer department feuds with public works. They

become isolated little kingdoms. We end up changing the problem to fit into a department. *Dallas Times Herald, December 7, 1977*

DONOVAN, Hedley (1914-)

D64 — Too often American business has created some physcial transformation of our living habits, usually for the better — and then walked away from all the social consequences and implications for our cities. I think business must not merely not walk away, but be willing to apply some of the same creative radicalism to the creation of good cities, even great cities, that it devotes to the creation of good, sometimes great, products. *The Troubled Environment*

DORSON, Richard M. (1916-)

D65 — Earlier generations thrilled to narratives of haunted homes and eerie revenants; urban society today does not need recourse to supernatural demons and ogres when natural ones walk the streets and enter domiciles. *Land of the Millrats*

DOS PASSOS, John (1896-1970)

D66 — Do you know how long God took to destroy the tower of Babel, folks? Seven minutes. There's more wickedness in one block in New York City than there was in a square mile in Nineveh, and how long do you think the Lord God of Sabbaoth will take to destroy New York City . . .? Seven seconds. *Manhattan Transfer*

D67 — There were Babylon and Nineveh; they were built of brick. Athens was gold marble columns. Rome was held up on broad arches of rubble. In Constantinople the minarets flame like great candles round the Golden Horn . . . Steel, glass, tile, concrete will be the materials of the skyscrapers. Crammed on the narrow island the millionwindowed buildings will jut glittering pyramid on pyramid like the white cloudhead above a thunderstorm. [of the Metropolis] *Ibid.*

DOSTOYEVSKY, Fyodor (1821-1881)

D68 — The most abstract and artificial town in the world. [of St. Petersburg] *Crime and Punishment*

DOUGHERTY, James (1937-)

D69 — At times the holy city is a symbol of spiritual tranquility, an inwardness grounded on communion with God. Or it may be set against an opposing, unholy city, to represent religious experience as a choice between alternative measures of life. Or it may represent a goal which, though unattained by those who conceive it, yet directs their actions and serves as the bond of their fellowship. Each of these versions of the holy city implies its devotees' taking an attitude toward that other city — not holy, not profane, but simply secular — which is the city we experience, the city where we live 'in time.' *The Fivesquare City*

D70 — Man's largest visible creation, his most manifold artifact: to name it — 'city' — is to conjure with the power of words to apprehend realities at the very limits of our comprehension. To the Romans an intangible commonweal, to the Anglo-Normans a thing they had only heard of in a book, 'city' enters our speech always with a charge of meaning that exceeds its literal reference to some assemblage of women and men, streets and structures. To speak of the city is to invoke not only that tangible presence, but also the accumulating aspirations which men have sought to realize in it and through it. From the beginning, man has seen his city as 'the center of the world.' Few discussions of urban life, whether of the physical *urbs*, or of the social *civitas*, or of their refraction in the mediums of art, can avoid the city's symbolic dimension, its power to focus our imaginations. *Ibid.*

DOUGLAS, Lloyd C. (1877-1951)

D71 — You might surmise that this is the typical tale of a sleepy American town that grew overnight to a big, dirty, dangerous, clamorous city; but that isn't so, as you shall see. Akron isn't typical at all; it isn't typical of anything; it doesn't follow any pattern; among municipalities it is what biologists call a sport; it is no more typical of American communities than Boulder City or Willow Run or Los Alamos . . . . *Rubber's Home Town*

DOUGLAS, Norman (1868-1952)

D72 — The present age, for all its

cosmopolitan hustle, is curiously surburban in spirit. *An Almanac*

DOUGLASS, Harlan Paul (1871-1953)

D73 — Somewhere between the country and city lies that which is neither, but which partakes on a petty scale of the nature of both — the little town. After the isolation of one leaves off, but before the congestion of the other begins, comes this neuter, sharing the contempt which follows its class. The world regards it as a sort of unsexed creature; or at best, as a negligible buffer state — a Belgium or a Poland — impotent between its mighty neighbours, with few rights which they are bound to respect. *The Little Town*

D74 — The city trying to escape the consequences of being a city while still remaining a city: urban society trying to eat its cake and keep it, too. [of suburbia] *The Suburban Trend*

DOUGLASS, Truman B. (1901-1969)

D75 — The Bible tells the story of many cities. There are Sodom, Gomorrah, Babylon — symbols of dissolution and disaster . . But there are also Jerusalem, Zion, the New Jerusalem — affirmations of the indefeasible hope that the city of man may yet become the City of our God. *Harper's Magazine, November, 1958*

D76 — To the anti-urban man the metropolis is the supreme manifestation of human pride, and many churchmen still like to refer to it as such. *Ibid.*

DOWNING, Andrew Jackson (1815-1852)

D77 — Hundreds and thousands, formerly obliged to live in the crowded streets of cities, now find themselves able to enjoy a country cottage, several miles distant, — the old notions of time and space being half annihilated; and these suburban cottages enable the busy citizen to breathe freely, and keep alive his love for nature, till the time shall come when he shall have wrung out of the nervous hand of commerce enough means to enable him to realize his ideal of the 'retired life' of an American landed proprietor. *Hints To Rural Improvers*

D78 — In no country, perhaps, are there so

many new villages and towns laid out every year as in the United States. Indeed, so large is the number, that the builders and projectors are fairly at a loss for names, — ancient and modern history having been literally worn threadbare by the godfathers, until all association with great heroes and mighty deeds is fairly beggared by this re-christening going on in our new settlements and future towns, as yet only populous to the extent of six houses. *Rural Essays*

D79 — There is not a village in America, however badly planned at first, or ill-built afterwards, that may not be redeemed, in a great measure, by the aid of shade trees in the streets, and a little shrubbery in the front yards, and it is never too late or too early to project improvements of this kind. *Ibid.*

DOXIADIS, Constantinos A. (1913-1975)

D80 — In many exploding cities we can say that a new, huge symbol is arising, based on private initiative. In effect it is the symbol of human greed. How else can we explain a situation where someone who buys a piece of land on which he is allowed to build five floors, claims he is concerned for the city's development when he succeeds in changing the regulations so as to build twenty floors, and make four times more money? Greed in effect is becoming the only symbol of the exploding cities. *Ekistics*

D81 — The urban crisis is a universal phenomenon. Whether mankind deals with large or small cities, with countries of high or low income, developed or undeveloped, it is invariably faced with an urban crisis. This may appear in different forms and may not always be understood as such. Very often, in fact, it is not even recognized as a crisis. The reason is that the symptoms may vary. In some cities the crisis may appear as a grave traffic problem, a waste of natural resources, a social, economic, technological or human problem. Any systematic study of the urban crisis will, however, show that it is indeed a very large and universal phenomenon which started in the 19th century and is developing at a much higher speed today. *Emergence and Growth of an Urban Region: The Developing Urban Detroit Area*

D82 — In fact, by 'city' we mean many things, and we should not use the term *city* but only the term *human settlement*. The era when the city was a unit of a habitat very clearly defined in space has passed. *How to Build the City of the Future*

D83 — We ought to learn from biology and go underground. In biology, the circulation systems are always on the inside. The idea in our cities is to take all things that have to do with machines and put them underground. This would leave the area above the ground to the walking people. Eventually, all urban transit would have to go underground, no matter what the cost. *Reader's Digest, March, 1972*

D84 — We must face the fact that modern man has failed to build adequate cities. In the past his problems were simpler, and he solved them by trial and error. Now human forces and mechanical ones are mixed and man is confused. He tries and fails. We say he will become adapted. Yes, he is running the danger of becoming adapted, since adaptation is only meaningful if it means the welfare of man. Prisoners, too, become adapted to conditions! For man to adapt to our present cities would be a mistake, since he is the great prisoner. Not only is man unsafe in his prison, but he is facing a great crisis and heading for disaster. *Saturday Review, March 18, 1967*

D85 — Man has not abandoned the city. He has enlarged it. One problem today is that too many people are still planning for the small cell city instead of the larger area. All cities everywhere are spreading out. You have more abandonment in the central sections of the U.S. because there is more room to spread out, and higher mobility because there are more autos. *U.S. News & World Report, April 10, 1972*

D86 — The longing for an idealistic conception of one city of man, of cosmopolis, becomes now a reality, if for no other reason at least because of a complete change of the number of people, of new dimensions and the shrinking of the earth due to new technologies. Thus we witness the beginning of the birth of ecumenopolis. *Quoted in Will the Church Lose the City?, Cully & Harper.*

DOYLE, (Sir) Arthur Conan (1859-1930)

D87 — It is my belief, Watson, founded upon my experience, that the lowest and vilest alleys of London do not present a more dreadful record of sin than does the smiling and beautiful countryside. *Adventures of Sherlock Holmes*

D88 — As I approached this great city [of Montreal] I recollected the time when only a line of frail palisades lay between its population and utter barbarism, and when a sudden rush of savages might have driven Europe entirely from these parts. I assure you that I felt as much veneration as I know you feel when you approach the historical centres of Europe. *The Future of Canadian Literature (address)*

D89 — London, that great cesspool into which all the loungers of the Empire are irresistibly drained. *Study in Scarlet*

DREISER, Theodore (1871-1945)

D90 — The thing that interested me then as now about New York — as indeed about any great city, but more definitely New York because it was and is so preponderantly large — was the sharp, and at the same time immense, contrast it showed between the dull and the shrewd, the strong and the weak, the rich and the poor, the wise and the

ignorant . . . the number from which to choose was so great here that the strong, or those who ultimately dominated, were so very strong, and the weak so very, very weak — and so very, very many. *The Color of a Great City*

D91 — I knew then and there that I loved Chicago. It was so strong, so rough, so shabby and yet so vital and determined. It seemed more like a young giant afraid of nothing, and that it was that appealed to me. *Dawn*

D92 — It is given to some cities and to some lands to suggest romance and to me Chicago did that hourly. It sang, I thought, and in spite of what I deemed my various troubles, I was singing with it . . . Chicago was so young, so blithe, so new. *Newspaper Days*

D93 — The city has its cunning wiles, no less than the infinitely smaller and more human tempter. There are large forces which allure with all the soulfulness of expression possible in the most cultured human. The gleam of a thousand lights is often as effective as the persuasive light in a wooing and fascinating eye. Half the undoing of the unsophisticated and natural mind is accomplished by forces wholly superhuman. *Sister Carrie*

D94 — A big city is not a little teacup to be seasoned by old maids. It is a big city where men must fight and think for themselves, where the weak must go down and the strong remain. Removing all the stumbling stones of life, putting to flight the evils of vice and greed, and all that, makes our little path a monotonous journey. Leave things be; the wilder the better for those who are strong enough to survive, and the future of Chicago will then be known. *The Titan*

D95 — The city of Chicago. This singing flame of a city, this all America, this poet in chaps and buckskin, this rude, raw Titan, this Burns of a city! By its shimmering lake it lay, a king of shreds and patches, a maundering yokel with an epic in its mouth, a tramp, a hobo among cities, with the grip of Caesar in its mind, the dramatic force of Euripides in its soul. A very bard of a city this, singing of high deeds and high hopes, its heavy brogans buried deep in the mire of circumstance. *Ibid.*

D96 — Here was the negro, the prostitute, the blackleg, the gambler, the romantic adventurer par excellence. A city with but a handful of the native-born; a city packed to the doors with all the riffraff of a thousand towns. Flaring were the lights of the bagnio; tinkling the banjos, zithers, mandolins of the so-called gin-mill; all the dreams and the brutality of the day seemed gathered to rejoice — and rejoice they did, in this new-found wonder of a metropolitan life in the West. *Ibid.*

D97 — Take Athens, of Greece! Italy, do you keep Rome! This was the Babylon, the Troy, the Nineveh of a younger day. Here came the gaping West and the hopeful East, to see. Here hungry men, raw from the shops and fields, idylls and romances in their minds, builded them an empire crying glory in the mud. [of chicago] *Ibid.*

DRURY, Allen (1918-)

D98 — Like a city in dreams, the great white capital stretches along the placid river from Georgetown on the west to Anacostia on the east. It is a city of temporaries, a city of just-arriveds and one-visitings, built on the shifting sands of politics, filled with people passing through. [of Washington] *Advise and Consent*

DRYDEN, John (1631-1700)

D99 — London, thou great emporium of our isle, / Oh, thou too bounteous, thou too fruitful Nile, / How shall I praise or curse to thy desert, / Or separate thy sound, from thy corrupted part? / *The Medal*

D100 — Oxford to him a dearer name shall be, / Than his own mother University. / Thebes did his green unknowing youth engage, / He chooses Athens in his riper age. / *Prologue to the University of Oxford*

D101 — So poetry, which is in Oxford made / An art, in London only is a trade. / *Ibid.*

DU BELLAY, Joachim

D102 — Now conquering Rome doth conquered Rome inter, / And she the vanquished is, and vanquisher. / To show us where she stood there rests alone / Tiber; and that too hastens to be gone. / Learn,

hence what fortune can. Towns glide away; / And rivers, which are still in motion, stay. / *Ruins of Rome*

D103 — Rome only might to Rome compared be, / And only Rome could make great Rome to tremble. / *Ibid.*

DUBOS, Rene Jules (1901-1982)

D104 — Man can be adapted to anything — to the dirt and noise of New York City — and that is what is tragic. As we can accept worse and worse conditions, we don't realize that there is something worse than extinction — the progressive degradation of human life.

D105 — Life in the modern city has become a symbol of the fact that man can become adapted to starless skies, treeless avenues, shapeless buildings, tasteless bread, joyless celebrations. *Quoted in The Exploding Cities*

D106 — The greatest crime committed in American cities may not be murder, rape or robbery, but rather the wholesale and constant exposure of children to noise, ugliness and garbage in the street, thereby conditioning them to accept public squalor as the normal state of affairs and diminishing their future enjoyment of life. *Reader's Digest, March, 1972*

DULLES, Allen W. (1893-1969)

D107 — Berlin, like Carthage, has represented the spirit of destructive conquest. It has lost its right to be the capital of the Germany of the future . . . The city is without a real history, without landscape, without architecture and without charm. *Goodbye, Berlin*

DUNBAR, William (1465?-1530?)

D108 — London, thou art the flower of cities all! / Gemme of all joy, jasper of jocunditie. Most mighty carbuncle of virtue and valor. / *In Honor of the City of London*

D109 — Thy famous Maire, by pryncely governaunce, / With sword of justice thee ruleth prudently. / No Lord of Parys, Venyce, or Floraunce / In dignitye or honour goeth to hym nigh. / *Ibid.*

DUNCAN, Isadora (1877-1927)

D110 — There is something about an open fire, bread and butter sandwiches, very strong tea, yellow fog without and the cultural drawl of English voices which makes London very attractive and if I had been fascinated before, from that moment I loved it dearly. *My Life*

DUNKERLEY, Harold (1921-)

D111 — There is for institutions a natural speed of evolution, a rather sluggish speed of evolution. But the big cities are changing in their social structure, in their economic structure, in *mores*, in their size and land area, in every respect; and with such rapidity that institutions are with great difficulty adapting to the challenge — sometimes not adapting, sometimes collapsing. *Quoted in The Exploding Cities*

DUNN, David

D112 — When we come to a large urban area, we forget to bring with us the most precious ingredient of life in a small place — humanness . . . . It's an old saying that what is everybody's business is nobody's business. City officials, the police, clubs, churches, schools and newspapers can't do all that's needed to make a town livable. They can help, but it is we ordinary citizens

— all of us together — who create the spirit of a community, whether it be New York or Eastport, Maine. *Try Giving Yourself Away*

DUNNE, Finley Peter (1867-1936)

D113 — Everything that's worth having goes to the city; the country takes what's left. Everything that's worth having goes to the city and is iced.

D114 — The wise people are in New York because the foolish went there first; that's the way wise men make a living.

DUNNE, John S. (1929-)

D115 — Cities were sacked in republican times as they had been in earlier periods, but the destruction of the city seems to have lost the significance it had when wars were fought over the presence of the goddess in the locality. *The City of the Gods*

D116 — A city that can exist in a fleet at sea or that can be transferred to another land is a far cry from the city in which gods and men had mingled at the center of the world. The departure from the earlier idea that the city is a sacred place, to be sure, is not so radical as to be already tantamount to the Copernican Revolution. Still the consciousness of the city's independence with respect to place is a clear anticipation of the modern consciousness of the insignificance of man's particular location in the universe. *Ibid.*

D117 — From the age of the gods to the age of God, from the gods of the living and the gods of the dead to the living God and the dead God, the city of man has remained the city of the gods . . *Ibid.*

D118 — [In ancient times] What motivated the sacking of the city was the very desire which seemingly inspired the original building of the city, the wish to consort with the gods . . *Ibid.*

D119 — When cities were a new thing and when the destruction of cities, the culminating act of warfare in ancient times as in modern times, was therefore a new thing, perhaps men had a more conscious notion than they do now as to why it is that cities are destroyed. Although it would appear to be an act of singular barbarism, almost as if it were the destruction of civilization itself, in that the city is the very embodiment of civilization, the Sumerians, the creators of the first civilization, listed 'the destruction of cities' as one of the divine institutions (*me's*) upon which civilization is founded. *Ibid.*

DURANT, Will (1885-1975)

D120 — Culture suggests agriculture, but civilization suggests the city. In one aspect civilization is the habit of civility; and civility is the refinement which townsmen, who made the word, thought possible only in the *civitas* or city. For in the city are gathered, rightly or wrongly, the wealth and brains produced in the countryside; in the city invention and industry multiply comforts, luxuries and leisure; in the city traders meet, and barter goods and ideas; in that cross-fertilization of minds at the crossroads of trade intelligence is sharpened and stimulated to creative power. In the city some men are set aside from the making of material things, and produce science and philosophy, literature and art. Civilization begins in the peasant's hut, but it comes to flower only in the towns. *The Story of Civilization*

DWIGHT, Timothy

D121 — In every village smil'd / The heav'n-inviting church, and every town / A world within itself, with order, peace, / And harmony, adjusted to all its weal. /

E

EBERHARDT, Isabelle

E1 — I love to dive into the bath of street life, the waves of the crowd flowing over me, to impregnate myself with the fluids of the people. *Quoted in The Destiny of Isabelle Eberhardt*

EDER, Richard (1932-)

E2 — In nineteenth-century America conquering the world meant going west. In the twentieth century, when Hollywood got started, it came to mean going to the city. The city had hope: it may seem a curiosity now. Certainly it would to anyone going to the movies these past years. When *My Sister Eileen* was made twenty years ago, it was taken for granted that two pretty sisters could come to New York from Columbus, Ohio, and get into only minor trouble. Nobody expected them to be robbed, raped, polluted, or driven to hang out in singles bars. *Horizon, May, 1977*

E3 — Like unsecured cargo on a pitching deck, American films ride our shifting notions of the urban reality always a little out of phase and harder than the lurches themselves . . . they make city life seem more terrible than it is. *Ibid.*

E4 — The great, sustained burst of Greek theater that still, after two and a half millennia, continues to move and govern us was born out of a city. Its themes, its sense of life, were inextricable from the notion of a city which, as it existed then, could be defined as the largest community that men could comprehend. Anything bigger was not a community but a league. Man's fate, the city's fate, and gods' fate — gods had fates in those days — were all part of an organic destiny. *Theater and Cities*

EDWARDS, Charles

E5 — The man of the country may feel himself a priest of nature: but gentleness and a love of the beautiful are also found in a maritime city. *The Merchants Magazine and Commercial Review*

EHRICKE, Krafft A. (1917-)

E6 — With their giant factories and food-producing facilities, the cities will maintain their own merchant fleet of spacecraft, their own raw material mining centers on other celestial bodies, and be politically independent city-states. *Bulletin of Atomic Scientists, November, 1971*

EISENHOWER, Dwight D. (1890-1969)

E7 — There are a number of things wrong with Washington. One of them is that everyone has been too long away from home. *(News Conference) May 11, 1955*

ELAZAR, Daniel J. (1934-)

E8 — The American city [in contrast to European cities] has its classic antecedent in the pattern of Israelite city-building described in the Bible, as befits the cities of an agrarian republic produced by the heirs of the Biblically-centered Reformation. Like the cities of ancient Israel, the American city is located within territorial political jurisdictions that take precedence over it — in this case, the state rather than the tribe, and in both cases, the nation above that. *Are We a Nation of Cities?*

E9 — Perhaps the central myth in the contemporary complex of American mythologies of urbanism is the myth that adheres to the very notion of 'a nation of cities.' The foundation of the central myth is the 'fact' that over 70 percent of all Americans now live in urban places. This 'fact,' however, must be considered in the context of the United States Census Bureau's definition of 'urban place:' any settlement of 25,000 population or more. Only when cities are thus defined is the United States a nation of cities. But, of course a town of 2,500 — or even 25,000 — is not what most of us mean when we speak of cities. *Ibid.*

E10 — Whatever changes the American people seem to be seeking, they are not directed toward the enhancement of the facilities that lead to an urbane or citified life, but rather to the introduction into the city of qualities associated with the rural life — whether trees, cleaner air, larger parks, or new family-style dwellings to reduce the overall density of population. *Ibid.*

ELEGANT, Robert (1928-   )

E11 — Hong Kong is the only major metropolis with a built-in time-fuse, a self-destruct mechanism set to explode in 1997 when the lease of the ceded New Territories expires and nine-tenths of the Colony reverts to China. In this unique city-port, East and West are intermixed to an unrivalled degree; here, two disparate ideologies co-exist in a burgeoning cosmopolis that combines the magic and mystery and colour of the Orient with the wonders of the technological age. It is, at one and the same time, the city of Suzy Wong and supersonic jets, of sampans and hydrofoils, fortune-tellers and fortune-hunters. *Hong Kong*

E12 — In Hong Kong you can buy almost anything from a 13-year-old virgin to a 1,300-year-old T'ang Dynasty statuette; both are certified as genuine and, upon occasion, they may genuinely be genuine. So why shouldn't you be able to buy a building inspector, policeman, tax inspector, or government factotum? That is the traditional view of a majority of the people in the Colony and, as the government has long since discovered, nothing — not even drug-addiction — is harder to break than the combination of centuries of deep-rooted Chinese Tradition and the laisser-faire, buccaneering tradition of the early British

merchant-settlers and their successors. *Tokyo*

ELIOT, George (1819-1880)

E13 — The breath of the manufacturing town, which made a cloudy day and a red gloom by night on the horizon, diffused itself over all the surrounding country, filling the air with eager unrest. Here was a population not convinced that old England was as good as possible. *Felix Holt: The Radical*

ELIOT, T.S. (1888-1965)

E14 — The chief danger about Paris is that it is such a strong stimulant, and like most stimulants incites to rushing about and produces a pleasant illusion of mental activity rather than the solid results of hard work. *(Letter To Robert McAlmon)*

E15 — I journeyed to London, to the timekept City, / Where the River flows, with foreign flotations. / There I was told: we have too many churches, / And too few chop-houses. There I was told / Let the vicars retire. Men do not need the Church / In the place where they work, but where they spend / their Sundays .. / In the City, we need no bells: / Let them waken the suburbs. / *The Rock*

E16 — Unreal City, / Under the brown fog of a winter dawn, / A crowd flowed over London Bridge, so many, / I had not thought death had undone so many. / Sighs, short and infrequent, were exhaled, / And each man fixed his eyes before his feet. / Flowed up the hill and down King William Street, / To where Saint Mary Woolnoth kept the hours / With a dead sound on the final stroke of nine. / *The Waste Land*

ELIZABETH (the Queen Mother) (1900-)

E17 — This seems to me the place to live. [of Vancouver]

ELLIS, Havelock (1859-1939)

E18 — The larger our great cities grow, the more irresistible becomes the attraction which they exert on the children of the country, who are fascinated by them, as the birds are fascinated by the lighthouse or the moths by the candle. *The Task of Social Hygiene*

ELLISON, Ralph (1914-)

E19 — It isn't the desire to run to the suburbs or to invade 'white' neighbourhoods that is the main concern with my people in Harlem. They would just like to have a more human life there. A slum like Harlem isn't just a place of decay. It is also a form of historical and social memory. *Quoted in The Exploding Cities*

E20 — To live in Harlem is to dwell in the very bowels of the city; it is to pass a labyrinthine existence among streets that explode monotonously skyward with the spires and crosses of churches and clutter under foot with garbage and decay. Harlem is a·ruin .... *Shadow and Act*

ELLUL, Jacques (1912-)

E21 — It is maddening perhaps, but we cannot conceive of Plato without Athens, or Racine without Paris. I am not trying to set the city up as an invariable conditioning factor, but we must recognize that the intellectual life cannot exist outside the city. It is true that Montaigne withdrew to the country to write his *Essays* but it cannot be denied that their substance was taken from his life in Bordeaux. *The Meaning of the City*

E22 — Like a vampire, it preys on the true living creation .... We cannot repeat too often that the city is an enormous man-eater .... The city devours men. Its very character is to receive from the outside; to consume, and to produce things usable only inside the city and to her gain .... There is something magical about her attractiveness, and it is impossible to explain men's passion for the city .... The irresistible current flowing in long unconscious waves to pull men toward her dead asphalt, without giving a thought for her force, her seductive power. *Ibid.*

ELSNER, Eleanor

E23 — It is a town of memories, for few cities have made history as has Cordoba; now it sits silently guarding the great treasure lying in its very heart — the mosque — and dreaming of past glories, waiting, maybe, for their return. *Spanish Sunshine.*

ELY, Richard T. (1854-1943)

E24 — The city needs religion, and without religion the salvation of the city is impossible .... You may read of a great religious awakening in the fifeenth and sixteenth centuries under the influence of which great leaders were unable to separate religion and politics. It is this kind of a religious awakening which our modern city needs. *(Public Address, Boston, December 4, 1899)*

E25 — As we think about the city during human history we recall Jerusalem, Athens, Rome, Florence, London, Paris, Berlin as sources of religion, learning, and art. Is it without significance that the words 'politie' and 'urban' are both derived from words

meaning city? Is it without significance that Christianity became known in a city, and that the word 'pagan' means a dweller in the country? Or is it without significance that the apostle John saw a redeemed society existing as a city? — 'and I John saw the holy city, New Jerusalem, coming down from God out of heaven, prepared as a bride adorned for her husband.' *The Coming City*

E26 — If I forget thee, O Chicago, O New York, O St. Louis, let my right hand forget her cunning. *Ibid.*

EMERSON, Ralph Waldo (1803-1882)

E27 — And now Rome is keeping its old promise to your eyes & mind, Rome which has always kept its promise, & which like Nature has that elasticity of application to all measures of spirit. These millennial cities in their immense accumulations of human works find it easy to impress the imagination by gradually dropping one piece after another of whim blunder & absurdity, — hay stubble & bladders, —

until nothing but necessity and geometry remains. *(Letter to Margaret Fuller)*

E28 — The cities drain the country of the best part of its population: the flower of the youth, of both sexes, goes into the towns, and the country is cultivated by a so much inferior class.

E29 — The history of any settlement is an illustration of the whole — first, the emigrant's camp, then the group of log cabins, then the cluster of white wooden towns — to the eye of the European traveller as ephemeral as the tents of the first stage of the swift succession — and almost as soon followed by the brick and granite cities, which in another country would stand for centuries, but which here must soon give place to the enduring marble. *(Letter)*

E30 — I seem to have been driven away from Rome by an unseen Angel with sword or whip for nothing would have served me so well & dearly as Rome. *Ibid.*

E31 — The most wonderful thing I see is this London . . . the centre of the world(.) the 'nation in brick'; the immense masses of life of power of wealth, and the effect upon the men of running in & out amidst the play of this vast machinery, the effect to keep them tense & silent, and to mind every man his own . . . *(Letter to Mrs. Emerson)*

E32 — [A city] terribly derisive of all absurd pretensions but its own. [of Paris]

E33 — While lecturing in New York in 1842 . . . Pity me & comfort me, O my friend, in this city of magnificence & of steam. For a national, for an imperial prosperity, everything here seems irrevocably destined. What a Bay! what a River! what climate! what men! What ample interior domain, lake mountain & forest! What manners, what histories & poetry shall rapidly arise & for how long, and, it seems, endless date! Me my cabin fits better, yet very likely from a certain poorness of spirit; but in my next transmigration, I think I should choose New York. *(Letter)*

E34 — We flee away from cities, but we bring / The best of cities with us, these learned classifiers / Men knowing what they seek, armed eyes of experts. / *The Adirondacs*

E35 — On the city's paved street / Plant gardens lined with lilacs sweet; / Let spouting fountains cool the air, / Singing in the sun-baked square. / *Art*

E36 — And what they call their city way / Is not their way, but hers. / *The Complete Works*

E37 — Cities degrade us by magnifying trifles; Life is dragged down to a fracas of pitiful cares and disasters. *The Conduct of Life*

E38 — Cities give us collision. London and New York take the nonsense out of man. *Ibid.*

E39 — New York is a sucked orange. *Ibid.*

E40 — What is the city in which we sit here, but an aggregate of incongruous materials, which have obeyed the will of some man? *Ibid.*

E41 — London is the epitome of our times, and the Rome of to-day. *English Traits*

E42 — All men keep the farm in reserve as an asylum where, in case of mischance, to hide their poverty, — or a solitude, if they do not succeed in society. And who knows how many glances of remorse are turned this way from the bankrupts of trade, from mortified pleaders in courts and senates, or from the victims of idleness and pleasure? Poisoned by town life and town vices, the sufferer resolves: 'Well, my children, whom I have injured, shall go back to the land, to be recruited and cured by that which should have been my nursery, and now shall be their hospital.' *Farming*

E43 — That uncorrupted behavior which we admire in animals and in young children belongs to him, to the hunter, the sailor, — the man who lives in the presence of Nature. Cities force growth and make men talkative and entertaining, but they make them artificial. *Ibid.*

E44 — Avarice, ambition, almost all talents, are restless and vagrant; they go up to the cities; but Religion is a good rooter. *The Journals of Ralph Waldo Emerson*

E45 — The City delights the Understanding. It is made up of finites: short, sharp, mathematical lines, all calculable. It is full of varieties, of successions, of contrivances. The Country, on the contrary, offers an unbroken horizon, the monotony of an endless road, of vast uniform and infinite vegetation; the objects on the road are few and worthless, the eye is invited ever to the horizon and the clouds. It is the school of the Reason. *Ibid.*

E46 — The enjoyment of travel is in the arrival at a new city, as Paris, or Florence, or Rome, — the feeling of free adventure, you have no duties, — nobody knows you, nobody has claims, you are like a boy on his first visit to the Common on Election Day. Old Civilization offers to you alone this huge city, all its wonders, architecture, gardens, ornaments, galleries, which had never cost you so much as a thought. *Ibid.*

E47 — Great cities, enormous populations, are disgusting like the population of cheese, like hills of ants, or swarms of fleas, — the more the worse. But if they contain Merlins and Corneliuses, Friar Bacons and Crichtons, if roadmakers, mathematicians, astronomers, chemists; good kings like Alfred; poets like Chaucer; inventors, farmers, and sailors, who know the elements, and can make them work; memories, imaginations, combinings, perseverances, arts, music, and not maggots; — then the more the merrier. Open the gates, let the miracle of generation go on. *Ibid.*

E48 — He has not seen Europe, who has not seen its cities. *Ibid.*

E49 — If a man loves the city so will his writings love the city, & if a man loves sweet fern & roams much in the pastures, his writings will smell of it. *Journals and Miscellaneous Notebooks*

E50 — If some persons are credible, a man cannot honestly get a livelihood by trade in the city. His integrity would be disqualification. *Ibid.*

E51 — Let the river roll which way it will, cities will rise on its banks. *The Journals of Ralph Waldo Emerson*

E52 — The sole terms on which the Infinite will come to cities is the surrender of cities to its will. *Ibid.*

E53 — Up, down, around, the kingdom of thought has no enclosures, but the Muse makes us free of her city. *Ibid.*

E54 — What care though rival cities soar / Along the stormy coast, / Penn's town, New York, and Baltimore, / If Boston knew the most! / *May-Day and Other Pieces*

E55 — Cities give not the human senses room enough. *Nature*

E56 — Nature is loved by what is best in us. It is loved as the city of God, although, or rather because there is no citizen. *Ibid.*

E57 — The hand that rounded Peter's dome, / And groined the aisles of Christian Rome, / Wrought in a sad sincerity; / Himself from God he could not free; / He builded better than he knew; — / The conscious stone to beauty grew. / *The Problem*

E58 — The farmer is a hoarded capital of health, as the farm is the capital of wealth; and it is from him that the health and power, moral and intellectual, of the cities come. The city is always recruited from the country. The men in cities who are the centres of energy, the driving wheels of trade, politics, or political arts, and the women of beauty and genius, are the children or grandchildren of farmers, and are spending the energies which their fathers' hardy, silent life accumulated in frosty furrows, in poverty, necessity, and darkness. *Society and Solitude*

E59 — The true test of civilization is, not the census, nor the size of cities, nor the crops—no, but the kind of man the country turns out. *Ibid.*

E60 — Whatever events in progress shall go to disgust men with cities, and infuse into them the passion for country life, and country pleasures, will render a service to the whole face of this continent. *The Young American*

E61 — The inhabitants of cities pay a high tax for their social advantages, their increased civilization, in their exclusion from the sight of the unlimited glory of the earth. Imprisoned in streets of brick and stone, in tainted air and hot and dusty corners, they only get glimpses . . . of the face of the green pastoral earth which the great Father of all is now adorning with matchless beauty as one wide garden. *Young Emerson Speaks*

E62 — Look at the great throng the city presents. Consider the variety of callings and pursuits. Here is one man toiling with a hod on his shoulders; and another with his saw and tools; a third with his books; a fourth driving bargains at the corners of the streets; another spreads his sail from the wharf toward the sea; another heals the sick; another draws a map; another is hasting to his entertainment and to dangerous pleasures; another is led to jail between officers; another takes his seat on a bench to judge him. They do not perceive, who make up this sad and cheerful scene, that they are placed in these circumstances to learn the laws of the universe. *Ibid.*

E63 — We live in a fair city [Boston]. It is full of commodious and spacious mansions. But the eye that sees the morning sun shine on long streets of decorated buildings is apt to forget how many obscure garrets, how many damp basements are here and there found amid this magnificence, that contain victims of great suffering, poor men and women reduced by consumptions or bedridden with rheumatisms, or worn with fruitless labors to meet demands the quarter day. *Ibid.*

ENGELS, Friedrich (1820-1895)

E64 — One day I walked with one of these middle-class gentlemen into Manchester. I spoke to him about the disgraceful unhealthy slums and drew his attention to the disgusting condition of that part of the town in which the factory worker lived. I declared that I had never seen so badly built a town in my life. He listened patiently and at the corner of the street at which we parted company, he remarked: 'And yet there is a great deal of money made here. Good morning, Sir!'

E65 — The greater the town, the greater its advantages. It offers roads, railroads, canals; the choice of skilled labour increases constantly, new establishments can be built more cheaply because of the competition among builders and machinists who are at hand, than in remote country districts, whither timber, machinery, builders, and operatives must be brought; it offers a market to which buyers crowd, and direct communication with the markets supplying raw material or demanding finished goods. Hence the marvellously rapid growth of the great manufacturing towns ... *The Condition of the Working Class in England in 1844*

E66 — This isolation of the individual, this narrow self-seeking is the fundamental principle of our society everywhere, it is nowhere so shamelessly barefaced, so self-conscious as just here in the crowding of the great city. The dissolution of mankind into monads, of which each one has a separate principle, the world of atoms, is here carried out to its utmost extremes. *Ibid.*

E67 — A town, such as London, where a man may wander for hours together without reaching the beginning of the end, without meeting the slightest hint which could lead to the inference that there is open country within reach, is a strange thing. This colossal centralisation, this heaping together of two and a half millions of human beings at one point, has multiplied the power of this two and a half millions a hundredfold; has raised London to the commercial capital of the world, created the giant docks and assembled the thousand vessels that continually cover the Thames. *Ibid.*

E68 — What is true of London, is true of Manchester, Birmingham, Leeds, is true of all great towns. Everywhere barbarous indifference, hard egotism on one hand, and nameless misery on the other, everywhere social warfare, every man's house in a state of siege, everywhere reciprocal plundering under the protection of the law, and all so shameless, so openly avowed that one shrinks before the consequences of our social state as they manifest themselves here undisguised, and can only wonder that the whole crazy fabric still hangs together. *Ibid.*

ENGLE, Paul (1908-)

E69 — I came to that dark water-wandered town, / Where, before proud stone was piled on stone / To mark the frantic limits of the

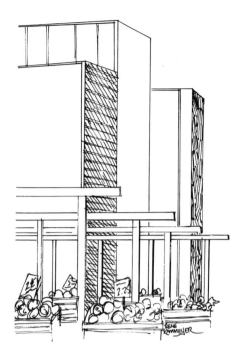

mind, / Oxen forded the mild, midland river. [of Oxford]

ENNIUS (239-169 B.C.)

E70 — It is through the ways of old and through the heroes of old that Rome stands fast.

EPICTETUS (50?-135?)

E71 — You will confer the greatest benefits on your city, not by raising its roofs, but by exalting its souls. For it is better that great souls should live in small habitations than that abject slaves should burrow in great houses. *Encheiridion*

ERICKSEN, E. Gordon (1917-)

E72 — The city is a settled aggregation of people who by their density tend toward heterogeneity and impersonality. *Urban Behavior*

E73 — Physical nearness coupled with social distance makes it necessary for urbanites to cultivate reserve and to disguise inner feelings. *Ibid.*

ERSKINE, Henry (1746-1817)

E74 — In the garb of old Gaul, wi' the fire of old Rome. *In the Garb of Old Gaul*

EURIPIDES (480-400 B.C.)

E75 — The first requisite to happiness is that a man be born in a famous city. *Ecomium on Alcibiades*

E76 — O children, my children, for you there will be a city, a home where you will always live, robbed of your mother, while for me there can only be my misery to live with .... *Medea*

E77 — Thou hast heard men scorn the city, call her wild / Of counsel, mad; thou hast seen the fire of morn / Flash from her eyes in answer to their scorn! / Come toil on toil, 'tis this that makes her grand. / Peril on peril! And common states that stand / In caution, twilight cities, dimly wise — / Ye know them; for no light is in their eyes! / Go forth, my son, and help. / *The Suppliants*

F

FADIMAN, Clifton (1904-)

F1 — Writing about American cities is like writing a history of Chester A. Arthur. It can be done, but is it worth it! *San Diego Union*

FALLACI, Oriana (1930-)

F2 — I'm going to show you the real New York — witty, smart, and international — like any metropolis. Tell me this — where in Europe can you find old Hungary, old Russia, old France, old Italy? In Europe you're trying to copy America, you're almost American. But here you'll find Europeans who immigrated a hundred years ago — and we haven't spoiled them. Oh, Gio! You must see why I love New York. Because the whole world's in New York . . . *Penelope at War*

FALTERMAYER, Edmund K.

F3 — Of all our cities, only New York, Chicago, and San Francisco can even lay claim to greatness, and only San Francisco is a joy to visit. *Redoing America*

FASI, Frank (Mayor, Honolulu) (1920-)

F4 — Your mother takes care of the family, keeps the house clean, keeps you out of trouble, tells you what you can do and cannot do and punishes you when you do something wrong. That's the same thing a Mayor does, except he must do it for an entire city. *(Speech before Cub Scouts, February 4, 1973)*

FAULKNER, William (1897-1962)

F5 — The plastic ass-hole of the earth. [of Los Angeles]

FEENEY, Leonard (1897-1978)

F6 — London . . . is a place full of fog, where bright ideas are always welcome, provided they come in under quota and fill out the proper form. *London Is a Place*

FEINSTEIN, Dianne (Mayor, San Francisco) (1933-)

F7 — You can build skyscrapers and a perfect art center, but if you don't have beauty shops, groceries and life on the streets, the city will disintegrate. The key to urban survival is keeping the working middle class. *San Francisco Examiner / Chronicle, April 10, 1977*

FELKER, Clay (1928-)

F8 — Let's not forget that so often when we talk about the city's problems — say, traffic congestion — we overlook the fact that they are also evidence of the city's vitality. Cities work, despite all prophecies of chaos and doom. *Christian Science Monitor, March 22, 1971*

FEMMINELLA, Francis X. (1929-)

F9 — From ancient times . . . men *have* linked notions regarding the evolution of culture, the attainment of freedom, and the growth of cities. Cities, meaning buildings and streets (*urbs*), and cities, meaning a community of citizens (*civitas*) began to develop in prehistoric times. The classical philosophers of Greece and Rome, and social thinkers even to the eighteenth and nineteenth centuries, recognized that the lives of urbanites were different from the lives of farm and village people; and they defended the city as a 'natural' development. *The Immigrant and the Urban Melting Pot*

FERNS, H.S. (1913-)

F10 — The centre and heart of modern Argentina is this city of Santa Maria de Buenos Aires, which died at birth, and after rebirth in 1580, remained for nearly two centuries the least of cities in an empire that could boast of great centres of civilization and power like Mexico, Havana, Lima, Quito, and Santa Fé de Bogotá. *Argentina*

FICHTE, Johann Gottlieb (1762-1814)

F11 — Living there is a race of men who are so bold that one does not get very far with them by being delicate. One has to talk back to them, and one may even have to become tough, if one wants to hold one's own. [of Berlin]

FIEDLER, Leslie (1917-   )

F12 — For millennia now mankind has been moving inexorably into cities — streaming from forest clearings and lonely farms, hillside hamlets and island villages to found Athens and Rome, Cairo and Jerusalem, Kiev and Odessa, Shanghai and Tokyo, Sao Paolo and Mexico City, San Francisco and New York — until the whole world promises or threatens (it can be, has been, felt either way) to turn into The City, Metropolis, Megalopolis. *Mythicizing the City*

FIELD, Eugene (1850-1895)

F13 — Have you ever heard of the Sugar-Plum Tree? / 'Tis a marvel of great renown! / It blooms on the shore of the Lollipop sea / In the garden of Shut-Eye Town. / *The Sugar-Plum Tree*

FIELD, Joanna (1900-   )

F14 — Possessing a rapacious, engulfing ego, their particular genius swallowed their world in its swift undertow and washed its cadavers out to sea. New York is a good place to be on the up-grade. *See Me at the Waltz*

FIELDING, HENRY (1701-1754)

F15 — Whoever considers the Cities of London and Westminster, with the late vast increases of their suburbs, the great irregularity of their buildings, the immense numbers of lanes, alleys, courts and bye-places, must think that had they been intended for the very purpose of concealment, they could not have been better contrived. *Inquiry into the Causes of the Late Increase of Robbers*

FIELDS, W.C. (1879-1946)

F16 — On the whole I'd rather be in Philadelphia.

F17 — Double Dubuque [of Los Angeles]

FINGER, Charles J. (1869?-1941)

F18 — One Sunday evening a Minneapolis minister started his sermon by saying, 'I take my text this evening from St. Paul'; whereupon his congregation rose en masse and filed out of the church, refusing to listen to any such doctrine. *Adventure under Sapphire Skies*

FINKELSTEIN, Louis

F19 — One of the most remarkable developments in the history of religion is the sudden emergence of Hebrew literary prophecy some 2700 years ago. Prophets had dwelt in Israel all the way back to Moses. But up to that time, none except Moses seems to have left any literary monuments. Their memories persist in stories about them, like the biographies of Elijah and Elisha in the Book of Kings, rather than in messages emanating from them . . . . The rise of the great cities of Samaria and Jerusalem gave the prophet a chance to repeat his message many times to various groups, and the city crowds contained individuals who were capable of retaining it. There was also an opportunity for the prophet to be surrounded by disciples who made it their business to preserve his words . . . For these and other reasons, the phenomenon of literary prophecy is probably associated closely with the emergence of the cities of Jerusalem and perhaps Samaria. *The Metropolis and Modern Life, E.M. Fisher, Ed.*

FISHER, Craig

F20 — Between the fall of the Roman Empire of the West in the fifth century and the beginning of social and economic expansion in the eleventh century, there was a period of six centuries during which the city ceased to be the most important social unit in Western Europe. There has been much debate as to how far the city as an institution disappeared, but it is clear that the most important, most complex social unit in these centuries was no longer the city but the monastery. *The Medieval City*

FISHER, Dorothy Canfield (1879-1958)

F21 — T.C. Hulme goes to New York City where he revels in human nonentity.

And glad to be there, relieved to have the tiresome mechanisms of daily life run invisibly by people of whose membership in his own race he need not be reminded. His cheap room was dingy, yes, but it was an anonymous back bent to shovel coal into the fire that kept it warm. That back could ache with overwork, could break in exhaustion, but because he would never know whose back it was, he would be safe from the nagging summons of moral responsibility. How restful city life was! *Seasoned Timber*

FISHER, Frank

F22 — One question about city planning must have come to the mind of anyone who has fingered the magnificent volumes in which the proposals of planners are generally presented. Why do those green spaces, those carefully placed skyscrapers, those pleasant residential districts, and equally pleasant factory and working areas, still remain dreams for the most part? Why are our cities hardly any less ugly and unpleasant than they were at the height of the nineteenth century's Industrial Revolution? *Commentary, January, 1954*

FITCH, Clyde (1865-1909)

F23 — What the City does is to bring out what's strongest in us. If at heart we're good, the good in us will win! If the bad is strongest, God help us! Don't blame the city! She gives the man his opportunity; it is up to him what he makes of it. *The City*

FITCH, James Marston (1909-   )

F24 — The automobile has not merely taken over the street, it has dissolved the living tissue of the city. Its appetite for space is absolutely insatiable; moving and parked, it devours urban land, leaving the buildings as mere islands of habitable space in a sea of dangerous and ugly traffic ... Gas-filled, noisy and hazardous, our streets have become the most inhumane landscape in the world. *The New York Times, May 1, 1960*

FITZGERALD, F. Scott (1896-1940)

F25 — As the toiler must live in the city's belly, so I was compelled to live in its disordered mind.

F26 — The city seen from the Queensboro Bridge is always the city seen for the first time, in its first wild promise of all the mystery and the beauty of the world. [of New York] *The Great Gatsby*

F27 — Full of vaunting pride the New Yorker had climbed here and seen with dismay what he had never suspected, that the city was not the endless succession of canyons that he had supposed but that *it had limits* — from the tallest structure he saw for the first time that it faded out into the country on all sides, into an expanse of green and blue that alone was limitless. And with the awful realization that New York was a city after all and not a universe, the whole shining edifice that he had reared in his imagination came crashing to the ground. *My Lost City*

FLAHERTY, Peter (Mayor, Pittsburgh) (1925-   )

F28 — You can't understand how lonely a Mayor feels with his problems. The people in the suburbs use our facilities but won't help pay for them. The Pittsburgh Zoo costs us $1 million a year. Three out of four people who go there come from outside the city. But when I ask the county commissioners for help, they look out the window. *Washington, March 23, 1971*

FLANNER, Janet (1892-1978)

F29 — Paris is now the capital of limbo. *The New Yorker, December 7, 1940*

FLEENER, Creedmore

F30 — Contrast with this the city life / With all its bustle and its roar; / Its howling greed, its angry strife / That tramples down each feeble life / Which vainly struggles to the fore; / Its brawling crime and snarling death; / Its cries of want and wild despairs; / Its dust and smoke which stifle breath; / Its foul effluvia of death; / Its catacombs of human lairs ... / *In Passing Through*

FLINN, John J. (1851-1929)

F31 — People of respectability tolerate things here which are perfectly shocking to the moral sense of respectable people elsewhere. Men, reckless of public opinion, and women, regardless of feminine delicacy, are continually creating social sensations . . . The painted woman drives an elegant equipage paid for, perhaps, by some prominent citizen; whole thoroughfares are given over, nay abandoned, to bagnios and brothels. [Cities in general]

FLORUS (2nd c. A.D.)

F32 — Of all cities which are chosen for a rest, if you will believe me, who know many, it is the most delightful [of Tarraco]

FLOWER, B.O. (1858?-1918)

F33 — The slums of our cities are the reservoirs of physical and moral death, an enormous expense to the state, a constant menace to society, a reality whose shadow is at once colossal and portentous. In time of social upheavals they will prove magazines of destruction; for, while revolution will not originate in them, once let a popular uprising take form and the cellars will reinforce it in a manner more terrible than words can portray. *Civilization's Inferno, or, Studies in the Social Cellar*

FOLLIET, Joseph

F34 — Ancient town have extended beyond all measure into such urban monsters as London, Paris, Berlin, or New York. The rhythms of city life, regulated according to the mathematical time divisions of the clock, no longer depend on day, season, or weather. Although the country goes on conditioning the city, it no longer exerts a determining influence. On the contrary, the country is influenced more and more by the city. Disappearing cultural peasant patterns provide subject matter only for museums and folkloric science and art. *The Effects of City Life upon Spiritual Life*

F35 — In the Graeco-Roman western world Christianity was at first an urban phenomenon. The countryside long remained pagan, and the French language still bears traces of this persistence. Words like *paien* (pagan) and *paysan* (a rural inhabitant), and the disparaging slang terms *pacant* (boorish) and *pequenot* (peasant-like) are derived from *pagus*, meaning the small country place, as contrasted with *civitas*, the city. *Ibid.*

FORD, Ford Madox (1873-1939)

F36 — New York is large, glamorous, easy-going, kindly and incurious — but above all it is a crucible — because it is large enough to be incurious. *New York Is Not America*

FORD, Gerald R. (1913-   )

F37 — New York City's officials have proved in the past that they will not face up to the city's massive network of pressure groups as long as any other alternative is available. If they can scare the whole country into providing that alternative now, why shouldn't they be confident they can scare us again into providing it three years from now? In short, it encourages the continuation of 'politics as usual' in New York — which is precisely not the way to solve the problem. Such a step would set a terrible precedent for the rest of the nation. *The New York Times, October 30, 1975*

FORD, Henry

F38 — We will solve the problems of the cities by moving away from the cities.

F39 — New York is a different country. Maybe it ought to have a separate government. Everybody thinks differently, acts differently — they just don't know what the hell the rest of the United States is. *Reader's Digest, October, 1973*

F40 — I will build a motor car for the great multitude. It will be large enough for the family but small enough for the individual to run and care for. It will be constructed of the best materials, by the best men to be hired, after the simplest designs that modern engineering can devise. But it will be so low in price that no man making a good salary will be unable to own one — and enjoy with his family the blessing of hours of pleasure in God's great open spaces. *Quoted in Road to Ruin*

FORRESTER, Jay W. (1918-   )

F41 — Urban difficulties are not a matter of location so much as a phase in the normal life cycle of occupied land. *Urban Dynamics*

F42 — I see no soluton for urban problems until cities develop the courage to plan in terms of maximum population, a maximum number of housing units, a maximum permissible building height and a maximum number of jobs. A city must also choose the type of city it wants to be. To become and remain a city that is all things to all people is impossible. *The Washington Post, June 8, 1975*

FORSTER, John (1812-1876)

F43 — There is fiercer crowded misery / In garret-toil and London loneliness / Than in cruel islands 'mid the far-off sea. / *Life and Adventures of Oliver Goldsmith*

FOSTER, Thomas

F44 — The zenith city of the unsalted seas. [of Duluth, Minn.] *(Speech)*

FRAME, Richard

F45 — A City, and Towns were raised then, / Wherein we might abide, / Planters also, and Husband-men / Had Land enough beside. / The best of Houses then was known, / To be of Wood and Clay, / But now we build of Brick and Stone, / Which is a better way. / *A Short Description of Pennsylvania in 1692*

FRANCE, Anatole (1844-1924)

F46 — The feeding-grounds of crime. [of slums]

F47 — Is it possible for the mind to conceive all the pain and suffering that lie pent within a great city? It is my belief that if a man succeeded in realizing it, the weight of it would crush him to earth.

FRANK, Lawrence K. (1890-1968)

F48 — Cities have been the chief, if not the only, laboratory for experimentation in living, for interrupting the continuity of traditions and encouraging new ideas, new patterns, and new expectations whereby human advances have been made. Cities have tolerated deviation from the norms of conduct, have allowed relations not elsewhere permitted; they have encouraged individuality, even permitted ruthless individualism; they have fostered creativity in almost all human activities, but especially in art, literature, music, the professions, and science. *The Promise of the City*

FRANK, Waldo (1889-1967)

F49 — On the one side, trains pour in the cattle and the hogs. On the other, trains pour in the men and women. Cattle and hogs from the West. Women and men from the East. Between, stockaded off by the dripping walls, the slaughter houses stand mysterious, and throb to their ceaseless profit. [of Chicago]

FRASER, J.F. (1868-1936)

F50 — The Argentines are town proud. You are not in Buenos Aires a couple of days before you are bombarded with the inquiry, 'Don't you think this is a beautiful city?' It is not that; but it is an interesting city. *The Amazing Argentine*

F51 — The Argentines call their city of Beunos Aires the Paris of the southern hemisphere. *Ibid.*

FRESCOBALDI, Matteo (1297?-1348)

F52 — As long as you were still adorned, O Florence, / by good and ancient citizens and dear, /people far and near / admired the Lion and its sons. [Lion: symbol of Florence] / Touted among even Muslims, / Whore you are now the world round. / *Dear Florence Mine*

FREUD, Sigmund (1856-1939)

F53 — The lie of salvation. [of Rome]

F54 — The women of Rome, strangely enough, are beautiful even when they are ugly, and not many of them are that. *The Letters of Sigmund Freud*

FRIEDMAN, Milton (1912-   )

F55 — Go bankrupt. That will make it impossible for New York City in future to borrow any money and force New York to live within its budget. The only other alternative is the obvious one — tighten its belt, pay off its debts, live within its means and become an honest city again. [of New York City's fiscal crisis] *The New York Times, July 30, 1975*

FRIEDRICHS, Robert W. (1923-   )

F56 — It was neither agriculture nor the marketplace . . . that led men to raise the first city wall and mark out the first crossroad. It was rather their consummate need to gather in worship. The city's first masters were her priests; her first permanent edifice, her temple. The crossroad and wall that stand as paradigm for the city stand also as paradigm for man's religious consciousness. *A Historical View*

FRONTENAC (Le Comte de) (1620-1698)

F57 — I never saw anything more superb than the position of this town. It could not be better situated as the future capital of a great empire. [of Quebec City] *Quoted in Count Frontenac and New France under Louis XIV*

FROST, Robert (1874?-1963)

F58 — I have been one acquainted with the night. / I have walked out in rain — and back in rain. / I have outwalked the furthest city light. / I have looked down the saddest city lane. / I have passed by the watchman on his beat. / And dropped my eyes, unwilling to explain. / *Acquainted with the Night*

FROUDE, J.A. (1818-1894)

F59 — The tendency of people in the later stages of civilization to gather into towns is an old story. Horace had seen in Rome what we are now witnessing in England — the fields deserted, the people crowding into cities. He noted the growing degeneracy. He foretold the inevitable consequences. *Oceana*

FRYE, Northrup (1912-   )

F60 — In Christianity the city is the form of the myth of *telos*, the New Jerusalem that is the end of the human pilgrimage. But there is no city in the Christian, or

Judaeo-Christian, myth of origin: that has only a garden, and the two progenitors of what was clearly intended to be a simple and patriarchal society. In the story which follows, the story of Cain and Abel, Abel is the shepherd and Cain a farmer whose descendants build cities and develop the arts. The murder of Abel appears to symbolize the blotting out of an idealized pastoral society by a more complex civilization. In Classical mythology the original society appears as the Golden Age, to which we have referred more than once, again a peaceful and primitive society without the complications of later ones. In both our main literary traditions, therefore, the tendency to see the ideal society in terms of a lost simple paradise has a ready origin. *Varieties of Literary Utopias*

FULK (of Chartres)

F61 — O what a splendid city, how stately, how fair, how many monasteries therein, how many palaces raised by sheer labor in its broadways and streets, how many works of art, marvelous to behold; it would be wearisome to tell of the abundance of all good things; of gold and of silver, garments of manifold fashion, and such sacred relics. Ships are at all times putting in at this port, so that there is nothing that men want that is not brought hither . . ." [of Constantinople]

FULLER, Thomas (1608-1661)

F62 — 'The beggars of Bath.' Many in that place; some native there, others repairing thither from all parts of the land; the poor for alms; the pained for ease. *Worthies*

FULLER, Thomas (1654-1734)

F63 — Tis the men, not the houses, that make the city. *Gnomologia*

F64 — Troy was not took in a day. *Ibid.*

F65 — The way to Babylon will never bring you to Jerusalem. *Ibid.*

FURNAS, J.C. (1905-   )

F66 — A hundred years ago Cincinnati was often called *Porkopolis* because so many hogs were butchered and processed there.

G

GALBRAITH, John Kenneth (1908-   )

G1 — From the earliest days of the Industrial City there was a strong desire by the few who could afford it to escape its smoke and grime and even more its unlovely landscape. So with the Industrial City came the suburb. With the reconstitution of a mercantile class and the appearance of the new managerial elite, the growth of the suburbs gained greatly in momentum. These settlements had no central function — they did not rule, sell or make. They were places where people found space. *Quoted in The Exploding Cities*

G2 — Perhaps the most urgent need for improved urban existence is to accept that the modern city is, by its nature, a socialist enterprise . . . . But this necessity is related to a yet further requirement. That is to see, far more clearly than at present, the essentially social character of the city as a whole. *Ibid.*

G3 — I am persuaded on this point: that much of the urban problem in the United States is the result of trying to run cities on the cheap; trying to run cities without adequate funds for the police, without adequate funds for sanitation, without adequate funds for housing, without adequate funds for recreation, without adequate funds for hospitals, without

adequate funds for welfare, without adequate funds for all the peculiar problems, the peculiarly expensive problems, of the modern metropolis. The one thing we have never understood was how expensive the very big city is . . . *Los Angeles Times, October 4, 1970*

G4 — The remarkable thing is not that [New York's] government costs so much, but that so many people of wealth have left. It's outrageous that the development of the metropolitan community has been organized with escape hatches that allow people to enjoy the proximity of the city while not paying their share of taxes. It's outrageous that a person can avoid income tax by moving to New Jersey or Connecticut. Fiscal funkholes are what the suburbs are. *The New York Times, July 30, 1975*

GALIANI, Abbé

G5 — The cafe of Europe. [of Paris]

GANS, Herbert J. (1927-   )

G6 — Although suburbia is often described as a hotbed of adultery in popular fiction, this is an urban fantasy. Levittown is quite monogamous, and I am convinced that most suburbs are more so than most cities. The desire for sexual relations with attractive neighbors may be ever-present, but when life is lived in a goldfish bowl, adultery is impossible to hide from the neighbors — even if there were motels in Levittown and baby-sitters could be found for both parties. Occasionally such episodes do take place, after which the people involved often run off together or leave the community. *An Anatomy of Suburbia*

G7 — The suburban critique considers life beyond the city limits harmful both to family life and to the happiness and mental health of the individual. The findings from Levittown suggest just the opposite — that suburban life has produced more family cohesion and a significant boost in morale through the reduction of boredom and loneliness. *Ibid.*

G8 — In this unpredictable world, nothing can be predicted quite so easily as the continued proliferation of suburbia. *The New York Times Magazine, January 7, 1968*

GARDNER, John W. (1912-)

G9 — One cannot blame racial tensions for our monumental traffic jams, for the inexorable advance of air and water pollution, for the breakdown in administration of the courts, for the shocking inefficiency and often corruption of municipal government. It is true that when urban systems malfunction, minorities and the poor are hit first and hardest, but the problem is deeper and broader and ultimately affects us all. *(Speech to National Press Club, Washington, December 9, 1969)*

G10 — The typical American city is in fragments — a variety of worlds wholly out of touch with each other.

G11 — We get richer and richer in filthier and filthier communities until we reach a final state of affluent misery — Croesus on a garbage heap.

G12 — In the slums of our great cities today boys and girls who could easily be brought to the full use of their powers are left stunted, inarticulate and angry. *No Easy Victories*

G13 — The plain fact is that most cities are not organized to cope with their problems. Their haphazard growth has brought such rampant administrative disorder that good government is scarcely possible. *Ibid.*

GARRICK, David (1717-1779)

G14 — London is good for the English, but Paris is good for everyone.

GASKELL, Elizabeth (1810-1865)

G15 — They are the mysterious problem of life to more than him. He wondered if any in all the hurrying crowd had come from such a house of mourning. He thought they all looked joyous, and he was angry with them. But he could not, you cannot, read the lot of those who daily pass you by in the street. *Mary Barton*

GASS, William (1924-)

G16 — This Midwest. A dissonance of parts and people, we are a consonance of Towns. Like a man grown fat in everything but

heart, we overlabor; our outlook never really urban, never rural either, we enlarge and linger at the same time, as Alice both changed and remained in her story. *In the Heart of the Heart of the Country*

GAUTIER, Theophile (1811-1872)

G17 — To arrive by night in a city of which one has dreamed for long years is a very simple accident of travel, but one which seemed calculated to excite curiosity to the highest degree of exasperation. To enter the abode of one's fancy with bandaged eyes is the most irritating thing in the world . . . . [of Venice] *Journeys in Italy*

GAY, John (1685-1732)

G18 — Remote from cities liv'd a swain, / Unvex'd with all the cares of gain; / His head was silver'd o'er with age, / And long experience made him sage. / *The Shepherd and Philosopher*

G19 — O happy streets! to rumbling wheels unknown, / No carts, no coaches, shake the floating town! / [of Venice] *Trivia*

GEDDES, Patrick (1854-1932)

G20 — He is no true town planner, but at best a too simple engineer, who sees only the similarity of cities, their common network of roads and communications. He who would be even a sound engineer, doing work to endure, let alone an artist in his work, must know his city indeed, and have entered into its soul as Scott and Stevenson knew and loved their Edinburgh; as Pepys and Johnson and Lamb, as Besant and Gomme their London. Oxford, Cambridge, St. Andrews, Harvard, have peculiarly inspired their studious sons; but Birmingham and Glasgow, New York or Chicago, have each no small appeal to observant and active minds. In every city there is much of beauty and more of possibility; and thus for the town planner as an artist, the very worst of cities may be the best. *Cities in Evolution*

G21 — The nature lover's revolt from city life, even though in youth strengthened and reinforced by the protest of the romantics and the moralists, of the painters and the poets, may be sooner or later overpowered by the attractions, both cultural and practical, which city life exerts. *Ibid.*

G22 — Not that which shows the palace of government as the origin and climax of every radiating avenue; the true city is that of a burgher people, governing themselves from their own town hall and yet expressing also the spiritual ideal which governs them.

G23 — Though the woof of each city's life be unique, and this it may be increasingly with each throw of the shuttle, the main warp of life is broadly similar from city to city. *Cities in Evolution*

G24 — A city is more than a place in space, it is a drama in time. Though the claim of geography be fundamental, our interest in the history of the city is supremely greater ... *Civics: As Applied Sociology*

G25 — To realise the geographic and historic factors of our city's life is thus the first step to comprehension of the present, one indispensable to any attempt at the scientific forecast of the future, which must avoid as far as it can the dangers of mere utopianism .... *Ibid.*

GELFANT, Blanche Housman

G26 — Behind the rise of the modern city novel has been the awareness — always growing stronger and more clearly articulated — that city life is distinctive and that it offers the writer peculiarly modern material and demands of him literary expression in a modern idiom. As a shaping influence upon the modern American literary mind, the city has made its impression not only as a physical place but more important as a characteristic and unique way of life.

GEORGE VI (of England) (1895-1952)

G27 — London ... that Mother City of the Commonweath which is proving herself to be built as a city at unity with itself. It is not walls that make the city, but the people who live within them, the walls of London may be battered, but the spirit of the Londoner stands resolute and undismayed. *(Radio Broadcast, September 23,1940)*

GEORGE, Dan (1899-)

G28 — No, it is not a good place to live. You have to look up to see the sky. [of New York] *Time, February 5, 1971*

GEORGE, Henry (1839-1897)

G29 — This life of great cities is not the natural life of man. He must, under such conditions, deteriorate, physically, mentally, morally. Yet the evil does not end here. This is only one side of it. This unnatural life of the great cities means an equally unnatural life in the country. Just as the wen or tumor, drawing the wholesome juices of the body into its poisonous vortex, impoverishes all other parts of the frame, so does the crowding of human beings into great cities impoverish human life in the country. *City and Country*

G30 — Clearly, it is because men cannot find employment in the country that there are so many unemployed in the city; for when the harvest opens they go trooping out, and when it is over they come trooping back to the city again. *Progress and Poverty*

G31 — The destruction of speculative land values would tend to diffuse population where it is too dense and to concentrate it where it is too sparse; to substitute for the tenement house, homes surrounded by gardens, and to fully settle agricultural districts before people were driven far from neighbors to look for land. The people of the cities would thus get more of the pure air and sunshine of the country, the people of the country more of the economies and social life of the city. *Ibid.*

G32 — In all the great American cities there is to-day as clearly defined a ruling class as in the most aristocratic countries of the world. Its members carry wards in their pockets, make up the slates for nominating conventions, distribute offices as they bargain together, and — though they toil not, neither do they spin — wear the best of raiment and spend money lavishly. They are men of power, whose favor the ambitious must court and whose vengeance he must avoid. *Ibid.*

G33 — In the United States it is clear that squalor and misery, and the vices and crimes that spring from them, everywhere increase as the village grows to the city, and the march of development brings the advantages of the improved methods of production and exchange. *Ibid.*

G34 — It is not the growth of the city that develops the country, but the development of the country that makes the city grow. And, hence, when, through all trades, men willing to work cannot find opportunity to do so, the difficulty must arise in the employment that creates a demand for all other employments — it must be because labor is shut out from land. *Ibid.*

G35 — A railroad company approaches a small town as a highwayman approaches his victim. The threat, 'If you do not accede to our terms we will leave your town two or three miles to one side!' ... is not merely to deprive the town of the benefits which the railroad might give, it is to put it in a far worse position than if no railroad had been built. ... And just as robbers unite to plunder in concert and divide the spoil, so do the trunk lines of railroads unite to raise rates and pool their earnings. *Ibid.*

G36 — The tax upon land values is the most just and equal of all taxes. It falls only upon those who receive from society a peculiar and valuable benefit, and upon them in proportion to the benefit they receive. It is the taking by the community, for the use of the community, of that value which is the creation of the community. *Ibid.*

GIBBON, Edward (1737-1794)

G37 — The decline of Rome was the natural and inevitable effect of immoderate greatness ... as soon as time or accident had removed the artificial supports, the stupendous fabric yielded to the pressure of its own weight. The story of its ruin is simple and obvious and instead of inquiring why the Roman empire was destroyed, we should rather be surprized that it had subsisted so long.

G38 — Had I been rich and independent, I should have prolonged and perhaps have fixed my residence in Paris.

G39 — It was at Rome, on the 15th of October, 1764, as I sat musing amidst the ruins of the Capitol, while the barefoot friars were singing vespers in the Temple of Jupiter, that the idea of writing the decline

and fall of the city first started to my mind. *Autobiography*

G40 — After a diligent inquiry, I can discern four principal causes of the ruin of Rome, which continued to operate in a period of more than a thousand years. I. The injuries of time and nature. II. The hostile attacks of the barbarians and Christians. III. The use and abuse of the materials. And IV. The domestic quarrels of the Romans. *The Decline and Fall of the Roman Empire*

G41 — Vicissitudes of fortune, which spares neither man nor the proudest of his works, which buries empires and cities in a common grave. *Ibid.*

G42 — If Julian [the Roman emperor, who was born in Paris in A.D. 331] could now revisit the capital of France, he might converse with men of science and genius capable of understanding and instructing a disciple of the Greeks; he might excuse the graceful follies of a nation whose martial spirit has never been enervated by the indulgence of luxury; and he must applaud the perfection of that inestimable art which softens and refines and embellishes the intercourse of social life. *Memoirs*

GIBSON, Kenneth (Mayor, Newark) (1932-   )

G43 — The city was, is and always will be the single most important source of economic, social, educational, cultural and political innovation and vitality. With all the difficulties we have today, we are this country's heart beat, and it strangles us at its own peril. *(Jersey City State College commencement, June 1971)*

G44 — We destroyed the cities of Western Europe in World War II and then rebuilt them. It didn't take so long. But we had the Marshall Plan to bring it about. That is the kind of effort we need now for the rebuilding of our own cities. It would not take so long, once we decided it could be done. *The Los Angeles Times, December 14, 1976*

G45 — Wherever the central cities are going, Newark is going to get there first. *The New York Times Magazine*

GIDE, André (1869-1951)

G46 — The glorious, pain-filled and tragic city. [of Prague]

G47 — I have found the secret of my boredom in Rome: I do not find myself interesting here. *The Journals of André Gide*

GIFFORD, Bernard (1943-   )

G48 — A city's greatness cannot be measured by the height of its tallest buildings; the length and breadth of its public transportation system; the number of nightclubs, sports stadiums or convention centers; or the presence of great museums of art and archeology beckoning us to peer into the past. All of these things are wonderful and their existence is a sign of a city's vitality and vibrancy. But they don't add up to greatness. A city's greatness is measured by its collective compassion toward its poor, its aged, its sick — the very people who are so often consigned to the junk heap of history by cynics and purveyors of benign neglect — those who inform us that the urban crisis is no more; that the problems of our major urban areas would disappear if we would only stop talking about them. *(Speech at Hunter College, May 20, 1975)*

GILBERT, W.S. (1836-1911) and A. SULLIVAN (1842-1900)

G49 — Our city we have beautified — we've

done it willy-nilly — / And all that isn't Belgrave Square is Strand and Piccadilly / [of London] *Utopia Limited or the Flowers of Progress*

GILDER, Richard Watson (1844-1909)

G50 — Stream of the living world / Where dash the billows of strife! / One plunge in the might torrent / Is a year of tamer life! / City of glorious days, / Of hope, and labor and mirth, / With room and to spare, on thy splendid bays, / For the ships of all the earth! / [of New York City] *The City*

GILMAN, Charlotte Perkins (1860-1935)

G51 — New York . . . that unnatural city where every one is an exile, none more so than the American. *The Living of Charlotte Perkins Gilman*

GINGER, Ray (1924-1975)

G52 — A modern city in the United States has the power to squelch, to destroy, to stamp out. Many of its defects are rooted in 'massive forces working obscurely in the background.' To be precise, there are three forces. First, cities have been increasingly regarded by Americans not as places to live in but as places to make money. Go to the Board of Trade, grab whatever you can, then go home to the little woman and the kids in Kenilworth. An Italian does not think that way about Florence, nor does a Frenchman think that way about Paris. *Modern American Cities*

GIRDNER, John H. (1856-1933)

G53 — My contention for less noise is based on the experience and observation of nearly twenty years' practice of my profession in New York City. And I am satisfied that the irritation caused by the din in which we live to-day is essentially health-destroying, and plays no unimportant part in producing disease of the brain and nervous system, and delaying the recovery of the sick. *North American Review, September 1896*

GISH, Lillian (1896-   )

G54 — An emotional Detroit. [of Hollywood]

GISSING, George (1857-1903)

G55 — A great gloomy city, webbed and meshed, as it were, by the spinnings of a huge poisonous spider . . . [of London] *Introduction to Bleak House*

G56 — London . . . a place of squalid mystery and terror, of the grimly grotesque, of labyrinthine obscurity and lurid fascination. *Introduction to Oliver Twist*

G57 — Not seldom I have a sudden vision of a London street, perhaps the dreariest and ugliest, which for a moment gives me a feeling of home-sickness. Often it is the High Street of Islington . . . no thoroughfare in all London less attractive to the imagination, one would say; but I see myself walking there — walking with the quick, light step of youth, and there, of course, is the charm. *The Private Papers of Henry Ryecroft*

G58 — Parks are but pavement disguised with a growth of grass. *Ibid.*

GLAAB, Charles N. (1927-   )

G59 — Americans have conducted a continuing dialogue about the worth of cities, and the weight of literary opinion — if not the opinion of thousands of promoters and pamphleteers in the aspiring, growing towns of America — has gone against the city. *The American City: A Documentary History*

GLASS, Andrew J. (1935-   )

G60 — As the Marshall Plan helped create the modern Europe, so the United States might in such a way help create the city of tomorrow. *The Urban Dilemma*

G61 — The immensely difficult task of educating the children of poverty has been left to the city — at the very time that its declining sources of revenue deny it the viable means to do so. The cities — plagued by outmoded facilities and a shortage of good teachers — must cope with the population explosion that is taking place in the slum areas which typically girdle a city's downtown core. The problem of providing meaningful 'equal opportunity' for the Negro youth is predominantly the problem of the city — and the beginning of the solution must lie in education. *Ibid.*

G62 — To assert that the city reflects a central problem in American life is simply to realize that increasingly the cities *are* American life — just as urban living is fast becoming the condition of man throughout the world. *Ibid.*

GLAZER, Nathan (1923-   )

G63 — Almost every urban problem in the United States has a racial dimension, and the racial dimension in almost every problem is the key factor. Only the problems of pollution — which affect all cities, whether racially mixed or not — seem to be free of a significant racial aspect. *Cities in Trouble*

G64 — The city is productive — it makes things everyone needs, it produces knowledge to make things more efficiently. According to the way economists figure these things, in modern societies cities are far more productive than the countryside. A country will be rich in proportion to the numbers of people that live in its cities, and in any modern society three-quarters or more of the population live in cities. *Ibid.*

G65 — No modern society with any degree of consumer freedom has figured out how to control the impact of the automobile. In American cities this is now visible in a high level of air pollution; in huge investments in road building, which damages or replaces older parts of the city with their various benefits of physical design and of complex integrated social structure, and which changes the open land around the city; in the drying up of public transportation; in the increasing difficulty of access to the older, inner parts of the city. *Ibid.*

G66 — People in small towns and in the countryside, even if they do not fear crime as much as those in the city do, also show a substantial degree of madness and unhappiness. But this may well be owing to the fact that today, even outside the cities, one cannot escape the disorienting effects of new standards and values and ways of life, for the city spreads its influence through the mass media. People in the small towns and the country not only know what the people in the city know; they suffer further from knowing they are not where the action is. *Ibid.*

G67 — Most people prefer automobiles as a form of public transportation, even when they are not — as in American cities — forced to it by a lack of public transportation. Architects, planners, sociologists ask gloomily, can the city live with the automobile? People have already answered — it must, because we won't give them up. *Ibid.*

G68 — Geographical proximity may lead to very little social contact. *Dead End,* in which the slum kids interact with the swells, is still fiction; most of such interaction occurs through the intermediary of the police. Puerto Ricans and Negroes in the shadows of expensive apartment houses in New York scarcely have any interaction with the wealthy — they generally use different stores, schools, churches, and open spaces. *Housing Problems and Housing Policies*

G69 — The most decisive of the social problems that we think of when we consider the urban crisis — the integration of Negroes into the American city and American society — is particularly immune to attack by means of the physcial improvement of the city. *The New York Times Magazine, November 21, 1965*

G70 — Los Angeles produces less than any other great city of the things that, from a grim, Protestant way of looking at things, anyone really *needs.* And yet it grows like mad. *Notes on Southern California: A Reasonable Suggestion as to How Things Can Be?*

G71 — Modern city planning has completely failed to plan for big cities in the twentieth century. It has failed because it has not yet broken loose from the small-town vision concerned with small-town values. What passes for city planning today is fundamentally a rejection of the big city and of all it means — its variety, its peculiarities, its richness of choice and experience — and a yearning for a bucolic society. *Why City Planning Is Obsolete*

GLAZIER, Willard (1841-1905)

G72 — By all means make your first approach to Pittsburgh in the night time, and you will behold a spectacle which has not a parallel on the continent. . . . around

the city's edge, and on the sides of the hills which encircle it like a gloomy amphitheatre, their outlines rising dark against the sky, through numberless apertures, fiery lights stream forth, looking angrily and fiercely up toward the heavens, while over all these settles a heavy pall of smoke. It is as though one had reached the outer edge of the infernal regions, and saw before him the great furnace of Pandemonium with all the lids lifted. *Peculiarities of American Cities.*

G73 — Pittsburgh illustrates more clearly than any other city in America the outcome of democratic institutions. There are no classes here except the industrious classes; and no ranks in society save those which have been created by industry. *Ibid.*

G74 — Pittsburgh is a smokey, dismal city, at her best. At her worst, nothing darker, dingier or more dispiriting can be imagined. *Ibid.*

GOETHE, Johann Wolfgang von (1749-1832)

G75 — I have observed, that in a great city even the poorest, the lowest can be himself, whereas in a small community even the richest does not feel he really lives, that he can breathe.

G76 — No settlement of ancient peoples was so badly located as Rome.

G77 — Now I am counting an additional birthday, truly a regeneration from the day when I entered Rome.

G78 — [To Eckermann] Now imagine a city like Paris where the best minds of a great empire are gathered together in the same place, where everything remarkable that all the realms of nature and the art of all parts of the earth can offer is open to study every day; imagine such a world city where every step on a bridge or square recalls a glorious past, and where at every street corner a fragment of history has taken place. *Conversations with Eckermann*

G79 — Now it stood written on my page in the Book of Fate, that on the evening of the 28th of September, by 5 o'clock, German time, I should see Venice for the first time, as I passed from the Brenta into the lagunes, and that, soon afterwards, I should actually enter and visit this strange island-city, this heaven-like republic. So now, Heaven be praised, Venice is no longer to me a bare and hollow name, which has so long tormented me, — me, the mental enemy of mere verbal sounds.

G80 — One does not like to reminisce here about Rome. Compared to the spaciousness here, the capital of the world in the Tiber valley seems to be an old, badly placed monastery. [of Naples]

G81 — The patriotism of antiquity becomes in most modern societies a caricature. In antiquity, it developed naturally from the whole condition of a people, its youth, its situation, its culture — with us it is an awkward imitation. Our life demands, not separation from other nations, but constant intercourse; our city life is not that of the ancient city-state.

G82 — A truly royal and classical city . . . unlike Berlin, which one sees only when one is inside, one sees Prague only from the outside or from above.

G83 — Venice can be compared only to itself.

G84 — Only in Rome have I felt what it really is to be a man. *Conversations with Eckermann*

GOLD, Herb (1924-   )

G85 — Oh to be in L.A. when the polyethyl-vinyl trees are in bloom!

GOLDBERGER, Paul

G86 — If it is best to read *Tender Is the Night* on the Riviera and *Homer* in Greece, then probably the right place for Dante is the New York subway. *The City Observed, New York*

G87 — New York is an arrogant city; it has always wanted to be all things to all people, and a surprising amount of the time it has succeeded. *Ibid.*

GOLDMARK, Peter C. (1906-1977)

G88 — When people started moving to the suburbs, they thought they would be going

far enough. They were afraid to go farther away because they wanted to have the advantages of the nearby big cities and the rural charm of the suburbs. Today, they have neither. The city doesn't have the amenities and there is little of the rural charm left in the suburbs. *The Dallas Times Herald, March 16, 1973*

GOLDONI, Carlo (1707-1792)

G89 — Paris is a world of itself: everything is on a large scale, the good and bad both in abundance. Whether you go to theaters, promenades, or places of pleasure, you find every corner full. Even the churches are crowded. In a town of eight hundred thousand souls there must necessarily be more of both good and bad people than anywhere else; and it rests with ourselves to make our choice. . . . *Memoirs*

GOLDSMITH, Oliver (1728?-1774)

G90 — I have found by experience, that they who have spent all their lives in cities, contract not only an effeminacy of habit, but of thinking.

G91 — Sweet Auburn! loveliest village of the plain. *The Deserted Village*

G92 — Where village statesmen talk'd with looks profound, / And news much older than their ale went round. / *Ibid.*

GOLDSTON, Robert (1927-   )

G93 — The city itself — the idea of a city, any city — is not merely a collection of buildings, however imposing, nor a massing of people, however many. The city has always been a shrine to which men flocked to worship — to worship to gods or God or themselves in their highest expressions of culture . . It is a place where people, much more isolated personally than in a town or village, consciously identify themselves with public symbols, with their fellow men on a more impersonal scale. *Barcelona: The Civic Stage*

G94 — If the city, any city, is looked upon as an environment strictly for exploitation, then that city is doomed as a city. It may survive as a gigantic commercial enterprise, accommodating the residence of transient business or workers (Manhattan seems headed for this category), or as a center devoted almost entirely to industrial production, housing only the industrial workers and the engineers and managers (Pittsburgh has long since become such a city) — but as a city, as a place to celebrate the human experience, to create, preserve and transmit a human culture, such huge centers will not survive. *Ibid.*

G95 — It would be pointless . . . to establish the fact that the citizens of, say, Florence, Italy, or Sacramento, California, enjoy a more satisfactory, more intimate and more humane way of life than do the citizens of Leeds, England, or Denver, Colorado, or Birmingham, Alabama. Of course they do. But neither Florence nor Sacramento are facing the terribly urgent and intense pressures of modern industrialization. *Ibid.*

G96 — Most cities in the modern world have become shrines to naked power, either the power of commerce (New York, Chicago, Marseilles, Nagasaki) or the power of the state (Washington, Moscow, Paris, Brasilia). And apologists for this condition have insisted that since an acceptable standard of living is the result of a concentration of economic and political power, the worship of power is, if regrettable, inevitable. *Ibid.*

G97 — The only secure and ennobling mission of the people of the cities has been the advancement of those arts and sciences (and their communication to the rest of the world) which are the highest expressions of human culture and which, hopefully, may one day produce a truly mature, truly humane worldwide civilization. *Ibid.*

G98 — The way of life of the people of Barcelona is still today one which the citizens of other cities may truly envy, and one from which they have very much to learn. Meantime, unself-consciously or otherwise, a delightful, human urban drama continues in this city-theater. The stage décor changes slowly over the decades and centuries, the actors change more rapidly; but there is never an intermission in the show. *Ibid.*

G99 — Where a former sense of mission has been destroyed (as in London or Paris or Boston), cities are in the process of decay and, perhaps, eventual disappearance as urbane places to live. Where the sense of

mission has been perverted to mere self-aggrandizement, (as in New York or San Francisco), the city becomes an urban jungle, a chaotic wasteland of personal greed and public disorder . . . Nor can the imposition from above of out-dated superhuman 'missions,' such as the advancement of the power of the state (as in Moscow or Washington), bring anything but eventual ruin to the citizens of such cities (as the fate of Berlin, Tokyo and a dozen other capitals in the past fifty years testifies) while surrounding them with urban wastelands of impersonal monuments to private or collective power. *Ibid.*

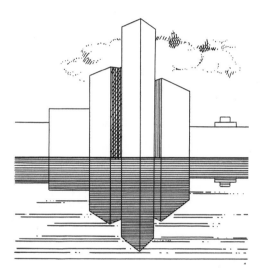

GOODMAN, Mitchell (1923-   )

G100 — Out of a snow — / white night sky / the speaking wind / drives whiteness down / to trim grim edges of / the city, to round / them. / *Snow on the City Three Days before Christmas*

GOODMAN, Paul (1911-1972) and Percival GOODMAN(1904-   )

G101 — Everybody praises diversified farming as a way of life. Yet the farm youth migrate to the city when they can. *Communitas*

G102 — To the farmers, the city families are the most valuable source of money income. *Ibid.*

GOODRICH, Lloyd (1897-)

G103 — The American artist's picturing of America has been romantic from its beginning. The painters of the Hudson River School devoted themselves to the wild and spectacular features of the continent — the wilderness, the mountains, the sea — and disregarded the works of man. The early genre painters focused on rural life, and avoided the city and industrialism . . . Even the naturalistic Winslow Homer turned his back on the city to paint nature and man at their most primitive. The American impressionists selected the idyllic aspects of our country; if they sometimes pictured New York, it was Fifth Avenue and not Seventh. Until the end of the nineteenth century few artists . . . had attempted to picture the American city. *Quoted in The Regionalists, Heller and Williams*

GORNICK, Vivian (1935-)

G104 — I lived once in the American desert. The solitude opens up. It becomes an enormous surrounding comfort. But the solitude in the city is a confusing and painful thing. *In Search of Ali-Mahmoud*

G105 — If the word for London is decency and the word for New York is violence, then, beyond doubt, the word for Cairo is tenderness. Tenderness is what pervades the air here. *Ibid.*

GOULD, Glenn (1932-)

G106 — Toronto, by general consensus, is the financial capital of Canada. The contending office towers that dominate the downtown district house major banking institutions, and most of them are located on or near Bay Street, which is the Canadian equivalent of America's Wall Street. People who are not particularly fond of Toronto insist that we go about the making of money with a religious devotion. *in Cities, John McGreevy*

G107 — Toronto does belong on a very short list of cities I've visited that seem to offer to me, at any rate, peace of mind — cities which, for want of a better definition, do not impose their 'cityness' upon you. Leningrad is probably the best example of the truly peaceful city. I think that, if I could come to grips with the language and the political system, I could live a very productive life in Leningrad. On the other hand, I'd have a crack-up for sure if I were compelled to live in Rome or New York — and of course, any Torontonian worthy of the name feels that way about Montreal, on principle. *Ibid.*

GOURMONT, Remy de (1856-1915)

G108 — The ever-present phenomenon ceases to exist for our senses. It was a city dweller, or a prisoner, or a blind man suddenly given his sight, who first noted natural beauty.

GRANHOLM, Ake

G109 — Every public opinion poll gives the same result: the typical Finn wants to live in a private house on its own plot of land, beside a lake, in the middle of Helsinki.

GRANT, Ulysses S. (1822-1885)

G110 — Venice would be a fine city if it were only drained.

GRASS, Gunter (1927-)

G111 — Inner City and Outer City, Old City, New City, and Old New City, Lower City and Spice City — what had taken several hundred years to build burned down in three days. Yet this was not the first fire to descend on the city of Danzig. For centuries Pomerelians, Brandenburgers, Teutonic Knights, Poles, Swedes, and a second time Swedes, Frenchmen, Prussians, and Russians, even Saxons, had made history by deciding every few years that the city of Danzig was worth burning. And now it was Russians, Poles, Germans, and Englishmen all at once who were burning the city's Gothic bricks for the hundreth time. *The Tin Drum*

GRAVES, Robert (1895-)

G112 — I was last in Rome in 540 A.D., when it was full of Goths and their heavy horses. It has changed a great deal since then. *Time, January 6, 1958*

GRAY, Thomas (1716-1771)

G113 — That most picturesque (at a distance) and nastiest (when near) of all capital cities. [of Edinburgh]

G114 — Ye towers of Julius, London's lasting shame, / With many a foul and midnight murther fed. / *The Bard*

G115 — Some village Hampden that, with dauntless breast, / The little tyrant of his fields withstood, / Some mute inglorious Milton here may rest, / Some Cromwell guiltless of his country's blood. / *Elegy Written in a Country Churchyard*

GRAYSON, David (1870-1946)

G116 — What we get in the city is not life, but what someone else tells us about life. *Adventures in Contentment*

GREELEY, Horace (1811-1872)

G117 — Secure to the family the inducements of a home, surrounded by fruits and flowers, rational village movements and sports, the means of education and independence. Get them out of the cities and would-be cities into scenes like those, and the work is done.

G118 — We cannot all live in the cities yet nearly all seem determined to do so. Millions of acres . . . solicit cultivation . . . yet hundreds of thousands reject this and rush into the cities.

G119 — Cities are the result of certain social necessities of civilized or semi-civilized Man, — necessities of Trade, of Manufacture, Interchange of Ideas, and of Government: they rest upon and are supported by the Country. *Coming to the City*

G120 — Whoever leaves the country to come to the city should feel sure that he has faculties, capacities, powers, for which the Country affords him no scope, and that the City is his proper sphere of usefulness. He shall be laboring to attain that sphere which he regards as his ultimate destination. No youth should migrate to a City without a thorough mastery of some good mechanical trade or handicraft such as is prosecuted in cities, although he may not intend to follow it except in case of dire necessity. *Ibid.*

GREEN, Constance McLaughlin (1897-1975)

G121 — The wreckage wrought by

Americans' instinct to exploit and move on has been incalculable. They have permitted an appalling waste of human resources. 'Ghost towns' still stand in every part of the country as a reproach to the nation — even when profitably revived as tourist centers. Exhaustion of natural resources — oil, timber, and minerals — coupled with extinction of the buffalo herds and other wild life, has been ruthless. *American Cities in the Growth of the Nation*

G122 — Like men the world over, Americans built their towns and cities where geographic conditions promised the first settlers and later promoters a profitable future. The single notable exception in American history is the capital of the United States, Washington in the District of Columbia, founded for the sole purpose of serving as the national capital. *Ibid.*

GREENE, Albert Gorton (1802-1868)

G123 — His knowledge hid from public gaze, / He did not bring to view, / Nor made a noise town-meeting days, / As many people do. / *Old Grimes*

GREER, Germaine (1939-   )

G124 — Once a week, at least once a week, I dream about Sydney. I know it is a Sydney dream, first of all, because of the smells — the smell of the sea, the smell of the frangipani — because of the sounds — the sounds of the birds crying — and because of the feeling that the sky is so far away. In Europe, the sky sits on your head like a grey felt hat; in Australia, the sky is a million miles away and all that lies beneath it belongs to you. *in Cities, John McGreevy*

GREER, Scott (1922-   )

G125 — The controversy which is sometimes brought, as to which offers the greater advantage, the country or the city, finds a happy answer in the suburban idea which says, both — the combination of the two — the city brought to the country. The city has its advantages and conveniences, the country has its charm and health; the union of the two (a modern result of the railway), gives to man all he could ask in this respect. *The Urbanization of the Suburbs*

G126 — The crisis of the city is . . ., in the beginning at least, an intellectual crisis. . . . The action crisis in the metropolis cannot be disengaged from the intellectual crisis for the very definition of a metropolitan problem is dependent upon one's picture of the city and the kind of life it should contain. *The Emerging City*

G127 — I would like to distinguish between urban problems and problems located in cities. When you say urban America, you can mean either America-as-urban or *cities* and problems peculiar to cities. Many of the things we call urban problems are not problems peculiar to cities; they are human problems. They are problems of poverty, segregation, the poor quality of public services, the shape of traffic and environmental pollution. You do not have to have a city for any of these things. *Decaying Urban America*

GREY, Earl

G128 — The English people of Montreal would be much gayer & happier & cultured if they allowed a little French sunlight to warm and illuminate their lives. *Quoted in Rideau Hall, R.H. Hubbard*

GRIFFIN, C.W. (1925-   )

G129 — More than any other major American city, Los Angeles illustrates the ludicrous conflict between frontier mythology and contemporary reality. *The Frontier Heritage of Urban America*

G130 — Nostalgia for frontier freedoms is manifest in almost every facet of American life — from the popularity of Wild West paperbacks, screen plays, and television shows, to the economic 'rugged individualism' extolled by businessmen living off cost-plus government contracts . . The vicarious reliving of frontier days is both psychological escape and protest against the increasing frictions and collisions accompanying urban growth. *Ibid.*

G131 — There is no place to hide from the stark realities of our crowded, city-centered society with its inevitable frictions, conflict, and turmoil. As pioneers on the urban frontier, can we outgrow the values of our

rural ancestors and adapt to civilized urban life? *Ibid.*

GRIMALD, Nicholas (1519-1562)

G132 — People-pestered London. *The Lover to His Dear*

GRIMES, Tammy (1934-   )

G133 — When you're a kid and decide to become a part of this profession [acting], not really knowing what the profession is all about, you only think in terms of coming to New York, to Broadway, that's final, that's the peak. When you make it in New York that means you've made it. *in Cities, John McGreevy*

GROPIUS, Walter (1883-1969)

G134 — Good planning I conceive to be both a science and an art. As a science, it analyzes human relationships; as an art, it coordinates human activities into a cultural synthesis. *The Scope of Total Architecture*

GROSS, Mason W. (1911-1977)

G135 — A city is a vast collection of memories and expressions of emotion, with its greatest concentration of human meanings at its center, and a gradual thinning out of emotional value until one reaches the drabness of the fringes. But these are not separate and distinct emotions: rather they build upon and reinforce each other, and thus we get that organization which characterizes a great city. But it is not a biological form of organization, and organism; it is an organization of meanings and values. I believe that the real source of fascination of the city is that it represents the widest and fullest expression of all the types of meaning which man has achieved. The city is what we mean by civilization. *(Speech, National Conference on Urban Life, March 28, 1962)*

GROVES, Charles

G136 — A city with eleven months and several odd days of Indian Summer. [of San Francisco]

GRUEN, Victor (1903-   )

G137 — The city is the sum total of countless features and places, of nooks and crannies, of vast spaces and intimate spots, an admixture of the public and private domain, of rooms for work and rooms for living, of rooms for trade, where money and wares change hands, and rooms where music and drama lift the soul, of churches and night spots, of landmarks expressing the spirit of the community, and homes for the comfort of the individual.

G138 — The symptoms of this disease known as the urban crisis are generally the following: a spreading of the intensively inhabited area in an amorphous manner reaching dozens of miles in all directions from the formerly established city centers; and simultaneously with this cancerous growth caused by urban fallout, a shrinking and drying up of those central areas which, in the established sense of the word: 'city,' represented urban and urbane values.

G139 — Basically, the aim of a new planning philosophy must be to sort out and make order — to separate flesh from machines, vehicles from people, and various types of vehicles from each other. To attain this aim, we must abandon the gridlike arrangement characteristic of today's urban pattern. *In Defense of the City*

G140 — Moving out to the suburbs did not bring us the advantages of contact with

nature, as we had once hoped. We have carried with us all the disadvantages of the city, at the same time losing most of the advantages of urban life. *Ibid.*

GUITERMAN, Arthur (1871-1943)

G141 — The finest thing in London is the Bobby, / Benignant information is his hobby. / *The Lyric Baedeker*

G142 — Those lions still are rude and wild, / For while they pose as meek and mild, / To keep their fierceness hid, / Down from their pedestals they'd leap, / As soon as New York went to sleep — / If New York ever did! / [of the stone lions in front of the New York public library.] *The New York Public Library in Fiction, Poetry and Children's Literature*

GUIZOT, Francois Pierre (1787-1874)

G143 — Rome has left us nothing but monuments impressed with the municipal stamp and intended for populations amassed upon a single spot. From whatever point of view you consider the Roman world, you find this almost exclusive preponderance of cities and the social non-existence of the country.

GULICK, Luther (1892-   )

G144 — Historically, it could be shown that the more important institutions of our free society originated in the thinking of men who lived in the larger population centers of their day. It could also be demonstrated that the historic struggles for freedom, including the violent revolutions of the eighteenth and nineteenth centuries, were centered in the great cities, and that the resulting political institutions were given an extensive trial, if not initiation, in urban areas. *Metropolitan Political Developments*

GUNTHER, John (1901-1970)

G145 — Moscow is the city where, if Marilyn Monroe should walk down the street with nothing on but shoes, people would stare at her feet first. *Inside Russia Today*

G146 — New York City, the incomparable, the brilliant star city of cities, the forty-ninth state, a law unto itself, the Cyclopean paradox, the inferno with no out-of-bounds, the supreme expression of both the miseries and the splendours of contemporary civilization. . . . New York is at once the climactic synthesis of America, and yet the negation of America in that it has so many characteristics called unAmerican. *Inside U.S.A.*

G147 — Both London and Paris were its colonies two thousand years ago, and Rome still ranks with them as a major capital. It is one of the most venerable cities in the world, although one of the youngest capitals of a modern nation — younger than Washington, D.C.. *Twelve Cities*

G148 — Cities have characteristic colors, I have always thought. Istanbul is blue and silver, London red, Marrakech pink, and Paris gray. Tokyo is the color of whitish cardboard or raw cement. A good many cities have distinctive smells as well — London of fog and wet leaves. Vienna of ozone, beer, and goulash. Tokyo has a faint, pervasive odor of fish fried in grease. *Ibid.*

G149 — I never saw a Brussels sprout in Brussels. *Ibid.*

G150 — Moscow, with its spotless streets, is far cleaner than New York; it is a great industrial city, but has no smog. Warsaw is a more harmonious community from several points of view than Los Angeles or Dallas. Tel Aviv, Berne, and Bruges are better administered than most American cities in an analogous category, and Vienna has more amenities than Baltimore or St. Louis. The gross physical squalor, dilapidation, noise, and filth in the outskirts of several important American cities would not be tolerated in Stockholm, Ankara, or even Madrid. No city in Europe has an entrance so brutally unkempt as, let us say, Bruckner Boulevard in New York. Even Beirut could show Detroit or Philadelphia a thing or two, and Jerusalem, even if it is an Oriental city, is better run and less offensive to the eye and ear than Pittsburgh or Atlanta. *Ibid.*

G151 — The pace of the city is still extremely slow. It is impossible to hurry the Viennese, which is one reason why the Hapsburg Empire fell. *Ibid.*

G152 — The principal sight of Warsaw is Warsaw. There is nothing here to compare with San Marco in Venice or the Tower of London, because the city itself is the major attraction. Warsaw was destroyed — destroyed in the literal sense like Carthage, leveled to the ground — by the German fury in World War II. *Ibid.*

G153 — Surely no capital in the world (except Paris, Leningrad, and the old Peking) is so lavishly, majestically laid out. [of Vienna] *Ibid.*

G154 — This is one of the least-known capitals in the world, one of the most inaccessible, and one of the pleasantest. The Jordanians are the most agreeable Arabs I know, and their principal city, remote and humdrum as it is, reflects this *gemutlich* quality. [of Amman] *Ibid.*

G155 — Tokyo, the largest city in the world by population, is two-faced, double-sided, pig and porcelain. Its dominant note is commerce — money-making, money-spending — but its fierce and incessant financial activity and perfervid concern with the material elements of society are cloaked by a good deal of Japanese charm and hocus-pocus. This is Wall Street — or the busiest imaginable commercial community — in a kimono. *Ibid.*

G156 — Vienna has nine daily newspapers, more than any American city by a large margin, and I do not quite understand how they survive since, it seems, nobody actually buys a paper, but reads them in their rattan frames in the coffee house. *Ibid.*

GUTHEIM, Frederick (1908-)

G157 — The existence of cities today is threatened by the disappearance of their traditional reasons for being, which largely determined their historical forms. Far from offering a means of defense against enemies, cities are particularly vulnerable to attack. Cities have no monopoly on trade as they had when the medieval markets flourished. People are not obliged to live in cities because the only jobs are there, or because transportation is lacking to allow them to live elsewhere. No city has a cultural monopoly; these are the days of mass media. The search for original art, music, theatre, dance takes one not merely to the central city but to many cities, suburbs, and summer festival centers, and ubiquitous transportation has led to the city that, like Wright's Broadacre City, 'is everywhere and nowhere.' *Urban Space and Urban Design*

G158 — The most important design characteristic of a city is coherence. This means more than order .. Indeed, order alone leads but to monotony and deadness. It provides no role for the imagination. Cities are alive, and their living quality must come through in the articulation of the various parts of the city, in its adaptations, in its growth. A city tells us things, and our body responds to the perception of whether they are places of good or bad air, hot or cold, comfortable or uncomfortable, or provide other bodily sensations. *Ibid.*

G159 — To the visually trained or sensitive person today, the assault of urban anarchy on the senses is remorseless and unremitting. It is an outstanding fact of modern life, an expression of brutalism as harsh and as significant as slave labor, atomic warfare or genocide — and it reveals the same disregard for life. Our cities are neither an expression of civilization nor a creator of civilized men. *Ibid.*

GUTHRIE, William N. (1868-1944)

G160 — The town / drench'd by a penetrant / wind-driven dust of rain, / fast-gluing to the walls soot-flakes / from grimy house-tops swept . . . / a viscous mire; compacting / the smoke-roof, propped by the towers, / spires, factory-chimneys, that threaten / under the mass enormous / to topple, and smother all life / with gloom and stifling dismay . . . / the dusk, wet, slime / of the hideous town. / *Songs of American Destiny*

GUTHRIE, Woodie (1912-1967)

G161 — There was a rich man and he lived in Detroitium, / Glory hallelujah, heirojarum. / And all the workers he did exploitium, / Glory hallelujah, heirojarum. / *There Was a Rich Man and He Lived in Detroitium*

GUTKIND, E.A. (1886-1968)

G162 — The last vestiges of a community have disappeared. They are hardly anything else than an agglomeration of innumerable and isolated details, of human atoms, and rows of boxes, called houses, interspersed between the industries. It is a total victory of laissez faire insensibility and recklessness over organic growth and even over organized development. *The Expanding Environment*

G163 — Cities are the power stations of our technical mass civilization. In these giant containers, ideas and habits, technical skills and inventions are transformed into new energy, spreading over vast areas and connected by the invisible bonds of similar pursuits and interests. The power lines and the pylons are symbolic media of this process. *The Twilight of Cities*

G164 — Every city official, every city planner, wants to grab as much land, as much tax money, as many inhabitants, as many outlying districts as possible for his own city. The hunt for these coveted prizes, this civic buccaneering and uneasy coexistence between cities has hardly anything in common with constructive and peaceful competition. *Ibid.*

G165 — It is not true that life in cities is less isolated than in the country. It is merely another sort of isolation. In the cities this isolation, this human desert, is superficially hidden by the agitation and variety on the surface, and in the country by the rhythm of nature, imposing a rigid equality of life in time and space upon the members of a rural community. *Ibid.*

G166 — The modern city is not a social community. At best it is an association of different classes of society on an economic basis, at worst an agglomeration of human atoms. Under such conditions no clear conception can arise of what a city should be. *Ibid.*

G167 — The old forces that have shaped our environment as we know it have lost their formative power, and the most momentous of the agencies that have given idea and form in the past to our cities and buildings are also those which are in an advanced state of decline. They are the Church, the State and Tradition. *Ibid.*

G168 — The twilight now descending upon towns, cities, and metropolises marks the end of a perennial revolution that has shaped and reshaped urban communities all over the world for more than five thousand years. The problems that have accumulated during these millennia, bringing about the present crisis, are manifold and their interaction is complex and farreaching. *Ibid.*

G169 — We are living today in cities which have neither center nor limits, cities whose central zone symbolizes the power of money. The city of the masses is just as amorphous as the masses themselves. The power of money is the fictitious center — the City of London, Wall Street in New York, the Banque de France in Paris — while the residential and industrial zones surrounding this center house the modern 'slaves' who are governed by this new despotic force. It is the old game of ruler and ruled, but with other symbols. *Ibid.*

H

HABBERTON, John (1842-1921)

H1 — Criminals when not actually plying their vocation generally go to large cities, for two reasons: first to spend their ill-gotten gains in pleasure, and secondly, that as a rule cities are the best hiding-places. *Our Country's Future*

H2 — A great city is a great sore — a sore which never can be cured. The greater the city, the greater the sore. It necessarily follows that New York, being the greatest city in the Union, is the vilest sore on our body politic *Ibid.*

HALL, Edward (1914-)

H3 — Apart from the ethnic enclave, virtually everything about American cities today is sociofugal and drives men apart, alienating them from each other. *The Hidden Dimension*

H4 — The implosion of the world population into cities everywhere is creating a series of destructive behavioral sinks more lethal than the hydrogen bomb. Man is faced with a chain reaction and practically no knowledge of the structure of the cultural atoms producing it. If what is known about animals when they are crowded or moved to an unfamiliar biotope is at all relevant to mankind, we are now facing some terrible consequences in our urban sinks. *Ibid.*

HALL, Peter (1932-)

H5 — The first problem with London is to define it. London has never taken kindly to attempts at delimitation whether by people who wanted to govern it, or by those who just wanted to fix it statistically; every time this was done, London promptly outgrew its administration or its figures. *London 2000*

HALL, Thomas Winthrop (1862-1900)

H6 — One of the million, that am I; / One of the million wondering why / And what it is, and if it pays, / This living in the city's ways. / *When Love Laughs*

HAMBLIN, Dora Jane (1920-) and M.J. GRUNSFELD

H7 — Rome is one of the few 'Roman' cities in the world which has neither *cardus* nor *decumanus*, those rigid and geometrically laid out central thoroughfares designed to meet one another at right angles and form the framework of the classic grid pattern which became the trademark of Roman city planning. The mother city just developed, without plan, up and down the passageways of its peculiar hill-strewn and river-cut terrain, its whimsical and meandering form stamped into a permanent pattern by the bare feet and tough hoofs of its first residents and visitors. *The Appian Way, A Journey*

HAMERTON, Philip G. (1834-1894)

H8 — There are natures that go to the streams of life in great cities as the hart goes to the waterbrooks. *The Intellectual Life*

HAMILTON, Alexander (1757-1804)

H9 — When the first principles of civil society are violated, and the rights of a whole people are invaded, the common forms of municipal law are not to be regarded. Men may then betake themselves to the law of nature; and if they but conform their actions to that standard, all cavils against them betray either ignorance or dishonesty. *The Farmer Refuted*

HAMILTON, Edith (1867-1963)

H10 — In Rome the true artist is the engineer. *The Roman Way*

HAMILTON, (Lord) Frederick

H11 — The atrociously uneven pavements, the general untidiness, the broad thoroughfares empty except for a lumbering cart or two, the low cotton-wool sky all gave the effect of unutterable dreariness. And this was the golden city of my dreams! This place of leprous fronted houses, of vast open spaces full of drifting snow flakes, and of immense emptiness. I never was so disappointed in my life. [of St. Petersburg]

HAMMERSTEIN, Oscar (1895-1960)

H12 — The last time I saw Paris, her heart was warm and gay, / I heard the laughter of her heart in every street cafe. / *The Last Time I Saw Paris*

HAMMURABI of Babylonia (1955-1913 B.C.)

H13 — If the brigand be not captured, the man who has been robbed, shall, in the presence of god, make an itemized statement of his loss, and the city and the governor, in whose province and jurisdiction the robbery was committed, shall compensate him for whatever was lost. *Hammurabi's Code of Laws*

H14 — My benign shadow is spread over my city. / In my bosom I carried the peoples of the land of Sumer and Akkad . . . / I am the king who is preeminent among kings; / My words are choice; my ability has no equal. /

HAMSUN, Knut (1859-1952)

H15 — I may as well state that I have visited four of the five continents . . . and I have truly seen quite a bit of the world; but I have never seen anything that could be called equal to the Kremlin in Moscow. I have seen beautiful cities — and I think Prague and Budapest certainly are among them — but Moscow is like a fairy land.

HANDLIN, Oscar (1915-)

H16 — Seen from above, the modern city edges imperceptibly out of its setting. There are no clear boundaries. Just now the white trace of the superhighway passed through cultivated fields; now it is lost in an asphalt maze of streets and buildings. As one drives in from the airport or looks out from the train window, clumps of suburban housing, industrial complexes, and occasional green spaces flash by; it is hard to tell where city begins and country ends. Our difficulties with nomenclature reflect the indeterminacy of these limits; we reach for some vague concept of metropolis to describe the release of urban potential from its recognized ambit. *The Historian and the City*

HANKINS, Marie L.

H17 — The wheel of fortune turns no where so swiftly as in the great metropolis. New Yorkers must go up or down, must sink or swim. They make fortunes in a year, or lose them in a day. A friendly push sends some to the top of the see-saw, an unlucky jounce precipitates others head long to the bottom, towards which we are always progressing. All the better for the lucky ones, and all the worse for those who fall. It is impossible to tell the future life of the child, by the circumstances in which fate appears to have placed it. Make the attempt, and you will soon see your mistake. *Women of New York*

HANNAY, J.O. (1865-1950)

H18 — Budapest — even Buda, which is the older part of the twin city — is singularly lacking in buildings of historic interest, even of architectural interest or beauty. The wanderer will not expect to find in Budapest a rival of Vienna, much less of Paris or Rome. But it is a little disappointing to discover that it cannot be regarded even as a serious rival of Prague in the historic and architectural interest of its buildings. *A Wayfarer in Hungary*

H19 — Cities ought always to be entered by ship instead of by train if this is possible. Especially is this the case when the traveller is approaching the city for the first time. He wants to get, and ought to get, the best possible impression to start with. Trains never give it. They deliberately choose to enter cities through the purlieus and mean streets. *Ibid.*

H20 — If I knew a really potent prophet and wanted him to curse Budapest — which is nearly the same thing as cursing the Israelites, since Budapest, as its inhabitants say bitterly, ought to be called Judah Pest — I should take him into the city by rail from Vienna, showing him the most unlovely outskirts in the world. He would then, even if he were as stubborn as Balaam was, certainly utter a curse or two. *Ibid.*

HANNEY, James

H21 — Pompous the boast, and yet a truth it speaks: / A modern Athens — fit for modern Greeks. / [of Edinburgh] *On Edinburgh*

HARDY, Thomas (1840-1928)

H22 — [London] appears not to *see itself*. Each individual is conscious of *himself*, but nobody is conscious of themselves collectively, except perhaps some poor gaper who stares round with a half-idiotic aspect.

HARLAS, F.X.

H23 — Our *raison d'etre* . . . the fireplace of our national literature. [of Prague]

HARRINGTON, Michael (1928-   )

H24 — A slum is not merely an area of decrepit buildings. It is a social fact. There are neighborhoods in which housing is run-down, yet the people do not exhibit the hopelessness of the other Americans. Usually, these places have a vital community life around a national culture or a religion. In New York City, Chinatown is an obvious example. Where the slum becomes truly pernicious is when it becomes the environment of the culture of poverty, a spiritual and personal reality for its inhabitants was well as an area of dilapidation. This is when the slum becomes the breeding ground of crime, of vice, the creator of people who are lost to themselves and to society. *The Other America*

HARRIS, Chauncy (1914-   ) and E. ULLMAN (1912-   )

H25 — Cities are the focal points in the occupation and utilization of the earth by man. Cities are also paradoxes. Their rapid growth and large size testify to their superiority as a technique for the exploitation of the earth, yet by their very success and consequent large size they often provide a poor local environment for man. The problem is to build the future city in such a manner that the advantages of urban concentration can be preserved for the benefit of man and the disadvantages minimized. *The Nature of Cities*

HARRIS, Frank (1856-1931)

H26 — London when you are twenty-eight and have already won a place in its life; London when your mantelpiece has ten times as many invitations as you can accept, and there are two or three pretty girls that attract you; London when everyone you meet is courteous-kind and people of importance are beginning to speak about you; London with a foretaste of success in your mouth while your eyes are open wide at its myriad novelties and wonders; London with its round of receptions and Court life, its theatres and shows, its amusements for the body, mind and soul: enchanting hours at a burlesque prolonged by a boxing-match at the Sporting Club; or an evening in Parliament where world-famous men discuss important policies; or a quiet morning spent with a poet who will live in English literature with Keats or Shakespeare or an afternoon with pictures of a master already consecrated by fame; London, who could give even an idea of its various delights? *My Life & Loves*

HARRIS, Louis

H27 — The image of the large city that emerges from our data is that of an economic, cultural-intellectual and recreational service center. The city's image today as a place to live and raise children is overwhelmingly negative. *The Los Angeles Times, March 24, 1978*

HARRIS, Sydney J. (1917-   )

H28 — The lusts of the flesh can be gratified anywhere; it is not this sort of license that distinguishes New York. It is, rather, a lust of the total ego for recognition, even for eminence. More than elsewhere, everybody here wants to be Somebody. *Strictly Personal*

HARRISON, Frederic (1831-1923)

H29 — The ancient city was a State — the collective centre of an organised territory, supreme within it, and owing no fealty to any other sovereign, temporal or spiritual, outside its own territory. The mediaeval city was only a privileged town within a fief or kingdom, having charters, rights, and fortifications of its own; but, both in religious and in political rank, bound in absolute duty to far distant and much more exalted superiors. *The Meaning of History*

H30 — A city where one cannot walk of an evening into the open, wherein millions live and die without seeing the spring flowers and the June foliage and the autumn harvest, from year's end, is an incubus of civilisation. *Ibid.*

H31 — A city, worthy of such a name, should offer to all its citizens noble public buildings, and impressive monuments within the reach of all. *Ibid.*

H32 — A country covered with houses is not a city. *Ibid.*

H33 — The essential thing in a great city is the power and variety that arises from the association of a very large body of organised families living a common life and combining for great social ends. A quarter of a million or less gives that variety and that power. When the number is extended to a million or to two or four millions the result is monotony rather than variety and disorganisation rather than association. *Ibid.*

H34 — How vast is the interval between one kind of town-life and another kind — say comparing Bagdad with Chicago, or Naples with Staleybridge. The differences in the humblest forms of rural life are far less apparent, whether we deal with different epochs or different races. *Ibid.*

H35 — The idea of Patriotism, Art, Culture, Social Organisation, Religion — as identified with the city, springing out of it, stimulated by it — is an idea beyond the conception of modern men. *Ibid.*

H36 — It is needless to describe the modern city: we all know what it is, some of us too well. The first great fact about the Modern City is that it is in a far lower stage of organic life. It is almost entirely bereft of any religious, patriotic, or artistic character as a whole. *Ibid.*

H37 — It would be childish to expect that Acts of Parliament can limit the growth of cities. *Ibid.*

H38 — Let us imagine ourselves citizens of some famous city of Greece or Italy in the earlier ages before the Roman empire — such a city as Athens, Corinth, Syracuse, or Rome some centuries before Christ. Our city would be at once our Country, our Church, our Religion — our school, academy, and university, — our museum, our tradeguild, our play-ground, and our club. *Ibid.*

H39 — The life that men live in the city gives the type and measure of their civilisation. The word civilisation means the manner of life of the civilised part of the community: i.e. of the city-men, not of the country-men, who are called rustics, and once were called pagans, or the heathens of the villages. Hence, inasmuch as a city is a highly organised and concentrated type of the general life of an epoch or people, if we compare the various types of the city, we are able to measure the strength and weakness of different kinds of civilisation. *Ibid.*

H40 — A Modern City is an amorphous amoeba-like aggregate of buildings, wholly without defined limits, form, permanence, organisation, or beauty — often infinitely dreary, monstrous, grimy, noisy, and bewildering. *Ibid.*

H41 — The Modern City is ever changing, loose in its organisation, casual in its form. It grows up, or extends suddenly, no man knows how, in a single generation — in America in a single decade. *Ibid.*

H42 — There is but one city of the modern world — the French capital, where any attempt is made to develop the noble instrument of city life. *Ibid.*

H43 — To defile the precincts of the [ancient] city, and almost every open corner of it was consecrated to some deity or hero, was to outrage the powers of heaven or of earth; to cast refuse or sewage into a stream was to incur the wrath of some river-god; to pollute one of the city fountains was to offer sacrilege to some water-nymph. To bring disease into some public gathering was to insult the gods and demi-gods; to place the dead within the precincts of a temple, or to bury the dead within the city, or in contact with human habitations, to leave the dead or any human remains unburied or scattered about in public places and abandoned as carrion, would have seemed to a Greek or a Roman the last enormity of blasphemous horror. *Ibid.*

HARTE, Bret (1836?-1902)

H44 — Blackened and bleeding, helpless, panting, prone / On the charred fragments of her shattered throne / Lies she who stood but yesterday alone. / Like her own prairies by some chance seed sown, / Like her own prairies in one brief day grown, / Like her own prairies in one fierce night mown. / *Chicago, The Great Conflagration*

H45 — Queen of the West! by some enchanter taught / To lift the glory of Alladdin's court. / *Ibid.*

HASKELL, Harry G. (Mayor, Wilmington, Delaware) (1921-)

H46 — A city doesn't go bankrupt with a bang — it just shrivels up. I'm afraid it is going to be the same old story in America: Until the situation gets really bad, no one will look for a solution. *Austin Statesman, April 28, 1971*

HASKINS, Henry S.

H47 — At length the dead cities, Troy, Mycenae, Argos, Amphipolis, Corinth, Sparta, will do a *danse macabre* with New York, Berlin, London, Paris.

HASSAN, Ihab (1925-)

H48 — In its earliest representations, the city — Ur, Nineveh, Thebes, or that heaven-defying heap turned into verbal rubble, which we call Babel — symbolized the place where divine powers entered human space. The sky gods came, and where they touched the earth, kings and heroes

rose to overwhelm old village superstitions, and build a city. *Cities of Mind, Urban Words: The Dematerialization of Metropolis in Contemporary Fiction*

HATHERILL, (Commander) G.H.

H49 — There are only about twenty murders a year in London and not all are serious — some are just husbands killing their wives. *(Scotland Yard news report, July 1, 1954)*

HAUSER, Philip (1909-)

H50 — What the small town may have contributed in the past is one side of the coin; the other side is urbanism and the greatest opportunity in the history of man for him to reach his full potential. Where the small town kept him prisoner, urbanism gives him freedom of choice — choice of education, choice of profession, choice of marriage. If the small town is passing, we can't bemoan it. *Newsweek, July 8, 1963*

HAWTHORNE, Julian (1846-1934)

H51 — Not often in English history have more men and women worth knowing gathered in London than during the last quarter of the nineteenth century. *Shapes That Pass*

HAWTHORNE, Nathaniel (1804-1864)

H52 — The city of all time, and of all the world. [of Rome]

H53 — Whatever had been my taste for solitude and natural scenery, yet the thick, foggy, stifled elements of cities, the entangled life of so many men together, sordid as it was, and empty of the beautiful, took quite a strenuous hold upon my mind. I felt as if there could never be enough of it. *The Blithedale Romance*

HAYDEN, Joseph (fl. 1896)

H54 — There'll be a hot time in the old town tonight. *A Hot Time in the Old Town*

HAYDON, Benjamin Robert (1786-1846)

H55 — So far from the smoke of London being offensive to me, it has always been to my imagination the sublime canopy that shrouds the City of the World. *Autobiography*

HAYES, Helen (1900-)

H56 — The saddest thing in America today is the decline of the cities. The American city was, and I trust again will be, one of man's most exciting creations. There was nothing more exciting and wondrous than the American city when I was growing up. *U.S. News & World Report, September 13, 1976*

HAZLITT, William (1778-1830)

H57 — The only place in which the child grows completely up into the man. [of London]

HEAD, (Sir) Edmund (1805-1868)

H58 — On the whole, therefore, I believe that the least objectionable place is the city of Ottawa. Every city is jealous of every other city except Ottawa. *(Memorandum)*

HEBBEL, Friedrich (1813-1863)

H59 — Even now, and in spite of the great darkness which envelops my soul, I am well aware of what it means to live in this city. One feels not only carried, but actually lifted up by the resilient ground one treads. It is very strange indeed. [of Paris]

H60 — Everything in Prague excites the fantasy but reason doesn't come off second-best; it must be wonderful to be born in this city, with its mysteries and miracles.

HECHT, Ben (1893?-1964)

H61 — There is hardly one in three of us who live in the cities who is not sick with unused self.

H62 — Chicago the jazz baby — the reeking, cinder-ridden, joyous Baptist stronghold, Chicago the chewing gum center of the world, the bleating slant-headed rendez-vous of sociopaths and pants makers — in the name of the seven Holy Imperishable Arts, Chicago salutes you. *Chicago Literary Times*

H63 — The city is so and so. Everyone feels this and this. No matter who they are or where they live, or what their jobs are they can't escape the mark of the city that is on them. *A Thousand and One Afternoons in Chicago*

HECKSCHER, August

H64 — What makes men want to gather in cities, once technology has removed the necessity of their doing so, is partly such a simple, age-old thing as a liking for companionship and gossip. But it is also — and perhaps chiefly — a delight in the amenities which the city alone provides. These include the color and the variety of life on the street, the unexpectedness with which things are always happening — the chance encounter and the 'strange and fatal' interview. *in The Urban Industrial Frontier*

HEGEL, Georg Wilhelm (1770-1831)

H65 — Only the modern city offers the mind the grounds on which it can achieve awareness of itself.

HEINE, Heinrich (1797-1856)

H66 — If you send a philosopher to London and place him at a corner of Cheapside, he will learn more than from all the books at the recent Leipzig Trade Fair ... If London is the right hand of the world, the active, the powerful right hand, then one may consider the street which leads from the Exchange to

Downing Street as the artery of the world. . . . But do not send a poet to London! This stark solemnity in all things, this tremendous uniformity, this mechanical movement, this vexation of joy, this exaggerated, egregious London crushes the imagination and tears the heart asunder.

HELDT, Henning

H67 — Miami Beach presents the strange picture of a community approximately half Jewish and half Gentile. At the lower end of the resort, familiarly known as South Beach, Jews own virtually every lot, home, and business. Gradually, year by year, the growing Jewish population and ownership of tourist hotels expands northward.

Anti-Semitic talk is probably more common in and around Miami than anywhere else in the country. *Miami, Heaven or Honky-Tonk*

H68 — To the average 'snow bird' alighting from train or plane in Miami's brilliant sunshine a few hours after leaving sleet and slush and biting winds, the city may well seem like a page out of childhood fairy books. There's little risk of disillusionment, either, for the tourist who's whisked over to Miami Beach — a city built on sand and enduring despite the Biblical injunction, a city unique in its ratio of three or four hotel beds to every one in a home. *Ibid.*

HELLER, Joseph (1923-   )

H69 — 'It's a hell of a feeling being lost in a great city,' the man said slowly. 'And the world is full of great cities.' His voice was deep and solemn. He spoke slowly, staring straight ahead, and his words seemed to emanate from a trance. 'The human mind is a great city in which a guy is always lost. He spends his lifetime groping, trying to locate himself.' *World Full of Great Cities*

HELPER, Hinton R. (1829-1909)

H70 — I may not be a competent judge, but this much I will say. That I have seen purer liquors, better segars, finer tobacco, truer guns and pistols, larger dirks and bowie knives and prettier courtezans, here in San Francisco, than in any other place I have ever visited; and it is my unbiased opinion that California can and does furnish the best

bad things that are obtainable in America. *The Land of Gold*

HEMINGWAY, Ernest (1899-1961)

H71 — If you are lucky enough to have lived in Paris as a young man, then wherever you go for the rest of your life, it stays with you, for Paris is a moveable feast.

HENRY IV (of France) (1553-1610)

H72 — Paris vaut bien une messe. [Paris is well worth a mass.]

HENRY, O. (1862-1910)

H73 — Little old Noisyville-on-the-Subway. [of New York City]

H74 — A town that's shut off from the world by the ocean on one side and New Jersey on the other. [of New York City]

H75 — The big city is like a mother's knee to many who have strayed far and found the roads rough beneath their uncertain feet. At dusk they come home and sit upon the door-step. *Options: Supply and Demand*

H76 — In the Big City a man will disappear with the suddenness and completeness of a candle that is blown out. *Sixes and Sevens*

H77 — Far below and around lay the city like a ragged purple dream . . . the wonderful, cruel, enchanting, bewildering, fatal, great city. [of New York City] *Strictly Business*

H78 — Take of London fog 30 parts; malaria 10 parts; gas leaks 20 parts; dewdrops gathered in a brick-yard at sunrise 25 parts; odor of honeysuckle 15 parts. Mix. The mixture will give you an approximate conception of a Nashville drizzle. *Ibid.*

H79 — If there ever was an aviary overstocked with jays it is that Yaptown-on-the-Hudson, called New York . . . . 'Little old New York's good enough for us' — that's what they sing. *A Tempered Wind*

H80 — In dress, habits, manners, provincialism, routine and narrowness, he acquired that charming insolence, that irritating completeness, that sophisticated crassness, that overbalanced poise that makes the Manhattan gentleman so delightfully small in his greatness. *The Voice of the City*

H81 — In the Big City large and sudden things happen. You round a corner and thrust the rib of your umbrella into the eye of your old friend from Kootenai Falls. You stroll out to pluck a Sweet William in the park — and lo! bandits attack you — you are ambulanced to the hospital — you marry your nurse; are divorced — get squeezed while short on U.P.S. and D.O.W.N.S. — stand in the bread line — marry an heiress, take out your laundry and pay your club dues — seemingly all in the wink of an eye. *Ibid.*

HERACLITUS (fl. 500 B.C.)

H82 — The people must fight to save its laws, as it fights to protect the walls of the city. *Fragment*

HERBERT, (Sir) Alan Patrick (1890-1971)

H83 — When laughing Ann trips down the street/ The sun comes out as well,/ The town is at her twinkling feet,/ The crier rings his bell,/ The young men leap like little fish,/ Policemen stand and purr,/ While husbands look behind and wish/ That they had married her./ *Laughing Ann*

HERBERT, George (1593-1633)

H84 — The chicken is the country's, but the city eats it. *Jacula Prudentum*

H85 — Cities are taken by the ears. *Works*

HERBERT, RAY

H86 — Put-downs, jokes and slaps at cities flourished during vaudeville's heyday when touring comics played New York and Chicago, and rattled off wisecracks about the hayseeds in Hoboken, Keokuk and Podunk. *The Los Angeles Times, December 14, 1981*

HERFORD, Oliver (1863-1935)

H87 — In the midst of life we are in Brooklyn.

HERODOTUS (5th c. B.C.)

H88 — I will tell the story as I go along of small cities no less than of great. Most of those which were great once are small today; and those which in my own lifetime have grown to greatness, were small enough in the old days.

H89 — In addition to its size it surpasses in splendour any city in the known world. [of Babylon]

HEROLD, DON

H90 — Funerals are a lost art in the big cities.

H91 — There is more sophistication and less sense in New York than anywhere else on the globe.

H92 — There is nothing distinctive about living in New York; over eight million other people are doing it.

HERRICK, Robert (1591-1674)

H93 — Great cities seldom rest: if there be none T'invade from far, they'll find worse foes at home. *Hesperides*

HERRICK, Robert (1868-1938)

H94 — The City was man! And already it was sowing its seed in the heart of youth, this night. It was moulding him as it moulds the millions, after its fashion, warming his blood with desire, — the vast, resounding, gleaming City. *A Life for a Life*

HERSHFIELD, Harry (1885-1974)

H95 — A city where everyone mutinies but no one deserts [of New York]

HESIOD (c. 720 B.C.)

H96 — Oft hath even a whole city reaped the evil fruit of a bad man. *Works and Days*

HEYWOOD, John (1497?-1580)

H97 — Foolish (Peevish) pity mars a city. *Spider & Flie*

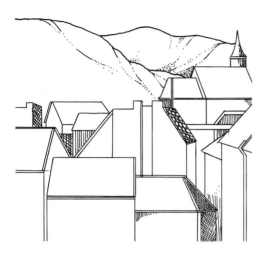

HEYWOOD, Thomas (1574?-1641)

H98 — Seven cities warred for Homer, being dead, Who, living, had no roof to shroud his head. *The Hierarchy of the Blessed Angels*

HICKEL, Walter J. (Secretary of the Interior) (1919-)

H99 — A man can live in a slum out in the open spaces and be happier than a man of means who lives in the city and can't get that 'spiritual renewal.' We've just made life miserable for ourselves in these urban areas. *The Los Angeles Times, March 13, 1970*

HIGBEE, Edward (1910-)

H100 — Most farmers on the urban fringe, even if they had not wanted to sell their land to an advancing suburbia, are eventually persuaded by a series of events to change their minds. Slowly they are overwhelmed by an endless rise of taxes to help defray the mounting costs of new schools and roads, as well as the wages of the inevitable bureaucracy that comes with urbanization. *The Squeeze*

HIGHET, Gilbert (1906-1978)

H101 — At first little more than the power of the sword carried Rome forward; but as it grew, it acquired the power of thought, the power of the law, and the power of religious

and poetic vision. These are the spiritual powers which it bequeathed to its heirs, the modern nations of the western world. *Sword & Spirit*

H102 — Rome. It has a resonance like a deep bronze bell. It clangs like a heavy shield struck by a heavy sword. It is the keynote of a noble theme in which other names are overtones: Caesar, triumph, legion, forum, senate, emperor, pope. The majestic word has rung through twenty-seven centuries. It is one of the greatest utterances of mankind: it is heard all round the world and will not soon be silenced. *Ibid.*

HILL, A.V.

H103 — It might be said that the word metropolis has outgrown the maternal metaphor and today merely refers to an urban region of more than a certain size. Detroit, for example, has nearly two million people. Is it therefore a metropolis? A mother city of what — automobiles? Or should the biological metaphor now be dropped? If metropolis is used merely as a measure of size, however, is not the English language being robbed of a pleasant word for an important idea? *The Effects of Scientific Progress on Metropolitan Communities*

HILL, Matthew Davenport (1792-1872)

H104 — In small towns there must be a sort of natural police, of a very wholesome kind, operating upon the conduct of each individual, who lives, as it were, under the public eye; but in a large town he lives, if he choose, in absolute obscurity, and we know that large towns are sought by way of refuge because of that obscurity, which to a certain extent gives impunity. *Report of the Select Committee on Criminal and Destitute Juveniles, 1852*

HILLARD, George S. (1808-1879)

H105 — To the gentle-hearted youth who is thrown upon the rocks of a pitiless city, and stands 'homeless amid a thousand homes,' the approach of evening brings with it an aching sense of loneliness and desolation, which comes down upon the spirit like darkness upon the earth. In this cause he is social, affectionate, sympathetic, and warm-hearted. *(Address to the Mercantile Library Association, 1850)*

HILLS, Carla A. (Secretary of Housing and Urban Development) (1934-   )

H106 — It is far less costly to recycle a city than to build a suburb. *(At Washington Press Club, October 18, 1975)*

HIMMELWRIGHT, A.L.A. (1865-c.1960)

H107 — The tower-like structures that have sprung up as if by magic within the past few years in the business portions of nearly all our large cities are indeed wonderful creations. These buildings are remarkable not only because they are unique in proportions and exemplify novel methods of construction, but also on account of their vast commercial importance.... When it is remembered that many of these buildings occupy areas less than one hundred feet square, the enormous value of building lots in the best business centres can be appreciated. *North American Review*

HINES, Gerald D. (1925-   )

H108 — The vehicle to improve the American city is the American corporation — that's where the money is. *The New York Times Magazine, November 11, 1976*

HINKSON, Katherine Tynan (1861-1931)

H109 — O you poor folk in cities, / A thousand, thousand pities! / Heaping the fairy gold that withers and dies; / One field in the June weather / Is worth all the gold ye gather, / One field in June weather — one Paradise. / *June Song*

HIRST, W.A. (1870-?)

H110 — In Buenos Aires There is a great wealth and the love of display is also great, and doubtless, like Paris, it exercises a dangerous fascination on the people at large, who are apt to think that there is no profit or pleasure anywhere except at Buenos Aires. It occupies in Argentina a more important position than does Paris in France, and probably the development of Rosario and Bahia Blanca will have a good effect in modifying its pretensions. It is a very magnificent city. *Argentina*

HITLER, Adolf (1889-1945)

H111 — Berlin is a big city, but not a real metropolis. Look at Paris, the most beautiful city in the world. Or even Vienna. Those are cities with grand style. Berlin is nothing but an unregulated accumulation of buildings. We must surpass Paris and Vienna.

H112 — The entire Ringstrasse affected me like a fairy tale out of the Arabian Nights. [of Vienna]

H113 — To create in Berlin a truly representative capital must be considered one of the foremost tasks of the Third Reich. To begin with, the railroad terminal and the approaches to the main highways should be so that even the Viennese would be overwhelmed by the thought: This is our capital. At the moment one cannot blame a Viennese, visiting Berlin, if he is disappointed in comparing it with the grandiose view his own city offers.

HOBBES, Thomas (1588-1679)

H114 — London has a great belly but no palate. *History of the Civil War*

HOBSON, John A. (1858-1940)

H115 — The biggest, and in some respects the most characteristic of machine-products is the modern industrial town. *The Evolution of Modern Capitalism. A Study of Machine Production*

H116 — If it is true that as the larger village grows into the town, and the town into the ever larger city, there is a progressive weakening of the bonds of moral cohesion between individuals, that the larger the town the feebler the spiritual unity, we are face to face with the heaviest indictment that can be brought against modern industrial progress, and the forces driving an increased proportion of our population into towns are bringing about a decadence of *morale* which is the necessary counterpart of the deterioration of national physique. *Ibid.*

H117 — The industrial town, left for its growth to individual industrial control, compresses into unhealthily close proximity large numbers ... with different and often antagonistic aims, with little knowledge of one another, with no important common end to form a bond of social sympathy. *Ibid.*

H118 — It is ... unlikely that any wide or lasting solution of the problem of congested town life will be found in a sharp local severance of the life of an industrial society which shall abandon the town to the purpose of a huge workshop, reserving the country for habitation.... It is only in the case of the largest, and densest industrial cities, swollen to an unwieldly and dangerous size, that such methods of decentralization can in some measure be applied. *Ibid.*

H119 — Perhaps the most potent influence in breaking the strength of the *morale* of the town worker is the precarious and disorderly character of town work.... Town work ... is more irregular than country work, and this irregularity has a most pernicious effect upon the character of the worker. *Ibid.*

HOCKING, William Ernest (1873-1966)

H120 — In the city you have neither heaven nor hell. You merely have smog overhead and pavement beneath your feet. *Wisdom for Our Time*

HOFFMAN, Abbie (1936-   )

H121 — It is in the streets that we will make our struggle. The streets belong to the people! Long live the flower-cong of the gutters! *Revolution for the Hell of It*

HOFSTADTER, Richard (1916-1970)

H122 — The U.S. was born in the country and has moved to the city.

HOLE, Dean

H123 — Limerick was, Dublin is, and Cork shall be / The finest city of the three. / *Literary Tour in Ireland*

HOLMAN, Joan

H124 — Cleveland — Two Hobokens back to back.

HOLMES, Nathanial (1815-1901)

H125 — It is not impossible that our City of St. Louis may be 'the future great city of the world,' but if we are to come to practical facts for our day and generation, and take the safe and sure way, I think we may be content to set it down as both the present and future great city of the Mississippi Valley. *in Saint Louis: Future Great City of the World*

HOLMES, Oliver Wendell (1809-1894)

H126 — Chicago sounds rough .... One comfort we have — Cincinnati sounds worse. *(at the Chicago Commercial Club, 1880)*

H127 — The heart of the world [of Boston]

H128 — The thinking center of the continent and therefore of the planet. [of Boston]

H129 — The axis of the earth sticks out visibly through the centre of each and every town or city. *The Autocrat of the Breakfast Table*

HOMER (c. 700 B.C.)

H130 — There will be a day when sacred Ilium shall be no more. [of Troy] *Iliad*

H131 — Far from gay cities, and the ways of men. *Odyssey*

H132 — He saw the cities of many people and learnt their ways. *Ibid.*

HOPE, Bob (1903-   )

H133 — You're going to have a great town here if you ever get it finished. [comment on Toronto, August 21, 1969]

HOPKINS, Gerard Manley (1844-1889)

H134 — Towery city and branchy between towers. *Duns Scotus' Oxford*

HOOD, Thomas (1799-1845)

H135 — Alas, for the rarity / Of Christian charity / Under the sun! / Oh, it was pitiful! / Near a whole city full, / Home had she none! / *The Bridge of Sighs*

HORACE (65-8 B.C.)

H136 — The chorus of writers, one and entire, / Detests the town and yearns for the sacred grove . . . *Epistles*

H137 — Every man cannot go to Corinth. *Ibid.*

H138 — I say that living in the country makes a man happy. You say the city. Small wonder, that one discontent with his own lot prefers another's. Each is absurd to pretend the place is at fault: it's innocent. The mind is to blame. It has to live with itself. Wherever it is. *Ibid.*

H139 — At Rome, you long for the country; when you are in the country, fickle, you extol the absent city to the skies. *Satires*

H140 — That bit of hell known as big city life . . . *Ibid.*

H141 — Smoke, wealth, and noise. [of Rome]

HORWITZ, Julius (1920-)

H142 — The soot is the ugliest sight in New York. The sky looks snatched from the viewer. As though your eyes have been ripped out of your head . . . . You wait for the soot to get swallowed up into the sky. For the sky to be clean. *The Inhabitants*

HOUSER, Philip (Director, Population Research Center, University of Chicago)

H143 — The major problem of the cities in 1972 is the complete inability of the cities to deal with their problems. Complete inability, because there isn't a city in the United States that has the sources of revenue to deal with its problems. The reason is that we in the United States are still dealing with the 18th century form of governments we inherited from England; England has long since got rid of it. *San Francisco Examiner & Chronicle, January 1-2, 1972*

HOUSMAN, Alfred Edward (1859-1936)

H144 — Oh, the pearl seas are yonder, / The gold and amber shore; / Shires where the girls are fonder, / Towns where the pots hold more. / *More Poems*

H145 — Today, the roads all runners come, / Shoulder-high, we bring you home, / And set you at your threshold down, / Townsman of a stiller town. / *To an Athlete Dying Young*

HOVEY, Richard (1864-1900)

H146 — Whose furthest footstep never strayed / Beyond the village of his birth / Is but a lodger for the night / In this old wayside inn of earth. / *More Songs from Vagabondia*

HOWAR, Barbara (1934-)

H147 — Those complicated people that make Washington the mysterious jungle it is, those famous men and women who to the rest of the world are glamorous and powerful; even ruthless, public figures, have in them a specialness that is inconsistent with the city's official image — a combination of worldly involvement and personal commitment that makes Washington genuine despite its reach for power. *Laughing All the Way*

HOWARD, Ebenezer (1850-1928)

H148 — The end I venture to now set before the people of [England] and of other countries is no less 'noble and adequate' than this, that they should forthwith gird themselves to the task of building up clusters of beautiful home-towns, each zoned by gardens, for those who now dwell in crowded, slum-infested cities. *The Garden Cities of Tomorrow*

H149 — A Garden City is a Town designed for healthy living and industry; of a size that makes possible a full measure of social life, but not larger; surrounded by a rural belt; the whole of the land being in public ownership or held in trust for the community. *Ibid.*

HOWARD, James J. (U.S. Congressman) (1927-)

H150 — The SST ... will provide for the jetsetters to get from New York to a cocktail party in London in less time than many commuters can get from Asbury Park to New York City to work. *(November 29, 1970)*

HOWARD, John T. (1911-)

H151 — It is appropriate to pause and consider the relationship between the automobile and the suburban low-density trend. It is popular to blame the automobile for suburbia — for the miles of sprawling, low-density, single-family tracts. This is like blaming the printing press for comic books — or for *The New York Times*. The automobile did not *cause* the suburban explosion; it merely *permitted* it. *The Crisis of the Cities*

HOWE, Edgar Watson (1853-1937)

H152 — Farmers worry only during the growing season, but town people worry all the year round. *Country Town Sayings*

HOWE, Frederic C. (1867-1940)

H153 — Our cities are what they are because we have not thought of the city as a city, of the town as a town, of the rights of everybody as opposed to the rights of anybody. A million men are thinking only of their individual lot lines, of their inviolable right to do as they will with their own, irrespective of its effect on the community. *The City as a Socializing Agency*

HOWE, Irving (1920-)

H154 — Almost every *idea* about the city

tempts us to forget what the young Dickens never forgot: the city is a place of virtuosity, where men can perform with freedom and abandonment. *The City in Literature*

H155 — The city enables the birth of new genres: who could imagine surrealism without Paris? *Ibid.*

H156 — For the novelist ... the city's proliferation of casual and secondary relationships offers new possibilities: the drama of the group and the comedy of the impersonal. The experiences of Ulysses for which Homer had to arrange complicated journeys, Joyce can pack into a day's wandering through a single city. *Ibid.*

H157 — If the city is indeed pesthole and madhouse, it is also the greatest show on earth, continuous performances and endlessly changing cast. *Ibid.*

H158 — The modern city first appears full-face — as physical concreteness, emblem of excitement, social specter, and locus of myth — in Dickens and Gogol. *Ibid.*

H159 — Our modern disgust with the city is foreshadowed in the 18th Century novelists. *Ibid.*

H160 — The suspicion of the city and all it represents seems to run so deeply in our culture that it would be impossible to eradicate it, even if anyone were naive enough to wish to. *Ibid.*

H161 — We may destroy our civilization, but we cannot escape it. We may savor a soured remorse at the growth of civilization, but that will yield us no large or lasting reward. There is no turning back: our only way is a radical struggle for the City of the Just. *Ibid.*

H162 — Western culture bears ... a deeply-grounded tradition that sees the city as both inimical and threatening. *Ibid.*

HOWE, Mark Anthony De Wolfe (1864-1960)

H163 — The village sleeps, a name unknown, till men / With life-blood stain its soil, and pay the due / That lifts it to eternal fame, — for then / 'Tis grown a Gettysburg or Waterloo. / *Distinction*

HOWELL, James (1594?-1666)

H164 — Dunmow bacon, and Doncaster daggers, Monmouth caps and Lemster wool, Derby ale and London beer. *English proverbs*

H165 — Paris, that huge (though durty) Theater of all Nations. *Instructions for Forreine Travel*

H166 — There are in Genoa mountains without wood, sea without fish, women without shame, and men without conscience. *Ibid.*

HOWELLS, William Dean (1837-1920)

H167 — The Bostonian who leaves Boston ought to be condemned to perpetual exile. *The Rise of Silas Lapham*

H168 — In the winter, the whole city sniffs, and if the Pipchin theory of the effect of sniffing upon the eternal interests of the soul be true, few people go to heaven from Venice. I sometimes wildly wondered if Desdemona, in her time, sniffed, and found little comfort in the reflection that Shylock must have had a cold in his head. There is comparative warmth in the broad squares before the churches, but the narrow streets are bitter thorough-draughts, and fell influenza lies in wait for its prey in all those picturesque, seducing little courts . . . *Venetian Life*

HUBBARD, Elbert (1856-1915)

H169 — Any part of the earth where ignorance and stupidity integrate, agglomerate and breed. [of the city]

H170 — Any place where men have built a jail, a bagnio, a gallows, a morgue, a church, a hospital, a saloon, and laid out a cemetery — hence a center of life. [of the city]

H171 — A herding region. [of the city]

H172 — There isn't much to be seen in a little town, but what you hear makes up for it.

H173 — The posthumous revenge of the Merchant of Venice. [of New York] *Roycroft Dictionary and Book of Epigrams*

HUBBARD, Frank McKinney (1868-1930)

H174 — Farmer Jake Bentley talks some o'movin' to the city so he kin keep a son. *Abe Martin's Broadcast*

HUDNUT, Joseph (1886-1968)

H175 — Architecture did not impose itself upon the practical activities of a city, was not an intruder into social or economic life, was not inconsistent with politics, war or individual ambition, but marched with all of these holding before all the shining symbols which revealed the direction and unity of the general life. *Architecture and the Spirit of Man*

H176 — Beneath the visible city laid out in patterns of streets and houses there lies an invisible city laid out in patterns of idea and behavior which channels the citizen with silent persistent pressures and, beneath the confusion, noise, and struggle of the material and visible city, makes itself known and reconciles us to all of these. *Ibid.*

H177 — The cathedral, once generator and guardian of cities, had cherished and consoled all who lived at its side. The palace, also a generator of cities, ennobled the citizens with an ordinance and art of living; the distant trading posts bound together with common enterprise and shared destiny those who gathered around them and even the fortress inspired in those who must live beneath its walls a loyalty from which they drew a communal strength. *Ibid.*

H178 — Civilized, polite, and urbane — each word rooted in a word that means the city. *Ibid.*

H179 — The factory came into the city not as architecture but as machine. Unlike the temple and the theater, the house and the market place, the factory was built, not out of love and the commerce of society but out of calculation and economic necessities. *Ibid.*

H180 — The literature of the world is filled with a poet's conspiracy against the city: with advertisements of the city's clamors and indecencies, with the illusion of the country's solace. Only God, we are reminded, can make a tree. As if He had no part in the making of poems and cities! *Ibid.*

H181 — Mound above mound, a thousand Troys laid on Troy, these lift us above the arid plain of biological and economic existence. *Ibid.*

H182 — Our poets are too ready to give the city to the devil. The city, I think, was the tool with which God made man. Perhaps it is the tool with which He is making man. *Ibid.*

H183 — Perhaps because I was born and brought up in the country I have always wanted to live near the heart of a great city. Even now I look forward to the day when I can live in a little flat, say, at the corner of Broadway and Forty-second Street. I should like to be clothed again in the strength and space of that city; to feel about me the encompassment and drift of its opinion. I am not alone in New York even when I am alone. The city furnishes and fortifies my mind. *Ibid.*

H184 — We are held in the city neither by pleasure nor by economic necessity but by a hunger which transcends both practical and sensuous experience, a hunger seldom revealed by appearances, seldom acknowledged in our consciousness. We are held in the city by our need of a collective life; by our need of belonging and sharing; by our need of that direction and frame which our individual lives gain from a larger life lived together. *Ibid.*

H185 — We did not guess when we admitted the factory to our cities that it would destroy their patterns; destroy them utterly and with that destruction provoke the questionings and discontents which color our present judgments of cities. *Ibid.*

HUDSON, William Henry (1841-1922)

H186 — The delight I experienced in my communings with Nature did not pass away, leaving nothing but a recollection of vanished happiness to intensify a present pain. The happiness was never lost, . . . so that in my worst times, when I was compelled to exist shut out from Nature in

London for long periods, sick and poor and friendless, I could yet always feel that it was infinitely better to be than not to be. *Far Away and Long Ago*

HUGHES, Langston (1902-1967)

H187 — Melting pot Harlem — Harlem of honey and chocolate and caramel and rum and vinegar and lemon and lime and gall. Dusky dream Harlem rumbling into a nightmare tunnel where the subway from the Bronx keeps right on downtown. *Freedomways*

H188 — Across / The Harlem roof-tops / Moon is shining / Night sky is blue / Stars are great drops / Of golden dew. / *Harlem Night Song*

H189 — I went to San Francisco. / I saw the bridges high / Spun across the water / Like cobwebs in the sky. / *The Langston Hughes Reader*

H190 — In the morning the city / Spreads its wings / Making a song / Of stone that sings. / In the evening the city / Goes to bed / Hanging lights / About its head. / *Ibid.*

H191 — O, sweep of stars over Harlem streets, / O, little breath of oblivion that is night, / A city building / A city dreaming / To a lullaby. / *Stars*

HUGO, Victor (1802-1885)

H192 — Cities are bibles of stone. This city possesses no single dome, roof or pavement which does not convey some message of alliance and of union, and which does not offer some lesson, example or advice. Let the people of all the world come to this prodigious alphabet of monuments, of tombs and of trophies to learn peace and to unlearn the meaning of hatred. Let them be confident. For Paris has proven itself. To have once been Lutece and to have become Paris — what could be a more magnificent symbol! To have been mud and to have become spirit!

H193 — Paris is nothing but an immense hospitality.

H194 — Paris is the ceiling of the human race.

H195 — You must love her, desire her, submit to her, frivolous though she is, frivolous, fickle, singing, dancing, painted, florid, deadly. [of Paris]

H196 — Cities produce ferocious men, because they produce corrupt men; the mountains, the forest, and the sea, render men savage; they develop the fierce, but yet do not destroy the human. *Les Misérables*

HUMBOLDT, W.H.

H197 — Just as Homer is unique among poets, so stands Rome among other cities, and Rome's empire among all others in the world.

HUMPHREY, Hubert H. (Senator) (1911-1978)

H198 — I long for the day when we look upon even a great metropolis as but a center, and around it like spokes on [a] wheel, going on out, are autonomous villages and communities that are viable, that can live by themselves. *(Before New Jersey Mayors, Princeton, May 17, 1972)*

H199 — I suggest we quit talking about the urban crisis and put it as the American crisis, because America is essentially urbanized. *(At U.S. Conference of Mayors, New Orleans, June 20, 1972)*

H200 — There are no answers to the problems of urban America if there are not answers to the problems of rural America — none. *(Before Oklahoma Legislature, Oklahoma City, March 23, 1972)*

H201 — No person can occupy the power of the Presidency of the United States without being knowledgeable about, and dedicated to, the well-being of the American cities. That's where we start. To govern America, you have to know how to govern a city; and to have cities that are ungovernable, is to have an America that is ungovernable. *The Dallas Times Herald, April 2, 1976*

H202 — President Ford is attempting to punish New York. What New York needs is a friendly doctor with a prescription, not a mortician that tells New York that it ought to die and then hope for a resurrection. *TV-radio interview, Washington, October 2, 1975*

H203 — The day before yesterday I flew out of New York City. There was a beautiful sunset, a lovely evening. It was about 4:30 or 5 o'clock, I should say. As our plane lifted off that airport, you could literally see waves of smoke and dirt over that great city. It was as if we were ashamed of the city and wanted to cover it up. This is not true only of New York; it is true of almost every great city in the United States. *Quoted in The Troubled Environment*

H204 — We are coming to understand more fully the most pressing problem facing us in our cities, and it is this: To eradicate the explosive combination of poor housing, poor schools, inadequate public services, high rates of unemployment and crime, prejudice and discrimination which comprise the slums of urban America. *Ibid.*

HUNEKER, James G. (1860-1921)

H205 — I know of no city where you formulate an expression of like or dislike so quickly as in Rome. You are its friend or foe within five minutes after you leave its dingy railway station. *Steeplejack*

H206 — The man who first called Brussels le petit Paris must have been imbibing many bottles of the fiery Burgundy for which the city is renowned. *New Cosmopolis*

H207 — Vienna, the magnificent! I fear the approach of the dithyrambic. Vienna is truly the city of magnificent distances; not even Washington deserves the title as much. Every vista has its picture, either a church, a monument, a palace, or a park. You range and range and seemingly never exhaust the possibilities of the city. *Ibid.*

H208 — With the possible exception of London, there is no place like New York for versatility in eating and drinking. Nearly all cuisines are represented. You can eat kosher or munch birds' nests in the Chinese style; while French, Russian, German, Dutch, Italian, Spanish, Hungarian, Polish, Austrian, Turkish, Syrian, Rumanian, Greek, Portuguese, Cuban, Mexican, Liberian — why drag out the list? — are to be found; everything from everywhere may be had in our city — everything but fried oysters as they cook them in Philadelphia. *Ibid.*

HUNGERFORD, Edward (1875-1948)

H209 — Dinner is New York's real function of the day. *The Personality of American Cities*

HUNTER, Robert (1874-1942)

H210 — The degeneration of the two-story frame and brick houses from the home of one family into a tenement for several families is a commonplace in the housing histories of all large cities . . . . The next step in the evolution is the tenement-house built for several families, and this varies in size from a two-story house covering fifty per cent of the lot to a four or five story tenement covering . . . a large percentage of the ground area. This is very much the same history as that of London, New York, and Boston. Their problems are, and will be, very likely, our problems. *Tenement Conditions in Chicago*

HUSTON, John

H211 — Dublin has a legacy from its past of subjugation and persecution, a brooding wistfulness which seems to linger still in the grey-faced buildings and in the procession

of bridges across its river. *Quoted in Cities, John McGreevy*

H212 — It is something of a habit with Dubliners to make a joke of poverty and misfortune. It is a way of showing their familiarity with both. Whatever his original racial origins, which could be Gaelic or Norman, Danish or English or Norse, the average Dubliner views life with a mixture of wry humour and a sort of serene fatalism. Perhaps it is due to the history of his native city — a long history of siege, pestilence, invasion, rebellion, slaughter, persecution, and civil war. Whatever the cause, he tends to believe that the worst is inevitable and must be endured. *Ibid.*

HUXLEY, Aldous (1894-1963)

H213 — No man could find a better spot on earth, if only he had some intelligent person to talk to. [of Los Angeles] *(in conversation)*

H214 — A large city cannot be experientially known; its life is too manifold for any individual to be able to participate in it. *Beyond the Mexique Bay*

HUXTABLE, Ada Louise (1921-)

H215 — A city, in its most real sense, is its buildings. Whatever the life, spirit, activity or achievements of the city may be, they are expressed in the mass of asphalt, brick, stone, marble, steel and glass that has accumulated during the city's existence. The structures that its inhabitants have erected for their use and pride — even the buildings that have come and gone — and the way in which those buildings are disposed upon the streets and squares are the source of its personality, its style, and its distinguishing stamp. *Classic New York*

H216 — Architects and city fathers would be surprised at the amount of public concern over a city's skyline. *Kicked a Building Lately?*

H217 — Suburban Christmas is a cheap plastic Santa Claus in a shopping center parking lot surrounded by asphalt and a sea of cars. Suburban spring is not a walk in the awakening woods, but mud in poorly built roads. Suburban life is no voyage of discovery or private exploration of the world's wonders, natural and man-made; it is cliche conformity as far as the eye can see, with no stimulation through quality of environment. *The New York Times Magazine, February 9, 1964*

H218 — City life and city problems have come to Antarctica. In some kind of record for nest-fouling, urban sprawl has turned McMurdo Station into an urban horror in a brief ten years. This may be a standing backjump record for ruining the environment. *Will They Ever Finish Bruckner Boulevard*

H219 — Every year sees megalopolis, the urban smear that is staining the entire American northeast and blurring city boundaries everywhere, relentlessly on its way to ecumenopolis, or a totally urbanized world . . . Ecumenopolis may take a little while, but we'll get there. We are getting to the moon first, of course, although only one thing is sure about that and none of the scientific prognostications mention it. When we get there, we'll make a mess of it. *Ibid.*

H220 — New York, the Death-Wish City. *Ibid.*

H221 — When it is good, New York is very, very good. Which is why New Yorkers put up with so much that is bad. *Ibid.*

HUYSMANS, J.K. (1848-1907)

H222 — A sinister Chicago. [of Paris] *A Rebours*

I

IBSEN, Henrik (1828-1906)

I1 — A community is like a ship; everyone ought to be prepared to take the helm.

I2 — To think that I should live cooped up in a great city, just to be pestered and plagued by people! *Peer Gynt*

IKRAM, S. Muhammad

I3 — In its origin and development, Islam was something of an urban phenomenon. Mecca, the birthplace of Islam, was the principal city of the Arabian peninsula ... Islam encouraged congregational prayer .. The Friday prayer had to be offered in a mosque, which was not normally found in villages. So the faithful were obliged to journey to the nearest town. This was even more the rule for the Ir'd prayers, offered on the occasion of principal Moslem celebrations. *The Metropolis and Modern Life*, E.M. Fisher, Ed.

IMBODEN, Max

I4 — Although Zurich exceeds the normal dimensions of a Swiss town by all standards, it has preserved ... the characteristic political and constitutional make-up of a Swiss commune: namely far reaching autonomy and a pronounced democratization of public life. *Zurich*

I5 — The structure of the city of Zurich demonstrates, as do most political and constitutional bodies in Switzerland, the tendency to strike a balance between the opposites, to unite divergent wishes in a middle solution. A way has been sought to reconcile the direct communal democracy handed down from the past with the exigencies of a modern city. It is clear that this attempt has in general been successful, when one sees how energetically Zurich has solved the problems presented to it. *Ibid.*

INGE, William Ralph (1860-1954)

I6 — It wasn't until I got to New York that I became Kansan. Everyone there kept reminding me that they were Jewish or Irish, or whatever, so I kept reminding them that I was midwestern. Before I knew it, I actually began to *brag* about being from Kansas! I discovered that I had something a bit unique, but it was the nature of New York that forced me to claim my past. *Behind the Scenes*

I7 — The modern town-dweller has no God and no Devil; he lives without awe, without admiration, without fear. *Outspoken Essays*

I8 — The nations which have put mankind and posterity most in their debt have been small states — Israel, Athens, Florence, Elizabethan England. *Wit and Wisdom of Dean Inge*

INGRAHAM, J.H. (1809-1860)

I9 — Adam and Eve were created and placed in a garden. Cities are the results of the fall.

INNOCENT II, (Pope) (?-1143)

I10 — The capital of the world [of Rome]

IRVING, Washington (1783-1859)

I11 — The renowned and ancient city of Gotham. [of New York]

I12 — Your true dull minds are generally preferred for public employ, and especially prompted to city honors; your keen intellects, like razors, being considered too sharp for common service. *Quoted in Knickerbocker's History of New York*

I13 — Those who see the Englishman only in town are apt to form an unfavorable opinion of his social character.... An immense metropolis, like London, is calculated to make men selfish and uninteresting. In their casual and transient meetings, they can but deal briefly in commonplaces. They present but the cold superficies of character — its rich and genial qualities have no time to be warmed into a flow. *The Sketch Book*

IRWIN, Will

I14 — The gayest, lightest-hearted, most pleasure-loving city in the Western continent. [of San Francisco]

IVO, (Saint)

I15 — I approve the life of those men for whom a city is but a prison, who find their paradise in solitude, who live there by the labor of their hands, or who seek to renew their souls by the sweetness of a life of contemplation — men who drink with the lips of their heart at the fountain of life.

J

JACKSON, Holbrook (1874-1948)

J1 — London is strangely elusive to the tourist. Indeed, I know of no place, save Paris, which eludes those who come to see her so effectively as London. *Southward Ho! and Other Essays*

JACKSON, (Rev.) Jesse L. (1941-   )

J2 — We blacks have populated the cities; we must now learn to run them. The need is urgent. The ethical collapse, the heroin epidemic, the large numbers of our people who are out of work and on welfare, and the disruptive violence in the schools all indicate that the cities may be destroying us. *Quoted in The San Francisco Examiner & Chronicle, June 27, 1976*

JACKSON, Kenneth T. (1939-   )

J3 — By almost any standard, Newark is America's sickest city. *The Effects of Suburbanization on the Cities*

J4 — Cities, by their very nature, ought to encourage the elevation of the human spirit. Anyone who has ever visited the Piazza San Marco in Venice, or shared the happy conviviality of Tivoli Gardens in Copenhagen, or marveled at the temptations of the Reeperbahn in Hamburg, or strolled at midnight along the Ramblas in Barcelona, or gone Sunday bicycling in Central Park in New York knows something of the potentialities and varieties of urban experience. *Ibid.*

J5 — It is one of the ironies of the twentieth century that in an age of cities, American cities are decaying. While real trolleys in Newark, Philadelphia, Pittsburgh, and Boston languish for lack of patronage and government support, millions of people flock to Disneylands and Six Flags to ride fake trains that don't go anywhere. Our environment is becoming bland and plastic; our world is full of McDonald's and Holiday Inns, each one looking exactly like the one before. Suburbs themselves, although parklike and pleasant, usually have as much distinctiveness and character as a shopping center. With a few exceptions, if you have seen one, you have seen them all. *Ibid.*

J6 — Professional sports nomenclature also offers a clue to the changing 'sense of community' in metropolitan America. The designation of a place or a team by a name — a specific name under which fans or residents can unite — is one piece of evidence that a community exists. Until about 1960, athletic teams were almost always known by the names of the central cities they represented: the New York Yankees, the Chicago White Sox, the Boston Celtics, the San Francisco Giants, the Cleveland Indians. In recent years, however, there has been a trend away from naming teams for cities, as if an association with the core city would limit box office appeal. Thus we have the Minnesota Twins, the California Angels, the Texas Rangers, the Golden State Warriors, the Indiana Pacers, the Kentucky Colonels, even the New England Patriots. *Ibid.*

JACOBS, Jane (1916-   )

J7 — The bureaucratized, simplified cities, so dear to present-day city planners and urban designers, and familiar also to readers of science fiction and utopian proposals, run counter to the processes of city growth and economic development. Conformity and monotony, even when they are embellished with a froth of novelty, are not attributes of developing and economically vigorous cities. They are attributes of stagnant settlements. *The Economy of Cities*

J8 — A city that is large for its time is always an impractical settlement because size greatly intensifies whatever serious practical problems exist in an economy at a given time. *Ibid.*

J9 — Every city has a direct economic ancestry, a literal economic parentage, in a still older city or cities. New cities do not arise by spontaneous generation. The spark of city economic life is passed on from older cities to younger. It lives on today in cities whose ancestors have long since gone to dust. New York, far from having sprung from the Erie Canal (a mere artifact of New York) is more likely the great-great-great-great-grandcity of Urartu, say, by a descent that traces back through London, Venice, Constantinople, Rome, and Vetulonia or Tarquinii, oldest of the Etruscan cities. *Ibid.*

J10 — The ballet of the good city sidewalk never repeats itself from place to place, and in any one place is always replete with new improvisations. *The Death and Life of Great American Cities*

J11 — Being human is itself difficult, and therefore all kinds of settlements (except dream cities) have problems. Big cities have difficulties in abundance. But vital cities are not helpless to combat even the most difficult of problems. *Ibid.*

J12 — Big cities and countrysides can get along well together. Big cities need real countryside close by. And countryside — from man's point of view — needs big cities, with all their diverse opportunities and productivity, so human beings can be in a position to appreciate the rest of the natural world instead of to curse it. *Ibid.*

J13 — But look what we have built.... low-income projects that become worse centers of delinquency, vandalism and general social hopelessness than the slums they were supposed to replace.... Cultural centers that are unable to support a good bookstore. Civic centers that are avoided by everyone but bums.... Promenades that go from no place to nowhere and have no promenaders. Expressways that eviscerate great cities. This is not the rebuilding of cities. This is the sacking of cities. *Ibid.*

J14 — Great cities are not like towns, only larger. They differ from towns and suburbs in basic ways, and one of these is that cities are, by definition, full of strangers. *Ibid.*

J15 — In small settlements everyone knows your affairs. In the city everyone does not — only those you choose to tell will know about you. This is one of the attributes of cities that is precious to most city people ... *Ibid.*

J16 — The main responsibility of city planning and design should be to develop — insofar as public policy and action can do so — cities that are congenial places for.... (a) great range of unofficial plans, ideas and opportunities to flourish, along with the flourishing of ... public enterprises. *Ibid.*

J17 — Nobody can keep open house in a great city. Nobody wants to. And yet if interesting, useful, and significant contacts among the people of cities are confined to acquaintanceships suitable for private life, the city becomes stultified. Cities are full of people with whom a certain degree of contact is useful and enjoyable, but you do not want them in your hair. And they do not want you in theirs either.

J18 — Streets and their sidewalks, the main public places of a city, are its most vital organs.... If a city's streets are safe from barbarism and fear, the city is thereby tolerably safe from barbarism and fear.... To keep the city safe is a fundamental task of a city's streets and its sidewalks. *The Death and Life of Great American Cities*

JAFFE, Norman (1932-)

J19 — This is a sad day. In terms of beauty New York is not a great city. In terms of activity it is an epic city. We need to keep buildings which are an expression of that epic quality. (on the demolition of Penn Station) *The New York Times, November 11, 1963*

JAMES I (of England) (1566-1625)

J20 — For it possible but the Country must diminish, if London do so increase, and all sorts of people do come to London? And where does this increase appear? Not in the heart of the City, but in the suburbs; not giving wealth or profit to the City, but bringing misery and surcharge both to City and Court. *(Speech)*

JAMES, Henry (1843-1916)

J21 — It is difficult to speak adequately or justly of London. It is not a pleasant place; it is not agreeable, or cheerful, or easy, or exempt from reproach. It is only magnificent.

J22 — It is rather ignoble to stay in Paris simply for the restaurants. [Before his departure for London]

J23 — It is the heart of the world, and I prefer to be the least whit in its whirl, than to live and own a territory in any other place. [of London]

J24 — There are new cities enough about the world, goodness knows, and there are new parts enough of old cities — for examples of which we need go no farther than London, Paris and Rome, all of late so mercilessly renovated. But the newness of New York — unlike even that of Boston, I seemed to discern — had this mark of its very own, that it affects one, in every case, as having treated itself as still more provisional, if possible, than any poor dear little interest of antiquity it may have annihilated. The very sign of its energy is that it doesn't believe in itself; it fails to succeed, even at a cost of millions, in persuading you that it does. *The American Scene*

J25 — We swept in the course of five minutes into the Grand Canal; whereupon she uttered a murmur of ecstasy as fresh as if she had been a tourist just arrived. She had forgotten the splendour of the great water-way on a clear summer evening, and how the sense of floating between marble palaces and reflected lights disposed the mind to freedom and ease. We floated along and far, and though my friend gave no high-pitched voice to her glee I was sure of her full surrender. She was more than pleased, she was transported; the whole thing was an immense liberation. *The Aspern Papers*

J26 — The British capital is the particular spot in the world which communicates the greatest sense of life. *London*

J27 — For the real London-lover the mere immensity of the place is a large part of its merit. A small London would be an abomination, as it fortunately is an impossibility, for the idea and the name are beyond everything an expression of extent and number. *Ibid.*

J28 — It is not what London fails to do that strikes the observer, but the general fact that she does everything in excess. Excess is her highest reproach, and it is her highest misfortune that there is really too much of her. She overwhelms you by quantity and number — she ends by making human life, by making civilization appear cheap to you. *Ibid.*

J29 — London is so clumsy and so brutal, and has gathered together so many of the darkest sides of life, that it is almost ridiculous to talk of her as a lover talks of his mistress, and almost frivolous to appear to ignore her disfigurement and cruelties. She is like a mightly ogress who devours human flesh; but to me it is a mitigating circumstance that the ogress herself is not human. *Ibid.*

J30 — The sentimental tourist's sole quarrel with his Venice is that he has too many competitors there. He likes to be alone; to be original; to have (to himself, at least) the air of making discoveries. The Venice of today is a vast museum where the little wicket that admits you is perpetually turning and creaking, and you march through the institution with a herd of fellow-gazers. There is nothing left to discover or describe, and originality of attitude is completely impossible. *Portraits of Places*

J31 — Something assures one that Quebec must be a city of gossip; for evidently it is not a city of culture. A glance at the few booksellers' windows gives evidence of this. A few Catholic statuettes and prints, two or three Catholic publications, a festoon or so of rosaries, a volume of Lamartine, a supply of ink and matches, form the principal stock. *Ibid.*

J32 — The great grey Babylon [of London] *The Princess Casamassima*

JAMES, William (1842-1910)

J33 — The first impression of New York ... is one of repulsion at the clangor, disorder, and permanent earthquake conditions. But this time, installed ... in the center of the cyclone, I caught the pulse of the machine, took up the rhythm, and found it simply magnificent ... The courage, the heaven-scaling audacity of it all, and the lightness withal, as if there was nothing that was not easy, and the great pulses and bounds of progress ... give a kind of drumming background of life that I never felt before. I'm sure that once in that movement, and at home, all other places would seem insipid. *(Letter to Henry James)*

J34 — Rome is simply the most satisfying lake of picturesqueness and guilty suggestiveness known to this child. Other places have single features better than anything in Rome, perhaps, but for an *ensemble* Rome seems to beat the world. *(Letter to Miss Frances R. Morse, December 25, 1900)*

J35 — No more fiendish punishment could be devised, were such a thing physically possible, than that one should be turned loose in society and remain absolutely unnoticed by all the members thereof. *The Principles of Psychology*

JAMESON, Anna (1794-1860)

J36 — Toronto is, as a residence, worse and better than other small communities — *worse* in so much as it is remote from all the best advantages of a high state of civilisation, while it is infested by all its evils, all its follies; and *better*, because, beside being a small place, it is a *young* place; and in spite of this affectation of looking back, instead of looking up, it must advance — it may become the thinking head and beating heart of a nation, great, and wise, and happy; — who knows? *Winter Studies and Summer Rambles in Canada*

JEBB, (Sir) Gladwyn (1900-   )

J37 — Many times have I consulted them as one consults an oracle. If we are to believe the ancients, the voice of the people must be taken very seriously indeed. [of cab drivers] *Cab Drivers*

JEFFERIES, Richard

J38 — Every fresh day's research into the city brings increasing disappointment.... Everything is planned, smoothed, and set to an oppressive regularity.... in short, Paris is the plainest city in Europe. *The Plainest City in Europe*

JEFFERS, Robinson (1887-1962)

J39 — But for my children, I would have them keep their distance / from the thickening center; corruption / Never has been compulsory, when the cities lie at the monster's / feet there are left the mountains. / *Cities, Nomadism, and Labor*

JEFFERSON, Thomas (1743-1826)

J40 — The city of London, though handsomer than Paris, is not so handsome as Philadelphia. *(Letter to John Page, 1786)*

J41 — A cloacina of all the depravities of human nature. [of New York City]

J42 — I think our governments will remain virtuous for many centuries; as long as they are chiefly agricultural; and this will be as long as there shall be vacant lands in any part of America. When they get piled upon one another in large cities, as in Europe, they will become corrupt as in Europe. *(Letter to James Madison, December 20, 1787)*

J43 — I view great cities as penitential to the morals, the health, and the liberties of man. *(Letter to Benjamin Rush)*

J44 — The mobs of great cities add just so much to the support of pure government, as sores do to the strength of the human body. It is the manners and spirit of a people which preserve a republic in vigour. A degeneracy in these is a canker which soon eats to the heart of its laws and constitution. *Notes on the State of Virginia, 1785*

JENNINGS, Leslie Nelson (1890-1972)

J45 — Who's ground the grist of trodden ways — / The gray dust and the brown — / May love red tiling two miles off, / But cannot love a town. / *Highways*

JEROME, (Saint) (340?-420)

J46 — While this (theological war) was being waged in Jerusalem, terrible news arrived from the West. We learnt how Rome had been besieged, how her citizens had purchased immunity by paying a ransom, and how then, after they had thus been despoiled, they had been beleaguered again, to forfeit their lives after having already forfeited their property. At the news my speech failed me, and sobs choked the words that I was dictating. She had been captured — the city by whom the whole world had once been taken captive.

J47 — The world sinks into ruin; the renowned city is swallowed up in one tremendous fire. We live as though we were going to die to-morrow.

JERROLD, Douglas (1803-1857)

J48 — Compared to the city, the country looks like the world without its clothes on.

JESUP, Scott W.

J49 — No logical induction, no mathematical demonstration can be clearer to our mind, than that here [in the American West] will come together the greatest aggregations of men in cities-outrivalling in splendor as in magnitude, all which past ages have produced . . . *The Great West*

J50 — New-York has long been, and for some decades of years it will continue to be, the necessary chief focal point of our nation. But, in all respects, it is not the true heart. In its composition and dealings, it is almost as foreign as American. *Westward the Star of Empire*

JIMÉNEZ, Juan Ramón (1881-1958)

J51 — The urban man is an uprooted tree, he can put out leaves, flowers and grow fruit but what a nostalgia his leaf, flower, and fruit will always have for mother earth! *Aristocracy and Democracy*

JONSON, Ben (1573-1637)

J52 — PEOPLE: / The Voice of Cato is the voice of Rome. / CATO: / The voice of Rome is the consent of heaven! / *Catiline, His Conspiracy*

J53 — To hear thy buskin tread, / And shake a stage; or, when thy socks were on, / Leave thee alone for the comparison / Of all that insolent Greece or haughty Rome / Sent forth, or since did from their ashes come. / *To the Memory of My Beloved Master William Shakespeare*

JOHNSON, James Weldon (1871-1938)

J54 — In the history of New York the significance of the name Harlem has changed from Dutch to Irish to Jewish to Negro. Of these changes the last has come most swiftly. Throughout colored America, from Massachusetts to Mississippi and across the continent to Los Angeles and Seattle, its name, which as late as fifteen years ago had scarcely been heard, now stands for the Negro metropolis. Harlem is, indeed, the great Mecca for the sight-seer, the pleasure-seeker, the curious, the adventurous, the enterprising, the ambitious, and the talented of the Negro world; for the lure of it has reached down to every island of the Carib Sea and has penetrated even into Africa. *The Making of Harlem*

JOHNSON, Lyndon B. (1908-1973)

J55 — The American city should be a collection of communities where every member has a right to belong. It should be a place where every man feels safe on his streets and in the house of his friends. It should be a place where each individual's dignity and self-respect is strengthened by the respect and affection of his neighbors. It should be a place where each of us can find the satisfaction and warmth which comes only from being a member of the community of man. This is what man sought at the dawn of civilization. It is what we seek today. *(Message to Congress, March 1965)*

J56 — The clock is ticking, time is moving . . ., we must ask ourselves every night when we go home, are we doing all that we should do in our nation's capital, in all other big cities of the country. *(after Watts Riot, August 1965)*

J57 — The first step is to break old patterns — to begin to think, work and plan for the development of entire metropolitan areas. *(State of the Union Message, January 4, 1965)*

J58 — The modern city can be the most ruthless enemy of the good life, or it can be its servant. The choice is up to this generation of Americans. For this is truly the time of decision for the American city.

J59 — Our society will never be great until our cities are great. In the next forty years we must rebuild the entire urban United States. . . . There is the decay of the centers and the despoiling of the suburbs. There is not enough housing for our people or transportation for our traffic. Open land is vanishing and old landmarks are violated . . . A few years ago we were concerned about the ugly American. Today we must act to prevent an ugly America. *My Hope for America*

J60 — There is nothing I know of that we need more urgently in the cities of this country than health care and housing for the elderly — unless it's for the young.

J61 — Where and how will they [the people] all live? By crowding further into our dense cities? In new layers of sprawling suburbia? In jerry-built strip cities along new highways? *(Message to Congress, February 22, 1968)*

J62 — If we permit our cities to grow without rational design; if we stand passively by, while the center of each becomes a hive of deprivation, crime, and hopelessness; if we devour the countryside as though it were limitless while our ruins — millions of tenement apartments and dilapidated houses — go unredeemed; if we become two people, the suburban affluent and the urban poor, each filled with mistrust and fear one for the other — if this is our desire and policy as a people, then we shall effectively cripple each generation to come. *(The Rebirth of our Cities: A Message to Congress, January 26, 1966)*

JOHNSON, Paul (1928-   )

J63 — The Church saved the cities [after the fall of Rome] . . . Over a huge area of western Europe, the function of the episcopate ensured urban continuity . . . The bishop was the first, and almost always the most influential, magistrate of the city. *A History of Christianity*

JOHNSON, Philip (1906-   )

J64 — Urban renewal, as this country knew it once, was what I always called 'urban removal.' That's all it was. The policy was an attempt to push problems of the inner city a bit further away to make it more profitable to erect skyscrapers. *U.S. News & World Report, June 5, 1978*

J65 — Why do we not build great cities? Why do we spend billions building roads but nothing in cities for the roads to end up in? We subsidize — pitifully enough — housing, but we do not subsidize the great amenities of the city that make housing meaningful. Planners today refer to themselves as 'housers.' Is nothing more important? Or are our housers despairing of ever getting more? Will there never be anything more? *Why We Want Our Cities*

JOHNSON, Samuel (1709-1784)

J66 — The happiness of London is not to be conceived but by those who have been in it. I will venture to say, there is more learning and science within the circumference of ten miles from where we now sit, than in all the rest of the kingdom. *The Life of Johnson, James Boswell*

J67 — I know not why any one but a school-boy in his declamation should whine over the Commonwealth of Rome, which grew great only by the misery of the rest of mankind. *Ibid.*

J68 — When a man is tired of London, he is tired of life; for there is in London all that life can afford. *Ibid.*

J69 — By seeing London I have seen as much of life as the world can show. *Tour to the Hebrides, James Boswell*

J70 — Grubstreet — The name of a street near Moorsfield, London, much inhabited by writers of small histories, dictionaries, and temporary poems. *Definition in The Dictionary*

J71 — Here malice, rapine, accident, conspire, / And now a rabble rages, now a fire; / Their ambush here relentless ruffians lay, / And here the fell attorney prowls for prey; / Here falling houses thunder on your head, / And here a female atheist talks you dead. / [of London] *London*

J72 — London! the needy villain's gen'ral home, / The common shore of Paris, and of Rome; / With eager thirst, by folly or by fate, / Sucks in the dregs of each corrupted state. / *Ibid.*

J73 — Prepare for death if here at night you roam, / And sign your will before you sup from home. / [of London] *Ibid.*

JOHNSTONE, Ernest Fenwick (1867-1938)

J74 — I dreamed that I went to the City of Gold, / To Heaven resplendent and fair, / And after I entered that beautiful fold / By one in authority there I ws told / That not a Vermonter was there. / *No Vermonters in Heaven*

JONES, Leroi (1934-   )

J75 — In a very real sense, Harlem is the capital of Black America. And America has always been divided into black and white, and the substance of the division is social, economic, and cultural. But even the name Harlem, now, means simply Negroes (even though some other peoples live there too). The identification is international as well:

even in Belize, the capital of predominantly Negro British Honduras, there are vendors who decorate their carts with flowers and the names or pictures of Negro culture heroes associated with Harlem like Sugar Ray Robinson. Some of the vendors even wear t-shirts that say 'Harlem, U.S.A.' and they speak about it as a black Paris. In Havana, a young Afro-Cuban begged me to tell him about the 'big leg ladies' of Lenox Avenue, hoping, too, that I could provide some way for him to get to that mystic and romantic place. *City of Harlem*

JORDAN, Vernon E., Jr. (1935-   )

J76 — The heart of any urban policy must be jobs. Everything flows from jobs if the city is to be rehabilitated, stabilized and revitalized. *(Before Urban League of Eastern Massachusetts, Boston, April 17, 1978)*

JOSEPHUS, Flavius (37?-100)

J77 — What corner of the earth had escaped the Romans, unless heat or cold made it of no value to them? From every side fortune had passed to them, and God . . . now abode in Italy. It was an immutable and unchallenged law among beasts and men alike, that all must submit to the stronger, and that power belonged to those supreme in arms. That was why their ancestors in soul and body had submitted to Rome . . .

had they not known that God was on the Roman side? *The Jewish War*

JOYCE, James (1882-1941)

J78 — He walked along the curbstone. Stream of life . . . Cityful passing away, other cityful coming, passing away too: other coming on, passing on. Houses, lines of houses, streets, miles of pavements, piled up bricks, stones. Changing hands. This owner, that. Landlord never dies they say. Other steps into his shoes when he gets his notice to quit. They buy the place up with gold and still they have all the gold. Swindle it somewhere. Piled up in cities, worn away age after age. Pyramids in sand. Built on bread and onions. Slaves. Chinese wall. Babylon. Big stones left. Round towers. Rest rubble, sprawling suburbs, jerry-built, Kerwan's mushroom house, built of breeze. Shelter for the night. No one is anything. [of Dublin] *Ulysses*

JUGURTHA (?-104 B.C.)

J79 — A city for sale, and doomed to speedy destruction, if it finds a purchaser. [of Rome]

JUVENAL, Decimus Junius (60?-140?)

J80 — If you can tear yourself away from the games of the Circus, you can buy an excellent home at Sora, at Prusino, for what you now pay in Rome to rent a dark garret for a year. And there you will have a little garden . . .

J81 — Neither for thought . . . nor for quiet is there any place in the city for a poor man. [of Rome] *Epigrams*

J82 — Here in town the sick die from insomnia mostly. / Undigested food, on a stomach burning with ulcers, / Bringing on listlessness, but who can sleep in a flophouse? / Who but the rich can afford sleep and a garden apartment? / That's the source of infection. The wheels creak by on the narrow / Streets of the wards, the drivers squabble and brawl when they're stopped, / More than enough to frustrate the drowsiest son of a sea cow. / [of Rome] *Satires III*

J83 — Every crime is here, and every lust, as they have been / Since the day, long since, when Roman poverty perished. / Over our seven hills, from that day on, they came pouring, / The rabble and rout of the West, Sybaris, Rhodes, Miletus, / Yes, and Tarentum too, garlanded, drunken, shameless. [of Rome] *Satires VI*

J84 — The scum of the swamps and the filth of the forest / Swirl into Rome, the great sewer, their sanctuary, their heaven. *Satires III*

J85 — What should I do in Rome? I am no good at lying. *Ibid.*

J86 — Where have we ever seen a place so dismal and lonely / We'd not be better off there, than afraid, as we are here, of fires / Roofs caving in, and the thousand risks of this terrible city . . .? / [of Rome] *Ibid.*

K

KAFKA, Franz (1883-1924)

K1 — On the picture the roofs fly away. The church coupolas are umbrellas in the wind. The whole city is about to fly off. But Prague remains — despite all inner discord. That is the wonderful thing about Prague. [of Oskar Kokoschica's painting of Prague]

K2 — Prague doesn't release you. This *Mutterchen* [little mother] has claws.

KAHN, Herman (1922-   )

K3 — If New York goes through some drastic unpleasant experience, maybe even being deprived of home rule, there'll be a reform in city behavior . . . . The crisis could really lead to a positive result. The bankruptcy of New York City will make people realize there's no such thing as a free lunch. *Interview, "W", October 14, 1975*

KARAMZIN, Nikolai (1766-1826)

K4 — So here it is, here is this city which during the course of so many centuries was the model of all Europe, the source of taste, of manners, whose name is pronounced with respect by the learned and the ignorant, by philosophers and artisans, by artists and peasants, in Europe and in Asia, in America and in Africa, whose name has been known to me as long as my own, about which I have read so many things in novels, have learned so many things from travellers, have

dreamed and thought so many things . . . [of Paris]

KAVANAUGH, James

K5 — Man does not live in the giant city / But in a name like New York / Where he's never seen a play / But subways in silence til he finds / The corner where a dog barks at him in recognition. // He is not as free as his San Francisco / Nor as energetic as his Chicago / As pragmatic as his Detroit or Pittsburgh / Liberated as his Los Angeles // As elegant as his Boston / Only as gentle and frightened as the little town he clings to. / *Man Does Not Live in the Giant City*

KAZIN, Alfred (1915-   )

K6 — No New York streets are named after Herman Melville, Henry James, Walt Whitman, or Edith Wharton. New York does not remember its own: it barely remembers Poe in Fordham, Mark Twain on lower Fifth Avenue, William Dean Howells on West Fifty-seventh Street, Stephen Crane in Chelsea, Dreiser and O'Neill in Washington Square, Willa Cather on Bank Street, Thomas Wolfe and Marianne Moore in far-off Brooklyn, Hart Crane on Columbia Heights, Allen Tate in the Village, Cummings in Patchin Place, Auden in St. Mark's Place, Lorca at Columbia. It will not remember Ellison and Bellow on Riverside Drive, Mailer in Columbia Heights, Capote in the U.N. Plaza, Singer on West Eighty-sixth Street any more than it remembers having given shelter to European exiles from Tom Paine to John Butler Yeats, Gorky to Nabokov. *New York from Melville to Mailer*

K7 — In the city, where the triumph of numbers is complete, the technical collaboration between men persists in the midst of the greatest loneliness and destructiveness. There is a meticulous unending confrontation between man and other men, between man and his *things*, even between things and *their* things. *Introduction to Seize the Day, by Saul Bellow*

KEATS, John

K8 — A box of your own in one of the fresh

air slums we're building around the edges of America's cities. [of suburbia]

KEATS, John (1795-1821)

K9 — To one who has been long in city pent, / 'Tis very sweet to look into the fair / And open face of heaven. / *To One Who Has Been Long in City Pent*

KELLER, Helen (1880-1968)

K10 — Cut off as I am, it is inevitable that I should sometimes feel like a shadow walking in a shadowy world. When this happens I ask to be taken to New York City. Always I return home weary but I have the comforting certainty that mankind is real and I myself am not a dream. *Quoted in The Empire City*

KELLY, A. William

K11 — In San Francisco nothing is natural — everything is forced; it is a hot-bed where all pursuits are stimulated by the fierce fire of one predominant lust. *An Excursion to California*

K12 — The world's progress furnishes no parallel for the precocious depravity of San Francisco. *Ibid.*

KELLY, Robert

K13 — And the critical rhythm of a city is the sequence of closing hours, the city's play with the order of the eternal sun.

KEMPTON, Murray (1918-   )

K14 — A neighborhood is where, when you go out of it, you get beat up. *America Comes of Middle Age*

KENNEDY, Edward M. (1932-   )

K15 — The time has come for the Federal government to give greater breathing room to the Mayors and let them do their jobs. If we can deregulate the airlines . . . we can also deregulate the Mayors so that they can serve the people of our cities. *United States Conference of Mayors, Atlanta, June 19, 1978*

KENNEDY, John F. (1917-1963)

K16 — All free men, wherever they may live,

are citizens of Berlin. And therefore, as a free man, I take pride in the words 'Ich bin ein Berliner' [I am a Berliner.] *Address at City Hall, West Berlin, June 26, 1963*

K17 — The cities — their needs, their future, their financing — these are the great unspoken, overlooked, underplayed problems of our times.

K18 — The freedom of the city is not negotiable. We cannot negotiate with those who say, 'What's mine is mine and what's yours is negotiable.' *Address to Nation, July 25, 1961*

K19 — I hear it said that West Berlin is militarily untenable — and so was Bastogne, and so, in fact, was Stalingrad. Any danger spot is tenable if men — brave men — will make it so. *Ibid.*

K20 — Peace and freedom walk together. In too many of our cities today, the peace is not secure because freedom is incomplete. *Commencement Address, American University, Washington D.C., June 10, 1963*

K21 — A strong America depends on its cities — America's glory and sometimes America's shame. *State of the Union Address, January 11, 1962*

K22 — There are many people in the world who really don't understand — or say they don't — what is the great issue between the free world and the Communist world . . . There are some who say that Communism is the wave of the future . . . . And there are some who say in Europe and elsewhere 'we can work with the Communists.' . . . And there are even a few who say that it's true that Communism is an evil system but it permits us to make economic progress. Let them come to Berlin! *Address at City Hall, West Berlin, June 26, 1963*

K23 — We will neglect our cities to our peril, for in neglecting them we neglect the nation. *Message to Congress, January 30, 1962*

K24 — The shame of our cities today is not political; it is social and economic. Blight and decay in urban government have been replaced by blight and decay in the cities themselves. *The New York Times Magazine, May 18, 1958*

KEY, Ellen (1849-1926)

K25 — A destroyed home life, an idiotic school system, premature work in the factory, stupefying life in the streets, these are what the great city gives to the children of the under classes. *The Century of the Child*

KHRUSHCHEV, Nikita S. (1894-1971)

K26 — I don't like the life there. There is no greenery. It would make a stone sick. [of New York City]

K27 — When we started building the Moscow Metro, we had only the vaguest idea of what the job would entail. We were very unsophisticated. We thought of a subway as something almost supernatural. I think it's probably easier to contemplate space flights today than it was for us to contemplate the construction of the Moscow Metro in the early 1930's. *Khrushchev Remembers*

KILGALLEN, Dorothy (1913-1965)

K28 — The world is grand, awfully big and astonishingly beautiful, frequently thrilling. But I love New York. *Girl around the World*

KILMER, Joyce (1886-1918)

K29 — Golden towns where golden houses are. *Roofs*

KINGSBURY, F.J. (1823-1910)

K30 — I think isolated rural life, where people seldom come in contact with dwellers in large towns, always tends to barbarism. I believe that poorer poeple in our cities, if planted in isolated situations in the country, would deteriorate and grow barbaric in habit and thought, even though they might be physically in better condition. What very unattractive people most of our rural population [are]. *The Tendency of Men to Live in Cities*

K31 — One would think after reading all . . . about the evils of cities from the time of Cain to the last New York election . . . and especially when we must admit that we know everything that is said to be true, and

that even then not the half nor the tenth part has been told, and we are almost driven to the conclusion that nothing short of the treatment applied to Sodom and Gomorrah will meet the necessities of the case, that every sane man and woman should flee without stopping for the open country; and the women especially should be careful how they look behind them, and be sure to remember Lot's wife, and nothing should induce them to turn their faces cityward again. *Ibid.*

KINGSLEY, Charles (1819-1875)

K32 — A ghastly, deafening, sickening sight it was. Go, scented Belgravian! and see what London is! and then go to the library which God has given thee — one often fears in vain — and see what science says this London might be! *Alton Locke, Tailor and Poet*

K33 — I assure you that, after years of thought, I see no other remedy for the worst evils of city life . . . if you cannot bring the country into the city, the city must go into the country. *Great Cities and their Influence for Good and Evil*

K34 — [The plague epidemics in the mediaeval cities] showed that the crowded city life can bring out human nobleness as well as human baseness; that to be crushed into contact with their fellow-men, forced at least the loftier and tender souls to know their fellow-men, and therefore to care for them, to love them, to die for them. Yes — from one temptation the city life is free, to which the country life is sadly exposed — that isolation which, self-contented and self-helping, forgets in its surly independence that man is his brother's keeper . . . . *Ibid.*

K35 — The social state of a city depends directly on its moral state, and . . . that the moral state of a city depends — . . . to an extent as yet uncalculated, and perhaps uncalculable — on the physical state of that city; on the food, water, air, and lodging of its inhabitants. *Ibid.*

K36 — Yes — were I asked to sum up in one sentence the good of great cities, I would point first to Bristol, and then to the United States, and say, That is what great cities can do. By concentrating in one place, and upon one subject, men, genius, information, and

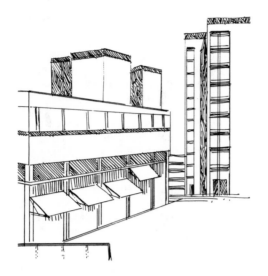

wealth, they can conquer new-found lands by arts instead of arms; they can beget new nations; and replenish and subdue the earth from pole to pole . . . *Ibid.*

KINSEY, Alfred (1894-1956)

K37 — The differences between the total [sexual] outlet of the rural males and the total outlet of the urban males were never very great. In general the differences would not be particularly significant if they did not all lie in the same direction of a lower frequency of total sexual outlet for the rural males. *Rural/Urban Background and Sexual Outlet*

KIPLING, Rudyard (1865-1936)

K38 — [New York's streets] are first cousins to a Zanzibar foreshore, or kin to the approaches of a Zulu kraal.

K39 — Chance-directed, dance-erected, laid and built / On the silt — / Palace, byre, hovel — poverty and pride — / Side by side; / And, above the packed and pestilential town / Death looked down. / [of Calcutta]

K40 — A mad city inhabited by perfectly insane people whose women are of a remarkable beauty. [of San Francisco]

K41 — She was well and healthy and alive, and she was dressed in flaming red and black, and her feet . . . were cased in red leather shoes. She stood in a patch of

sunlight, the red blood under shoes, the vivid carcasses tacked around her, a bullock bleeding its life not six feet away from her, and the death factory roaring all around her. She looked curiously, with hard, cold eyes, and was not ashamed.

Then said I: 'This is a special Sending. I've seen the city of Chicago!' And I went away to get peace and rest.

K42 — We must go back with Policeman Day — / Back from the City of Sleep! / *The City of Sleep*

K43 — I have struck a city, — a real city, — and they call it Chicago. The other places do not count. San Francisco was a pleasure-resort as well as a city, and Salt Lake was a phenomenon. This place is the first American city I have encountered. It holds rather more than a million people with bodies, and stands on the same sort of soil as Calcutta. Having seen it, I urgently desire never to see it again. It is inhabited by savages. Its water is the water of the Huglei, and its air is dirt. Also it says that it is the 'boss' town of America. *From Sea to Sea*

K44 — Canada possesses two pillars of Strength and Beauty in Quebec and Victoria. The former ranks by herself among those Mother-cities of whom none can say 'This reminds me.' To realize Victoria you must take all that the eye admires most in Bournemouth, Torquay, the Isle of Wight, the Happy Valley of Hong Kong, the Doon, Sorrento, and Camps Bay; add reminiscences of the Thousand Islands, and arrange the whole round the Bay of Naples, with some Himalayas for the background. *Letters to the Family*

K45 — Winnipeg has Things in abundance, but has learned to put them beneath her feet, not on top of her mind, and so is older than many cities . . . . She is a little too modest. *Ibid.*

K46 — But that's all shove be'ind me — long ago an'fur away, / An' there ain't no 'buses runnin' from the Bank to Mandalay; / An' I'm learnin' 'ere in London wot the ten-year soldier tells: / 'If you've 'eard the East a-callin', you won't never 'eed naught else.' / *Mandalay*

K47 — I walk my beat before London Town, / Five hours up and seven down, / Up I go till

I end my run / At Tide-end-town, which is Teddington. / *The River's Tale*

K48 — Into the mist my guardian prows put forth / Behind the mist my virgin ramparts lie, / The Warden of the Honour of the North / Sleepless and veiled am I. / [of Halifax] *The Seven Seas*

K49 — Mithras, God of the Morning, our trumpets waken the Wall! / 'Rome is above the Nations, but Thou art over all!' *A Song to Mithras*

K50 — Comfort it is to say: 'Of no mean city am I!' [of Bombay] *To the City of Bombay*

KITTO, H.D.F.

K51 — 'Polis' is the Greek word which we translate 'city-state.' It is a bad translation, because the normal polis was not much like a city, and was very much more than a state. *The Polis*

KNEBEL, Fletcher (1911-　)

K52 — No other city in the United States can divest the visitor of so much money with so little enthusiasm. In Dallas, they take away with gusto; in New Orleans, with a bow; in San Francisco, with a wink and a grin. In New York, you're lucky if you get a grunt. *Look, March 26, 1963*

KNEF, Hildegard (1925-　)

K53 — Everything in Berlin is actually double. An East Zoo and a West Zoo, an East Opera and a West Opera, and just as many theatres in the East as in the West.
The wall dividing the city went up in 1961. Little can be said about something as monstrous as that. The soul of the city is divided, and even though we do not think of it continuously, there is still this sense of division in the back of our minds. *Quoted in Cities, John McGreevy*

KNICKERBOCKER, Conrad

K54 — An American city is a place where the post office looks like the Parthenon, the home of the town's richest citizen is a replica of Blenheim Palace, and everybody else lives like a Texas rancher. *Life, December 24, 1965*

K55 — American city life has never stood still for more than a nanosecond. It is always in the process of becoming. If the past has little influence, the future is thereby closer. Americans have not so much built their cities and their noncities as assembled them from do-it-yourself kits. *Ibid.*

K56 — American urban freedom produces wild and wooly scenes. Drive down Kansas City's Main Street and suddenly there's a big airplane aimed right at the car. A crash? No, just an old plane fuselage that has been wedged into a parking lot and converted into a cocktail lounge. Only in an American city can one leap off a jetliner and 36 seconds later be shoveling quarters into a slot machine while wiser heads read self-help gambling books at the cigar counter. Only in America can one witness from a descending jet what appears to be a daily reenactment of the German gas attack at Ypres, but is merely the San Fernando Valley on a good day when everybody has his car out. Millions of Angelenos live at the bottom of this sea of hydrocarbonous gas while, above the mountains, the sky gleams a pure, cruel blue. *Ibid.*

K57 — Architecturally and spiritually, Los Angeles was the first city to say the hell with it as a place; better to be a state of mind in which any life style goes and it is still the pluperfect example of its kind. *Ibid.*

K58 — Worrying about cities has become the most fashionable form of national self-torture, succeeding bootlegging, necking in rumble seats and the other great social concerns of the past. Mention the word 'city' to thinking Americans and their eyeballs roll back in their heads. They clench their teeth and their fingers begin to twitch. 'Yes,' they gasp. 'Terrible. Cancer in the air we breath. Detergents in our drinking water. Entire Himalayan ranges of pop-top cans. One-hundred-car freeway accidents. Thirty million people suddenly with no lights. Can't walk in the park.' *Ibid.*

KNOTT, James Proctor (1830-1911)

K59 — Duluth! The word fell upon my ear with a peculiar and indescribable charm, like the gentle murmur of a low fountain stealing forth in the midst of roses, or the soft sweet accent of an angel's whisper in the bright, joyous dream of sleeping innocence. T'was the name for which my soul had panted for years, as the hart panteth for the waterbrooks. [Congressman Knott's eulogy of Duluth] *Speech on the St. Croix and Bayfield Railroad Bill, U.S. House of Representatives*

KNOX, John (1505-1572)

K60 — In Geneva . . . I neither fear man nor am ashamed to say that this is the most perfect school of Christ that ever was in the earth since the days of the apostles. In other places, I confess Christ to be truly preached; but manners and religion to be so sincerely reformed, I have not yet seen in any other place.

KOCH, Edward I. (Mayor of New York) (1924-   )

K61 — I do not exaggerate when I say that New York is unique in the history of human kindness. New York is not a problem. New York is a stroke of genius. From its earliest days, this city has been a lifeboat for the homeless, a larder for the hungry, a living library for the intellectually starved, a refuge not only for the oppressed but also for the creative. New York is and has been the most open city in the world, and that is its greatness and that is why in large part it faces monumental problems today. *Inauguration Address, New York, January 1, 1978*

KOLLEK, Teddy (1911-   )

K62 — Jerusalem is not New York, London, Paris or even Rome. It is not just a great city or an historical city. It is a place where everyone seems to feel he has a share, a stake — and a say. Because Jerusalem is a city holy to millions, every new house that goes up adds itself to history and thus often becomes controversial. Yet I feel there is also a deep human value in preserving Jerusalem, independent of its political future, because I am overcome by sadness whenever a long-established thing of beauty and character disappears. *For Jerusalem*

KONING, Hans (1912-   )

K63 — Being a born Amsterdammer, I can say with conviction that our so-called commercialism is an exaggeration, just as any Parisian knows there are plenty of Paris restaurants that serve mediocre food and plenty of Parisians who let whole days drift by without thinking about sex. I wouldn't deny, however, that this is, and always has been, a city of merchants. *Amsterdam*

K64 — Nothing is more dangerous, I suppose, than to try to sum up the individuality of a city in a single word. But if I had to settle for one adjective that distils Amsterdam's peculiar genius, it would be the Dutch word *gezellig*. Attempts at precise translation are likely to spawn a series of near-misses; but in essence, *gezellig* means both cosy and convivial, both intimate and sociable. The blend of these various shades of meaning adds up to an aspect of a character that is more pronounced in Amsterdammers than in other inhabitants of Holland — and surely more pronounced than in city dwellers of other lands. If it weren't for Amsterdam, in fact, one might logically assume that big-city life and *gezelligheid* — the noun for this bent of personality and preference — just do not mix. *Ibid.*

K65 — 'Town air makes free,' Amsterdammers said in the 17th Century; 'sea air makes freer.' *Ibid.*

KOTKER, Norman (1931-   )

K66 — Originally all cities were holy. Just as primitive farmers sanctified the whole earth, primitive townsfolk revered the enclosure within which they lived, imagining it a sacred space, like a church, where a sacred drama was continually being enacted between themselves and their god. In Sumer, and later in Babylonia, every city contained within its walls a ziggurat, a temple shaped like a mountain, where the patron god of the city lived. *Horizon*

KOTLER, Milton (1935-   )

K67 — Corporate power has moved its structure and influence to the cities, after a historic collusion with state governments. No longer do public land grabs and privileged tax structures suffice for corporate power. Instead, they require centralization, intellect and skill for the administration of its productive technology.

For these and other reasons, the corporation has come full force to the city. Their procession requires favorable opinion to withstand public misgiving. Thus, they have come to control the media, the schools, the press, the university — either by way of ownership, contract, or public service.

KREYMBORG, Alfred (1883-1966)

K68 — Harlem has a black belt where darkies dwell in a heaven where white men seek a little hell. *Harlem*

K69 — Manhattan's a hell where culture rarely grew; / But it lets two lives do all they care to do. / *Two Lives and Six Million*

KRISCHKE, Traugott

K70 — In no other city of Europe had two forces loved and hated each other as strongly as the Czechs and Germans in Prague, and in no other city in Europe had the Jews such an important task of mediating between them.

KRISHNAMURTI, J.,

K71 — Life in a city is strangely cut off from the universe; man-made buildings have taken the place of valleys and mountains; and the roar of traffic has been substituted for that of boisterous streams. At night one hardly ever sees the stars, even if one wishes to, for city lights are too bright; and during the day the sky is limited and held. Something definitely happens to the city dwellers; they are brittle and polished, they have churches and museums, drinks and theatres, beautiful clothes and endless shops. There are people everywhere, on the streets, in the buildings, in the rooms. A cloud passes across the sky, and so few look up. There is rush and turmoil! *Life in a City*

KRISTOL, Irving (1920-)

K72 — Urban problems are real, but the conglomeration of urban problems into something called an urban crisis is largely the function of . . . television, which has to make a national issue out of every event . . . Cities have always had problems. When you call it a crisis, it's a matter of labeling. *The Los Angeles Times, April 8, 1975*

K73 — How much of a disaster would it be if some of our major cities were to become preponderantly Negro? I rather doubt we would answer this question candidly, but I am sure we would find the prospect disturbing, probably, as the 19th-century 'proper' Bostonian found the fact of his city becoming preponderantly Irish. *The Negro and the City*

K74 — In comparison with previous waves of immigration to the great cities, Negroes are 'making out' not badly at all. They need, and are entitled to, assistance from the white society that has made them — almost our oldest settlers — into new immigrants. But the first step toward effective help would seem to be a change in white attitudes. Until now, we have spent an enormous amount of energy and money trying to assimilate Negroes into 'our' cities. Is it not time we tried helping them to assimilate into 'their' cities? *Ibid.*

KROPOTKIN, Peter (1842-1921)

K75 — Factories grew up and they abandoned the fields. They gathered where the sale of their produce was easiest, or the raw materials and fuel could be obtained with the greatest advantage. New cities rose, and the old ones rapidly enlarged; the fields were deserted. Millions of labourers, driven away by sheer force from the land, gathered in the cities in search of labour, and soon forgot the bonds which formerly attached them to the soil. And we, in our admiration of the prodigies achieved under the new factory system, overlooked the advantages of the old system under which the tiller of the soil was an industrial worker at the same time. We doomed to disappearance all those branches of industry which formerly used to prosper in the villages; we condemned in industry all that was not a big factory. *Fields, Factories and Workshops*

K76 — The two sister arts of agriculture and industry were not always so estranged from one another as they are now. There was a time, and that time is not so far back, when both were thoroughly combined; the villages were then the seats of a variety of industries, and the artisans in the city did not abandon agriculture; many towns were nothing else but industrial villages. *Ibid.*

KUH, Katherine (1904-   )

K77 — Artists have always painted the city. But in our industrialized century the metropolis, grown to overwhelming proportions, has become a central motif in contemporary art. Its inhumanity, loneliness, confusion, and sheer beauty are favorite themes for present-day artists, who sometimes reproduce its chaotic disorder, sometimes escape from this turmoil with works of precision and clarity.

KUTUZOV, Mikhail (1745-1813)

K78 — Napoleon is a torrent which as yet we are unable to stem. Moscow will be the sponge that will suck him dry. *Address to Russian Army, September 13, 1812*

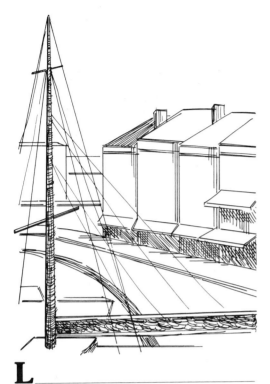

L

LA BRUYERE, Jean de

L1 — If you suppress the exorbitant love of pleasure and money, idle curiosity, iniquitous purpose, and wanton mirth, what a stillness would there be in the great cities.

L2 — There is something which has never been seen yet, and which, to all appearances, never will be, and that is a little town which isn't divided into cliques, where the families are united, and the cousins trust each other; where a marriage doesn't start a civil war, and where quarrels about precedence don't arise every time a service, a ceremony, a procession, or a funeral are held; where gossip and lying and malice have been outlawed; where the landlord and the corporation are on speaking terms, or the ratepayers and their assessors; where the dean is friendly with the canons, and the canons don't despise the chaplains, and the chaplains tolerate the men in the choir.

LACTANTIUS, Firmianus (4th c. A.D.)

L3 — The fall and ruin of the world will soon take place, but it seems that nothing of the kind is to be feared as long as the city of Rome stands intact. But when the capital of the world has fallen . . . who can doubt that the end will have come for the affairs of men and for the whole world? It is that city which sustains all things. *The Divine Institutions*

LAING, R.D.

L4 — In a way there are as many Glasgows as there are eyes to see it. It is a diamond with as many facets as there are people in it. With all its many sides and divisions, Glasgow is still a place where you can enjoy a sense of community that is very rare in the great cities of the world nowadays. *Quoted in Cities, John McGreevy*

L5 — Walking around Glasgow one might not sense the wildness, the passion of the city. We haven't tribal dances or Mardi Gras or Saturnalia or even a Witches' Sabbath now; no more gladiators or Christians fed to the lions; but — for men, at least — we have the next best thing in these times of tranquility and peace, the football matches. *Ibid.*

LAMB, Charles (1775-1834)

L6 — Oh, her lamps of a night! her rich goldsmiths, print-shops, toy-shops, mercers, hardware-men, pastry-cooks, St. Paul's Churchyard, the Strand, Exeter Change, Charing Cross, with a man upon a black horse! These are thy gods, O London! *(Letter to Thomas Manning)*

L7 — Separate from the pleasure of your company, I don't much care if I never see a mountain in my life. I have passed all my days in London, until I have formed as many and intense local attachments, as any of you mountaineers can have done with dead nature. The lighted shops of the Strand and Fleet Street, the innumerable trades, tradesmen and customers, coaches, waggons, playhouses, all the bustle and wickedness round about Covent Garden, the very women of the town, the watchmen, drunken scenes, rattles . . . I often shed tears in the motley Strand from fullness of joy at so much life. *(Letter to Wordsworth)*

L8 — We can be nowhere private except in the midst of London. *(Letter to Thomas Manning)*

LAMB, Frederick S.

L9 — It seems strange that the American mind, usually so quick to appreciate the pecuniary value of any movement, has not seen the civic advantage of Municipal Art. There is a competition of cities just as there is a competition of individuals, and this competition has remained unrealized by the citizens of Greater New York. In fact, until recently, everything has been done, or left undone to make our city as unattractive as possible. *Municipal Affairs*

LAMPARD, Eric (1922-   )

L10 — As a type of community, the city may be regarded as a relatively permanent concentration of population, together with its diverse habitants, social arrangements and supporting activities, occupying a more or less discrete site, and having a cultural importance which differentiates it from other types of human settlement and association. In its elementary functions and rudimentary characteristics, however, a city is not clearly distinguishable from a town or even a large village. Mere size of population, surface area or density of settlement are not in themselves sufficient criteria of distinction, while many of their social correlates (division of labor, nonagricultural activity, central-place functions and creativity) characterize in varying degrees all urban communities from the small country town to the giant metropolis. *Encyclopedia Britannica*

LAND, Andrew

L11 — The gloom and glare of towns. *Ballade of the Midnight Forest*

LANDOR, Walter Savage (1775-1864)

L12 — All the cities of the earth should rise up against the man who ruins one.

L13 — The sweetest souls, like the sweetest flowers, soon canker in cities, and no purity is rarer there than the purity of delight. *Imaginary Conversations*

LANDRIEU, Moon (Mayor of New Orleans) (1930-   )

L14 — [In New Orleans] we've taxed everything that moves and everything that

stands still; and if anything moves again, we tax that, too.

L15 — Years ago, all the Mayor had to concern himself with was housekeeping chores. But that isn't where it's at today. No mayor can survive just as a housekeeper. Now he has to be a salesman, an innovator and a negotiator. *The Austin Statesman, April 28, 1971*

LANGER, Suzanne (1895-   )

L16 — The ordinary city-dweller knows nothing of the earth's productivity; he does not know the sunrise and rarely notices when the sun sets; ask him what phase the moon is in, or when the tide in the harbor is high, or even how high the average tide runs, and likely as not he cannot answer you. Seed time and harvest time are nothing to him. If he has never witnessed an earthquake, a great flood or a hurricane, he probably does not feel the power of nature as a reality surrounding his life at all. His realities are the motors that run elevators, subway trains, and cars, the steady feed of water and gas through the mains and of electricity over the wires, the crates of food-stuff that arrive by night and are spread for his inspection before his day begins, the concrete and brick, bright steel and dingy woodwork that take the place of earth and waterside and sheltering roof for him . . . Nature, as man has always known it, he knows no more. *Philosophy in a New Key*

LAQUIAN, Aprodicio (1935-   )

L17 — The city may be a crucible for social change, but not many developing countries can afford the necessary investment to turn the new urban dweller into a productive asset. *Town Drift*

LARCOM, Lucy (1824-1893)

L18 — Farewell! thou busy city, / Amid whose changing throng / I've passed a pleasant sojourn, / Though wearisome and long. / My soul is sad at leaving / The dear ones, not a few, / I've met within thy mazes, / So noble and so true. / *Farewell to New England*

LARDNER, John (1912-1960)

L19 — As a city, New York moves in the

forefront of today's great trend of great cities toward neurosis. She is confused, self-pitying, helpless and dependent. *The New York Times, February 1, 1953*

LATIMER, Hugh (1485?-1555)

L20 — All things are sold for money at Rome; and Rome is come home to our own doors. *(5th Sermon before Edward VI)*

L21 — Is there not reigning in London as much pride, as much covetousness, as much cruelty, as much oppression, as much superstition, as was in Nebo? Yes, I think, and much more, too. Therefore I say, Repent, O London, repent, repent! *Sermon on the Ploughers*

LATINI, Brunetto (1212?-1294)

L22 — When going through cities, / Go, I advise you, / In a stately manner (cortesemente). / Ride handsomely, / Head slightly bowed. / It's not urbane / To move without restraint. // And don't stare at the height / Of every house you pass. / Guard against moving / Like a man from the country; / Don't squirm like an eel, / Go self-assuredly / Through the streets and people. / *Il Tesoretto*

LATROBE, Charles J. (1801-1875)

L23 — Sharpers of every degree; peddlers, grog sellers, horse stealers . . . rogues of every description, white, black, brown and red . . . half-breeds, quarter-breeds, and men of no breeds at all. [of Chicago]

LATTING, Patience (Mayor of Oklahoma City) (1918-   )

L24 — We have been building cities for industries, business, automobiles too long. We have built cities for everybody but people. Now let's build cities for human beings. *(Speech at Southern Methodist University, April 23, 1971)*

LAURIER, (Sir) Wilfrid (1841-1919)

L25 — The subject is a delicate one. I would not wish to say anything disparaging of the capital, but it is hard to say anything good of it. Ottawa is not a handsome city and does not appear destined to become one either. *(Address, May 14, 1884)*

LAWRENCE, D.H. (1885-1930)

L26 — I knew, even while I looked at it, that it was the place where I was born, the ugly colliery townlet of dirty red brick. Even as a child, coming home from Moorgreen, I had looked up and seen the squares of miners' dwellings, built by the Company, rising from the hill-top in the afternoon light like the walls of Jerusalem, and I had wished it were a golden city. *Autobiographical Fragment*

L27 — The English are town-birds through and through, today, as the inevitable result of their complete industrialization. Yet they don't know how to build a city, how to think of one, or how to live in one.

L28 — The great city means beauty, dignity and a certain splendour. This is the side of the Englishman that has been thwarted and shockingly betrayed. *Letters to Bertrand Russell*

L29 — We live in towns from choice, when we subscribe to our great civilized form. The nostalgia for the country is not *so* important. What is important is that our towns are *false* towns — every street a blow, every corner a stab. *Ibid.*

L30 — The new cities of America are much more genuine cities, in the Roman sense, than is London or Manchester. *Phoenix*

L31 — Nottingham is a vast place sprawling towards a million, and it is nothing more than an amorphous agglomeration. There *is* no Nottingham, in the sense that there is no Siena. *Ibid.*

L32 — The real tragedy of England, as I see it, is the tragedy of ugliness. The country is so lovely: the man-made England is so vile. *Ibid.*

L33 — London seems to me like some hoary massive underworld, a hoary ponderous inferno. The traffic flows through the rigid grey streets like the rivers of hell through their banks of dry, rocky ash. *Selected Letters of D.H. Lawrence*

LAWRENCE, Gertrude (1901-1952)

L34 — In London I had been by terms poor and rich, hopeful and despondent, successful and down-and-out, utterly miserable and ecstatically dizzily happy. I belonged to London as each of us can belong to only one place on this earth. And, in the same way, London belonged to me. *A Star Danced*

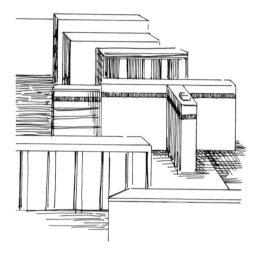

LE CORBUSIER (1887-1965)

L35 — A beautiful catastrophe. [of New York]

L36 — A city in the process of becoming. Today it belongs to the world. Without anyone expecting it, it has become the jewel in the crown of universal cities. . . . Crown of noble cities, soft pearls, or glittering topazes, or radiant lapis, or melancholy amethysts! [of New York]

L37 — The city of to-day is a dying thing because it is not geometrical. To build in the open would be to replace our present hap-hazard arrangements, which are all we have to-day, by a uniform lay-out. Unless we do this there is no salvation. *The City of Tomorrow and Its Planning*

L38 — The desire to rebuild any great city in a modern way is to engage in a formidable battle. Can you imagine people engaging in a battle without knowing their objectives? Yet that is exactly what is happening. The authorities are compelled to do something, so they give the police white sleeves or set them on horseback, they invent sound signals and light signals, they propose to put

bridges over streets or moving pavements under the streets; more garden cities are suggested, or it is decided to suppress the tramways, and so on. And these decisions are reached in a sort of frantic haste in order, as it were, to hold a wild beast at bay. That BEAST is the great city. It is infinitely more powerful than all these devices. And it is just beginning to wake. What will to-morrow bring forth to cope with it?

We must have some rule of conduct.

We must have fundamental principles for modern town planning. *Ibid.*

L39 — The great city expresses man's power and might . . . Antiquity has left us, in its various remains, a demonstration of this fact. There have been golden moments when the power of the mind dominated the rabble. We have already seen it clearly in regard to Babylon and Pekin, and they are but examples among many; great cities and smaller ones, even quite small ones, which during certain noble periods were illumined by talent, science and experience. Everywhere there are remains, or units still intact, which provide us with a model: Egyptian temples, the rectilinear cities of North Africa (e.g., Kairouan), the sacred cities of India, the Roman cities of the Empire, or those built in the great tradition: Pompeii, Aigues-Mortes, Monpazier. *Ibid.*

L40 — The structure of cities reveals two possibilities; a progressive growth, subject to chance, with resultant characteristics of slow accumulation and a gradual rise; once it has acquired its gravitational pull it becomes a centrifugal force of immense power, bringing the rush and the mob. Such was Rome; such are now Paris, London, or Berlin. *Ibid.*

L41 — Town planning has now become a sort of dumping ground for every difficult and unresolved problem such as the birth-rate, the social equilibrium, alcoholism, crime, the moral of the great city, civic affairs and so forth. *Ibid.*

L42 — The towns of to-day can only increase in density at the expense of the open spaces which are the lungs of a city.

We must increase the open spaces and diminish the distances to be covered. Therefore, the centre of the city must be constructed vertically. *Ibid.*

L43 — A hundred times have I thought New York is a catastrophe and fifty times: It is a beautiful catastrophe. *The New York Herald Tribune, August 6, 1961*

LE GALLIENNE, Richard (1866-1947)

L44 — Ah London! London! our delight, / Great flower that opens but at night, / Great city of the midnight sun, / Whose day begins when day is done. / *A Ballad of London*

L45 — Out of the cleansing night of stars and tides, / Building itself anew in the slow dawn, / The long sea-city rises: night is gone, / Day is not yet; still merciful, she hides / Her summoning brow, and still the night-car glides / Empty of faces; the night-watchmen yawn / One to the other, and shiver and pass on, / Nor yet a soul over the great bridge rides. / *Brooklyn Bridge at Dawn*

L46 — Paris, half Angel, half Grisette, / I would that I were with thee yet; / But London waits me, like a wife, / London, the love of my whole life. / *Paris Day by Day*

L47 — Yet all the while my Lord I meet / In every London lane and street. / *The Second Crucifixion*

LEADBELLY (folksinger) (1885-1949)

L48 — Home of the brave, land of the free / I don't want to be mistreated by no bourgeoisie, / Lord, it's a bourgeois town! / Tell all the colored folks to listen to me, / Don't try to buy no home in Washington D.C. / 'Cause it's a bourgeois town! // Eeee — it's a bourgeois town / I got the bourgeois blues, / Gonna spread the news all around! *(Song)*

LEE, J. Bracken (Mayor of Salt Lake City) (1899-)

L49 — I don't know of any qualifications (to be mayor). You just run for office. If you get enough votes, you could be elected if you couldn't read or write.

LEE, Rose Hum (1904-1964)

L50 — Cities are basically population aggregates which are large, heterogeneous, and densely settled within a limited land area. *The City*

LEFRAK, Samuel J. (1918-)

L51 — In the cities we centralize goods, services and people. You can take a short stroll, buy a newspaper, a painting, consult your lawyer, visit a museum, go to a show or library, and enjoy a good meal. Suburbia is filled with thousands of individual homes, each with an inefficient heating and cooling system, and dependent on the automobile and roads.... The suburbanite may claim that his castle is sacrosanct, but the high costs and inadequate transportation will hasten a return to the cities. We have to begin rebuilding our cities now in order to meet the demands of the future. *(Before Annual Real Estate Conference, July, 1975)*

LEHRER, Tom (1928-)

L52 — If you visit American city / You will find it very pretty. / Just two things of which you must beware: / Don't drink the water and don't breathe the air. / *Pollution*

L53 — Lots of things there that you can drink, / But stay away from the kitchen sink; / The breakfast garbage that you throw into the Bay, / They drink at lunch in San Jose. / *Ibid.*

LELYVELD, Joseph

L54 — Like no other city, Calcutta smothers the senses; overexposed and darkened, they cease to register. This happens even after Calcutta has exacted a measure of acceptance and fond sentiment. The evening pall of smoke with its putrefying and fruity odours, a little bougainvillaea and a lot of burning cow dung, can stir a feeling that passes for contentment. The endless jumble of undernourished bodies, some supine, others twisted into knots of stringy muscle, may register itself finally as something other than a scream; something like a dirge, with its own kind of dignity. But then, when the alarming sights, smells and sounds have receded into a recognisable, nearly comfortable reality, some commonplace incident shows how strange your commonplace has become, and throws you into a state of super-saturation. *Calcutta*

L55 — There is a slogan that a civic-minded bank has been putting up on billboards all around the city. 'Calcutta is Forever,' it proclaims. Or perhaps warns. When I first saw it, I amused myself with the thought that it was vaguely Dantesque. But if the Panchanantala Road bustee area is forever, the allusion would not be strained. It is, to be precise, one hell of a place. *Ibid.*

L'ENFANT, Pierre (1754-1825)

L56 — No nation had ever before the opportunity offered them of deliberately deciding on the spot where their Capital City should be fixed, or of combining every necessary consideration in the choice of situation, and although the means now within the power of the Country are not such as to pursue the design to any great extent, it will be obvious that the plan should be drawn on such a scale as to leave room for that aggrandizement and embellishment which the increase of the wealth of the nation will permit it to pursue at any period however remote. *Letter to George Washington, September 11, 1789*

LEO X (Pope) (1475-1521)

L57 — I should even go so far as to say that all this new Rome which we now see, large and beautiful as it is, adorned with palaces, churches and other edifices, is all built with lime made from ancient marbles.

LEO XII (Pope) (1760-1829)

L58 — Athens, that home of all learning. *Aeterni Patris*

LEOPARDI, Giacomo (1798-1837)

L59 — For I have seen and known too much, black city walls where pain and hatred follow hatred and pain. *La Vita Soletaria*

LERMONTOV, Mikhail (1814-1841)

L60 — Moscow is not an ordinary city like thousands of others; it is no silent immensity of cold stones piled one upon the other to form symmetrical patterns . . . no, indeed! It has its own soul, its own life . . . every stone is graven with its own inscription, carved by time and destiny, an inscription beyond the comprehension of the crowd but rich and rewarding in thought, feeling, and inspiration for the scholar. *A Panorama of Moscow*

LERNER, Max (1902-)

L61 — The phrase 'small town' has come itself to carry a double layer of meaning, at once sentimental and condescending. There is still a belief that democracy is more idyllic at the 'grass roots,' that the business spirit is purer, that the middle class is more intensely middling. There is also a feeling that by the fact of being small the small town somehow escapes the corruptions of life in the city and the dominant contagions that infest the more glittering places. History, geography, and economics gave each American town some distinctive traits of style that are imbedded in the mind, and the memory of this style is all the more marked because of the nostalgia felt, in a largely urban America, for what seems the lost serenity of small-town childhoods. *America as a Civilization*

LETTS, Winifred Mary (1882-)

L62 — I saw the spires of Oxford / As I was passing by, / The gray spires of Oxford / Against a pearl-gray sky. / *The Spires of Oxford*

LEVANT, Oscar (1906-1972)

L63 — Strip away the phony tinsel (and) you can find the real tinsel underneath. [of Hollywood]

LEVENSON, Sam 1911-1980)

L64 — What poor as well as rich families leave on the sidewalks these days for the Sanitation Department to cart away looks to me like the stuff people used to load on moving vans, not on dump trucks. I see lamps, umbrellas, TV sets, playpens, baby carriages, bicycles, tables, refrigerators — all cut down in the prime of life.

We have been educated to use; we shall now have to be reeducated to reuse, restore, renew and conserve. *Quoted in Reader's Digest*

LEVEY, Stanley

L65 — This capital city of high-tension activity. [of New York] *The New York Times, November 2, 1957*

LEVIN, Meyer (1905-1981)

L66 — For what is a ghetto? A tolerated

corner in a city that belonged to another people.

LEVINE, Philip (1928-)

L67 — A winter Tuesday, the city pouring fire, / Ford Rouge sulfurs the sun, Cadillac, Lincoln, / Chevy gray. The fat stacks / of breweries hold their tongues. Rags, / papers, hands, the stems of birches / dirtied with words. / *Coming Home, Detroit, 1968*

LEVINSON, Leonard Louis (1905?-1974)

L68 — Chicago — a pompous Milwaukee.

LÉVI-STRAUSS, Claude (1908-)

L69 — [We are] accustomed to associate our highest values, both material and spiritual, with urban life. *Quoted in The Exploding Cities*

L70 — The urban phenomenon, reduced to its ultimate expression . . . filth, chaos, promiscuity, congestion: ruins, huts, mud, dirt: dung, urine, pus, humours, secretions and running sores: all the things against which we expect urban life to give us organised protection, all the things we hate and guard against at such great cost. [of Indian cities] *Ibid.*

LEWIS, Cecil Day (1904-1972)

L71 — The flowers of the town are rotting away. *A Time to Dance*

LEWIS, Sinclair (1885-1951)

L72 — The retreat of all failures . . . [of Los Angeles]

L73 — Back in 1905, in America, it was almost universally known that though cities were evil and even in the farmland there were occasionally men of wrath, our villages were approximately paradise. They were always made up of small white houses under large green trees; there was no poverty and no toil worth mentioning; every Sunday, sweet-tempered, silvery pastors poured forth comfort and learning. . . . But it was Neighborliness that was the glory of the small town. In the cities, nobody knew or cared; but back home, the Neighbors were one great big jolly family. They lent you money, without questioning, to send Ed to

business college; they soothed your brow in sickness — dozens of them, twenty-four hours a day, kept charging in and soothing your brow without a moment's cessation; and when you had nevertheless passed beyond, they sat up with your corpse and your widow. *Main Street*

LIEBLING, A.J. (1904-1963)

L74 — The Second City. [of Chicago]

LILENCRON, Detlev von (1844-1909)

L75 — Whole Prague is a golden net of poems.

LILLE, Alain de (1128-1202)

L76 — A thousand roads lead men forever to Rome. *Liber Parabolarum*

LILLEY, William (III)

L77 — The biggest problem in American life today is the city. It is dying — spiritually, socially, economically, politically, even physically. In every way, the city has become a contradiction of the American ideal: its politics are unstable; its economy without promise; its communities unsafe and its people without hope, mobility or independence. Most striking of all, the new urban demographics refute the American rules of social diversity and cultural pluralism. Today, a child's coloring book for American communities would carry only one instruction for the cities: color them black. For the American city, once the country's melting pot for all races and nationalities, is rapidly becoming the exclusive and unhappy domain of the American Negro. *The American Cities*

LINCOLN, C. Eric (1924-)

L78 — Anyone who expected the election of a black Mayor to end the problems of crime, poverty, housing, unemployment and the countless other frustrations of the cities is both politically and intellectually naive. There is no magic in being black. *U.S. News & World Report, April 7, 1975*

LINDSAY, John V. (Mayor of New York) (1921-)

L79 — A government which can spend $12 billion on an antiballistic missile system, $5 billion on a single airplane (the SST), a quarter of a billion dollars to prop up an aerospace giant (Lockheed), cannot claim a lack of money to save our cities. It may not care to make the city an equal partner in America — but to say it cannot do so is hypocrisy. *to New York Democratic State Committee Advisory Council, September 17, 1971)*

L80 — The mayor has to be an activist, and I think that he's got to be willing to use the power of his office in order to lead, to innovate, to bring about changes, and to try new things. *(News Conference, October 10, 1969)*

L81 — Washington responds more vigorously to the threatened bankruptcy of a single corporation than it does to the devastation of 50 Brownsvilles across the country. This is not only the shame of our nation; it is the single greatest threat to our economic stability. *to American Insurance Association, May 19, 1971*

L82 — We (the cities) do not plead for charity. We don't look for a hand-out. We don't even ask Washington to bail us out. We simply seek the return of our own money

to our own cities where the problems are. We seek assistance based on desperate need, proven effort and demonstrated ability to manage our own affairs. *to House Ways and Means Committee, June 11, 1971*

L83 — Antipathy to the city predates the American experience. When industrialization drove the European working man into the major cities of that continent, books and pamphlets appeared attacking the city as a source of crime, corruption, filth, disease, vice, licentiousness, subversion, and high prices. The theme of some of the earliest English novels — Moll Flanders abounds in it — is that of the innocent country youth coming to the big city and being subjected to all forms of horror until justice — and a return to the pastoral life — follow. *The City*

L84 — In the American psychology, the city has been a basically suspect institution, reeking of the corruption of Europe, totally lacking that sense of spaciousness and innocence of the frontier and the rural landscape. *Ibid.*

L85 — The cities are not the problem. They are the solution. The city is not the creator of social problems, and it doesn't spread them. It solves them; for the city is the machine of social change. *The Plainview Texas Herald, October 16, 1972*

L86 — If we cannot move forward in the cities, we will move backward in America. If we fail now, the cost will far outweigh today's financial deficits. They will be measured in despair, in hatred, in bitterness and in strife. *Time, January 11, 1971*

L87 — New York has total depth in every area. Washington has only politics; after that, the second biggest thing is white marble. *Vogue, August 1, 1963*

LINDSAY, Vachel (1879-1931)

L88 — Let not your town be large, remembering / That little Athens was the muses' home, / That Oxford is the heart of London still, / That Florence gave the Renaissance to Rome. / *On the Building of Springfield*

L89 — Record it for the grandson of your son — / A city is not builded in a day: / Our little town cannot complete her soul / Till countless generations pass away. / *Ibid.*

LINKLETTER, Art (1912-)

L90 — Suburbs are things to come into the city from. *A Child's Garden of Misinformation*

LINOWITZ, Sol M. (1913-)

L91 — Today we are near the end of a long countdown for our cities — cities that are over-crowded, dirty, crime-ridden, poor and discouraged, cities that have become prisons which trap millions of people in hopeless and abject poverty. We stand at the edge of a crisis, but we seem incapable of summoning the will and the resources to rebuild the cities and reclaim the lives of the people living in them. *The Los Angeles Times, November 13, 1973*

L92 — The American people have been indifferent to the festering problems of our cities. Lacking strong moral leadership in this vital area and unwilling to pay the price in either human effort or in dollars to make urban America livable again, Americans have simply turned their backs on our cities, content to believe that as long as the cities remain quiet, all is well. Perhaps the American people are also operating on the theory that if they pretend the ghettos aren't there, they will go away. *The State of the Cities*

LIPPMANN, Walter (1889-1974)

L93 — The true view of cities is to regard them as places where the activities of the whole nation come to a head. . . . There is no way to separate the cities from the nation. Upon the cities are concentrated the extreme consequences, the concrete results, of that revolution in the manners of men's life which modern science is working.

L94 — The cities exist, but they are still felt to be alien, and in this uncertainty as to what the cities might yield up, men turn to the old scenes from which the leaders they have always trusted have come. *Men of Destiny*

LITTELL, Franklin H.

L95 — A parasitical growth, and the religion which serves it tries artificially to recollect the vision of a simple rural and village life which no longer exists. [of suburbia]

LITTLE, Rich (1938-)

L96 — Mr. President, how do you keep the Russians from invading Poland?
   Change its name to Cleveland. *(Joke)*

LIVY, Titus Livius (59 B.C.-17 A.D.)

L97 — If any people should be permitted to consecrate its own origins and attribute them to the gods, the military glory of the Roman people is such that when they call Mars their father and the father of their founder, the nations of men might as well put up with it as calmly as they endure Rome's domination.

L98 — The fates were resolved, I believe, upon the founding of this great city and the beginning of the mightiest of empires, next after that of heaven. [of Rome] *Ab Urbe Condita Libri*

L99 — Once Rome's neighbors had considered her not so much as a city as an armed camp in their midst threatening the general peace; now they came to revere her so profoundly as a community dedicated wholly to worship, that the mere thought of offering her violence seemed to them like sacrilege. *History I*

LLOYD, Roger

L100 — The City is an orderly arrangement of purified relationships between persons, and it exists, and is there to be verified, wherever the relationships of nature have paid the price of becoming relationships in Christ. *The Manchester Guardian Weekly*

LLOYD GEORGE, David (1863-1945)

L101 — Who is the landlord? The landlord is a gentleman who does not earn his wealth. He does not even take the trouble to receive his wealth. He has a host of people around him to do the actual spending for him. He never sees it until he comes to enjoy it. His sole function, his chief pride, is stately consumption of wealth produced by others. *(Speech at Limehouse, July 30, 1909)*

LONG, Norton (1910-)

L102 — The older conception of the walled city as a shared common enterprise has been weakened by the breaching of its walls and its transformation into an open economy. The nation-state has increasingly insisted that national citizens, even noncitizens, be accorded all or almost all the rights and privileges accorded local citizens. What is the point of belonging to an organization that all may join and none need join to enjoy all its privileges. *The Unwalled City*

LONGFELLOW, Henry Wadsworth (1807-1882)

L103 — Even cities have their graves! *Amalfi*

L104 — I have an affection for a great city. I feel safe in the neighborhood of man, and enjoy the sweet security of streets. *The Great Metropolis*

L105 — To say the least, a town life makes one more tolerant and liberal in one's judgement of others. *Hyperion*

L106 — Better like Hector in the field to die, / Than like a perfumed Paris turn and fly. / [of Troy] *Morituri Salutamus*

L107 — In the valley of the Pegnitz, where across broad meadow-lands / Rise the blue Franconian mountains, Nuremberg, the ancient, stands. / *Nuremberg*

L108 — One if by land, and two if by sea; / And I on the opposite shore will be, / Ready to ride and spread the alarm / Through every Middlesex village and farm. / *Tales of a Wayside Inn*

L109 — A town that boasts inhabitants like me / Can have no lack of good society. / *Ibid.*

L110 — White swan of cities, slumbering in thy nest / So wonderfully built among the reeds / Of the lagoon, that fences thee and feeds, / As sayeth thy old historian and thy guest! / [of Venice] *Venice*

LONGSTREET, Stephen (1907-)

L111 — Los Angeles has always been the goal of the footloose and the curious, the polymorphous hustler. *All Star Cast*

L112 — In Chicago, fire was always a simple certainty. *Chicago, 1860-1919*

L113 — Mudtown was another favorite name for early Chicago in the 1830s. Its mud was notorious for deepness, stickiness, color, and smell. A private letter said: 'Stunk like original sin, clung like piglets to a sow's dugs . . . .' *Ibid.*

LORCA, Federico Garcia (1899-1936)

L114 — Dawn in New York bears / four pillars of slime / and a storm of black pigeons / that dabble dead water. // Dawn in New York grieves / on the towering stairs / seeking on ledges / pangs traced upon nard. / *Dawn*

L115 — Seville is a tower / Full of fine archers. // Seville for hurting / And Cordoba to die. // A city lying in ambush / with endless rhythms / Which, by twist and by

coil, / She weaves into a labyrinth, / Or
blood-red grapevine's / Tentacle. / *Sevilla*

LORIMER, George Horace (1868-1937)

L116 — We don't have much use for poetry
in Chicago, except in streetcar ads. *The
Saturday Evening Post*

LOVE, Edmund (1912-   )

L117 — New York attracts the most talented
people in the world in the arts and
professions. It also attracts them in other
fields. Even the bums are talented. *Subways
Are for Sleeping*

LOWELL, Amy (1874-1925)

L118 — The sight of a white church above
thin trees in a city square / Amazes my eyes
as though it were the Parthenon.
/ *Meeting-House Hill*

L119 — A near horizon whose sharp jags /
Cut brutally into a sky / Of leaden heaviness,
and crags / Of houses lift their masonry /
Ugly and foul, and chimneys lie / And snort,
outlined against the gray / of lowhung cloud.
I hear the sigh / The goaded city gives, not
day / Nor night can ease her heart, her
anguished labours stay. / *New York at Night*

L120 — All Naples prates of this and that,
and runs about its little business, shouting,
bawling, incessantly calling its
wares. *Sea-Blue and Blood-Red*

L121 — The city is squalid and sinister, /
With the silver-barred street in the midst. /
Slow-moving, / A river leading nowhere.
/ *Sword Blades and Poppy Seeds*

LOWELL, James Russell (1819-1891)

L122 — Cities rob men of eyes and hands
and feet, / Patching one hole of many
incomplete; / The general preys upon the
individual mind, / And each alone is helpless
as the wind. / *The Pioneer*

L123 — I du believe in Freedom's cause, / Ez
fur away ez Payris is; / I love to see her stick
her claws / In them infarnal Phayrisees; / It's
wal enough again a king / To dror resolves
an' triggers, — / But libbaty's a kind o'thing
/ Thet don't agree with niggers. / *The Pius
Editor's Creed*

LOWELL, Robert (1917-1977)

L124 — Oh Florence, Florence, patroners of
the lovely tyrannicides! *Florence*

L125 — Man is the root of everything he
builds; / no nature, except the human, loves
New York. / *The Heavenly Rain*

**LUBBOCK, John (Lord Avebury)
(1834-1913)**

L126 — In London we may suffer, but no one
has any excuse for being dull. *The Pleasures
of Life*

LUCANUS (39-65)

L127 — Troy was.

LUCRETIUS, Titus (c. 99-55 B.C.)

L128 — Parent of Rome! by gods and men
beloved, / Benignant Venus! thou, the
sail-clad main / And fruitful earth, as round
the seasons roll, / With life who swellest, for
by thee all live, / And, living, hail the
cheerful light of day . . . / *Invocation to
Venus*

**LUGAR, Richard G. (Mayor of Indianapolis)
(1932-   )**

L129 — The problems of the cities are
considerable; but they are unlikely to be
worked out satisfactorily by indulging in an
excess amount of self-pity and merely
indicating that we are charitable wards that
must be picked up by somebody else.

LUTHER, Martin (1483-1546)

L130 — Whoever goes to Rome for the first
time is looking for a rogue; whoever goes
again will find him; and whoever goes the
third time will return with him. *Quoted in
Rein's Luther*

LYNCH, Kevin (1918-   )

L131 — Every citizen has had long
associations with some part of his city, and
his image is soaked in memories and
meanings. *The Image of the City*

L132 — Looking at cities can give a special
pleasure, however commonplace the sight

may be. Like a piece of architecture, the city is a construction in space, but one of vast scale, a thing perceived only in the course of long spans of time. City design is therefore a temporal art, but it can rarely use the controlled and limited sequences of other temporal arts like music. *Ibid.*

LYNES, Russell (1910-   )

L133 — Beautiful as our skyscraper cities may be, no one has ever had the temerity to call them tasteful. *The Tastemakers*

LYONS, Louis M. (1897-1982)

L134 — That Boston is peculiar is one of the accepted facts of life in America. It is a baffling peculiarity that reaches through every aspect of the city's existence. *Boston, Study in Inertia*

M

McALMON, Robert (1895-1956)

M1 — I knew all too well that Paris is a bitch; and that one shouldn't become infatuated with bitches; particularly when they have wit, imagination, experience and tradition.

MACAPAGAL, Diosdado (1910-)

M2 — Truly the City of Man. It is humanity in microcosm, reflecting the infinite variety as well as the infinite capacity for good or evil of the human race. [of New York City]

MACAULAY, Thomas Babington (1800-1859)

M3 — In lordly Lacedaemon, / The city of two kings. / *The Battle of Lake Regillus*

M4 — One of us two, Herminius, /Shall never more go home. / I will lay on for Tusculum / And lay thou on for Rome! / *Ibid.*

M5 — As to the effect of the manufacturing system on the bodily health, we must beg leave to estimate it by . . . the proportion of births and deaths. We know that, during the growth of this atrocious system . . . there has been a greater diminution of mortality — and that this diminution has been greater in the manufacturing towns than anywhere else. *Edinburgh Review*

M6 — The harvests of Arretium, / This year, old men shall reap. / This year, young boys in Umbro / Shall plunge the struggling sheep; / And in the vats of Luna, / This year, the must shall foam / Round the white feet of laughing girls / Whose sires have marched to Rome. / *Horatius*

M7 — Round turned he, as not deigning / Those craven ranks to see; / Nought spake he to Lars Porsena, / To Sextus nought spake he; / But he saw on Platinus / The white porch of his home; / And he spoke to the noble river / That rolls by the towers of Rome. / *Ibid.*

M8 — Thrice looked he at the city; / Thrice looked he at the dead; / And thrice came on in fury, / And thrice turned back in dread. / [of Rome] *Ibid.*

M9 — Wherever literature consoles sorrow or assuages pain; wherever it brings gladness to eyes which fail with wakefulness and tears, and ache for the dark house and the long sleep, — there is exhibited in its noblest form the immortal influence of Athens. *Milford's History of Greece*

M10 — She (the Roman Catholic Church) may still exist in undiminished vigour when some traveller from New Zealand shall, in the midst of a vast solitude, take his stand on a broken arch of London Bridge to sketch the ruins of St. Paul's. *On Ranke's History of the Popes*

McBRIDE, Mary Margaret (1899-1976)

M11 — Terrible things happen to young girls in New York City. *A Long Way From Missouri*

McCARTHY, Mary (1912-)

M12 — A wholly materialistic city is nothing but a dream incarnate. Venice is the world's unconscious: a miser's glittering hoard, guarded by a Beast whose eyes are made of white agate, and by a saint who is really a prince who has just slain a dragon. *Venice Observed*

McCORD, David

M13 — A pedestrian is a man in danger of his life; a walker is a man in possession of his soul. *Quoted in Reader's Digest*

McDERMOTT, John J. (1932-   )

M14 — On the one hand, we lament the city as being without nature. On the other hand, the nature we have in mind and about which we are nostalgic is stripped of its most forbidding qualities: loneliness, unpredictability, and the terrors of the uninhabitable. *The Culture of Experience*

McDONAGH, Edward

M15 — You find it driving to work, alongside all those other people, but alone with your thoughts. The car has become a secular sanctuary for the individual, his shrine to the self, his mobile Walden Pond. *Time, May 10, 1963*

McFARLAND, James

M16 — In cities densely populated / The poor are apt to dwell, / And to describe their misery, / Is more than tongue can tell . . . / We find no form of diction, / To adequately describe the poverty / Of a tenement-house eviction. / *Miscellaneous Poems*

McGINLEY, Phyllis (1905-1978)

M17 — To condemn Suburbia has long been a literary cliche. . . . I have yet to read a book in which the suburban life was pictured as the good life or the commuter as a sympathetic figure. He is nearly as much a stock character as the old stage Irishman: the man who 'spends his life riding to and from his wife,' the eternal Babbit who knows all about Buicks and nothing about Picasso, whose sanctuary is the club locker room, whose ideas spring ready-made from the illiberal newspapers. His wife plays politics at the P.T.A. and keeps up with the Joneses. *A Short Walk from the Station*

McHARG, Ian L. (1920-   )

M18 — It is my proposition that, to all practical purposes, western man remains obdurately pre-Copernican, believing that he bestrides the earth round which the sun, the galaxy, and the very cosmos revolve. This delusion has fueled our ignorance in time past and is directly responsible for the prodigal destruction of nature and for the encapsulating burrows that are the dysgenic city. *Values, Process and Form*

MACHIAVELLI, Niccolo (1469-1527)

M19 — Whoever becomes the ruler of a free city and does not destroy it, can expect to be destroyed by it, for it can always find a motive for rebellion in the name of liberty and of its ancient usages, which are forgotten neither by lapse of time nor by benefits received; and whatever one does or provides so long as the inhabitants are not separated or dispersed, they do not forget that name and those usages, but appeal to them at once in every emergency, as did Pisa after so many years held in servitude by the Florentines. *The Prince*

MacKAYE, Benton (1879-1975)

M20 — Look over yonder there at the Hudson Highlands (you do not even need your field glasses). In those hills there lives a man who recently made his first visit to New York. He had lived a long life within fifty miles from Times Square, and in spite of the Sunday supplement had no real notion of a metropolis. Yonder in the Appalachian hinterland there dwells another world. This world is the indigenous America. It is being invaded (but is not yet captured) by metropolitan America. *The New Exploration*

M21 — A railway may stop running, or a city may disappear: but the earth itself, as a receiver and storer of solar energy, as a hoarder and container of soils and metals and potential vegetation-that does not alter: it can never basically alter. . . . *Ibid.*

MacKAYE, M.

M22 — Phoenix . . . is Palm Beach, Red Gap and Mr. Babbitt's Zenith all rolled into one. *Saturday Evening Post*

McKEE, H.S. (1868-1956)

M23 — The most conspicuous fact about Los Angeles lies in its being a residential and not an industrial community. The half million people who reside here did not come here in any considerable numbers to engage in business; they came to reside.

MACLEISH, Archibald (1892-   )

M24 — Be proud New-York of your prize

domes / And your docks & the size of your
doors & your dancing / Elegant clean big
girls & your / Niggers with narrow heels &
the blue on their / Bad mouths & your bars
& your automo- / biles in the struck steel
light & your / Bright Jews & your
sorrow-sweet singing / Tunes & your signs
wincing out in the wet, / Cool shine & the
twinges of / Green against evening . . . .
/ & Forty-Second Street

McLUHAN, Marshall (1911-1980)

M25 — The circuited city of the future
will . . . be an information megalopolis.
What remains of the configuration of former
'cities' will be very much like World's Fairs
— places in which to show off new
technology, not places of work or residence.
They will be preserved museumlike . . . like
so many Williamsburgs.

M26 — The full-blown city coincides with
the development of writing — especially of
phonetic writing, the specialist form of
writing that makes a division between sight
and sound. *Understanding Media*

M27 — The steam railroad as an accelerator
proved to be one of the most revolutionary
of all extensions of our physical bodies,
creating a new political centralism and a
new kind of urban shape and size. It is to the
railroad that the American city owes its
abstract grid layout, and the nonorganic
separation of production, consumption, and
residence. It is the motorcar that scrambled
the abstract shape of the industrial town,
mixing up its separated functions to a
degree that has frustrated and baffled both
planner and citizen. It remained for the
airplane to complete the confusion by
amplifying the mobility of the citizen to the
point where urban space as such was
irrelevant. *Ibid*.

MacNAMARA, Edward

M28 — A place where the inmates are in
charge of the asylum. [of Hollywood]

McPHERSON, Aimee Semple (1890-1944)

M29 — God's great blueprint for man's
abode on earth. [of Los Angeles]

McPHERSON, Simon John

M30 — The city has always been the
decisive battle ground of civilization and
religion. It intensifies all the natural
tendencies of man. From its fomented
energies, as well as from its greater weight
of numbers, the city controls. Ancient
civilizations rose and fell with their leading
cities. In modern times, it is hardly too
much to say, 'as goes the city so goes the
world.'

McQUEEN, Steve (1930?-1980)

M31 — I'd rather wake up in the middle of
nowhere than in any city on earth.

MADDEN, Carl H. (1920-1978)

M32 — The urban crisis — mainly a
problem of class, race, unemployment,
poverty, education, and crime — is also a
problem of land use. Our lack of appropriate
land-use policies is in part responsible for
the present state of affairs. We have brought
both suburban sprawl and inner city blight
upon ourselves by our lack of vision and our
absolutist views of ownership and use of the
land. *Land as a National Resource*

MAIER, Henry W. (Mayor of Milwaukee) (1918-   )

M33 — Basically, the . . . central cities of the
country have to handle the young and the
attendant costs and the aged and the
attendant costs and the poor and the
attendant costs. These three classes in our
society — services to the poor, education for
the young, recreation for the young and aid
to the aged — are the most expensive
business we (in the cities) have. *TV-radio
Interview, June 18, 1972*

M34 — The crisis in our cities cannot be
solved by Presidential proclamation that
the urban crisis is over. Nor can it be solved
by the 'Vietnamization' of our urban
problems — the pulling out of
vitally-necessary Federal programs and
paying the cities to try to cope with an
already over-burdened property tax, the
most unpopular and unfair in the
land. *(Before Ad Hoc Senate Committee,
Washington, June 14, 1973)*

M35 — We, along with other cities, are part of a deepening trend. That trend is toward an ever-growing concentration of the poor, and the relatively poor, in the central cities of America. New York just got hit first with its current fiscal crisis. It's time to factor out the real causes of the dilemma. All large cities are in the trend New York is in. It's a matter of time. *The New York Times, September 29, 1975*

MAILER, Norman (1923-   )

M36 — New York cannot begin to solve its budgetary problems until it becomes the 51st state. *(Interview, May 12, 1969)*

M37 — Chicago is the great American city. New York is one of the capitals of the world and Los Angeles is a constellation of plastic, San Francisco is a lady, Boston has become Urban Renewal, Philadelphia and Baltimore and Washington wink like dull diamonds in the smog of Eastern Megalopolis, and New Orleans is unremarkable past the French Quarter. Detroit is a one-trade town, Pittsburgh has lost its golden triangle, St. Louis has become the golden arch of the corporation, and nights in Kansas City close early. The oil depletion allowance makes Houston and Dallas naught but checkerboards for this sort of game. But Chicago is a great American city. Perhaps it is the last of the great American cities. *Miami and the Siege of Chicago*

M38 — Only a great city provides honest spectacle, for that is the salvation of the schizophrenic soul. Chicago may have beasts on the street, it may have a giant of fortitude for Mayor who grew into a beast — a man with the very face of Chicago — but it is an honest town, it does not look to incubate psychotics along an air-conditioned corridor with a vinyl floor. *Ibid.*

M39 — By the most brutal view, New York City is today a legislative pail of dismembered organs strewn from Washington to Albany. *The New York Times Magazine, May 18, 1965*

M40 — How is one to speak of the illness of a city? A clear day can come, a morning in early May like the pride of June. The streets are cool, the buildings have come out of shadow, and silences are broken by the voices of children. It is as if the neighborhood has slept in the winding sheet of the past. Forty-years go by — one can recollect the milkman and the clop of a horse. It is a great day. Everyone speaks of the delight of the day on the way to work. It is hard on such mornings to believe that New York is the victim 'etherized on a table.' *The New York Times Magazine, May 18, 1965*

M41 — The ills of New York cannot be solved by money. New York will be ill until it is magnificent. For New York must be ready to show the way to the rest of Western civilization. Until it does, it will be no more than the victim of the technological revolution no matter how much money it receives in its budget. Money bears the same relation to social solutions that water does to blood. *The New York Times Magazine, May 18, 1965*

MAKELY, William (1932-   )

M42 — The man who says 'It's a nice place to visit, but I wouldn't want to live there' feels the tug of city life just as strongly as the man who says 'What is there beyond the Hudson' — about the tug toward the city. 'The grass is always greener,' because quite often it is brown, but the idea is the same: curiosity to know what goes on in the city — what strange delights keep the urban dweller in his madhouse of crowding and noise and smoke — draws in anyone who has not completely closed his mind. *City Life*

MALAMUD, Bernard (1914-   )

M43 — In New York who needs an atom bomb? If you walked away from a place they tore it down. *The Tenants*

MANET, Edouard (1832-1883)

M44 — The country only has charms for those not obliged to stay there.

MANN, Thomas (1875-1955)

M45 — One of the most magical cities on earth — in its old beauty she surpasses much of what is Italian. [of Prague]

M46 — Hardest of all to bear, at times completely insufferable, was the thought that he would never see Venice again, that this was a leave-taking for ever. Since it had been shown for the second time that the city affected his health, since he was compelled for the second time to get away in all haste, from now on he would have to consider it a place impossible and forbidden to him, a place which he was not equal to, and which it would be foolish for him to visit again. *Death in Venice*

MANSFIELD, C.B.

M47 — Buenos Aires! What a misnomer! the first thing that greeted our eyes on landing was the skinless carcass of a horse lying on the beach on one side of the landing-place; the second, another ditto on the other side; and the 'good air' of the town was the stench thereof. . . . There is something most delicious about the air of this place, notwithstanding the horrible stenches from the putrid flesh all about the town. *Paraguay, Brazil, and the Plate*

MANSFIELD, Katherine (1888-1923)

M48 — Yes, large towns are the absolute devil! Oh, how glad I shall be to get away — the difficulty to work is really appalling — one gets no distraction. By distraction I mean the sky and the grass and trees and little birds. I absolutely pine for the country . . . I could kiss the grass. *Katherine Mansfield: The Memories of LM*

MAO TSE-TUNG (1893-1976)

M49 — Can the countryside defeat the cities? The answer is that it is difficult, but it can be done . . . The question of China's cities and countryside today is qualitatively different from that of the cities and countryside in capitalist countries abroad. In capitalist countries, the cities rule the countryside in reality as well as in outward form, and when the head constituted by the cities is cut off, the four limbs of the countryside cannot continue to exist. It is impossible to conceive of a protracted guerilla war carried on by the peasants in the countryside against the cities in a country such as England, America, France, Germany, Japan, etc. Such a thing is also impossible in a small semi-colonial country . . . *Quoted in Schram, The Political Thought of Mao Tse-tung*

M50 — If we rely fundamentally on organizing a resolute, prolonged and widespread war of resistance against the enemy who has occupied our cities, if we wage war on many interlocking fronts, encircle the cities and isolate them, meanwhile gradually increasing our own strength over a long period, and so transform the relations between the enemy and ourselves; and if we coordinate these tactics with changes in the international situation — in this case, we will be able to drive out the enemy progressively and to regain control of the cities. There is not the slightest doubt that it is difficult, even in China today, for the countryside to oppose the cities. For the cities as a whole are concentrated, whereas the countryside is scattered. *Ibid.*

M51 — It is very necessary for educated young people to go to the countryside to be re-educated by the poor and lower-middle peasants. Cadres and other people in the cities should be persuaded to send their sons and daughters who have finished junior or senior middle school, college or university to the countryside. *Ibid.*

M52 — With regard to attacking cities, resolutely to seize all weakly defended fortified enemy points and cities. To seize at opportune moments all moderately defended fortified enemy points and cities if circumstances permit. As for strongly defended fortified enemy points and cities, to wait until conditions are ripe and then take them. *Ibid.*

MARAGALL, Juan (1860-1911)

M53 — Oh! Happy the city with a mountain beside it, for it can admire itself from on high. [of Barcelona]

MARAINI, Fosco (1912-)

M54 — The flourishing city that now stands on the site of so many other cities may have little remaining of the past. But cities are made not only of stone. There is an immortal continuity in the people of Tokyo that transcends the endings and beginnings of the physical city. *The Great Cities/Tokyo*

M55 — Understandably, Tokyo is not a city to speak of in terms of beauty — at least in any conventional terms. But it has a magic all its own. It takes you by the neck, shakes you, turns you inside out and then only slowly does it reveal its heart. *Ibid.*

M56 — Anyone with some familiarity with the history of Jerusalem throughout the centuries can thank the gods for one thing only: that blood isn't indelible, that it melts away with the rain, dries in the sun and disappears. If blood were indelible, Jerusalem would be red, all red. *Jerusalem, Rock of Ages*

M57 — Certainly Rome was stronger, more splendid than Jerusalem, Babylon knew greater luxury, London and New York are infinitely bigger and richer, Paris may be more learned, Florence more sophisticated, Vienna gayer, but all had or have limits to their floruit, they were and are not, or were not and are. Jerusalem, accursed or holy as one pleases, has existed for three thousand years, truly marked by destiny, herself immortal dealer of destinies. *Ibid.*

M58 — In Jerusalem man and stone meet, converge. The stones of Jerusalem are scored with contact with men, and here men sign themselves in stone. The stones of

Jerusalem are no ordinary stones; each one has a past that may have been dramatic and terrible; if they could speak, they would tell not only of crystallization and erosion, like those of rivers and mountains, but also of tears and the warmth of bodies, sometimes of merrymaking, more often of what men have shrieked out *in extremis*. *Ibid.*

MARCHAND, Jean (1918-)

M59 — The best thing about Ottawa is the train to Montreal.

MARIANI, John

M60 — If Monaco were a planet unto itself, Liechtenstein would be a solar system, Andorra a galaxy, and Rhode Island would take on the dimensions of a virtual universe. In fact, Monaco would easily fit twice into New York's Central Park, and only Vatican City can claim by comparison that less is more. *MD Magazine, August, 1982*

MARIATEGUI, Jose Carlos (1894-1930)

M61 — Any great modern capital has had a complex formation, deeply rooted in tradition. Lima, however, has had a somewhat arbitrary beginning. Founded by a conquistador, a foreigner, Lima appears to have originated as the military tent of a commander from some distant land. Lima did not compete with other cities to win its title as capital. The creature of an aristocratic age, Lima was born into nobility and was baptized City of Kings. *Seven Interpretive Essays on Peruvian Reality*

MARINEO, Lucio Siculo (1444?-1536)

M62 — Citizens of all ages were gifted in both the liberal and applied arts by which the city flourished. People without jobs did not exist, they all had their occupations. For this reason there were no poor people, and all the people lived correctly and with plenty of money. [of Barcelona]

MARION, Frances (1886-1973)

M63 — San Franciscans look upon the city of the Queen of the Angels as California's floating kidney transplanted from the Middle West. *1914 through 1924*

MARKEY, Morris (1899-   )

M64 — As I wandered about Los Angeles, looking for the basic meaning of the place, the fundamental source of its wealth and its economic identity, I found myself quite at sea. The Chamber of Commerce people told me about the concentration of fruit, the shipping, the Western branch factories put up by concerns in the East. But none of these things seemed the cause of a city. They seemed rather the effect, rising from an inexplicable accumulation of people — just as the immense dealings in second-hand automobiles and the great turnover of real estate were an effect. It struck me as an odd thing that here, alone of all the cities in America, there was no plausible answer to the question, 'Why did a town spring up here and why has it grown so big?'

MARKHAM, Edwin (1852-1940)

M65 — Why build these cities glorious / If man unbuilded goes? / In vain we build the world, unless / The builder also grows. / *Man-Making*

MAROT, Clement (1495?-1544)

M66 — Paris, thou hast made me oft afeard / And pursued me even unto death. /

MARQUIS, Don (1878-1937)

M67 — Most of the people living in New York have come here from the farm to try to make enough money to go back to the farm.

M68 — Go down into the city. Mingle with the details; . . . your elation and your illusion vanish like ingenuous snowflakes that have kissed a hot dog sandwich on its fiery brow. *The Almost Perfect State*

MARTIAL, Marcus Valerius (c. 40-c. 104)

M69 — The country in town. *Epigrams*

M70 — In all the city there is no man who is so near yet so far from me . . . [as my next-door neighbor]. *Ibid.*

MARTIN, John Bartlow (1915-   )

M71 — The city roared with life, traffic sped up the Outer Drive, trucks rumbled down Western Avenue, and elevated trains roared by overhead on the wondrous El, reared against the sky. Randolph Street in the theatrical district blazed with light nightlong. . . . And always there was the wonderful lake, a limitless inland sea. It was all rather innocent foolishness. Today the El no longer seems romantic to me, just an obsolete nuisance. The slums are not picturesque, just appalling; Randolph Street and Rush Street not glamorous, just tinsel cheap; gangsterism not exciting, just dreary and dangerous. But this change is in me, not in the city, and I have no doubt that only yesterday some other young man got off a train from Indiana, longing for excitement and opportunity, and found it here. [of Chicago] *The Saturday Evening Post, October 15, 1960*

MARTINDALE, Don (1915-   )

M72 — A blase attitude develops in the city as a product of the rapidly changing context of contrasting experiences. *The Theory of the City*

M73 — Communities are organized for defense and for mutual economic advantage. When a community reaches a point of culmination — the limits of the economic advantage that occasioned the population aggregation — it must either stabilize, re-cycle, or disintegrate. *Ibid.*

M74 — Every device in the city facilitating trade and industry prepares the way for further division of labor and further specialization of tasks. As a result there is a continuous breakdown of older traditional, social and economic structures based on family ties, local associations, culture, caste, and status with the substitution of an order resting on occupation and vocational interests. *Ibid.*

M75 — In city social life, punctuality, calculabilty and exactness are required by the very complexity of life, intimately connected with money economy and intellectualism. *Ibid.*

M76 — The individual is no longer required to take up arms and man its walls — and with this the city no longer figures in his hopes and dreams as a unit of survival, as a structure that must marshal his supreme loyalties since it may ask his very life. The destruction of the city no longer represents the extinction of the institutions of social life. *Ibid.*

M77 — The metropolitan man is subject to an unusual volume of stimulation and he develops a mentality protecting himself against elements in the external environment which would uproot him. This means that he must react with his head rather than his heart — to yield to deep emotional reactions is to be crushed. His environment intensifies his awareness, not his feeling, leading to a dominance of intelligence. Intellectuality, which extends in many directions with the specialization of the urban environment, is characteristic of the city. *Ibid.*

M78 — The modern city is losing its external and formal structure. Internally it is in a state of decay while the new community represented by the nation everywhere grows at its expense. The age of the city seems to be at an end. *Ibid.*

M79 — The observation that man thinks, feels, responds differently in the city than outside it is old as the city itself. *Ibid.*

M80 — The theory of the city somehow cannot account for what every journalist, poet, and novelist knows — the city is a living thing. *Ibid.*

M81 — There are moments in every city dawn when the circles, rectangles, polygons, and triangles — the geometry of the city — seem to float in the mist, like the essence of the human spirit emancipated from the earth. There are times, on starlit nights, when its towers and spires ram upward as if to tear the darkness loose from its riveting stars and the city seems to be a strident assertion of mankind against time itself. *Ibid.*

M82 — The ultimate armed units of modern society are not tribes, or castle-dwelling nobles, nor cities, but states. The modern city is militarily negligible even as politically it has become a subordinate unit. With atomic weapons the city may have become the great death trap of modern man. *Ibid.*

MARVELL, Andrew (1621-1678)

M83 — Hence Amsterdam — Turk, Christian, Pagan, Jew, / Stable of sects and mint of schism grew: / That bank of conscience where not one so strange / Opinion but finds credit and exchange. /

MARY I (Queen of England) (1516-1558)

M84 — When I am dead and opened, you shall find 'Calais' lying in my heart. *Quoted in Holinshed's Chronicle*

MARYANNA, Sister

M85 — I never tire of singing my own 'Manhattan Magnificat'. . . . Often I look out of my sixth floor window at midnight or an early hour of the morning at the squares of gold and topaz and I pray for all the worry-weary souls behind those windows — and the glad and gay ones, too. For there is gaiety in this sprawling metropolis. You hear it in the cheep of sparrows in the park, the laughter of children in playgrounds, the banter of taxi drivers lightly insulting other motorists, and it is a truer gaiety than that which glitters in the night spots or theatres, where visitors so often seek it. *The New York Daily News, April 9, 1960*

MARX, Groucho (1890-1977)

M86 — I'm leaving because the weather is too good. I hate London when it's not raining. *(news item, June 28, 1954)*

MARX, Karl (1818-1883) and Friedrich ENGELS (1820-1895)

M87 — The bourgeoisie has subjected the country to the rule of the towns. It has created enormous cities, has greatly increased the urban population as compared with the rural, and has thus rescued a considerable part of the population from the idiocy of rural life. Just as it has made the country dependent on the towns, so it has made barbarian and semi-barbarian countries dependent on the civilized ones, nations of peasants on nations of bourgeois, the East on the West. *The Class Struggle and the Change from Feudalism to Capitalism*

MARX, Karl (1818-1883)

M88 — The more rapidly capital accumulates in an industrial or commercial town, the more rapidly flows the stream of exploitable human material and the more miserable are the improvised dwellings of the labourers. *Das Kapital*

M89 — Ancient classical history is the history of cities, but cities based on landownership and agriculture; Asian history is a kind of undifferentiated unity of town and country (the large city, properly speaking, must be regarded merely as a princely camp superimposed on the real economic structure); the Middle Ages (Germanic-feudal period) starts with the countryside as the locus of history, whose further development then proceeds through the opposition of town and country; modern history is the urbanization of the countryside, not, as among the ancients the ruralization of the city. *Grundrisse*

MARX, Leo (1919-)

M90 — Most American cities, after all, have been built since the onset of industrialization, and unlike London, Paris, or Rome, they embody relatively few features of any social order other than that of industrial capitalism. If the American city is perceived chiefly as the locus of a particular socio-economic order, that view accords with the historical fact that millions of Americans have moved to cities, not because they preferred urban to rural life, but rather because of the inescapable coercion of a market economy. *The Puzzle of Anti-Urbanism*

MASEFIELD, John (1878-1967)

M91 — Friends and loves we have none, nor wealth, nor blest abode, / But the hope, the burning hope, and the road, the lonely road. / Not for us are content, and quiet, and peace of mind, / For we go seeking a city that we shall never find. / *The Seekers*

M92 — Oh London Town's a fine town, and London sights are rare, / And London ale is right ale, and brisk's the London air. / *London Town*

M93 — One road leads to London, / One road runs to Wales, / My road leads me seawards / To the white dipping sails. / *Roadways*

MASTERMAN, C.F.G. (1873-1927)

M94 — As of Nineveh there remains but a heap, and of Tyrus a spit of sandy shore, and of Sagesta but one solemn temple looking down the valley to the sea, so a triumphant imagination can fling off the yoke of the present, to see in solid England dynamic instead of static forces, all the cities in motion and flow towards some unknown ends. *The Condition of England*

M95 — The Crowd consciousness and the city upbringing must of necessity act as a disintegrating force, tearing the family into pieces. *Ibid.*

M96 — The . . . characteristic *physical* type of town dweller: stunted, narrow-chested, easily wearied; yet voluble, excitable, with little ballast, stamina, or endurance — seeking stimulus in drink, in betting, in any unaccustomed conflicts at home or abroad. Upon these city generations there has operated the now widely spread *mental* change; each individual has been endowed with the power of reading, and a certain dim and cloudy capacity for comprehending what he reads. *The Heart of the Empire*

M97 — Gazing . . . upon the multitudinous desolation of a great city in its interminable acreage of crowded humanity, one realizes as never before the Burden of London — London as it has been called, 'the visible type of a universe hastening confusedly to unknown ends and careless of individual pain.' Here are lives not even kindled by the resourcefulness, subtlety, and individual enterprise of the avowed criminal; but in incredible multitude, shabby, ineffective, battered into futility by the ceaseless struggle of life. *Ibid.*

M98 — 'Merrie England' is emphatically a place of villages and small towns, with open spaces and the perpetual presence of the natural world. Englishmen packed for their lives in the labyrinths of drab streets that make up the greater part of London acquire a life of 'mechanic pacing to and fro,' varied only by occasional outbursts of brutalising and unlovely pleasure. *Ibid.*

M99 — Virtually ... the only forces operating among the new city race, the only attempts at spiritual or collective effort with which any dweller in it is ever likely to come into contact, are the forces of the older creeds of Christianity ... the Churches to-day present to the observer the most hopeful machinery to the warfare against the degenerating influences of modern town life. *Ibid.*

MASTERS, Edgar Lee (1869?-1950)

M100 — Go into any community of the kind I am speaking of and you'll find this process going on. The town is being made a ganglion of the city. Telephone and telegraph wires make it part of the metropolis, the radio, the automobile, the airplane, the city newspaper, the magazines carrying Paris fashions, the standard cigar stores, the standard grocery stores, the standard drug stores, machine gas stations, everything that the city can boast of, the small town of today can boast of. The privately owned canning companies, lumber mills, are taken over by large corporations who run them more cheaply and more efficiently. Industrialism is in the saddle; it is America. This is a country of monopolies and the

small towns long preserved from this influence are being drawn into the net. *The New York Times Book Review, September 9, 1924*

MATHER, Cotton (1663-1728)

M101 — Come hither, and I will show you, an admirable Spectacle! 'Tis an Heavenly CITY.... A CITY to be inhabited by an Innumerable Company of Angels, and by the Spirits of Just Men ... Put on thy beautiful Garments, O America, the Holy City! *Theopolis Americana: An Essay on the Golden Street of the Holy City 1710*

MAUGHAM, W. Somerset (1874-1965)

M102 — In great cities men are like a lot of stones thrown together in a bag: their jagged corners are rubbed off till in the end they are as smooth as marbles. *The Summing Up*

M103 — Though you may be reminded of Venice and Amsterdam, it is only to mark the difference. The colors are pale and soft. They have the quality of a pastel and there is a tenderness in them that painting can seldom reach. [of Leningrad] *A Writer's Notebook*

MAUROIS, Andre (1885-1967)

M104 — Few people in the world, or in America for that matter, realize that Kansas City is one of the prettiest cities on earth ...

M105 — If, in New York, you arrive late for an appointment, say, 'I took a taxi.' *The New York Times*

MAVERICK, Maury (1895-1954) and Robert E.G. HARRIS

M106 — For the millions who have come to the Los Angeles area in the past quarter of a century and for the additional millions on the way, the end of the rainbow is more fact than fancy. Those who have lived in Los Angeles usually will proclaim that here, more than anywhere else, they know or care about, is a place where the ordinary guy can cut in on the jackpot. Ask those from Tennessee or anywhere else why they came: they will shed a tear for home sweet home, but will stay in Los Angeles. *Los Angeles, Rainbow's End*

M107 — When its sense of the community emerges, Los Angeles will begin its maturity. Now it is adolescent, with the glandular imbalance of a youngster who has grown too rapidly and wants glamour more than wisdom or enduring strength. *Ibid.*

MAXWELL, Neville (1926-)

M108 — [The Chinese] don't like the city. The cities that they are left with are the bequest of the period of imperial investment, the domination of coastal China. They have to live with them; but as far as they are concerned there will be no — or very few — new ones. *Quoted in The Exploding Cities*

MAXWELL, W.H.

M109 — Curse all parades! Tell Sergeant Skelton to go to Bath, and let the Adjutant go after him! *Hector O'Halloran*

MAYER, Martin (1928-)

M110 — The city's prime function is that of the marketplace. The market facilitates, then encourages, division of labor, which in turn extends the market. Necessarily, the city imports the food sold in its market, which means it must generate a surplus of manufactured goods or salable services (not infrequently, government services) to trade for what to eat. *The Builders*

MAYO, A.D. (1823-1907)

M111 — All dangers of the town may be summed up in this: that here, withdrawn from the blessed influences of Nature, and set face to face against humanity, man loses his own nature and becomes a new and artificial creature — an inhuman cog in a social machinery that works like a fate, and cheats him of his true culture as a soul. *Symbols of the Capital*

M112 — An American city is essentially a different thing from an European capital. The old cities abroad are the growth of another state of human affairs, and represent quite another phase in the history of human progress than our own . . . thus an European city is a nation within a nation, a conglomeration of institutions rooted in the soil of centuries, firmly interlaced into a corporate structure that resists the convulsions of ages. . . . But an American city is only a convenient hotel, where a free country people come up to tarry and do business, with old recollections of nature haunting them amid its toil and confusion. *Ibid.*

M113 — Happiness does not depend so much on what we have as on a certain freshness of nature that illuminates every corner of our life with a light from within; and how we preserve that freshness amid the monotonous toils and discouraging collisions of the city. *Ibid.*

M114 — Our young countrymen are born with a fever in their blood which drives them from the farm, or the factory, or the mine, where actual production is the result of their efforts, and economy of health, property, and soul is promoted, to the town where ninety percent of the merchants fail, and the mechanic toils with a pit of starvation ever yawning beneath his feet, and an ever increasing series of middle men enhances the cost of living, and pitiless competition of labor and perpetual temptation imperil integrity of mind and purity of life. Our country girls push for the city as by a natural instinct, seeming to relish better the intoxicating charm of being one colored wave of the torrent that rolls along a Broadway than the centre of a neighborhood among the fields. *Ibid.*

M115 — We cannot build cities 'to order'; they are and will be the huge receptacles for all varieties of humanity, and represent the worst as surely as the best in our American character. All the teacher of Christianity can do is to take men and women in towns as he finds them and, in spite of disheartening influences, keep on forever warning, instructing and inspiring virtue. *Ibid.*

MEAD, Margaret (1901-1978)

M116 — If the small city is to make its most distinctive contribution, it must remain a *small* city, a city where distances are not too great, a city where all the interested citizenry take part in the same activities, a city big enough for surprises and new encounters but small enough so that all the citizenry feel a connection with the political, economic, artistic and intellectual life of the city. *The Crucial Role of the Small City in Meeting the Urban Crisis*

MEADOWS, Paul (1913-   )

M117 — The conventional view of the community in the city has been handicapped by a romantic ideological bias and by a theoretical orientation to a limited range of empirical data and to macro-social interests. The community in the modern city is a sea of social life which needs better conceptual nets to capture the human phenomena of interaction and change which characterize the contemporary urban scene. *The Idea of Community in the City*

MEANY, George (President of the AFL-CIO) (1894-1980)

M118 — [President Nixon said] a few weeks ago we've solved the problems of our cities — of our inner cities. Well, by God, he had better go to some of our inner cities. *The National Observer, May 5, 1973*

MEHRING, Franz (1846-1919)

M119 — A prison for speculative minds. [of the city]

MEIER, Richard L. (1920-   )

M120 — One of the most mystifying complications that has come out of technology and that we find concentrated in the urban scene is the special form of harassment which results from man's being the target of too many 'messages' — too much communication from too many sources. *Living with the Coming Urban Technology*

M121 — Among all the cities in the Third World, planners and urbanists have the most to learn from Seoul. With the help and advice of international advisors, Seoul has pulled a Korean society five times its size up the steep path of economic development faster than any city ever before recorded. *Urban Futures Observed in the Asian World*

MELVILLE, Herman (1819-1891)

M122 — Debased into equality: / In glut of all material arts / A civic barbarism may be: / Man disennobled — brutalised / By popular science — atheised / Into a smatterer — / *Clarel*

M123 — A city of Dis (Dante's) clouds of smoke — the damned — coal barges — coaly waters. [of London] *Manuscript Papers 1849*

M124 — A man-of-war is to whalemen as a metropolis to shire-towns. *Neversink*

M125 — The ship was like a great city. *Ibid.*

MENCKEN, Henry Louis (1880-1956)

M126 — In Chicago originality still appears to be put above conformity.... I give you Chicago. It is not London-and-Harvard. It is not Paris-and-buttermilk. It is American in every chitling and sparerib, and it is alive from snout to tail.

M127 — Philadelphia is the most pecksniffian of American cities, and thus probably leads the world. *The American Language*

M128 — When arc-lights began to light the streets, along about 1885, they attracted so many beetles of gigantic size that their glare was actually obscured. These beetles at once acquired the name of electric-light bugs, and it was believed that the arc carbons produced them by a kind of spontaneous generation, and that their bite was as dangerous as that of a tarantula. [of Baltimore] *Happy Days*

M129 — [New York] is the place where all the aspirations of the Western World meet to form one vast master aspiration, as powerful as the action of a steam dredge. It is the icing on the pie called Christian civilization. *Prejudices: Sixth Series*

M130 — It is this colossal opportunity to escape from life that brings yokels to the cities, not mere lust for money. *Prejudices: Fourth Series*

M131 — In Chicago there is a mysterious something that makes for individuality, personality and charm.... a city which offers free play for prairie energy.... some imaginative equivalent for the stupendous activity they were bred to. *Smart Set*

MENEN, Aubrey (1912-   )

M132 — The true New Yorker does not really seek information about the outside world. He feels that if anything is not in New York it is not likely to be interesting. *Holiday*

MERCIER, Louis-Sebastien (1740-1814)

M133 — Characters in Paris are more sharply distinct than in the provinces, and some more eccentric. There is a kind of peaceful quality in the life of the smaller towns, where day follows day smoothly as a river flows; but the capital is a storm-tossed sea, eternally troubled by contrary winds. *The Waiting City: Paris*

MERCOURI, Melina (1925-)

M134 — Athens is like a great mother who opens her heart to Greeks from every part of the country. Even though she has already stretched beyond what is physically bearable, in her heart Athens always has room for one more Greek. *Quoted in Cities, John McGreevy*

MEREDITH, George (1828-1909)

M135 — The air seems dead in this quiet country, we're out of the stream. I must rush up to London to breathe. *The Charm of London*

MERRIAM, Eve (1916-)

M136 — Sing a song of subways, / Never see the sun; / Four-and-twenty people / In room for one. / *The Inner City Mother Goose*

MERRYMAN, Mildred Plew (1892-)

M137 — Sputter, city! Bead with fire / Every ragged roof and spire; . . . . / Burst to bloom, you proud, white flower, / But — remember that hot hour / When the shadow of your brand / Laps the last cool grain of sand — / You will still be just a scar / On a little, lonesome star. / *To Chicago at Night*

MERTON, Thomas (1915-1968)

M138 — Through every precinct of the wintry city / Squadroned iron resounds upon the streets; / Herod's police / Makes shudder the dark steps of the tenements / At the business about to be done. / [of Bethlehem] *The Flight into Egypt*

M139 — City, when we see you coming down, / Coming down from God / To be the new world's crown: / How shall they sing, the fresh, unsalted seas / Hearing your harmonies!/ *The Heavenly City*

M140 — Cities that stood, by day, as gay as lancers / Are lost, in the night, like old men dying. [of European cities] *The Night Train*

METTERNICH, Clemens von (1773-1859)

M141 — When Paris sneezes, Europe catches cold.

M142 — Lamentable illusions hang like a thick cloud over the poor city of Vienna. She believes that she holds the same position that Paris occupied in France; she thinks she can dictate to the Empire. It is a gross error. Vienna is merely the outer shell of a nut which constitutes the main body. She is only the leading town in the smallest province of the Empire and she only becomes the capital of it if the Emperor remains Emperor and lives there with the government of the Empire. For her to be the capital it is, therefore, necessary that there should be an Emperor and an Empire. *Memoirs*

MEYNELL, Alice (1847-1922)

M143 — O heavenly colour, London town / Has blurred it from her skies; / And, hooded in an earthly brown, / Unheaven'd the city lies. / *November Blue*

MEYNELL, Hugo (1727-1808)

M144 — The chief advantage of London is, that a man is always so near his burrow. *Quoted in Boswell's Johnson*

MICHELET, Jules (1798-1874)

M145 — The city population of France, which is but one-fifth of the nation, furnishes two-fifth of the criminals. *Le Peuple*

MICHENER, James (1907?-)

M146 — The city of Toledo, a bejeweled museum set within walls, is a glorious monument and the spiritual capital of Spain; but it is also Spanish tourism at its worst. Anyone who remains in this city overnight is out of his mind ... *Iberia*

M147 — Salamanca's Plaze Mayor is the finest in Spain and one of the four best in the world. St. Mark's in Venice has a richer expanse; and the barbaric Asian splendour of the Registan in Samarkand is without equal. But the Plaza Mayor is unique in that its spacious area is bordered on all four sides by what amounts to one continuous building, four stories high and graced with an unending arcade of great architectural beauty. *Ibid.*

MIDDLETON, Thomas (1570?-1627)

M148 — London's the dining-room of Christendom. *City Pageant*

MIES VAN DER ROHE, Ludwig (1886-1969)

M149 — Less is More. [of modern architecture]

MILLAY, Edna St. Vincent (1892-1950)

M150 — Always I climbed the wave at morning, / Shook the sand from my shoes at night, / That now am caught beneath great buildings, / Stricken with noise, confused with light. / *Exiled*

MILLER, Arthur (1915-   )

M151 — The city is fundamentally a practical, utilitarian invention; it always was. *The Brooklyn Bridge (TV Documentary)*

MILLER, Henry (1891-1980)

M152 — Old, crumbling walls and the pleasant sound of water running in the urinals. [of Paris]

M153 — One needs no artificial stimulation, in Paris, to write. The atmosphere is charged with creation.

M154 — The city is loveliest when the sweet death racket begins. Her own life lived in defiance of nature, her electricity, her frigidaires, her soundproof walls. Box within box she rears her dry walls, the glint of lacquered nails, the plumes that wave across the corrugated sky. Here in the coffin

depths grow the everlasting flowers sent by telegraph.... This is the city, and this the music. Out of the little black boxes an unending river of romance in which the crocodiles weep. All walking toward the mountain top. All in step. From the power house above God floods the street with music. It is God who turns the music on every evening just as we quit work. *Black Spring*

M155 — New York has a trip-hammer vitality which drives you insane with restlessness, if you have no inner stabilizer *The Colossus of Maroussi*

M156 — [Paris] takes hold of you, grabs you by the balls, you might say, like some lovesick bitch who'd rather die than let you out of her hands. *Quoted in Horizon, November, 1980*

M157 — When spring comes to Paris the humblest mortal alive must feel that he dwells in paradise. *The Tropic of Cancer*

MILLER, J. Marshall

M158 — Too many people try to build buildings for all eternity. We should design structures — perhaps whole cities — to be written off more quickly. Since housing needs change from generation to generation, we ought to plan a disposable city rather than attempt to make our cities monuments.

MILLER, Joaquin (1839-1913)

M159 — A circus, a fair. [of Paris]

MILLER, (Senator) John Franklin (1831-1886)

M160 — If we continue to permit the introduction of this strange people, with their peculiar civilization, until they form a considerable part of our population, what is to be the effect upon the American people and Anglo Saxon civilization? Can the two civilizations endure side by side as two distinct and hostile forces? ... Can they meet half way, and so merge in a mongrel race, half Chinese and half Caucasian, as to produce a civilization half pagan, half Christian, semi-oriental, altogether mixed and very bad? *Congressional Record*

MILLER, Jonathan

M161 — I've always felt that the most exotic form of tourism is to be given the chance of revisiting the city in which one actually lives, really seeing it for the first time. You see, the problem of a big city is that the visitor is always seeing the official sites, the spectacles, observing it from points of view from which it was meant to be seen. And those of us who live here gradually grow indifferent to what it looks like, and it becomes more or less invisible. So what one needs is to look at the city in a way it was never meant to be looked at. *Quoted in Cities, John McGreevy*

MILLIKAN, Stella Hall

M162 — Indianp'lis is the city throughout the middle West / As an inland railroad center she is known to be the best; / She is hustling, bustling, thriving, and she's growing ev'ry day, / Indianap'lis, Indianap'lis, in the good old U.S.A. / *Indianapolis (song)*

MILLS, C. Wright

M163 — The city is a structure composed of such little environments, and the people in

them tend to be detached from one another. The 'stimulating variety' of the city does not stimulate the men and women of 'the bedroom belt', the one-class suburbs, who can go through life knowing only their own kind. If they do reach for one another, they do so only through stereotypes and prejudiced images of the creatures of other milieux. *The Power Elite*

M164 — The growth of the metropolis, segregating men and women into narrowed routines and environments, causes them to lose any firm sense of their integrity as a public. The members of publics in smaller communities know each other more or less fully, because they meet in the several aspects of the total life routine. The members of masses in a metropolitan society know one another only as fractions in specialized milieux: the man who fixes the car, the girl who serves your lunch, the saleslady, the women who take care of your child at school during the day. *Ibid.*

M165 — As skyscrapers replace rows of small shops, so offices replace free markets. Each office within the skyscraper is a segment of the enormous file, a part of the symbol factory that produces the billion slips of paper that gear modern society into its daily shape. From the executive's suite to the factory yard, the paper webwork is spun; a thousand rules you never made and don't know about are applied to you by a thousand people you have not met and never will ... And at night, after the people leave the skyscrapers, the streets are empty and inert, and the hand is unseen again. *White Collar*

MILLSTEIN, Gilbert

M166 — He speaks English with the flawless imperfection of a New Yorker *Esquire, January, 1962*

MILNE, Alan Alexander (1882-1956)

M167 — James James / Morrison Morrison / Weatherby George Dupree / Took great / Care of his Mother / Though he was only three. / James James / Said to his Mother, / 'Mother,' he said, said he: / 'You must never go down to the end of the town, if you don't go down with me.' / *When We Were Very Young*

MILTON, John (1608-1674)

M168 — Behold now this vast city; a city of refuge, the mansion-house of liberty, encompassed and surrounded with His protection. [of London] *Arepoagitica*

M169 — Tower'd cities please us then, / And the busy hum of men. / *L'Allegro*

M170 — As one who long in populous city pent, / Where houses thick and sewers annoy the air, / Forth issuing on a summer's morn to breathe / Among the pleasant villages and farms / Adjoin'd, from each thing met conceives delight. / *Paradise Lost*

M171 — Pandemonium, city and proud seat of Lucifer. *Ibid.*

M172 — Athens, the eye of Greece, mother of arts / And eloquence, native to famous wits / Or hospitable, in her sweet recess, / City or suburban, studious walds and shades; / See there the olive grove of Asademe, / Plato's retirement, where the Attic bird / Trills her thick-warbled notes the summer long. / *Paradise Regained*

M173 — Some time let gorgeous Tragedy / In sceptred pall come sweeping by, / Presenting Thebes, or Pelops' line, / Or the tale of Troy divine. / *Il Penseroso*

MINER, Horace (1912-)

M174 — Everyone knows what a city is, except the experts. For them, the city is many things, among which none is clearly dominant. *The City in Modern Africa*

MIRO, Joan (1893-1974)

M175 — Ah, what vitamins! this city is a tonic! This city is a doctor! [of New York] *Quoted in Close-Up by John Gruen*

MITTERRAND, Francois (1916-)

M176 — When one asks me the cities I prefer, I put New York in the ranks of Venice, Ghent, Florence, Jerusalem. The first time I saw New York it was from the sky. How dazzling! I had flown there overnight, and the rising sun had not dissipated the mist of the early morning. Manhattan, gray and golden in its geometric relief, had a full softness. I have returned there five or six times. By plane I have always experienced the same shock, the same impression of entering the future through the window. *Time, May 25, 1981*

MIZNER, Wilson (1876-1933)

M177 — A parking lot for used cities. [of Los Angeles]

MOHOLY-NAGY, Sibyl

M178 — All cities are only cities in relationship to the territory they are in. In relationship to Alexandria they are but villages, for Alexandria is the city of the whole civilized world. *Matrix of Man*

M179 — Cities, like men, are embodiments of the past and mirages of unfulfilled dreams. They thrive on economy and waste, on exploitation and charity, on the initiative of the ego and the solidarity of the group. They stagnate and ultimately die under imposed standardization, homogenized equality, and a minimum denominator of man-made environment. Most decisive of all, cities, like mankind, renew themselves unit by unit in a slow, time-bound metabolic process. *Ibid.*

M180 — Man has built and loved cities because in the urban form he constructs the superimage of his ideal self. The common denominator of cities, from Nineveh to New York, is a collective idol worship, praying for power over nature, destiny, knowledge, and wealth. *Ibid.*

M181 — Prophets of divine over human power have fared badly in cities — witness Lot, Confucius, Jesus, Savonarola, Joseph Smith, as well as the first Sumerian victimn, Urukagina, who lived in the middle of the third millennium B.C. *Ibid.*

M182 — Their most popular spokesmen have declared all cities moribund. Our 'urban nightmares' can only be saved by 'universal planning principles and over-all solutions.' Popular success on the civic wailing wall depends on the carrying power of piercing Cassandra cries that time is running out. It never does. *Ibid.*

MONTAGUE, C.E. (1867-1928)

M183 — Let everything — almost

everything — change with a will, in any city that you love. People gush and moan too much about the loss of ancient buildings of no special note — 'landmarks' and 'links with the past.' In towns, as in human bodies, the only state of health is one of rapid wasting and repair. *The Right Place*

M184 — We all see more of architecture than of any other art. Every street is a gallery of architects' work, and in most streets, whatever their age, there is good work and bad. Through these amusing shows many of us walk unperceivingly all our days, like illiterates in a library, so richly does the fashionable education provide us with blind sides. *Ibid.*

MONTAIGNE, Michael Eyquem de (1533-1592)

M185 — Eloquence flourished most in Rome when public affairs were in the worst condition.

M186 — I am only a Frenchman by virtue of that great city. [Paris]

M187 — Accustom him to everything, that he may not be a Sir Paris, a carpet-knight, but a sinewy, hardy, and vigorous young man. *Essays, I*

M188 — There's no place here on earth that the heavens have embraced with such influence of favors and grace, and with such constancy. Even her ruin is glorious with renown and swollen with glory. [of Rome] *Essays, III*

MONTESQUIEU, C.L. de (1689-1755)

M189 — The sight of a town whose towers and mosques rise out of a water, and of a multitude of people where one would expect to find only fish, will always excite astonishment. [of Venice] *Persian Letters*

MOODY, William Vaughn (1869-1910)

M190 — Shrill and high, newsboys cry / The worst of the city's infamy. / [of New York] *In New York*

MOORE, Clyde

M191 — Cities are growing so fast their arteries are showing through their

outskirts. *Reader's Digest, November, 1963*

MOORE, Flossie (Chicago thief)

M192 — Any gal what can't make herself twenty thousand dollars a year in Chicago oughta be ashamed of herself.

MOORE, Paul (Jr.) (1919-)

M193 — I do not believe it is the will of God that New York shall die, nor that Yonkers dies, nor Newburgh, Poughkeepsie nor any other place. Yet they are all doomed. Someone has to say it. Our cities will die within the next 20 years — as surely as Sodom and Gomorrah. Our sin is not as colorful as Sodom's but deeper. It is the sin of Cain, the murder of our bothers. New York murders her children in the tenements, on the streets, in the schools; while those who can escape understandably seek an illusory Eden in the suburbs. *(At his installation as Episcopal Bishop of New York, September 23, 1972)*

MOORE, Thomas (1779-1852)

M194 — Go where we may, rest where we will, / Eternal London haunts us still. / *Rhymes on the Road*

MOORE, Thomas (1870-1944)

M195 — Where the blue hills of old Toronto shed / Their evening shadows o'er Ontario's bed; / Should trace the grand Cataraqui, and glide / Down the white rapids of his lordly tide.... / *To the Lady Charlotte Rawdon, from the Banks of the St. Lawrence*

MOOREHEAD, Alan

M196 — One of the nice things about living in Rome is that you don't at all despise or avoid the things that the ordinary tourists do. *Holiday, August, 1959*

MORAN, (Lord) (1882-1977)

M197 — The atmosphere of Ottawa after Washington is like Belfast after Dublin. *in Churchill: Taken from the Diaries of Lord Moran*

MORAND, Paul (1886-1976)

M198 — New York's supreme beauty, its

truly unique quality [which] gives it nobility, excuses it, makes its vulgarity forgettable . . .

M199 — If the planet grows cold, this city will nevertheless have been mankind's warmest moment. [of New York] *New York*

MORGAN, Elaine (1920-   )

M200 — The city is, among other things, the place where the ethologist gets deeply discouraged and the economist comes into his own. *Falling Apart*

M201 — Civilization survived the death of a thousand Ozymandiases with no trouble at all. Individual cities might relapse into chaos and anarchy and sink into the sand, but the *idea* of the city seemed imperishable. *Ibid.*

M202 — The really glaring difference between the city and the zoo is that the modern city has no walls and that even when cities did have walls they were not designed to keep the insiders in but to keep outsiders out. . . . Nobody ever coined a platitude by saying 'all roads lead from Rome.' To depict the whole conurbation as a vast cage full of unwilling captives is to turn the actual situation precisely inside out. *Ibid.*

MORGAN, Henry

M203 — The housing shortage is an ugly rumor — circulated by people who have no place to live.

MORGAN, Neil (1924-   )

M204 — San Diego — not Los Angeles or San Francisco — is the kind of place that those in other parts of the world are most likely to think of when they picture California: a bucolic setting of sunshine and water, not yet shrouded in smog or grown into anonymous infinity, still full of dreams, still obsessed with the hope of greatness tomorrow. *San Diego: The Unconventional City*

MORGENSTERN, Joseph

M205 — Where people are encouraged to be good consumers and to want goods but are themselves unwanted goods. [of the city] *Newsweek, May 18, 1970*

MORLEY, Christopher (1890-1957)

M206 — The nation's thyroid gland. [of New York City]

M207 — For students of the troubled heart / Cities are perfect works of art. / *John Mistletoe*

M208 — O praise me not the country — / The meadows green and cool, / The solemn glow of sunsets, the hidden silver pool! / The city for my craving. / Her lordship and her slaving, / The hot stones of her paving / For me, a city fool! / *O Praise Me Not This Country*

M209 — All cities are mad: but the madness is gallant. All cities are beautiful: but the beauty is grim. *Where the Blue Begins*

MORRIS, Charles

M210 — A house is much more to my taste than a tree, / And for groves, O! a good grove of chimneys for me. / *The Contrast*

M211 — In town let me live then, in town let me die / For in truth I can't relish the country, not I. / If one must have a villa in summer to dwell, / Oh give me the sweet shady side of Pall Mall. / *Ibid.*

MORRIS, Desmond (1928-)

M212 — In terms of quantity of space, the city park is a joke. It would have to cover thousands of square miles to provide a truly natural amount of wandering space for the huge city population it serves. The best that can be said for it is that it is decidedly better than nothing. *The Human Zoo*

M213 — When the pressures of modern living become heavy, the harassed city-dweller often refers to his teeming world as a concrete jungle. This is a colorful way of describing the pattern of life in a dense urban community, but it is also grossly inaccurate, as anyone who has studied a real jungle will confirm.

Under normal conditions, in their natural habitats, wild animals do not mutilate themselves, masturbate, attack their offspring, develop stomach ulcers, become fetishists, suffer from obesity, from homosexual pair-bonds, or commit murder. Among human city-dwellers, needless to say, all of these things occur. . . . Clearly, then, the city is not a concrete jungle, it is a human zoo. *Ibid.*

MORRIS, George Pope (1802-1864)

M214 — A stillness and a sadness / Pervade the City Hall, / And speculating madness / Has left the street of Wall; / The Union Square looks really / Both desolate and dark, / And that's the case, or nearly, / From Battery to Park. / [of New York City] *Dark Days*

MORRIS, James (1926-)

M215 — And on from thence to Isfahan, / The golden garden of the sun, / Whence the long dusty caravan / Brings cedar and vermilion. / *Cities*

M216 — Anything may happen to Berlin in the second half of our century; but whoever rules her, until the shades of that dreadful capital are exorcized at last, until the very memory of it is dim, all the brilliance and bluster of the new city will be sham, and its spirit will never be easy. *Ibid.*

M217 — As Beirut is to the world of the Arabs, so Rotterdam is to the Ruhr. *Ibid.*

M218 — Ask any ill-informed Londoner for his impressions of the Arab world and he will at once enumerate for you, with a pitying smile, all the characteristics of this lovely city: flightiness, prevarication, political naivete, stubborness, instability. Here it all comes true. Mingle these sorry ingredients thoroughly, add a flash of humour and a basinful of charm, flavour with brave memories and a trace of ineffectual nobility, soothe with a glimpse of magnificent architecture, and you have the essence of Damascus. *Ibid.*

M219 — Bangkok is not, like Venice, exclusively wet-bob. She has her streets and railways, her automobiles and her trolley-cars: but she still feels unmistakably subject to the Senior Lord River, and her very name means 'Water-Flower Village.' *Ibid.*

M220 — Beirut is the impossible city, in several senses of the adjective. She is impossible in the enchantment of her setting, where the Lebanese mountains meet the Mediterranean. She is impossible in her headiness of character, her irresponsible gaiety, her humid prevarications. She is impossible economically, incorrigibly prospering under a system condemned by many serious theorists as utterly unworkable. Just as the bumble-bee is aerodynamically incapable of flying, so Beirut, by all the rules and precedents, has no right to exist. *Ibid.*

M221 — Beneath the lacquered surface of Munich there remains, I cannot help fancying, some hint of strut, arrogance, or dangerous gullibility. This does not feel either a gentle or a sceptical city. Its smiles, though ubiquitous, do not seem heartfelt. It has no wry humour like Berlin, and no sense of liberal ease, like Hamburg. In Munich I do not often catch an eye, as I do every day in Damascus or La Paz, New York or Warsaw, into whose passing glance there steals some instant glow of sympathy, the natural collusion of one human being with another. *Ibid.*

M222 — The city has long been rebuilt, and a new population has flooded in to replace the victims of the holocaust: but for all the bright new buildings and the broad boulevards, no Pompeii is more surely frozen in its attitude of disaster, and no Mont Pelee more permanently scarred. [of Hiroshima] *Ibid.*

M223 — Cuzco was the heart of a civilization so strange, precise and rarefied that nothing remotely like it has ever been seen again. *Ibid.*

M224 — Dublin seems made for charm, comfort and easy-going affluence. But it is not there. *Ibid.*

M225 — Every city has its function, and Geneva is a kind of civic nursing home. *Ibid.*

M226 — The feeling has faded in New York, as that old refuge ages and hardens, and has never quite bloomed in Sydney: but here in Jacques Cartier's city where the noble St. Lawrence strikes for the heart of the continent, and their great expresses pound away to Winnipeg and Vancouver and the wildernesses of the north-west — here in Montreal you can still understand what it means to stand on the edge of a new world. *Ibid.*

M227 — For at least a century Baghdad sheltered the greatest conglomeration of wealth and learning on earth — she was at once the Alexandria and the Manhattan of her time — and to this day, of all the cities of Islam, she retains the most potent allure. *Ibid.*

M228 — (New Delhi) . . . for of all the planned capitals, from Washington to Brasilia, this is perhaps the most successful. *Ibid.*

M229 — The horizons of Cairo are wide, and visionary, and heavy with symbolism. She is a city half African, half Arab, Muslim with pagan undertones, softened over the generations by a sporadic soft breath of humanism playing upon her from the north. You can call her a hybrid city, or a mongrel; but she can perhaps serve as an archetype of a half-caste society of the future, a melange of colours and tastes and prejudices and heritages, fused into a fitful unity, like an ingot white-hot but flickering in the furnace. *Ibid.*

M230 — If you drive in Athens in the evening from your aircraft or your ship, she

does not feel at all pellucid, pure or glistening — adjectives the old travellers loved to bestow on her. On the contrary, she gives you an instant dismal impression of honkytonk intensity, a whiff of Soho, a meaner Beirut. *Ibid.*

M231 — In Cape Town, if you muffle your perceptions a little, and allow your imagination to overlap your realism, you can conceive what South Africa might be like, were it not for its burdens of tragedy. *Ibid.*

M232 — Istanbul is melancholy because she is an imperial capital without an empire, an older London, perhaps, or a less buoyant Vienna. *Ibid.*

M233 — It is sad but fitting that the northern gateway of South Africa, that pariah among the nations, should be the swollen mining camp of Johannesburg, for she is the most miasmal of African cities. Greedy, harsh and angular, she stands on the bleak uplands of the high veldt like an emblem of materialism, an unfailing confirmation of the traveller's preconceptions. *Ibid.*

M234 — Jerusalem is the official capital of Israel, and Haifa up the coast is a more serene and elegant city, but in the streets of Tel Aviv are enshrined, once and for all, the formidable efforts of the Zionists to achieve a homeland of their own. Here, better than anywhere else in the world, you may consider what it means to be a Jew, ponder the tragic significance of this astonishing people, and wonder whether this smallish seaside town, half resort, half business center, will ever be a great city in a great nation, or whether the heart of Jewry lies elsewhere still. *Ibid.*

M235 — Like London, she has never been conquered. Like Peking, she is the heart of a civilization. Like Stockholm, she does not care for brute strength. Like Paris, she is always fun. And like Rome, she is a city of religion. Above all it is the serene genius of Buddhism that sustains Bangkok, colouring her architecture with grace, style and delicacy, and making of her a city that few visitors can remember without affection and respect. It is not an awful or oppressive faith, the Buddhism of Bangkok. *Ibid.*

M236 — Like man, like city. Pizarro was a character of fascinating bestiality, and Lima is a metropolis of heartless charm. *Ibid.*

M237 — Like Venice, she is a city of canals and curious prospects, but unlike Venice, she never shows off. [of Amsterdam] *Ibid.*

M238 — Madrid is a city unique to herself, lapped as she always is, in the heart of her arid plateau, by this eerie but beautiful feeling: in Europe, but not of her, a sort of island capital, aloof behind the rampart of the Pyrenees and the surrounding moat of the sea. She feels very proud, and very courteous, and somehow never far from tragedy. *Ibid.*

M239 — More people live in Hong Kong than in all the rest of the world put together . . . *Ibid.*

M240 — The name Addis Ababa means 'New Flower', because she was founded in the odour of hope towards the end of the last century; and to this day the city feels young and unexpectedly charming, graced alike by the superb manners and the green fingers of the Ethiopians. *Ibid.*

M241 — Never did a city better live up to her reputation or more handsomely justify the picture-postcard flattery. In her splendour of situation, encouched among bays and humped hills, she has only half a dozen rivals on earth — Hong Kong perhaps, Venice, Wellington, San Francisco, Naples, Sydney if you happen to be Australian, possibly Beirut, Cape Town at a pinch. [of Rio de Janiero] *Ibid.*

M242 — No man is an island, and even less is any city. *Ibid.*

M243 — Of all the big cities of Europe, Geneva is perhaps the most boring: the most pallid, the most unprovocative, the most suburban, the most Swiss. *Ibid.*

M244 — Only at the Levantine end of the Mediterranean could a Beirut exist, with all these undertones of antiquity, graft and tolerance. Is she really a great city, this wayward paragon? Scarcely, by the standards of Berlin or San Francisco, Tokyo or Moscow: but she is great in a different kind. She is great like a voluptuous courtesan, a shady merchant-prince, the

scent of jasmine or the flash of a dazzling scandal. She has scarcely achieved greatness, nor even had it thrust upon her: but greatness has often spent a night in her arms, and a little lingers. *Ibid.*

M245 — A sad, severe, gorgeous city, like an old proud emperor, or a retired eunuch of distinction. [of Istanbul] *Ibid.*

M246 — She [Algiers] is a desiccated, heartless city, for all her lovely gardens, and you may glimpse her character most starkly during the blazing hours of early afternoon, when an ominous calm seems to fall like a blanket upon her streets, and the whole place seems to be cherishing some dread and menacing secret — as Albert Camus's Oran, down the coast, once cherished the awful secret of the plague. *Ibid.*

M247 — She is not beautiful, but she is inescapably exhilarating, not always for the best reasons: a jazzy, high-spirited, ever bubbly place, whose inhabitants are dressed in dazzling multi-colored togas, and love to dance a slow, blaring shuffle known as High Life . . . Nothing is altogether commonplace in Accra. She is a city of excesses. *Ibid.*

M248 — She reigns still as the supreme repository of their ancient traditions, their culture and their custom, their religions and their high-flown patriotism, their golden heritage and their resilient pride. She is a shrine, a palace, a memorial, a talisman, a poem, a picture. She is, to ninety million Japanese, the very soul and melody of Nippon. [of Kyoto] *Ibid.*

M249 — Some cities give an instant impression of provinciality, however urbane they are, however cultivated: such are Stockholm, San Francisco, Brussels, Karachi. Some, though, strike you the moment you arrive with the pulse and posture of history: and such a one is Delhi. *Ibid.*

M250 — The summit of the American Middle West (if one can use the word of a region so uniformly flat), its crown and symbol, the prime product of its energies, the pride of its heart, is the city of Chicago, on the shores of Lake Michigan. *Ibid.*

M251 — There is no more self-centered capital on earth than this proud, colourless little metropolis on the fringe of the Arctic Ocean. [of Reykjavik] *Ibid.*

M252 — They have tamed Leningrad and harnessed her, driven away her emperors, turned her palaces into museums and her academies for young ladies into political offices — coarsened her exquisite restaurants, exiled her fan-makers and her riding-masters, swamped her book shops with dialectical materialism, deconsecrated her cathedrals, humbled her hierarchies, stifled her frivolities, left her great avenues peeling and pining. Yet she rides above her fate like the queen she is . . . still a Cleopatra among cities. *Ibid.*

M253 — This is not an earnest city. Proper Victorians would have hated it. Harvard economists or British Civil Servants, examining its improbable methods, its flibberty-gibbet charm, its blatancy and its blarney — men of sombre purpose, deposited one scented evening in Beirut, would probably pronounce her irredeemable. *Ibid.*

M254 — Those of us given to whistling in the streets do so out of a variety of impulses. In Paris we whistle because it is expected of us, in London because it isn't. We whistle in Moscow out of self-defence, in New York out of stimulation, in Tokyo out of despair. And if we whistle our way through Bogota, the capital of Colombia, the impulse is partly well-being, for this is a hospitable place, but partly, alas, bravado. Bogota is a finely civilized old city, but she lacks peace of mind. She is dignified but highly strung, like an Edinburgh with twitches. *Ibid.*

M255 — Though her appearance is lovely and her culture profound, she is not one of your rapturous cities. Her effluences are essentially homely and comfortable, and of all the cities of Europe, none remains more resolutely European. [of Amsterdam] *Ibid.*

MORRIS, William (1834-1896)

M256 — Forget six counties overhung with smoke, / Forget the snorting steam and piston stroke, / Forget the spreading of the hideous town; / Think rather of the pack-horse on the down, / And dream of London, small and white and clean, / The clear Thames bordered by its gardens green. / *The Earthly Paradise*

MORRISON, Toni (1931-)

M257 — This missing quality in city fiction is not privacy or diminished individual freedom, not even the absence of beauty. Nor is the quality present in stories about the country, nature, serenity, or peace, for the country holds as many terrors for the Black American writer as the city does. What is missing in city fiction and present in village fiction is the ancestor. The advising, benevolent, protective, wise Black ancestor is imagined as surviving in the village but not in the city. *City Limits, Village Values: Concepts of the Neighborhood in Black Fiction*

MORROW, Elsie

M258 — At best, Springfield [Illinois] is a very typical American city, with a special flavor and pleasantness. At worst it is a town which has grown old without ever having grown up. It is something between a backward country settlement and a cosmopolis. *Saturday Evening Post*

MORTON, Henry Vollam (1892-1979)

M259 — The perfect place for a writer is in the hideous roar of a city, with men making a new road under his window in competition with a barrel organ, and on the mat a man waiting for the rent. [of London] *In the Steps of St. Paul*

MORYSON, Fynes (1566-1630)

M260 — Londoners, and all within the sound of Bowbell, are in reproch called Cocknies, and eaters of buttered tostes. *An Itinerary*

M261 — A traveler to Rome must have the back of an ass, the belly of a hog, and a conscience as broad as the king's highway. *Ibid.*

MOSCONE, George (Mayor of San Francisco) (1930-)

M262 — I hate to say it, but crime is an overhead you have to pay if you want to live in the city. *Newsweek, December 20, 1976*

MOSES, Robert (1888-1981)

M263 — Academic planners and those who

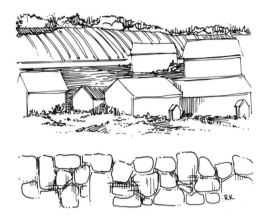

cannot stand urban competition or tolerate a certain amount of noise, tension, hurry, and the anonymity of urban life, advocate decentralization of cities and dispersion of population. But their prejudices will not materially influence the logic of the situation. There are good reasons why most cities persist. Those which decline do so because they no longer serve a function in the larger economy of the nation. *Working for the People*

M264 — Cities were in many cases originally created for protection. This is about the only logic of urban growth which is no longer significant. *Ibid.*

M265 — The city man is a weekend salt-water fisherman by instinct. He requires something unpaved, unencumbered and monotonous to keep him sane. Perhaps it is an admission against interest to say that there are many of us who simply cannot take the city the week around. *Ibid.*

M266 — The city, rebuilt, modernized and humanized, will always be the great magnet which draws from the hinterland the eager, the young, the curious, the ambitious, the talented. These, from the dawn of history, have gravitated to big places where the incentives are most dramatic, where competition is strongest and rewards great. Ours is an emerging new people of many stocks and talents in a land of extraordinary variety. Country and city, we are knitted together. *Ibid.*

M267 — In our cities the shallows murmur,

but the deeps are dumb. There are more churchgoers than cabaret hounds, but they make less noise. The jazz joints, with their raucous snare drums and trumpeters, are more obtrusive but much less important than the long-drawn aisles and fretted vaults where, as the poet said, the pealing anthem swells the note of praise. *Ibid.*

M268 — An Oriental bazaar where shrewd merchants charge all the traffic will bear, a catchpenny mechanical Coney Island run by barkers and concessionaires for absentee owners . . . and a garden community of homes, stores, and public beaches operated by and for substantial citizens and respectable visitors. [of Miami]

M269 — The physical beauties of a city can, no doubt, be exagerated, but no balanced observer will ignore them. Europeans coming to New York City for the first time are ecstatic about the view of lower Manhattan in the early morning from a great liner as it passes through upper New York Bay; mid-Manhattan seen from the Triborough Bridge at sundown; the jeweled diadem spread before the jet flyer at night; the clean gossamer cobwebs of its suspension bridges; the successive bustle and tomblike silences of its streets; the fantastic daring, imagination, and aspiration of its builders. *Are Cities Dead?*

M270 — The suburbs. . . . often are leaderless. I worry more about the suburbs than about the cities. In the cities we are at least aware of and are trying to undo the errors of the past. In the suburbs these felonies are being compounded and perpetuated. *Working for the People*

M271 — The trouble with the prophets of doom of cities is that they do not think like the people who live in them. *Ibid.*

M272 — We should not pay too much attention to the dweller in the shadow of the 'El' who would rather be a lamppost in Chicago than the whole Painted Desert. Or to the confirmed Gothamite who boasts that the city is the finest summer resort and that, as Mr. Dooley remarked: 'Ivrything that's worth havin' goes to th' city; the counthry takes what's left.' *Ibid.*

M273 — You need not live in a city, but you must be nearby or visit now and then if you expect to be recognized as a civilized man. *Ibid.*

MOTLEY, Willard (1912-1965)

M274 — The sparrow sits on a telephone pole in the alley in the city. / The city is the world in microcosm. / The city lies in splendor and squalor. / There are many doors to the city. Many things hide behind the many doors. More lives than one are lived in the city, more deaths than one are met within the city's gate. / The city doesn't change. / The people come and go, the visitors. They see the front yard. But what of the city's back yard, and the alley? Who knows the lives and minds of the people who live in the alley? / Knock on any door down this street, in this alley. / *Knock on Any Door*

MOWBRAY, A.Q.

M275 — The city is the culmination of man's attempt to become civilized; it offers the individual the fullest opportunity to realize his potential as a human being. It is the repository of our faith in the possibility of achieving a humane society and the arena in which his faith is translated into action toward that end. *Road to Ruin*

M276 — If a rebirth of intercity railroad passenger service is needed to save our countryside, a rebirth of intracity mass-transit facilities is needed to save our cities. If we abandon the city to the automobile and the freeway, it will become a wasteland in which no one will wish to live, to work, or even to visit. Complete dependence on the automobile for urban transportation will destroy the city as surely as bombs. *Ibid.*

M277 — The measure of a modern, industrialized nation can be taken by observing the quality of its works in the two extremes of its environment — cities and wilderness bespeak its attitude toward the living earth. The United States is swiftly destroying its cities and its wilderness with highways. *Ibid.*

M278 — There are those who say the American Dream is a split-level in the suburbs with a half-acre, a guaranteed annual income, and membership in the Best Club. Others maintain it's just a matter of

all the booze and broads you can handle. Not so. The American Dream is to drive from coast to coast without encountering a traffic light. *Ibid.*

MOYNIHAN, Daniel P. (1927-   )

M279 — The simple fact is that most American cities are broke. Their fiscal basis has simply given out. They are dependent to an extraordinary degree on a tax structure that is not flexible, that is increasingly retrograde, and, at certain points, becomes counter-productive.

MUILENBURG, James (1896-1974)

M280 — One wonders whether the prophets do sufficient justice to the problems of political and economic power and responsibility with which the city is necessarily involved. On the other hand, they cannot be said to condemn the city as such; they are quick to give us a bill of particulars. The city becomes the instrument of exploitation and oppression. *Biblical Images of the City*

MUMFORD, Lewis (1895-   )

M281 — In the city, time becomes visible.

M282 — Even before the city is a place of fixed residence, it begins as a meeting place to which people periodically return: the magnet comes before the container, and this ability to attract non-residents to it for intercourse and spiritual stimulus no less than trade remains one of the essential criteria of the city, a witness to its inherent dynamism, as opposed to the more fixed and indrawn form of the village, hostile to the outsider. *The City in History*

M283 — The final mission of the city is to further man's conscious participation in the cosmic and historic process. Through its own complex and enduring structure, the city vastly augments man's ability to interpret these processes and take an active, formative part in them, so that every phase of the drama it stages shall have, to the highest degree possible, the illumination of consciousness, the stamp of purpose, the color of love. The magnification of all the dimensions of life, through emotional communion, rational communication, technological mastery, and above all, dramatic representation, has been the supreme office of the city in history. And it remains the chief reason for the city's continued existence. *Ibid.*

M284 — The first germ of the city, then, is in the ceremonial meeting place that serves as the goal for pilgrimage: a site to which family or clan groups are drawn back, at seasonable intervals, because it concentrates, in addition to any natural advantages it may have, certain 'spiritual' or supernatural powers, powers of higher potency and greater duration, of wider cosmic significance, than the ordinary processes or life. *Ibid.*

M285 — From the beginning, then, the city exhibited an ambivalent character it has never wholly lost: it combined the maximum amount of protection with the greatest incentives to aggression: it offered the widest possible freedom and diversity, yet imposed a drastic system of compulsion and regimentation which, along with its military aggression and destruction, has become 'second nature' to civilized man and is often erroneously identified with his original biological proclivities. *Ibid.*

M286 — Though the great city is the best organ of memory man has yet created, it is also — until it becomes too cluttered and disorganized — the best agent for discrimination and comparative evaluation, not merely because it spreads out so many goods for choosing, but because it likewise creates minds of large range, capable of coping with them. *Ibid.*

M287 — Through its concentration of physical and cultural power, the city heightened the tempo of human intercourse and translated its products into forms that could be stored and reproduced. Through its monuments, written records, and orderly habits of association, the city enlarged the scope of all human activities, extending them backwards and forwards in time. By means of its storage facilities (buildings, vaults, archives, monuments, tablets, books), the city became capable of transmitting a complex culture from generation to generation, for its marshalled together not only the physical means but the human agents needed to pass on and enlarge

this heritage. That remains the greatest of the city's gifts. *Ibid.*

M288 — Woman's presence made itself felt in every part of the [neolithic] village: not least in its physical structures, with their protective enclosures, whose further symbolic meanings psychoanalysis has now tardily brought to light. Security, receptivity, enclosure, nurture — these functions belong to woman; and they take structural expression in every part of the village, in the house and the oven, the byre and the bin, the cistern, the storage pit, the granary, and from there pass on to the city, in the wall and the moat, and all inner spaces, from the atrium to the cloister. House and village, eventually the town itself, are woman writ large. *Ibid.*

M289 — The city is a fact in nature, like a cave, a run of mackerel or an ant-heap. But it is also a conscious work of art, and it holds within its communal framework many simpler and more personal forms of art. Mind takes form in the city; and in turn, urban forms condition mind.... With language itself, it [the city] remains man's greatest work of art. *The Culture of Cities*

M290 — Nobody can be satisfied with the form of the city today. Neither as a working mechanism, as a social medium, nor as a work of art does the city fulfill the high hopes that modern civilization has called forth — or even meet our reasonable demands. *The Future of the City*

M291 — This ancient port, founded by the Phoenicians twenty-five hundred years ago, and occupied at one time or another by the Greeks, the Romans, the Provençals, and all the races of the Levant, is a pungent bouillabaise of a city. [of Marseilles] *The Highway and the City*

M292 — Our national flower is the concrete cloverleaf.

M293 — The hope of the city lies outside itself. Focus your attention on the cities-in which more than half of us live — and the future is dismal. But lay aside the magnifying glass which reveals, for example, the hopelessness of Broadway and Forty-second Street, take up a reducing glass and look at the entire region in which

New York lies. The city falls into focus. Forests in the hill-counties, water-power in the mid-state valleys, farmland in Connecticut, cranberry bogs in New Jersey, enter the picture. To think of all these acres as merely tributary to New York, to trace and strengthen the lines of the web in which the spider-city sits unchallenged, is again to miss the clue. But to think of the region as a whole and the city merely as one of its parts — that may hold promise. *Regions to Live In*

M294 — Regional planning does not mean the planning of big cities beyond their present areas; it means the reinvigoration and rehabilitation of whole regions so that the products of culture and civilization, instead of being confined to a prosperous minority in the congested centers, shall be available to everyone at every point in a region where the physical basis for a cultivated life can be laid down. *Ibid.*

M295 — The city in its complete sense, . . . is a geographic plexus, an economic organization, symbol of collective unity. The city fosters art and is art; the city creates the theater and is the theater. It is in the city, the city as theater, that man's more purposive activities are focused, and work out, through conflicting and cooperating personalities, events, groups, into more significant culminations. *What Is a City?*

M296 — Limitations on size, density, and area are absolutely necessary to effective social intercourse; and they are therefore the most important instruments of rational economic and civic planning. *Ibid.*

M297 — Most of our housing and city planning has been handicapped because those who have undertaken the work have had no clear notion of the social functions of the city. *Ibid.*

MUNRO, William (1875-1957)

M298 — The city has more wealth than the country, more skill, more erudition within its bounds, more initiative, more philanthropy, more science, more divorces, more aliens, more births and deaths, more accidents, more rich, more poor, more wise men and more fools. *Encyclopedia of the Social Sciences*

M299 — Off hand one might say that . . . (the

city) . . . is a large body of people living in a relatively small area. That, however, would be a very inadequate definition, for it would convey no intimation of the fact that the city has a peculiar legal status, a distinct governmental organization, a highly complicated economic structure, and a host of special problems which do not arise when an equal number of people live less compactly together. A comprehensive definition of the modern city must indicate that it is a legal, political, economic, and social unit all rolled into one. *The Government of American Cities*

MURPHEY, Rhoads (1919-)

M300 — China has succeeded, apparently, no better than other developing countries in correcting this imbalance by creating enough new economic opportunity and other advantages in rural areas to make them more attractive, or by producing rapid enough growth of urban employment and basic services such as housing to absorb the millions of would-be migrants. What the Chinese alone have apparently been able to do is arbitrarily to control the growth of at least the largest cities. *The Fading of the Maoist Vision*

M301 — Cities would take their natural place and not appear as unnatural, congested spots or boils on the body-politic as they are today . . . If the hearts of the city-dwellers remain rooted in the villages, if they become village-minded, all other things will automatically follow, and the boil will quickly heal. *Ibid.*

M302 — Even if they could be made to do so, there is little reason to think that the Chinese, despite the inspiration of Maoist ideals, are immune to the blandishments of consumerism, any more than many of them have appeared able to resist the attractions of the city and its bourgeois rewards. The Chinese revolution aimed to destroy the city, and then to re-mold it. Instead it appears that the city threatens to destroy the revolution. *Ibid.*

M303 — Goodness develops only in the village, evil in the city. The city is the place of commerce and trade. People relate to one another only with the aim of making profits. They are superficial and pretentious. As a result, the city is a sink of iniquities. The village is different. There people are self-reliant and have deep emotional ties with each other. *Ibid.*

M304 — If the village perishes, India will perish too. Therefore we have to concentrate on the village being self-contained, manufacturing mainly for use. Provided the character of village industry is maintained, there would be no objection to villagers using even the modern machines and tools that they can make and can afford to use. *Ibid.*

M305 — It is not difficult to see the modern industrial city as a mistake, a wrong turn which has failed to produce a net improvement in total human welfare or which has instead become a new monster. *Ibid.*

M306 — It is really not possible to get a complete or coherent picture of urban planning in China. We have only a few partial samples of plans, and few specific descriptions of what urban planners intended except in the most general terms. We do not know in any detail what trends and changes have operated in planning circles over the past thirty years. In fact, we do not really know who the 'planners' are, or whether there is a recognized branch of urban planning represented in the administrative structure or in the universities. *Ibid.*

M307 — The Maoist blueprint for a better world may be reduced, as Mao himself has done, to two goals: eliminate the distinctions between mental and manual labor, and eliminate the differences between city and country-side. The two are of course interrelated, since mental labor, and the elites who engage in it, are almost entirely urban. In keeping with traditional Chinese attitudes, but further reinforced by the Communist Party's struggle for power, originally against the cities, the Maoist attitude toward cities and the elites they breed is negative. *Ibid.*

M308 — The modern industrial city may produce new material wealth, but perhaps at the cost of the human soul. *Ibid.*

M309 — Perhaps the most striking aspect of China's effort at planned control of city growth has been the policy of assigning

urban people to work in the countryside. In the Chinese context this accomplishes two purposes: it restricts the growth of urban populations by siphoning off a significant part of the yearly increase, and it educates or re-educates urban people in 'correct' attitudes, kindling or recharging their commitment to serve the people, who are primarily in rural areas. . . . Cities breed bourgeois values, and the only way to root them out, to cleanse the poisons which city life generates, is to labor with the untainted peasants in the country-side. *Ibid.*

M310 — Unlike cities in the West, especially since the end of the European Middle Ages, traditional Chinese cities were not for the most part agents of change, but rather makers and supporters of the status quo. *Ibid.*

MURRAY, Ken

M311 — A place where you spend more than you make, on things you don't need, to impress people you don't like. [of Hollywood]

MUSKIE, Edmund S. (Senator) (1914-   )

M312 — As we approach the 200th anniversary of our nation's beginnings, we must make a new beginning in urban government. That may even require that we take another lead from our forefathers by calling a multitude of 'urban constitutional conventions' — conventions where

Governors and Mayors, legislators and community leaders can raise and resolve some of the hardest problems our cities and suburbs face. With a little luck and a lot of reform, we might end up with government subunits in every city and a government superunit in every metropolitan area. *(Before American Jewish Committee, New York, May 14, 1971)*

M313 — In a nation where three-quarters of the people live in urban areas, the state of the Union is determined by the state of the cities. *(Before City Council, Philadelphia, January 20, 1972)*

M314 — The problem of the cities is perhaps the most critical domestic issue with which this country has been confronted since the Civil War, if not since the founding of the Republic.

M315 — The urban problem is the nation's problem. The urban problem is the concentration of all the pressure and problems and unmet needs of our society. We cannot abandon the cities without destroying the nation. *(At U.S. Conference of Mayors, New Orleans, June 20, 1972)*

MUSSOLINI, Benito (1883-1945)

M316 — This Berlin–Rome connection is not so much a diaphragm as an axis, around which can revolve all those states of Europe with a will towards collaboration and peace. *(Speech, Milan, November 1, 1936)*

N

NAFTALIN, Arthur (Mayor of Minneapolis) (1917-)

N1 — The plain and simple and unchallengeable fact is that our state governments are in default as regards their responsibilities to the urban centers, and there is no evidence to suggest that this historic pattern of indifference will be reversed. To round out the dismal picture, while the national and state governments remain in default, the local governments are in a state of paralysis. *(Before American Psychological Association, September 7, 1969)*

NAIPAUL, V.S. (1932-)

N2 — No city or landscape is truly rich unless it has been given the quality of myth by writer, painter, or by its association with great events. *An Area of Darkness*

NAPOLEON I (1769-1821)

N3 — The History of Rome is pretty much the history of the world. *(To Gaspard Gourgaud at St. Helena)*

N4 — Secrets travel fast in Paris. *Sayings of Napoleon*

NAPOLEON III (1808-1873)

N5 — I want to be a second Augustus, because Augustus ... made Rome a city of marble. [of Paris] *Quoted in Histoire de l'Administration Parisienne, A. des Cilleuls*

NASH, Ogden (1902-1971)

N6 — The Bronx? / No Thonx! /

N7 — City people always want the most faucets / And the comfortablest caucets. / *I'm a Stranger Here Myself*

NATHAN, Robert (1894-)

N8 — It is but just that there should rise, / At peace beneath our Western skies, / From out the hearts of free-born men, / This little town again. / *Lidice*

NEALE, John Mason (1818-1866)

N9 — Jerusalem the golden, / With milk and honey blest, / Beneath thy contemplation / Sink heart and voice opprest. / I know not, oh, I know not, / What joys await us there, / What radiancy of glory, / What bliss beyond compare. / *Jerusalem the Golden*

NEBUCHADNEZZAR (?-562 B.C.)

N10 — That no assault should reach Imgur-Bel, the wall of Babylon; I did, what no earlier king had done, for 4,000 ells of land on the side of Babylon, at a distance that it (the assault) did not come nigh, I caused a mighty wall to be built on the east side of Babylon. I dug out its moat, and I built a scarp, with bitumen and bricks. A mighty wall I built on its edge, mountain-high.

NESBIT, Edith (1858-1924)

N11 — But the plane tree's kind to the poor dull city — I love him best of all!

NEUBERGER, Richard L. (1912-1960)

N12 — To some extent, Juneau dramatizes the universality of American customs and behavior. It is 1,000 miles from America's continental soil; it is on the fringe of the last great frontier under our flag. Yet it is not so profoundly different from its sister Pacific Coast capitals of Olympia, Salem, and

Sacramento — or those of any others of the forty-eight states. *The New York Times Magazine, October 10, 1948*

N13 — Torn between her peaceful past and a brawling future as the Pittsburg of the West, Portland just can't make up her mind. . . . As a result of this strange ambivalence, Portland is a combination of the rustic and the metropolitan. *Saturday Evening Post*

N14 — Seattle is the capital of a Colonial Empire. Its lumber companies, railroads, canneries, and utilities are owned in Wall Street . . . Seattle is not merely a slave; it is a master as well. Kept in Colonial subjugation by the Eastern titleholders to its raw materials, Seattle, in turn, exercises imperial rule over Alaska. . . . Alaska is a suburb of Seattle. *Seattle, Slave and Master*

NEUTRA, Richard J. (1892-1970)

N15 — Animal species survive by adjustment to their habitat or else they perish. Our human species may itself perish by its own explosive and insidious inventions. The atom bomb is only the most spectacular of them. Man is a tinkerer, and through the uncoordinated technical avalanches of the Victorian age, the metropolis has become his most gigantic, puzzling tinker-toy. If man is to survive in the city, comprehensive design and systematic redevelopment will have to replace tinkering and profiteering. *The Adaptation of Design to the Metropolis*

NEVINS, Allan (1890-1971)

N16 — Italy was always a mother of cities and of traditions of civility. Indeed it may almost be said that the city is the product of a Mediterranean world of 'urbanity,' and that Northern Europe in comparison — at any rate down to the emergence of Paris in the thirteenth century of our era — was a home of 'rurality' and scattered tribes and the countryside. *Golden Ages of the Great Cities*

N17 — We face a new era in the history of our great western cities — the North Atlantic era, in which all the countries fronting on the Atlantic and its main arms will be more closely united culturally as well as politically. As an Atlantic community comes into being — and it must be created — New York and Philadelphia will be less American; London will be less English; Paris and Rome will be less French and less Italian. *Ibid.*

NEWMAN, Oscar (1935-)

N18 — The size of a public housing project is the strongest *physical* indicator of the crime rate. The strongest indicator of all is the social characteristics of the residents. The lower the income, the higher the crime rate, regardless of the form of the housing or where it is located. *Quoted in The Exploding Cities*

NEWMAN, Randy (1943-)

N19 — And they hide their faces / And they hide their eyes / 'Cause the city's dyin' / And they don't know why / Oh, Baltimore / Man, it's hard just to live / [song lyrics]

NEWTON, Byron Rufus (1861-1938)

N20 — Purple-robed and pauper-clad, / Raving, rotten, money-mad; / A squirming herd in Mammon's mesh, / A wilderness of human flesh; / Crazed with avarice, lust, and rum, / New York, thy name's delirium. / *Owed to New York*

NEWTON, John (1725-1807)

N21 — Glorious things of thee are spoken, / Zion, city of our God. / *Glorious Things*

NICIAS of Athens (?- 413 B.C.)

N22 — It is men who make a city, not walls or ships without crews. *(Speech to his army after his defeat by the Syracusans)*

NIETZSCHE, Friedrich Wilhelm (1844-1900)

N23 — As an artist, a man has no home in Europe save in Paris. *Ecce Homo*

NIEUWENHYS, Constant (1920-)

N24 — The city of the future will no longer be a place to earn money, but to play in.

NIKHILANANDA, Swami

N25 — From time out of mind, cities have played an important part in the propagation of spiritual ideas. The modern city, however, differs in certain important respects from the city of olden times. The metropolis no longer contains a homogeneous population belonging to the same race or blood and professing the same religious faith. *in The Metropolis and Modern Life, E.M. Fisher, Ed.*

NIN, Anaïs (1903-1977)

N26 — Each stone [in Paris] has a history, and each street bulges with lives well-lived, deeply loved.... It is ... the capitol of intelligence and creativity, enriched by the passage of all the artists in the world.

N27 — I miss the animal buoyancy of New York, the animal vitality. I did not mind that it had no meaning and no depth. *The Diaries of Anaïs Nin*

NIXON, Richard M. (1913-   )

N28 — As one indication of the rising cost of local government, I discovered the other day that my home town of Whittier, California — with a population of only 67,000 — has a budget for 1971 bigger than the entire Federal budget in 1791. *(State of the Union Address, January 22, 1971)*

N29 — There are 200 million Americans now. By the end of the century there will be 300 million. Where are those 100 million going to be? You can't pour them into New York, into Los Angeles, into Chicago and choke those cities to death ... it is necessary for America to grow toward its heartland, toward the center. *(before American Farm Bureau Federation, December 16, 1969)*

N30 — Through time, cities have been centers of culture and commerce, and nowhere has this been more true than in America. But today, many of our great cities are dying. We must not let this happen. We can do better than this. We must do better than this. Only if the American city can prosper can the American dream really prevail. *(University of Nebraska speech, January 14, 1971)*

NOLAND, Thomas

N31 — Paris is a whore — she is loved by all and loves no one.

NORRIS, Frank (1870-1902)

N32 — There are just three big cities in the United States that are *story cities* — New York, of course, New Orleans, and best of the lot, San Francisco.

NORRIS, Kathleen (1880-1966)

N33 — There is no solitude in the world like that of the big city. *Hands Full of Living*

NOYES, Alfred (1880-1958)

N34 — Go down to Kew in lilac-time, in lilac-time, in lilac-time; / Go down to Kew in

lilac-time (it isn't far from London!) / And
you shall wander hand in hand with love in
summer's wonderland; / Go down to Kew in
lilac-time (it isn't far from London!) / *Barrel
Organ*

NUGENT, R.C.

N35 — Though Cato lived, though Tully
spoke, / Though Brutus dealt the godlike
stroke, / Yet perished fated Rome. / *Epistle
to a Lady*

O

OATES, Joyce Carol (1938-   )

O1 — New York City — that most mythical of cities — tends to emerge in recent literature as hellish, or at any rate murderous; yet its presence is the occasion for some of the most subtle and intelligently graceful prose of our time. *Imaginary Cities: America*

OBOLENSKY, L.E.

O2 — This is the Czech Athens. [of Prague]

O'DWYER, William

O3 — I like to think of New York as being the greatest city in the world, not because of its population, its skyscrapers, its universities, or its financial leadership. I like to think of New York as being the greatest city in the world because we have demonstrated here, as nowhere else in the world, that the people of all races, religions, creeds, and color can live as neighbors and contribute the finest in their cultures to the composite culture of the city. *Quoted in Our Fair City, Robert Allen*

O'FAOLAIN, Sean (1900-   )

O4 — Where the used-car lots succeed one another like a string of past lives. [of Los Angeles] *Holiday Magazine, December, 1960*

OGBURN, William F. (1886-1959)

O5 — The city has done things to us. More crimes are committed in the city than in the country. Not so many people get married. Families have fewer children. More women are employed outside the home. Suicides are more frequent in cities. City people are more nervous and more of them go insane. There is more wealth in the cities. . . . We don't know many of our neighbors in the cities. There is not so much gossip. There is more music, more books, more education. All these differences between city and country life, the machine has caused. *You and Machines, 1934*

OGDEN, William Butler (first mayor of Chicago) (1805-1877)

O6 — When you're dealing with Chicago property, the proper way to do it is to go in for all you can get . . . and forget all about it. It will take care of itself.

O'HARA, Frank (1926-1966)

O7 — I can't even enjoy a blade of grass unless I know there's a subway handy. *Meditations in an Emergency*

OLDENBURG, Claes (1929-   )

O8 — Chicago has a strange metaphysical elegance of death about it.

OLMSTED, Frederick Law (1822-1903)

O9 — It is hardly a matter of speculation, I am disposed to think, but almost of demonstration, that the larger a town becomes because simply of its advantages for commercial purposes, the greater will be the convenience available to those who live in and near it for cooperation, as well with reference to the accumulation of wealth in the higher forms, — as in seats of learning, of science, and of art, — as with reference to merely domestic economy and the emancipation of both men and women from petty, confining, and narrowing cares. *Public Parks and the Enlargement of Towns*

O10 — Now, knowing that the average length of the life of mankind in towns has been much less than in the country, and that the average amount of disease and misery and of vice and crime has been much greater in towns, this would be a very dark prospect for civilization, if it were not that modern Science has beyond all question determined many of the causes of the special evils by which men are afflicted in towns, and placed means in our hands for guarding against them. *Ibid.*

O11 — Probably the advantages of civilization can be found illustrated and demonstrated under no other circumstances so completely as in some suburban neighborhoods where each family abode stands fifty or a hundred feet or more apart from all others, and at some distance from the public road. *Ibid.*

O12 — There can be no doubt . . . that, in all our modern civilization, as in that of the ancients, there is a strong drift townward. *Ibid.*

O'NEIL, Thomas P.

O13 — Philadelphia's past was great and gay. But today 'The City of Brotherly Love,' founded by William Penn in 1682 on the banks of the Delaware and the Schuylkill, is like a tired old roue, who bores you with tales of the past while dozing in the present and fumbling with the future. *Philadelphia, Where Patience Is a Vice*

OPPENHEIM, James (1882-1932)

O14 — I must see what I really am, and what I am for, and what this city is for . . .

O15 — Up in the heights of the evening skies I see my City of Cities float / In sunset's golden and crimson days: I look and a great joy clutches my throat! / Plateau of roofs by canyons crossed: windows by thousands

fire-furled — / O gazing, how the heart is lost in the Deepest City of the World. / [of New York City] *New York from a Skyscraper*

OSBORN, Frederic J. (1885-1978)

O16 — It has been found that whatever the town planner may desire, people have a marked tendency to segregate themselves by class or income. *Greenbelt Cities*

O17 — The pride of London suffered when its growth was outpaced by that of New York; France felt a loss of prestige when Berlin exceeded Paris; Birmingham and Glasgow watched each other's populations as two Forsytes watched each other's bank balances. To me all this seems as misguided as if cities were to boast of having the highest infant death-rate or incidence of tuberculosis. *Ibid.*

OSBORNE, Albert (1866-1913)

O18 — Bruges is an easy city to get acquainted with. Its personality is not complex, awakening many and different emotions. It expresses itself simply and frankly. It is like a beautiful person who is now old and withdrawn from the activities of life, though still full of kindly interest in the world about him — a ruddy-faced old man, who wears a ready smile, and is full of wisdom and peace, whose presence is a benediction; for at Bruges you are happy and at rest. *Picture Towns of Europe*

O19 — You meet towns precisely as you meet people, and look forward to the meeting in the same way. Some places, such as most of the provincial towns of France, are utterly commonplace and come to bore one in just the same way as does the prolonged presence of uninteresting people. Some towns homely, but companionable; some pique the curiosity by a certain intangible, vague sense of mystery; some allure by their beauty; others attract by their strangeness, just as does some person who is singled out from your acquaintances because of a strangeness in his ways or words or lines of thought which interest because they bring to you something new or different. *Ibid.*

OSBORNE, William A. (1919-)

O20 — The growth of American cities can, paradoxically enough, be traced to the farm. It was the rural peoples of Europe as well as the United States who turned the trick. By their migration they had swelled American cities to such proportions, that, by the turn of the century, the United States had transformed itself from a nation of farmers to a nation of city dwellers. . . . The American city has really been a revolving door in the migratory movements of this country. *Migration: The Revolving Door of Urban America*

OSMAN, John (1909-1978)

O21 — Christianity destroyed Athens. Paul of Tarsus in his address to the Athenians on Mars Hill dramatizes the manner in which Christianity destroyed civic deities. Indeed the journeys of Paul among the ancient cities of the Mediterranean were directed toward this end. *The City Is a Civilization*

O22 — The city is not a jungle stalked by terror although cities have jungles. The city is not a laboratory for social research although much can be learned from it. The city is not a prison filled with hatred although it can be indifferent. The city is not a place of dehumanization although parts of it are inhumane. Cities are not uncivilized although there are barbarians who live in cities. . . . There is evil in the city, but the city is not inherently bad. Men make the city. *Ibid.*

O23 — Urbanization is changing our character, modifying our culture, and transforming our institutions. Among these institutions are the church and the synagogue. Religion today is challenged to create an urban civilization. It is a task for religion. The task should not be abdicated. Religion has abandoned the city and left its redemption to business and industry. Only religion can redeem. Only religion can regenerate our cities by making them a place for spiritual growth. *Ibid.*

OVID, Publius (43 B.C.-17 A.D.)

O24 — From my own home, I turn to the sights of splendid Rome, and in my mind's eye I survey them all. Now I remember the fora, the temples, the theaters covered with marble, the colonnades where the ground has been leveled — now the grass of the Campus Martius and the views over noble gardens, the lakes, the waterway, the Aqua Virgo. *Letters from Pontus*

O25 — If you would trace it back to its beginning, Rome was but little; nevertheless, in that little town was hope of this great city. The walls were already standing, bounds too cramped for future people. *Fasti*

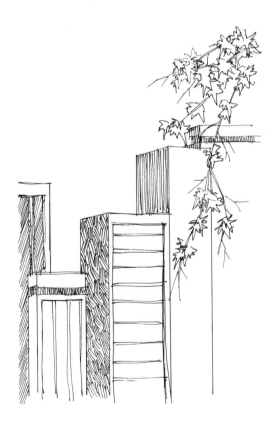

O26 — Other peoples have been allotted a certain defined portion of the earth; for the Romans, the boundaries of the City are the boundaries of the world. *Ibid.*

O27 — Now are empty fields where Troy was, and the soil ready for sickle and fat with Phrygian blood, brings forth abundantly. *Heroides*

P

PALLADIO, Andrea (1518-1580)

P1 — The main traffic and commercial streets of the town should be wide and adorned with stately buildings; for in this way the visitors will get a more impressive idea of the town and often think that the other parts of it are equally beautiful.

PANDIT, Vijaya Lakshmi (1900-   )

P2 — You know, what happens to anybody who has been in these two places (Moscow and Washington, D.C.) and looked at them objectively, is the horrifying thought — if I may use that word in quotes — that they are so similar. *Quoted in The Scotsman, August 29, 1955*

PAOLUCCI, Anne

P3 — Cities do not have to be big sprawling metropolises or megalopolises to provide the leisure which produces the life of intellect. On the contrary, the two cities that have produced the greatest number of poets, painters, philosophers, scientists, historians, and architects have been relatively small cities by modern standards: Athens in the fourth and fifth centuries before Christ and Florence in Renaissance Italy. *Cities as a Lure for Intellectuals*

PARK, Robert E.

P4 — People go to the city, as the farmer goes to town, not merely to market their products or their talents, as the case may be, but to meet people and to get the news. As the ultimate source of common culture is, in a manner of speaking, common talk, the market place, wherever it is, has been, and still remains, a cultural center for the territory tributary to it.

P5 — The city, in short, shows the good and evil in human nature in excess. It is this fact, perhaps, more than any other, which justifies the view that would make of the city a laboratory or clinic in which human nature and social processes may be conveniently and profitably studied. *The American Journal of Sociology*

P6 — The city is something more than a congeries of individual men and of social conveniences — streets, buildings, electric lights, tramways, and telephones; something more, also, than a mere constellation of institutions and administrative devices — courts, hospitals, schools, police, and civil functionaries of various sorts. The city is, rather, a state of mind, a body of customs and traditions, and of the organized attitudes and sentiments that inhere in these customs and are transmitted with this tradition. *Ibid.*

P7 — The attraction of the metropolis is due in part, however, to the fact that in the long run every individual finds somewhere among the varied manifestations of city life the sort of environment in which he expands and feels at ease; finds, in short, the moral climate in which his peculiar nature obtains the stimulations that bring his innate dispositions to full and free expression. *The City*

P8 — Cities, and particularly the great cities, are in unstable equilibrium. The result is that the vast casual and mobile aggregations which constitute our urban populations are in a state of perpetual agitation, swept by every new wind of doctrine, subject to constant alarms, and in consequence the community is in a chronic condition of crisis. *Ibid.*

P9 — The city, particularly the modern American city, strikes one at first blush as so little a product of the artless processes of nature and growth, that it is difficult to recognize it as a living entity. *Ibid.*

P10 — Great cities have always been the melting-pots of races and of cultures. Out of the vivid and subtle interactions of which they have been the centers, there have come the newer breeds and the newer social types. *Ibid.*

P11 — In the city every vocation, even that of a beggar, tends to assume the character of a profession and the discipline which success in any vocation imposes, together with the associations that it enforces, emphasizes this tendency — the tendency, namely not merely to specialize, but to rationalize one's occupation and to develop a specific and conscious technique for carrying it on. *Ibid.*

P12 — The authority of the Pope and the dominance of Rome itself (in its own religious world) are but the incidental products of this functioning through a long period of time. It is not the Pope that made Rome. Rather one might say: 'Rome made the Pope.' *The City and Civilization*

P13 — I may say that the contributions which cities have made to civilization have not been in the preservation nor perfection of any specific racial stock or any particular cultural type. On the whole, the influence of cities has been to destroy the existing racial stock by interbreeding; and in other respects the influence of the urban environment has been dysgenic than otherwise. Neither have the cities made any considerable contribution to morals as we ordinarily understand that term. Quite the contrary. Cities have been proverbially and very properly described as 'wicked.' *Ibid.*

P14 — The city and the urban environment represent man's most consistent and, on the whole, his most successful attempt to remake the world he lives in more after his heart's desire. But if the city is the world which man created, it is the world in which he is henceforth condemned to live. Thus, indirectly, and without any clear sense of the nature of his task, in making the city man has remade himself. *The City as a Social Laboratory*

P15 — The city magnifies, spreads out, and advertises human nature in all its various manifestations. It is this that makes the city interesting, even fascinating. It is this,

however, that makes it of all places the one in which to discover the secrets of human hearts, and to study human nature and society. *Ibid.*

PARKER, Theodore

P16 — [The city] has always been the fireplace of civilization, whence light and heat radiated out into the dark.

PASCAL, Blaise (1623-1662)

P17 — I see indeed that truth is the same at Toulouse and at Paris. *(Letter to Fermat)*

P18 — We do not worry about being respected in the towns through which we pass. But if we are going to remain in one for a certain time, we do worry. How long does that time have to be?

PATCHEN, Kenneth (1911-1972)

P19 — And there I did weep, / Men a-crowin' like asses, / And livin' like sheep. / Oh, can't hold the han' of my love! / Can't hold her little white han'! / Yes, I went to the city / And there I did bitterly cry, / Men out of touch with the earth, / And with never a glance at the sky. / Oh, can't hold the han' of my love! / Can't hold her pure little han'! / *I Went to the City*

PATMORE, Coventry (1823-1896)

P20 — That, maugre all God's promises could do, / The chosen People never conquer'd quite; / Who therefore lived with them, / And that by formal truce and as of right, / In metropolitan Jerusalem. / *The Unknown Eros*

PATRICK (Saint) (389?-461?)

P21 — They mocked those who crowded into the cities; they were of the opinion that the city people were not living the life of human beings, but of birds sitting high up in their nests. [of Visigoths]

PAUL, Elliot (1891-1958)

P22 — The last time I see Paris will be on the day I die. The city was inexhaustible, and so is its memory. *The Last Time I Saw Paris*

PAYNE, Robert (1911-)

P23 — According to a pleasant Rome fiction Rome was founded by a chieftain named Romulus on April 21, 753 B.C., at about eight o'clock in the morning. *The Horizon Book of Ancient Rome*

PEABODY, Elizabeth

P24 — What absurdity can be imagined greater than the institution of cities. Cities originated not in love but in war. It was war that drove men together in multitudes and compelled them to stand so close and build walls around them.

PEGGE, S. (1704-1796)

P25 — When it's dark in Dover, / 'tis dark all the world over. *Kenticisms*

PENDLE, George (1906-1977)

P26 — To some, even today, the far-off city of Buenos Aires is another Paris. Much of its late nineteenth-century architecture comes straight from the Madeleine and Neuilly . . . To others, 'B.A.' still signifies British businesses and clubs, the London bank, *Buenos Aires Herald*, English-named suburbs, cricket and polo at Hurlingham, amateur performances of English plays. *Argentina*

PENN, William (1644-1718)

P27 — Let the rivers and creeks be sounded in order to settle a great towne. Be sure to make your choice where it is most navigable, high, dry and healthy. Let every house be pitched in the middle of its plot so that there may be ground on each side for gardens or orchards or fields, that it may be a green country towne that will never be burnt and always be wholesome. [of plan for Philadelphia]

P28 — The country life is to be preferred, for there we see the works of God, but in cities little else but the works of men. *Reflections and Maxims*

PEPYS, Samuel (1633-1703)

P29 — But Lord! how everybody's looks, and discourse in the street, is of death, and nothing else; and few people going up and down, that the town is like a place distressed and forsaken. [The time of the Great Plague of London]

P30 — The city which is in every respect another London. [of Bristol] *Ibid.*

P31 — Here out of the window it was a most pleasant sight to see the City from one end to the other with a glory about it, so high was the light of the bonfires, and so thick round the City, and the bells rang everywhere. [of London] *Ibid.*

P32 — Though he be a fool, yet he keeps much company, and will tell all he sees or hears, so a man may understand what the common talk of the town is. *Ibid.*

PERICLES (?- 429 B.C.)

P33 — Our city is the centre of learning for all of Greece. Each individual man is educated and conducts himself decently and graciously. There is no other city but ours which comes out of each battle unscathed . . . It is even better than its reputation . . . We are not dependent on Homer or any other poet for their praise . . . Courageously we gain access to every ocean and every country; everywhere we leave behind reminders of our benevolence or our destruction. [of Athens]

P34 — I would have you day by day fix your eyes upon the greatness of Athens, until you become filled with the love of her; and when you are impressed by the spectacle of her glory, reflect that this empire has been acquired by men who knew their duty and had the courage to do it. *Funeral Oration*

PERRY, Clarence Arthur (1872-1944)

P35 — The truth is that the natural nest of the human family is not merely six solid walls, but this box plus a surrounding medium through which sunshine and air can penetrate and in which social activities of vital import to its members can be carried on. When we consider how ruthlessly the city has disrupted the family nest, it is easy to understand the misery peculiar to present urban living. *Housing for the Machine Age*

PERRY, George S.

P36 — A large part of the fun of making the acquaintance of Baltimore lies in trying to unravel its endless contradictions. Almost any sweeping statement you make about its character will be wrong. Most of its 101 consistencies are not simple, direct paradoxes, but oblique, chain-stitched contradictions which in the end lead one not merely around but over and under Robin Hood's barn. *Cities of America*

P37 — In the American mind, Reno remains to gambling and divorces what Pittsburgh means to steel and Hollywood to movies. *Saturday Evening Post*

P38 — Kansas City is a kind of interior American crossroads and melting pot where the Southerner, the Northerner, the Easterner and the Westerner meet and become plain John American, with America unfolding ... 'in oceans of glory' in every direction. It got its start on the riches of Boston banks and Western lands and Northern furs. It is not only America's approximate geographical heart, but the center of gravity for her taste and emotion. The soap opera, movie or national magazine that doesn't 'take' in Kansas City won't live long in the nation. *Ibid.*

PETERSON, Vergilia (1904-1966)

P39 — In Reno, there is always a bull market, never a bear market, for the stocks and bonds of happiness. *A Matter of Life and Death*

PETRARCH (1304-1374)

P40 — Cologne received me ... a place famous for its location and for its river, famous also because of its population. It is strange to see how fine the manners are in this barbaric country, how beautiful the view of the city, how proud the deportment of the women.

P41 — Paris actually never really lived up to its reputation, much of which it owes to the exaggerations of its inhabitants. But there is no doubt that it was something great once ... The shouting and the hustling of people in the streets is no more; the walls reverberate, the woods are silent.

PHAEDRUS (1st. c. A.D.)

P42 — Troy fell because Cassandra was not believed. *Fables*

PHILIP, (Prince, of England) (1921-   )

P43 — It is not a bad idea to remind the people who live in towns and get their milk in tins or bottles and butter in packets, that it all starts with the cow ...

PHILLIPS, Jewell Cass (1900-   )

P44 — Cultural contributions of the great cities of antiquity — Memphis, Thebes, Nineveh, Babylon, Athens, and ancient Rome, to mention only a few — were tremendous, but the real foundations of American municipal government are to be found in the self-governing institutions of the Anglo-Saxons, probably having their origin in Britain during the fifth century A.D. *Municipal Government and Administration in America*

PHILLIPS, (Sir) Richard

P45 — Great cities contain in their very greatness, the seeds of premature and rapid decay. London will increase, as long as certain causes operate which she cannot control. Such have been the causes of the decay of all overgrown cities. Ninevah, Babylon, Antioch, and Thebes are become heaps of ruins, tolerable only to reptiles and wild beasts. Rome, Delhi, and Alexandria, are partaking the same inevitable fate; and London must some time, from similar causes, succumb under the destiny of every thing human. *Monthly Magazine*

P46 — No question is so common as, whence come the inhabitants of all the new houses built in the suburbs of London? *Ibid.*

PHILLIPS, Wendell (1811-1884)

P47 — The time will come when our cities will strain our institutions as slavery never did.

PICARD, Max

P48 — Noise is manufactured in the city, just as goods are manufactured. The city is the place where noise is kept in stock, completely detached from the object from which it came. *A Certain World*

PICKFORD, Mary (1893-1979

P49 — Last night I had a dream about Toronto. I was on my bicycle, cruising about in front of the old house. And, as usual in my dreams, I was a little girl again. A little girl in Toronto, with long golden curls. *Toronto Telegram, June 22, 1968*

PIDGIN, Charles F. (1844-1923)

P50 — Yes, 'tis Boston, 'tis Boston, 'round which the world revolves, / Yes, 'tis Boston, 'tis Boston, where port and beans are grub; / Yes, 'tis Boston, 'tis Boston, that one to leave resolves, / But, no! he cannot do it, he cannot quit the Hub. / Because, when far away from Boston, no Boston joys I see, / Because the Boston music, Boston sights and Boston ways suit me; / Because the Boston culture, cranks, east winds, to me they all are prime, / Because 'tis Boston, Boston first and last, and Boston all the time. / *The Loyal Boston Man (Song)*

PIERCE, Warren H.

P51 — Chicago is rough and tough, rowdy and exciting. It hasn't grown up yet — and sometimes it is not funny to watch the growing pains. But that is Chicago.

P52 — A hodge-podge of races and nationalities. [of Chicago] *Chicago, Unfinished Anomaly*

P53 — This is unbroken city. It is a social and economic entity. It lives, eats, and breathes as a single body politic. Yet within its area are more than three hundred independent, tax levying, governmental units. Probably nowhere on earth exists as complex a political Balkans concentrated in a similar metropolitan area. [of Chicago] *Ibid.*

PIERCY, Marge (1936-)

P54 — Fiction builds us alternative cities superimposed on the city whose streets we walk or drive. Some of these paper cities seem close to our own, evoking the pleasure of reading a story set in a Boston you remember, or an Upper West Side of a Manhattan you live in. But some of these cities are exotic, threatening, enticing — cities of the dead and cities of the unborn. *The City as Battleground: The Novelist as Combatant*

PIGGOTT, Stuart (1910-)

P55 — By origin and primary definition, civilization was the exclusive property of city dwellers or citizens. The antithetic division of mankind into civilized and barbarian peoples was a natural concept within the classical tradition of Greek and Roman thought. *The Role of the City in Ancient Civilizations*

PIKE, (Rev.) James A. (1913-1969)

P56 — San Francisco also has the lowest percentage of church involvement of any major city — perhaps twenty-five percent (at the most) of the total population, including all Jews, Protestants, Roman Catholics, and members of other religions, are related to religious institutions. San Francisco is almost tops in the number of suicides and the consumption of alcohol, as well. Now some people say, 'No wonder! So few go to church — that is why all these evils happen.' Actually, I think these problems are functions of the more basic one. People don't reaffiliate with *any* group when they move to the city. *Morality in the Secular City*

PINERO

P57 — Paris is the middle-aged woman's paradise. *The Prince and the Butterfly*

PITT, William (Earl of Chatham) (1708-1778)

P58 — The parks are the lungs of London. *Speech in House of Commons*

PIUS II (Pope) (1405-1464)

P59 — It delights me, O Rome, to look on thy ruins, from whose wreck thy former glory still appears. But these, thy people, burn the hard marbles torn from thy old walls to make lime. If this sacrilegious people continue thus for three hundred years more, there will remain no vestige of greatness.

PIZARRO, Francisco (1470?-1541)

P60 — Town of Kings. [of Lima]

PLATO (427?-347 B.C.)

P61 — Socrates is charged with corrupting the youth of the city, and with rejecting the gods of Athens and introducing new divinities. *Apologia*

P62 — Fields and trees are not willing to teach me anything; but this can be effected by men residing in the city. *The Phaedrus*

P63 — Any city, however small, is in fact divided into two, one the city of the poor, the other of the rich; these are at war with one another; and in either there are many smaller divisions, and you would be altogether beside the mark if you treated them all as a single State. *The Republic*

P64 — A city will never know happiness unless its draughtsmen are artists who have as their pattern the divine . . . They will take as their canvas a city and human character, and first they will make their canvas clean — not at all an easy matter. But you know that it is just here that they will be different from all others. They will not consent to lay a finger on city or individual, or draft laws, until they are given, or can make for themselves, a clean canvas. *Ibid.*

P65 — It will be for the rulers of our city,

then, if anyone, to use falsehood in dealing with citizen or enemy for the good of the State; no one else must do so. And if any citizen lies to our rulers, we shall regard it as a still graver offense than it is for a patient to lie to his trainer about his physical condition, or for a sailor to misrepresent to his captain any matter concerning the ship or crew, or the state of himself or his fellow sailors. *Ibid.*

P66 — Let there be one man who has a city obedient to his will, and he might bring into existence the ideal polity about which world is so incredulous. *Ibid.*

P67 — Until the race of philosophers become masters of a city there will be no cessation of evils for city or citizens, nor will the constitution receive fulfillment in deed. *Ibid.*

PLIMPTON, George (1927-)

P68 — Here is focused almost everything we should be proud of, and perhaps a little scared of, too: power, imagination, energy, competitiveness. It's a place where invariably even the extraordinary is commonplace. [of New York] *Quoted in Cities, John McGreevy*

P69 — I don't suppose any city in the world has as bad a reputation or a press as New York City. Calcutta, perhaps. But with New York, everywhere you go, people wonder when the city's going to collapse from financial instability or when it's going to slide gracefully into the Atlantic Ocean. They want to know when it's going to burn itself out of existence. *Ibid.*

P70 — I've lived in a number of capitals around the world, London and Paris, and in a number of culturally exotic cities, such as Venice and Bangkok, but I've always become just a little tired of them after a while. They become mere backgrounds and lose their presence and their force. But not New York. You can't live in this city without feeling its impact day after day. *Ibid.*

PLINY the Elder (23-79)

P71 — In the marvels of her buildings, the city has almost surpassed the brilliant successes won by Roman arms . . . [of Rome]

PLUMMER, Desmond (Chairman of Greater London Council) (1914-   )

P72 — Cities are indeed national assets, but they are not permanent assets. Like all assets, they need to be preserved and developed. And it is time that central governments recognized more clearly that investment in the future of their cities is as vital to national prosperity as it is to the well-being of the cities themselves. *(At Conference of the World's Great Cities, Tokyo, November 28, 1972)*

PLUNKITT, George Washington (1842-1924)

P73 — I've told you how I got rich by honest graft. Now, let me tell you that most politicians who are accused of robbin' the city get rich the same way. *Plunkitt of Tammany Hall, William L. Riordan*

PLUTARCH (46-120)

P74 — In Rome itself there were most alarming revolutionary tendencies — the result of the unequal distribution of wealth ... Money had accumulated in the hands of people whose families were unknown and of no account. So only a spark was needed to set everything on fire and,

since the whole state was rotten within itself, it was in the power of any bold man to overthrow it.

P75 — Moral habits, induced by public practices, are far quicker in making their way into men's private lives, than the failings and faults of individuals are in infecting the city at large. *Lives*

P76 — Themistocles said that he certainly could not make use of any stringed instrument; could only, were a small and obscure city put into his hands, make it great and glorious. *Ibid.*

P77 — A city, like a living thing, is a united and continuous whole. *Moralia*

P78 — Leo Byzantius said, 'What would you do, if you saw my wife, who scarce reaches up to my knees? ... Yet,' went he on, 'as little as we are, when we fall out with each other, the city of Byzantium is not big enough to hold us.' *Political Precepts*

P79 — Pyrrhus was used to say that Cineas had taken more towns with his words than he with his arms. *Pyrrhus*

POE, Edgar Allan (1809-1849)

P80 — Lo! Death has reared himself a throne / In a strange city lying alone / Far down within the dim West, / Where the good and the bad and the worst and the best / Have gone to their eternal rest. *The City in the Sea*

P81 — The city was in a great measure depopulated — and in those horrible regions, in the vicinity of the Thames, where amid the dark, narrow, and filthy lanes and alleys, the Demon of Disease was supposed to have had his nativity, Awe, Terror, and Superstition were alone to be found stalking abroad. [of London] *King Pest*

P82 — The grandeur that was Rome. *To Helen*

POLIZIANO, Angelo (1454-1494)

P83 — Nor would I desist from paying tribute to Dante, who with fair Beatrice to guide him sped through the nether and upper realms to the loftiest peaks of the mountains; and Petrarch who renews the triumph of love; those who in ten days create a hundred tales and those who reveal the origins of an obscure love. Hence, eternal glory reflects forever upon you, inexhaustible in genius, unsurpassed in art, Mother Florence! *Orpheus*

POLO, Marco (1254?-1324)

P84 — City of Heaven . . . because of its size and beauty, and because one can find so much entertainment, joy, and delight there, that the inhabitants truly may well believe that they are living in Paradise. [of Hangchow]

P85 — Everything in the world that is rare and precious finds its way into this city . . . [of Peking]

P86 — They produce gold-encrusted silks in Baghdad, and damask and velvet which is decorated with animal figures. Almost all the pearls which are brought to Europe from India are mounted here in this city, where one can study Mohammedan law, as well as magic, physics, astronomy and physiognomy. Baghdad is the most elegant and largest city to be found in this part of the world.

P87 — The whole city is arranged in squares just like a chess-board, and disposed in a manner so perfect and masterly that it is impossible to give a description that should do it justice. [of Peking] *The Book of Marco Polo*

POPE, Alexander (1688-1744)

P88 — Dear, damn'd, distracting town, fare-well! / Thy fools no more I'll tease: / This year in peace, ye critics, dwell, / Ye harlots, sleep at ease! / [of London] *A Farewell to London*

P89 — See the wild waste of all-devouring years, / How Rome her own sad sepulchre appears, / With nodding arches, broken temples spread, / The very tombs now vanish'd like their dead. / *Moral Essays*

P90 — Where London's column, pointing at the skies / Like a tall bully, lifts the head, and lies. / *Ibid.*

PORTER, Russell B.

P91 — The essence of Flint is speed. The tempo of the production line where the speed-up was one of the grievances of the sit-down strikers who tied up the mammoth General Motors automobile plant throughout the country, has spread to the entire life of the city . . . *The New York Times Magazine, January 31, 1957*

PORTMAN, John (Jr.)

P92 — The city has developed with very little concern for people amenities. You look at cities today and you find there's no place for people. There are places for buildings, places for automobiles, for trucks and taxicabs; but there's no nature left, there's no tranquility, there's nothing for the human spirit except dejection. *Dallas Times Herald, August 25, 1971*

P93 — The cities have gone down so far, and crime has become such a major topic for so many years, that the perceptions in the minds of people are that cities are unsafe. And really it is more a perception than a reality because . . . in Atlanta, for instance, only 6 percent of the crime is committed in the central city. However, the perception in the minds of the people would probably be more like 70 percent. *The Los Angeles Times, November 20, 1978*

POTOK, Chaim (1929-)

P94 — Different cities boil within each of us. There is so much we hate — the dirt, the poverty, the prejudice; there is so much we love — the one or two friendships that somehow crossed boundaries, the libraries where we joined ourselves to the dreams of others, the places where we composed dreams of our own, the museums where we learned how to defeat time, certain streets, alleys, staircases, apartment-house roofs, certain radio stations we would listen to deep into the night, certain newspapers we read as if they were a testament to the ages. We remember the terrors and joys of our early urban wanderings. We write, and continue the journey. *Culture Confrontation in Urban America: A Writer's Beginnings*

POUND, Ezra (1885-1972)

P95 — O God, what great kindness / have we done in times past / and forgotten it; / That thou givest this wonder unto us, / O God of waters? . . . / [of Venice]

POWERS, W.A.

P96 — Like a resplendent chandelier, Paris in winter is made up of many parts. It is a classic Degasesque ballet dancer rehearsing in the Opera, the Champs-Elysees in the rain, the academic seriousness of study at the Beaux-Arts, the Bohemian bonhomie of all of St. Germain-des-Pres, the light eating and deep conversation of Les Deux Magots, a formal concert by the visiting Viennese, the ever-changing patterns of the river Seine by night, the smile of service, the master music, youth and a dog, fresh flowers and wet pavements in the Etoile, the Gare des Invalides and its magnificent clock, the illuminated night tracery of leafless plane trees, the mysterious solace of the bridges, the glistening, triumphant majesty of the nighttime vistas ... the heart-lifting silhouette of the Eiffel Tower, a businesslike bus and a proud set of arches ... It is Notre Dame ... it is Paris ... Fairest Lady of Europe. *Town and Country*

POWYS, John Cowper (1872-1963)

P97 — Certainly when one contemplates the general condition of mental life in a large city, it seems as though it needed an inhuman obstinacy to avoid being sucked down by the vortex of vulgar sensationalism that seethes around us at every moment. *The Meaning of Culture*

PRIESTLEY, J.B. (1894-   )

P98 — A stone forest. [the city]

P99 — London to most of us never becomes real at all; it is merely a dream, a phantasmagoria, a changing pattern of sight and sound, with little bits of reality here and there, like currants in a vague and enormous pudding. *All About Ourselves and Other Essays*

PRINGLE, H. and K. PRINGLE

P100 — Thus the evolution of Niagara Falls is in line with the traditional pattern of the American City: from small village to industrial control to middle-class domesticity. *Saturday Evening Post*

PRIOR, Matthew (1664-1721)

P101 — To cities and to courts repair, /

Flattery and falsehood flourish there; / There all thy wretched arts employ, / Where riches triumph over joy, / Where passion does with interest barter, / And Hymen holds by Mammon's charter; / Where truth by point of law is parried, / And knaves and prudes are six times married. *Turtle and Sparrow*

PRITCHETT, V.S. (1900-   )

P102 — The very name London has tonnage in it. *London Perceived*

PROCACCINO, Mario A. (New York City Comptroller) (1912-   )

P103 — In my opinion, the job of a mayor is like that of a judge; and that is to stand in the middle of an opposing conflict, to act as mediator first. *(News Conference, New York, October 10, 1969)*

PROCOPIUS (c.499-565)

P104 — The two seas which are on either side of it, that is to say the Aegean and that which is called the Euxine [Black Sea], which meet at the east part of the city and dash together as they mingle their waves, separate the continent by their currents, and add to the beauty of the city while they surround it. It is therefore encompassed by three straits connected with one another, arranged so as to minister both to its elegance and its convenience, all of them most charming for sailing on, lovely to look at, and exceedingly safe for anchorage. [of Constantinople] *The Buildings of Justinian*

PROPERTIUS (c.48-15 B.C.)

P105 — By her own wealth is haughty Rome brought low. *Elegies*

PROWSE, William Jeffrey (1836-1870)

P106 — Though the latitude's rather uncertain, / And the longitude likewise is vague, / Still the people I pity who know not the City, / The beautiful City of Prague. / *The City of Prague*

PUSHKIN, Alexander S. (1799-1837)

P107 — I love you, child of Peter / I love you calm and stern / [of St. Petersburg] *The Bronze Horseman*

PYLE, Ernie (1900-1945)

P108 — It is a city law that all public benches must be green, and made of wood. And they must be repainted once a year. They're more than just something to sit on.... I think it's mighty nice to have a place like St. Petersburg where you don't need either a Blue Book status or eighty billion red corpuscles to have a good time. [of St. Petersburg, Florida] *Home Country*

Q

QUILLEN, Robert (1887-1948)

Q1 — A hick town is one where there is no place to go where you shouldn't be.

QUINCY, Josiah (1772-1864)

Q2 — The interests of the average citizen are better and more fully cared for, his wants more fully met, in the great city of Europe than in that of America.

QUINN, (Father) Bernard

Q3 — While residing in a small town I had often heard people say what a friendly place it was, how kind and neighborly the people were, and what a fine place it was in which to live. From my own experience I had to agree. And yet, evidently not everyone in the town shared the same favorable image. On the highway sign at town entrance one night someone crossed out the town name and painted over it the word HELL.

QUINN, Sally (1941-   )

Q4 — Washington is ... a company town. Most of the interesting people in Washington either work for the government or write about it. *We're Going to Make You a Star*

R

RAABE, Wilhelm (1831-1910)

R1 — The mad, the solemn city, the city of martyrs, musicians and beautiful girls. [of Prague]

RABAN, Jonathan (1942-)

R2 — A natural territory for the psychopath with histrionic gifts. [of the city] *Soft City*

R3 — When I finally arrived in London to stay I felt twice life-size . . . one might see or hear anything in that immense ambiguous ripple of population and power. For me it promised release and a libidinous surge of adrenalin. I wanted London as I'd once lain awake wanting a glossy enamel split-cane trout rod. *Ibid.*

RABELAIS (1494?-1553)

R4 — Small town, great renown. [of Chinon, Rabelais's native town] *Pantagruel*

R5 — I have, I said, found in Holy Scripture that Cain was the first builder of towns. *Works*

RALPH, Julian (1853-1903)

R6 — The worst feature, that which seems almost to caricature the worst products of partisan politics, is seen in the Mayor's office. The Mayor of Chicago has to hide behind a series of locked doors, and it is almost as difficult to see him as it would be to visit the Prefect of Police in Paris . . . The reason for this extraordinary and undemocratic condition of affairs is that the Mayor of Chicago is the worst victim of the spoils system that has yet been created in America. The chase for patronage fetches up at his door, and all the avenues employed in it end at his person. He is almost the sole source and dispenser of public place of every grade. *Harper's New Monthly, April, 1892*

R7 — The most interesting among the experiences of all those who come here is that of the immigrants. They come like cattle, herded in the holds of ships, and then penned in a great house on Ellis Island, and separated into groups — this group for this railroad, that group for the other railroad — a helpless, confused huddle of foreigners tied to their babies and bundles, and awakening in the minds of all kindly folks who see them a blending of pity and amazement. The pity is for their helplessness, and the amazement is as to what kind of homes they must have left in Europe, and as to how they can have mustered the courage to come so far into a new and strange land. [of New York] *Harpers's Young People, December 18, 1894*

RAMSAY, W.M. (1851-1939)

R8 — Christianity spread first along the great roads that led to Rome, as every free and natural current of thought did, owing to the circumstances of the period, and from the center was distributed to the outlying parts of the Empire. *Roads and Travel in the New Testament*

RAND, Ayn (1905-1982)

R9 — The skyline of New York is a monument of a splendor that no pyramids or palaces will ever equal or approach. But America's skyscrapers were not built by public funds nor for a public purpose; they were built by the energy, initiative and wealth of private individuals for personal profit. *The Virtue of Selfishness*

RANSOM, John Crowe (1888-1974)

R10 — Athens, a fragile kingdom by the foam, / Assumed the stranger's yoke; but then behold how meek / Those unbred Caesars grew, who spent their fruits of Rome / Forever after, trying to be Greek. / *Triumph*

RAPHAEL, Adam

R11 — Now I know subjective opinions can vary, but personally I reckon LA as the noisiest, the smelliest, the most uncomfortable, and most uncivilised major city in the United States. In short a stinking sewer. *The Guardian, July 22, 1968*

RAPKIN, Chester (1918-   )

R12 — The towndweller throughout time has voiced a disquieting ambivalence about the city — his proudest and most significant creation in history. He has insisted that it is the source of civilization and has moulded his language to reflect this view; he has lamented that it is a generator of corruption and has railed against its evil influence. He has marvelled at the beauty of its towers and been revolted by its hovels. He has resented its changes and sought ways to perfect it. In recent years, it has spawned more detractors than defenders, some of whom have even challenged the right of the city to continue to exist or proposed major alterations as conditions of survival. But the cities, defying the predictions and the judgments, have continued to grow. *Current Trends and Future Prospects of the American City*

RAPPORT, Samuel and Patricia SCHARTLE

R13 — America is a nation of home towns. To thousands, home is not just a house and a family, but a street, a neighborhood where shade trees and party lines are shared and a cup of sugar is yours for the borrowing. *America Remembers. Our Best-Loved Customs and Traditions*

RASKIN, Eugene (1909-   )

R14 — The city has in most respects outgrown the reasons for its existence. It no longer fulfills the functions which brought it into being; on the contrary, most of these functions are better served outside the city.

We simply do not need the city any more. *Sequel to Cities*

R15 — In this the latter part of the 20th Century, we must face the fact that . . . in the case of defense, for example, the city represents a target hazard rather than an advantage. In the day of nuclear rockets one is more vulnerable in the city than anywhere else. The city walls no longer exist, and if they did, would be of no use. If the bomb doesn't get you, falling buildings will, — or broken gas and water mains, fire or panic. If it's a safe place you want, turn the clock back 500,000 years and look for a deep cave. *Ibid.*

R16 — The replacement of the Urban Society by its successor, the Post-Urban Society, is already taking place. We are shifting, and not so slowly, to a pattern of existence that is independent of cities, that gets along just fine without cities, and to a way of life whose members, a generation or two from now will look back upon the urban period of man's history with perhaps some romantic fondness, but certainly more than a tinge of horror. *Ibid.*

R17 — There is something a bit touching about urban experts these days. It does not occur to them that the city has outlived its evolutionary role, that the evidences of its demise are crystal clear around us, and that it is beyond help. Blind to reality, they go on making plans, like the officers of the sinking Titanic charting tomorrow's course, while water rises past their ears. *Ibid.*

R18 — Today's technology makes it possible for you to live anywhere you want to. You don't have to live in town; certainly you don't have to live in a big city. Of course, being able to get along without the city is nothing new, — there have always been people who were self-sufficient in the wilderness or on the farm. However, the principal characteristic of their scale of living was 'doing without.' Today it can be truthfully said that you can, if you like, sally forth into the wilderness and take with you every convenience and amenity that the city has to offer. And leave the city itself behind. *Ibid.*

R19 — We have had cities only for the last five thousand years, or one half of one percent of our time on Earth. Far from being permanent, it is therefore quite reasonable to expect that like every other phase of human evolution, cities too will one day yield to the great flushing action of history, and like the great lizards, vanish from the scene. *Ibid.*

RASMUSSEN, Steen Eiler (1898-   )

R20 — To search for the ideal city today is useless. For all cities are different. Each one has its own spirit, its own problems, and its own pattern of life. As long as the city lives, these aspects continue to change. Thus to look for the ideal city is not only a waste of time but may be seriously detrimental. In fact, the concept is obsolete; there is no such thing.

RAUDEBAUGH, Charles

R21 — A city is at once a time and a place. San Francisco is perched as breathtakingly in time as it is in space. Physically, it is set upon seven hills at the tip of a slender peninsula which divides an oceanlike bay from the greatest sea of the globe. Historically, it is on the partition line between the Period of Western Civilization and the Period of the Pacific. *San Francisco, the Beldam Dozes*

RAUSCHENBUSCH, Walter (1861-1918)

R22 — The larger our cities grow the less hold does religion seem to have over the multitude of men and the general life. . . . For one thing, the people of our great cities are cut off from nature and from nature's God. All that they see and touch was made by man. To men in Chicago the heavens do not declare the glory of God, for they are covered with smoke. *The State of the Church in the Social Movement*

REDFIELD, Robert (1897-1958)

R23 — With the exception of the few isolated survivors, the rise of the civilizations transformed the precivilized peoples. We may think of civilization as a remaking of man in which the basic type, the folk man, is altered into other types. . . . This remaking of man was the work of the city. *The Primitive World and Its Transformations*

REED, John (1887-1920)

R24 — Who that has known thee but shall burn / In exile till he come again / To do thy bitter will, O stern / Moon of the tides of men! / [of New York] *Proud New York*

REEVES, Richard (1936-   )

R25 — So our cities are dying. And they will go on dying until the federal income tax is used to pay for solution to national problems. . . . More than money is needed, however. The creativity of the nation is necessary; the United States has to figure out how to make an urban society work. *Quoted in Reader's Digest*

REPPLIER, Agnes (1855-1950)

R26 — Philadelphians are every whit as mediocre as their neighbors, but they seldom encourage each other in mediocrity by giving it a more agreeable name. *Philadelphia: The Place and the People*

R27 — It would be hard to say when or why the American mind acquired the conviction that the lonely farmhouse or the sacrosanct village was the proper breeding-place for great Americans. *Times and Tendencies*

R28 — Lovers of the town have been content, for the most part, to say they loved it. They do not brag about its uplifting qualities. They have none of the infernal smugness which makes the lover of the country insupportable. *Ibid.*

R29 — With all history to contradict us, it is hardly worthwhile to speak of city life as entailing 'spiritual loss,' because it is out of touch with Nature. It is in touch with humanity, and humanity is Nature's heaviest asset. *Ibid.*

RESTON, James (1909-   )

R30 — America is now an overdeveloped urban nation, with an underdeveloped system for dealing with its city problems. *The New York Times, January 9, 1966*

R31 — Look down on it in the early morning from the pinnacle of the Washington Monument. The geometric pattern of its streets stretches out in the early sun to a rim of blue water and green hills. From this peephole in the sky it looks like an architect's dream, a World's Fair model city turned on by an electric switch, a study in shine and shade and movement, a fabulous and incongruous mixture of long, straight modern boulevards and classical pillared buildings out of Greece and Rome. *The New York Times Magazine, June 1, 1941*

REYNOLDS, Malvina (1900-1978)

R32 — There's a green one and a pink one / A blue one and a yellow one / And they're all made out of ticky-tacky / And they all look just the same. / *(Satirical song on suburban housing)*

RIBER, Lorenzo (1882-1958)

R33 — Abode of the rich, pleasant is Barcelona; / There a port opens its amorous arms; / The land bubbles always with sweet waters. /

RIBICOFF, Abraham A. (Senator) (1910-)

R34 — The crisis in the cities isn't over. Anyone who lives or works in or visits the cities knows the crisis is still with us. [On President Nixon's assertion that the city crisis is over.] *(Radio Address, March 10, 1973)*

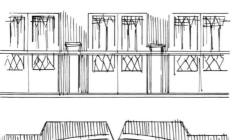

RICE, Wallace (1859-1939)

R35 — O great city of visions, waging the war of the free, / Beautiful, strong and alert, a goddess in purpose and mien. / *Chicago*

RICHARDSON, Anna S. (1865-1949)

R36 — No mother should permit her daughter to go to a strange city unless she can provide the girl with funds to pay board and room for a month, which will amount to not less than twenty dollars, and the price of her return ticket in case she fails to find work in that time. The mother who recklessly allows her unskilled daughter to enter a strange city armed only with a week's board and high hopes, is guilty of criminal neglect as the guardian of her child's future. *The Girl Who Earns Her Own Living*

RICHARD I (of England) (1157-1199)

R37 — Dear Lord, I pray Thee to suffer me not to see Thy Holy City, since I cannot deliver it from the hands of Thy enemies. [of Jerusalem]

RIESENBERG, Felix (1879-1939)

R38 — [A place where] there is no room to die. [of the city]

RIESMAN, David (1909-)

R39 — The whole American ethos, which once revolved about the dialectic of pure country versus wicked but exciting city, seems to me now aerated by the suburban outlook. This produces an homogenization of both city and country, but without full integration. *The Suburban Dislocation*

RIIS, Jacob (1849-1914)

R40 — The measure of civilization. [of slums]

R41 — Since the family home is the basis upon which our modern civilization rests, and since, with the universal drift toward the cities that characterizes this civilization in the age of steam, it is coming to be more and more an urban home. . . . New York is the type of the other great cities. What has happened there will happen elsewhere. Local conditions may differ in New York,

Boston, Chicago, Philadelphia, or St. Louis, as they differ in London, Glasgow, Paris, Berlin and Naples, but essentially the same problems have to be solved in them all, in the housing of their crowded populations. It amounts to this, whether or not the readjustment from the old plan to the new, in which the city home is to be the central fact, can be made safely; whether in it *the home* can be protected. *Forum, March-August, 1895*

R42 — The color line must be drawn through the tenements to give the picture its proper shade. The landlord does it with an absence of pretence, a frankness of despotism, that is nothing if not brutal. The Czar of all the Russias is not more absolute upon his own soil than the New Landlord in his dealings with colored tenants. *How the Other Half Lives*

R43 — A map of the city, colored to designate nationalities, would show more stripes than on the skin of a zebra, and more colors than any rainbow. *Ibid.*

RILEY, James Whitcomb (1849-1916)

R44 — Without the farmer the town cannot flourish. Ye men of the streets, be cordial to our rustic brethren. They are more potent than bankers and lawyers, more essential to the public good than poets and politicians. Do all you can for them. Farmers should vibrate wisely and heartily between the Public Square and the farm — and *we* of the town should do the same.

RILKE, Rainer Maria (1875-1926)

R45 — But cities seek their own, not others' good; / they drag all with them in their headlong haste. / They smash up animals like hollow wood / and countless nations they burn up for waste. /

R46 — And here about me is Rome . . . Rome which is having its blossom time, with full hanging wisteria, with thousands of new roses daily, with all its beautiful fountains that are like eternal life, serenely new, without age, without exhaustion. *Letters of Rainer Maria Rilke 1892-1910*

R47 — When one has Paris around one for the first time, one must let it act more like a

bath, without trying to do too much about it oneself; save to feel and let it happen. *Ibid.*

RIVERS, Joan (1937-   )

R48 — Everybody's into health in Beverly Hills. You're not considered legally dead until you lose your tan.

R49 — It's all sex and violence. You can get your purse snatched and rear end pinched simultaneously. [of New York]

R50 — New York is very rough. They write themes on: 'What I stole over my summer vacation.'

ROBERTS, Cecil (1892-1976)

R51 — If Greece has taught us that marble bleeds, Rome shows us that dust flowers. *And So to Rome*

ROBINSON, Charles M. (1869-1917)

R52 — There is other value in municipal beauty than that indicated by money value. There is a sociological value in the larger happiness of great masses of people, whose only fields are park meadows, whose only walls are city streets, whose statues stand in public places, whose paintings hang where all may see, whose books and curios, whose drives and music, are first the city's where they live. The happier people of the rising City Beautiful will grow in love for it, in pride for it. They will be better citizens, because better instructed, more artistic, and filled with civic pride. *Atlantic Monthly, May, 1899*

R53 — There is only one American city which has been laid out as a whole on an artistic design prohibitive to haphazard growth. That city is Washington. *Ibid.*

R54 — And when the heavens rolled away and St. John beheld the new Jerusalem, so a new vision of a new London, a new Washington, Chicago, or New York breaks with the morning's sunshine upon the degradation, discomfort, and baseness of modern city life. There are born a new dream and a new hope. *Modern Civic Art*

ROBINSON, Edwin A. (1869-1935)

R55 — I know my Boston is a counterfeit, — / A frameless imitation, all bereft / Of living

nearness, noise, and common speech . . .
/ *Torrent and the Night Before*

ROBSON, William A. (1895-1980)

R56 — There is much to love and to admire in the great city. It is the home of the highest achievements of man in art, literature and science: the source from which the forces of freedom and emancipation have sprung. It is the place where the spirit of humanism and of democracy have grown and flourished, where man's quest for knowledge and justice has been pursued most constantly, and truth revealed most faithfully and fearlessly. *Great Cities of the World, Their Government, Politics, and Planning*

ROCKEFELLER, David (1915-)

R57 — I wonder what the rest of the world would think of a political system that allowed its largest city to go into bankruptcy. [of New York during the fiscal crisis] *(Before Senate Banking Committee, Washington, June 12, 1978)*

ROCKEFELLER, Nelson A. (Governor of New York) (1908-1979)

R58 — New York (City) is still the cultural and financial capital in this country — and we've got to keep it that way. *(State of the State Address, Albany, January 23, 1972)*

R59 — We don't need Band-aids on the problems [of Federal aid to cities and states] . . . We need a blood transfusion.

RODALE, Robert (1930-)

R60 — We are, in effect, returning to the Middle Ages, when men wouldn't dare venture out without their armor. The modern American puts on his car in the morning, thereby changing from a soft-skinned target for autos into a missile himself. *Quoted in Reader's Digest*

RODIN, Auguste (1840-1917)

R61 — The Rome of the North. [of Prague]

ROGERS, David H. (Mayor of Spokane)

R62 — It's time to recognize that the mayors are not the village idiots, but probably have

more knowledge and ability on urban affairs than any other group. *(Interview, February, 1969)*

ROGERS, Will (1879-1935)

R63 — In a real estate man's eye, the most exclusive part of the city is wherever he has a house to sell.

R64 — Rome had senators. Now I know why it declined. [of Washington D.C.]

R65 — Hardly a day goes by, you know, that some innocent bystander ain't shot in New York City. All you got to do is be innocent and stand by and they're gonna shoot you. The other day, there was four people shot in one day — four innocent people — in New York City. Amazing. It's kind of hard to *find* four innocent people in New York. That's why a policeman don't have to aim. He just shoots anywhere. Whoever he hits, that's the right one. *Quoted in Reader's Digest*

ROHATYN, Felix G. (1928-)

R66 — A balanced Federal budget is not a moral imperative, but a livable urban civilization is. Basically, only the President of this country can light the candle that will lead the cities of this country out of the darkness they are in. . . . *(Before Association For A Better New York)*

ROLLAND, Romain (1886-1944)

R67 — Big cities are monstrous organisms, where, like the microbes of all maladies, those of the mind multiply rapidly. New-comers, if they do not succumb at once . . . must undergo a long and painful period to acclimatize their blood to these poisons. *Journey Within*

R68 — Rome is the *imperator* who governs forces. She does not give up her secret; perhaps she has none. But she unveils yours for you. Whoever knows her, knows nothing of her, but discovers himself. *Ibid.*

ROMNEY, George W. (Secretary of Housing and Urban Development) (1907-)

R69 — The flight of the affluent from the city to the suburbs, together with the influx of the poor into the central city, has created a white suburb noose around an impoverished black central core. *(United States Conference of Mayors, June 14, 1971)*

RONSARD, Pierre de (1524-1585)

R70 — A town set in the fields of Savoy which, by fraud, drove out its former rulers, the miserable abode of every apostasy, of stubbornness, pride, and heresy. [of Geneva]

ROOSEVELT, Theodore (1858-1919)

R71 — Let us show, not merely in great crises, but in every day affairs of life, qualities of practical intelligence of hardihood and endurance, and above all, the power of devotion to a lofty ideal. [of American cities]

ROSE, Billy (1899-1966)

R72 — The present mayor of Peoria / Works in a five-and-ten cent storia.... / They chased the laundry out of Peoria, / The legislature passed a lawria / And bought a bathtub for Peoria. / *I Wish I Was in Peoria*

ROSE, Daniel

R73 — The endlessly sprawling American suburb is the most economically wasteful human settlement known to man ... Besides, if safe, big cities are just more fun to be in. *(At New School Center for New York City Affairs, October, 1973)*

ROSENFELD, Issac (1918-1956)

R74 — A Walt Whitman storehouse of democracy come alive, a Sears catalogue of people and occupations endlessly varied in repetitive similarities. [of Chicago]

ROSSETTI, Christina Georgina (1830-1894)

R75 — One day in the country / Is worth a month in town. / *Summer*

ROURKE, Francis E. (1922-   )

R76 — As the city was being treated with such persistent disdain in the formal literature of political philosophy during the nineteenth and early twentieth centuries, the general population was simultaneously voting with its feet for urban life — moving into the city in ever increasing numbers in

response to economic and other incentives. The trend toward urbanization was certainly not reversed by the hostility shown the city in the American political tradition. Indeed much of this antagonism may rather be viewed as a peevish reaction against a development that could not be prevented. *Ethics*

ROUSE, James

R77 — Although the business of city building is the largest single industry in America, there is no large corporation engaged in it. City building has no General Motors or General Electric — no IBM, no Xerox; no big capital resources to invest in the purchase of large land areas; no big research and development program unfolding new techniques to produce a better environment. *(Testimony before Subcommittee of U.S. Congress)*

R78 — If we harness it to the tools we have forged for developing and redeveloping our cities, we will revolutionize our urban civilization in our lifetimes. We can wipe out the suffocating oppressiveness of slum and blight and sprawl. We can replace the nobodyness with communities that make a man and his family important. *Quoted in Great Cities for a Great Society*

ROUSSEAU, Jean-Jacques (1712-1778)

R79 — Cities are the abyss of the human

species. At the end of a few generations in them races perish or degenerate, and it is necessary to renew them. This renewal always comes from the country. *Emile*

R80 — Of all animals man is least capable of living in flocks. Penned up like sheep, men soon lose all. The breath of man is fatal to his fellows. . . . Cities are the burial pit of the human species. *Ibid.*

R81 — As the State or City constitutes a moral person whose life consists in the cooperation and union of its members, the first and most important of its concerns is that of its own preservation. *Geneva Manuscript*

R82 — All things considered, I do not see that it is henceforth possible for the sovereign to preserve the exercise of its rights among us unless the City is very small. *The Social Contract*

R83 — If the State cannot be reduced to a proper size, there is still one remaining expedient. It is not to tolerate a capital, to locate the government alternatively in each town, and to convene the assemblies of the country in each of them by turn. *Ibid.*

R84 — In a well-run City, everyone rushes to assemblies. *Ibid.*

R85 — In Madrid, there are superb drawing rooms, but not a window that closes; and people sleep in ratholes. *Ibid.*

R86 — It is always an evil to unite several towns in a single City, and that anyone who wants to create such a union should not imagine that its natural drawbacks can be avoided. *Ibid.*

R87 — Just as the regimen of healthy people is not suited to the sick, one must not want to govern a corrupt people by the same laws that are suited to a good people. Nothing proves this maxim better than the duration of the Republic of Venice, the semblance of which still exists uniquely because its laws are only suited to wicked men. *Ibid.*

R88 — Most of them mistake a town for a City, and a bourgeois for a citizen. They do not know that houses make the town, but citizens make the City. *Ibid.*

ROWAN, Jan (1924-)

R89 — To be able to choose what you want to be and how you want to live, without worrying about social censure, is obviously more important to Angelenos than the fact that they do not have a Piazza San Marco. *Progressive Architecture, February, 1968*

ROYALL, Anne (1769-1854)

R90 — No conception can be more fallacious, or any idea more wide of the truth, than that entertained by one who has never seen this city. Our hearts swell with national pride at the mention of its name — Washington! Washington city is repeated with a sort of holy enthusiasm; nothing evil or low mingles with the sound; it conveys sentiments at once the most elevated, the most pleasing. But how are we disappointed upon coming to this Idol of America! In every other country, in every other town or city, some semblance is maintained in that attention which is due to the poor and to the rich. But if you are poor, you have no business in Washington. *Sketches of History, Life and Manners in the United States*

ROYKO, Mike (1932-)

R91 — Chicago's city motto is *urbs in horto,* meaning 'city in a garden.' I've been campaigning for years to have it changed to *ubi est mea,* which means 'Where's mine?' *Quoted in Cities, John McGreevy*

RUKEYSER, Muriel (1913-1980)

R92 — Whatever can come to a city can come to this city. / Under the tall compulsion / of the past / I see the city / change like a man changing / I love this man / with my lifelong body of love / I know you / among your changes / wherever I go / Hearing the sounds of building / the syllables of wrecking / A young girl watching / the man throwing red hot rivets / Coals in a bucket of change / How can you love a city that will not stay? / I love you / like a man of life in change. / [of New York] *Waterlily Fire*

RUNYON, Damon (1880-1946)

R93 — A place where everyone will stop

watching a championship fight to look at an usher giving a drunk a bum's rush. [of New York City]

RUSKIN, John (1819-1900)

R94 — Our cities are a wilderness of spinning wheels instead of palaces; yet the people have not clothes. We have blackened every leaf of English greenwood with ashes, and the people die of cold; our harbors are a forest of merchant ships, and the people die of hunger. *The Crown of Wild Olive*

R95 — That great foul city of London there, — rattling, growling, smoking, stinking — a ghastly heap of fermenting brickwork, pouring out poison at every pore, — you fancy it is a city of work? Not a street of it! It is a great city of play; very nasty play, and very hard play, but still play. *Ibid.*

R96 — In all healthy states, the city is the central expression of the national religion, the throne of its legal authority, and the exponent and treasure-house of its artistic skill. A perfect city exhibits always these three functions in perfection, and the nobleness of its cathedral, the dignity of its king's palace (or councilhouse if it be a republic), and the beauty of its architecture and publicly seen painting, concentrate within its sacred walls the final energies and the loftiest pleasures of which the nation is capable. *The Guild of St. George*

R97 — In the faith and practice of unchristian licence, the modern cities of all European states have alike in these days become, literally, cities of the plain, or pits of the plain into which, in precise opposition to the former going up of the tribes as to the mountain of the Lord, the iniquity of the tribes sinks by instinctive drainage into a slimepit of central corruption, where sin reacting upon sin, and iniquity festering upon iniquity, curdle and coagulate into forms so monstrous, that the eye hath not seen, nor the ear heard them. *Ibid.*

R98 — The markets of a city which proposes to itself the gathering together only of the wise for counsel and of the skilful in art will never be found to exhaust the resources of the neighbouring country, but a city to which all the fools in the kingdom resort for pleasure, all the luxurious for channels of

extravagance, and all the vicious for varieties of temptation, will soon be found to require for its supply the greater part of the produce of neighbouring provinces, . . . *Ibid.*

R99 — It is chiefly by private, not by public, effort that your city must be adorned. *Lectures on Architecture and Painting*

R100 — At all events, cities have hitherto gained the better part of their good report through our evil ways of going on in the world generally; chiefly and eminently through our bad habit of fighting with each other. *Modern Painters*

R101 — It is a sorrowful proof of the mistaken ways of the world that the 'country,' in the simple sense of a place of fields and trees, has hitherto been the source of reproach to its inhabitants, and that the words 'countryman, rustic, clown, paysan, villager,' still signify a rude and untaught person, as opposed to the words 'townsman' and 'citizen.' . . . Whereas I believe that the result of each mode of life may, in some stages of the world's progress, be the exact reverse; and that another use of words may be forced upon us by a new aspect of facts, so that we may find ourselves saying: 'Such and such a person is very gentle and kind — he is quite rustic; and such and such another person is very rude and ill-taught — he is quite urbane. *Ibid.*

R102 — Thorough sanitary and remedial action in the houses that we have; and then the building of more, strongly, beautifully, and in groups of limited extent, kept in proportion to their streams and walled round, so that there may be no festering and wretched suburb anywhere, but clean and busy street within and the open country without, with a belt of beautiful garden and orchard round the walls, so that from any part of the city perfectly fresh air and grass and sight of far horizon might be reachable in a few minutes' walk. This the final aim. *Sesame and Lilies*

R103 — Along the iron veins that traverse the frame of our country, beat and flow the fiery pulses of its exertion, hotter and faster every hour. All vitality is concentrated through those throbbing arteries into the central cities; the country is passed over like a green sea by narrow bridges, and we are thrown back in continually closer crowds on city gates. *Seven Lamps of Architecture*

R104 — Until that street architecture of ours is bettered . . . I know not how we can blame our architects for their feebleness in more important work; their eyes are inured to narrowness and slightness; can we expect them at a word to conceive and deal with breadth and solidity? They ought not to live in our cities; there is that in their miserable walls which bricks up to death men's imaginations. . . . An architect should live as little in cities as a painter. Send him to our hills, and let him study there what nature understands by a buttress, and what by a dome. *Ibid.*

R105 — If, in the square of the city, you can find a delight, finite, indeed, but pure and intense, like that which you have in a valley among the hills, then its art and architecture are right; but if, after fair trial, you can find no delight in them, nor any instruction like that of Nature, I call on you fearlessly to condemn them. *The Stones of Venice*

R106 — The Venice of modern fiction and drama is a thing of yesterday, a mere efflorescence of decay, a stage dream which the first ray of daylight must dissipate into dust. *Ibid.*

R107 — We are forced, for the sake of accumulating our power and knowledge, to live in cities: but such advantage as we have in association with each other is in great part counterbalanced by our loss of fellowship with Nature. *Ibid.*

R108 — All lovely architecture was designed for cities in cloudless air; for cities in which piazzas and gardens opened in bright populousness and peace; cities built that men might live happily in them, and take delight daily in each other's presence and powers. *The Study of Architecture*

R109 — You who have ever been to Paris,

know; And you who have not been to Paris — go! *A Tour through France*

RUSSELL, Bertrand (1872-1970)

R110 — Astrakhan seemed to me more like hell than anything I had ever imagined. The town water-supply was taken from the same part of the river into which ships shot their refuse. Every street had stagnant water which bred millions of mosquitoes; every year one third of the inhabitants had malaria. There was no drainage system, but a vast mountain of excrement at a prominent place in the middle of the town. *The Autobiography of Bertrand Russell 1914-1944*

R111 — The College of the City of New York was an institution run by the City Government. Those who attended it were practically all Jews or Catholics; but to the indignation of the former, practically all the scholarships went to the latter. The Government of New York City was virtually a satellite of the Vatican. *Ibid.*

R112 — Most of Shanghai is quite European, almost American; the names of streets, and notices and advertisements are in English (as well as Chinese). The buildings are magnificent offices and banks; everything looks very opulent. But the side streets are still quite Chinese. It is a vast city about the size of Glasgow. The Europeans almost all look villainous and ill. *Ibid.*

R113 — The town is just like a mediaeval town — narrow streets, every house a shop with a gay sign hung out, no traffic possible except Sedan chairs and a few rickshaws. The Europeans have a few factories, a few banks, a few missions and a hospital — the whole gamut of damaging and repairing body and soul by western methods. [of Cheng-Sha] *Ibid.*

RUSSELL, G.W.E. (1853-1919)

R114 — Oxford is the home of lost causes. *Half-Lengths*

S

SAALMAN, Howard (1928-)

S1 — A city is a living and growing organism, but not without its delicate side. It frequently needs more room in which to exercise its economic muscles. It is subject to fatigue, shortness of breath, hardening and blockage of the arteries, and occasionally to apoplexy. Aspirins and tranquilizers usually do not alleviate its ailments. It may require careful surgery of the heart, veins, and arteries and a steady diet of capital investment. *Haussmann: Paris Transformed*

SAFDIE, Moshe (1938-)

S2 — You say the word 'house' and it means so many different things to different people. One person sees it on an open road in the countryside; another sees a village. One thinks of a farm; another of a cliff dwelling in the urban landscape. Environment is a culture and culture is archetypal; it grows from deep within you, embodies long-lived feelings toward shelter, family, community, and self. *Beyond Habitat*

SALA, G.A. (1828-1895)

S3 — 'See Naples and then die,' says the proverb. My view . . . is that you should see Canal-street, New Orleans, and then try to live as much longer as ever you can. *America Review*

SALLUST (86-34 B.C.)

S4 — A city for sale, and destined soon to disappear, if it can find a buyer. [of Rome] *Jugurtha*

SALTUS, Edgar (1855-1921)

S5 — A nightmare in stone. [of New York City]

SALUTATI, Coluccio (1331-1406)

S6 — What city, not merely in Italy, but in all the world, is more securely placed within its circle of walls, more proud in its palazzi, more bedecked with churches, more beautiful in its architecture, more imposing in its gates, richer in piazzas, happier in its wide streets, greater in its people, more glorious in its citizenry, more inexhaustible in wealth, more fertile in fields? [of Florence] *Invective against Antonio Loschi of Vicenza*

SANDBURG, Carl (1878-1967)

S7 — Hog Butcher for the World, / Tool Maker, Stacker of Wheat, / Player with Railroads and the Nation's / Freight Handler; / Stormy, husky, brawling, / City of the Big Shoulders. / *Chicago*

S8 — The fog comes / on little cat feet. / It sits looking / over harbor and city / on silent haunches / and then moves on. / *Fog*

S9 — In the evening there is a sunset sonata comes to the cities. / There is a march of little armies to the dwindling of drums. / The skyscrapers throw their tall lengths of walls into black bastions on the red west. / The skyscrapers fasten their perpendicular alphabets far across the changing silver triangles of stars and streets. / *Good Morning, America*

S10 — Omaha, the roughneck, feeds armies, / Eats and swears from a dirty face. / Omaha works to get the world a breakfast. / *Omaha*

S11 — By day the skyscraper looms in the smoke and sun and has a soul. / Prairie and valley, streets of the city, pour people into it and they mingle / among its twenty floors and are poured again back to the streets, prairies and valleys. / *Skyscraper*

S12 — New York is a city of many cats. / Some say New York is Babylon. / There is a rose and gold mist New York. / *Three Slants at New York*

SANSOM, William (1912-1976)

S13 — How is a Frankfurter different from a Hamburger — both from historically Free Cities? The answer is that the Hamburger, with his northern climate and seamanship, is a breezy fellow: whereas the Frankfurter, similarly free but climatically temperate, is *easy*. And the man from Stuttgart? A Swabian, a countrified southerner, he is less integrated in the pan-German energy, slower and more bourgeois. The *Beau de Cologne*? He is a man of wine from the Rhine, elastic and modern, living it up and hardening in the process. The Darmstadter? Small-town, but infected by his strong artistic patronage and near-century of aesthetic duties, and now citizen of the centres of modern music and all-German architectural planning. The Mainzer? French influenced: with a wit symptomized by the involved playfulness of the most splendidly contrived Carnival in Germany. *Grand Tour Today*

SANTAYANA, George (1863-1952)

S14 — The mind of the Renaissance was not a pilgrim mind, but a sedentary city mind, like that of the ancients.

S15 — Dear old Boston, what an unlovely place it is! *The Letters of George Santayana*

S16 — Boston is a moral and intellectual nursery always busy applying first principles to trifles. *Santayana, the Later Years*

SARTRE, Jean-Paul (1905-1980)

S17 — The American street is a straight line that gives itself away immediately. *Literary and Philosophical Essays*

S18 — Chicago, blackened by its smoke, clouded by the Lake Michigan fog, is a dark and gloomy red. Pittsburgh is more gloomy still. And there is nothing more immediately striking than the contrast between the formidable power, the inexhaustible abundance of what is called the 'American Colossus' and the puny insignificance of those little houses that line the widest roads in the world. But on second thought, there is no clearer indication that America is not finished, that her ideas and plans, her social structure and her cities have only a strictly temporary reality. *Ibid.*

S19 — For [Europeans] a city is, above all, a past; to [Americans] it is mainly a future; what they like in the city is everything it has not yet become and everything it can be. *Ibid.*

S20 — I came to understand that the American city was, originally, a camp in the desert. People from far away, attracted by a mine, a petroleum field or fertile land, arrived one fine day and settled as quickly as possible in a clearing, near a river. They built the vital parts of the town, the bank, the town hall, the church, and then hundreds of one-storey frame houses. The road, if there was one, served as a kind of spinal column to the town and then streets were marked out like vertebrae, perpendicular to the road. It would be hard to count the American cities that have that kind of parting in the middle. *Ibid.*

S21 — In New York, and even in Chicago, the skyscraper is on home ground, and imposes a new order upon the city. But everywhere else it is all out of place; the eye is unable to establish any unity between these tall, gawky things and the little houses that run close to the ground; in spite of itself it looks for that line so familiar in European cities, the sky-line, and cannot find it. That is why the European feels at first as though he were travelling through a rocky chaos that resembles a city — something like Montpellier-le-Vieux — rather than a city. *Ibid.*

S22 — It is customary, in the United States, for the fashionable neighbourhoods to slide from the centre to the outskirts of the city; after five years the centre of town is 'polluted.' If you walk about there, you come upon tumble-down houses that retain a pretentious look beneath their filth; you find a complicated kind of architecture, one-storey frame houses with entrances formed by peristyles supported by columns, gothic chalets, 'Colonial houses,' etc. These were formerly aristocratic homes, now inhabited by the poor. Chicago's lurid Negro section contains some of these Greco-Roman temples; from the outside they still look well. But inside, twelve rat- and louse-plagued Negro families are crowded together in five or six rooms. *Ibid.*

S23 — The most striking aspect of the American city is the vertical disorder. *Ibid.*

S24 — New York and Chicago do not have neighbourhoods, but they do have a neighbourhood life; the American is not familiar with his city; once he is ten 'blocks' away from his home, he is lost. *Ibid.*

S25 — One quickly begins to like American cities. Of course they all look alike. And when you arrive at Wichita, Saint Louis or Alburquerque, it is disappointing to realize that, hidden behind these magnificent and promising names, is the same standard checkerboard city with the same red and green traffic lights and the same provincial look. But one gradually learns to tell them apart. Chicago, the noble, lurid city, red as the blood that trickles through its abattoirs, with its canals, the grey water of Lake Michigan and its streets crushed between clumsy and powerful buildings, in no way resembles San Francisco, city of air, salt and sea, built in the shape of an amphitheatre. *Ibid.*

S26 — These perfectly straight cities bear [in America] no trace of organization. Many of them have the rudimentary structure of a polypary. Los Angeles, in particular, is rather like a big earthworm that might be chopped into twenty pieces. *Ibid.*

S27 — [Detroit] . . . they like to recall in their books and films the time when their community was only an outpost. And that is why they pass so easily from city to outpost; they make no distinction between the two. Detroit and Minneapolis, Knoxville and Memphis were born temporary and have stayed that way. They will never, of course, take to the road again on the back of a truck. But they remain at the melting point: they have never reached an internal temperature of solidification. *Ibid.*

S28 — We Europeans change within changeless cities, and our houses and neighbourhoods outlive us; American cities change faster than their inhabitants do, and it is the inhabitants who outlive the cities. *Ibid.*

S29 — What are the impressions of a European who arrives in an American city? First, he thinks he has been taken in. He has heard only about sky-scrapers; New York and Chicago have been described to him as 'up-right cities.' Now his first feeling is, on the contrary, that the average height of an American city is noticeably smaller than that of a French one. The immense majority of houses have only two storeys. Even in the very large cities, the five-storey apartment house is an exception. *Ibid.*

SASS, Herbert (1884-1958)

S30 — Charleston today has so much feminine grace and charm that the masculine power and drive which preceded and created this beauty are overlooked. *Charleston Grows*

SCAMMON, Richard M. (1915-) and Ben J. WATTENBERG (1933-)

S31 — A middle-aged, middle-income, high-school educated, white Protestant, who works with his hands, decreasingly ethnic . . . Generally metropolitan, and increasingly suburban, following the pattern of the American postwar hegira: from farms to cities, from cities to suburbs. [of the average voter] *The Real Majority*

SCHILLER, Ronald

S32 — What is needed to deal effectively with the twin problems of urban overcrowding and rural blight is a comprehensive national population resettlement plan that will enable us to *design* our future instead of resigning ourselves to it. *Quoted in Reader's Digest*

SCHLESINGER, Arthur Meier (1888-1965)

S33 — If we consider only the sordid aspects of urban life the American city of the period [1878-1898] seems a cancerous growth. But the record as a whole was distinctly creditable to a generation which found itself confronted with the phenomenon of a great population everywhere clotting into towns. No other people had ever met such an emergency so promptly or, on the whole, so successfully. The basic facilities of urban living — transit, lighting and communication — were well taken care of by an outburst of native mechanical genius which helped make these years the Golden Age of Invention. *The Rise of the City*

SCHMITT, Peter J.

S34 — As the nineteenth century came to a close, many people, like English sparrows, seemed to thrive on city life. Others returned as failures to the family farm, praising country life; but an increasing number of city dwellers turned 'back to nature,' rather than 'back to the farm,' mainly to escape the minor irritants of urban life. Poverty, crime, and disease disturbed them less than did the press of crowds along antiquated sidewalks, the rattle of iron wheels on cobblestone streets, or soft-coal smog. Such folk heartily approved the opportunities for social and economic success, the educational and religious benefits, and the cultural advantages that accompanied urban life. They simply realized, as every suburban mother knew, that the city is no place to raise a family. *Back to Nature*

SCHNEIDER, Kenneth R. (1927-   )

S35 — Although America has become a nation of cities, we did not really want it that way. Like Jefferson, we never quite trusted city life. But we did want industry, which we seemed to trust. The cities themselves were required to bring together the wealth, labor, materials, and consumers. So Carnegie built Detroit, even though he detested the 'unnaturalness' of city life. *On the Nature of Cities*

S36 — The city is a structure of human behavior and, if good, a structure of freedom. Such conditions are discernable, designable, buildable. Such conditions can be constitutionalized in the form of the city. When society begins to seriously debate social and environmental rights, the lines for a constitution of cities will become clearer. *Ibid.*

SCHNEIDER, Wolf (1925-   )

S37 — The city is the world that man builds for himself, and it is a weird fact, of

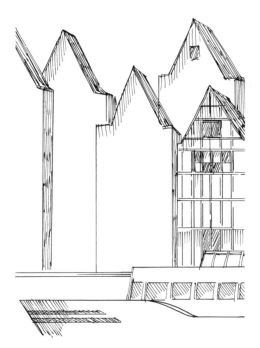

incalculable consequence, that this man-made world is on the verge of destroying nature on this earth. *Babylon Is Everywhere*

S38 — The city of Hangchow — what do we know about it? Hardly more than that it is located in China, even though it was once the largest and richest city in the world. *Ibid.*

S39 — Democracy developed within the Greek *polis*; but then every dictator has turned his metropolis into a citadel of tyranny. The city is the cradle of culture as well as of crime, the centre of misery as well as luxury. It is the conflux of vitality and nervous energy, the focal point of power and the source of decline. In the city man shows his noblest features and his most horrible grimaces. Wall against wall, roof touching roof, the city's huddled buildings contain happiness and tears, arrogance and humiliation, birth and death. *Ibid.*

S40 — Enjoying the crowds, the satisfaction of 'being there' feeling oneself a part of that power complex which is called city, freedom from the country, being protected in the world of people, culture, and comfort, more money for less work, and the opportunity to spend the money in a most pleasurable way — all that is the attraction of the city. *Ibid.*

S41 — The first houses built for the purpose of renting on a commercial basis were probably to be found in the city of Carthage. This was a big step in city history, an important factor in the development of *large* cities. *Ibid.*

S42 — In spite of the fact that certain city areas today cover a space comparable to an entire Roman province, and come close to the number of inhabitants of the whole Roman empire — about 55 million — we have not yet seen a modern city achieve the importance of ancient Rome. *Ibid.*

S43 — It is only in our day that Venice is seen in a romantic light. In the days of the Doges it was as cruel as any city of antiquity or the Middle Ages. *Ibid.*

SCHOPENHAUER, Arthur (1788-1860)

S44 — The most inexcusable and disgraceful of all noises is the cracking of whips — a truly infernal thing when it is done in the narrow resounding streets of a town. I denounce it as making a peaceful life impossible; it puts an end to all quiet thought.

SCHUMANN, Robert (1810-1856)

S45 — It is true: this Vienna, with its St. Stephen's tower, its beautiful women, its air of pageantry, girdled by the countless convolutions of the Danube and reaching out to the lush plain which rises gradually into the towering mountains beyond, this Vienna with all its memories of the great German masters, must be fruitful ground for the musician's imagination.

SCHWARTZ, Joel

S46 — The history of suburban America reaches back one hundred and thirty years. For at least that long, urban dwellers have tried to escape the city's grime, immigrants, and disorder and searched for outlying retreats with institutional structures to protect their preserves when distance alone did not suffice. *Evolution of the Suburbs*

S47 — Traditionally, 'suburbs' have been the haunts of the poor on land not yet taken up by the rich. In 'preindustrial' cities across the globe, established caste groups clung to the civic centers where palace,

cathedral, and guild hall dispensed wealth and prestige. The less affluent found lodging where they might, while the poor and outcast huddled beyond the walls, whether London's Cheapside or Paris' swamp, the Marais. *Ibid.*

SCOTT, Hugh (Senator) (1900-)

S48 — The tendency to make the capital a catch-all for a variety of monuments to honor the immortals, the not-so-immortals, the greats, the near-greats, and the not-so-greats must stop. We must be on our guard lest the nation's capital come to resemble an unplanned cemetery. *The New York Times, September 11, 1960*

SCOTT, John (1730-1783)

S49 — I hate that drum's discordant sound, / Parading round, and round, and round: / To me it talks of ravaged plains, / And burning towns, and ruined swains, / And mangled limbs, and dying groans, / And widows' tears, and orphans' moans; / And all that Misery's hand bestows / To fill the catalogue of human woes. / *I Hate That Drum's Discordant Sound*

SCOTT, Mel (1906-)

S50 — Here was an enthralling amalgam of classic Greece, imperial Rome, Renaissance Italy, and Bourbon Paris, as improbable in the Midwest as a gleaming iceberg would be in the Gulf of Mexico, yet somehow expressive of the boastfulness, the pretentions, the cultural dependence, the explosive energy, and the ingenious optimism of industrial America. [of the Columbian Exposition in Chicago, 1893] *American City Planning*

SCOTT, (Sir) Walter (1771-1832)

S51 — When I hae a saxpence under my thumb, / Then I get credit in ilka town; / But when I am poor, they bid me gae by, / O, poverty parts good company. / *The Abbot*

SENECA, Marcus Annaeus (54? B.C.-39 A.D.)

S52 — In this City, even in its broadest streets, the flow of pedestrian traffic is continuous, and consequently, when any obstruction occurs which checks the current of this rushing human torrent, there is a formidable crush. The City's population is of a magnitude that requires the simultaneous use of the auditoria of three theatres and the importation of food-supplies from all over the World. [of Rome] *De Clementia I*

SENIOR, Nassau (1790-1864)

S53 — These towns . . . have been erected with the utmost disregard of everything except the immediate advantage of the speculating builder. A carpenter and builder unite to buy a series of building sites (i.e., they lease them for a number of years) and cover them with so-called houses. In one place we found a whole street following the course of a ditch, because in this way deeper cellars could be secured without the cost of digging cellars not for storing wares or rubbish, but for dwellings of human beings. Not one house of this street escaped the cholera. In general the streets are unpaved, with a dungheap or ditch in the middle; the houses are built back to back, without ventilation or drainage, and whole families are limited to a corner of a cellar or a garret. [of Manchester]

SENNACHERIB (?-681 B.C.)

S54 — The city and its houses, from its foundation to its top, I destroyed, I devastated, I burned with fire. The wall and the outer wall, temples, and gods, temple towers of brick and earth, as many as they were, I razed and dumped them into the Arakhtu Canal. Through the midst of that city I dug canals, I flooded its site with water, and the very foundations, thereof I destroyed. I made its destruction more complete than that by a flood.

SEVAREID, Eric (1912-   )

S55 — A separate nation in spirit. [of New York City]

SEWARD, Thomas (1708-1790)

S56 — Seven wealthy towns contend for Homer dead, / Through which the living Homer begged his bread. / *On Homer*

SHAKESPEARE, William (1564-1616)

S57 — Let Rome in Tiber melt, and the wide arch / Of the rang'd empire fall! Here is my space. / *Antony and Cleopatra*

S58 — Shall they hoist me up / And show me to the shouting varletry / Of censuring Rome? Rather a ditch in Egypt / Be gentle grave unto me! rather on Nilus' mud / Lay me stark naked, and let the water-flies / Blow me into abhorring! / *Ibid.*

S59 — Under the canopy . . . The city of kites and crows. *Coriolanus*

S60 — What is the city but the people? *Ibid.*

S61 — In the most high and palmy state of Rome, / A little ere the mightiest Julius fell. / The graves stood tenantless and the sheeted dead / Did squeak and gibber in the Roman streets. / *Hamlet*

S62 — Are yet two Romans living such as these? The last of all the Romans, fare thee well! / It is impossible that ever Rome / Should breed thy fellow. Friends, I owe more tears / To this dead man than you shall see me pay. — / I shall find time, Cassius, I shall find time. / *Julius Ceasar*

S63 — But were I Brutus, / And Brutus Antony, there were an Antony / Would ruffle up you spirits, and put a tongue / In every wound of Caesar, that should move / The stones of Rome to rise and mutiny. / *Ibid.*

S64 — Not that I loved Caesar less, but that I loved Rome more. *Ibid.*

S65 — Now is it Rome indeed and room enough. *Ibid.*

S66 — You blocks, you stones, you worse than senseless things! / O you hard hearts, you cruel men of Rome, / Knew you not Pompey? / *Ibid.*

S67 — I hope to see London once ere I die. *King Henry IV, Part II*

S68 — It hath been prophesied to me many years / I should not die but in Jerusalem. / Which vainly I suppos'd the Holy Land. / But bear me to that chamber; there I'll lie: / In that Jerusalem shall Harry die. / *Ibid.*

S69 — In the quick forge and working-house of thought, / How London doth pour out her citizens. / *King Henry V*

S70 — Then that in all you writ to Rome, or else / To foreign princes, 'Ego et Rex meus' / Was still inscrib'd. / *King Henry VIII*

S71 — The early village cock / Hath twice done salutation to the morn. / *King Richard III*

S72 — In Venice they do let heaven see the pranks / They dare not show their husbands; their best conscience / Is not to leave't undone, but to keep't unknown. / *Othello*

S73 — The strongest castle, tower, and town, / The golden bullet beats it down. / *Sonnets to Sundry Notes of Music*

S74 — Hail, Rome, victorious in thy mourning weeds! *Titus Andronicus*

S75 — Water drops have worn the stones of Troy, / And blind oblivion swallow'd cities up, / And mighty states characterless are grated / To dusty nothing. / *Troilus and Cressida*

SHARP, Dallas Lore (1870-1929)

S76 — And this our life, exempt from public haunts and those swift currents that carry the city dweller resistlessly into the movie show, leaves us caught in the quiet eddy of little unimportant things — digging among the rutabagas, playing the hose at night. *The Hills of Hingham*

SHAW, Albert (1857-1947)

S77 — The abolition of the slums, and the destruction of their virus, are as feasible as the drainage of a swamp and the total dissipation of its miasmas. The conditions and circumstances that surround the lives of the masses of people in modern cities can be so adjusted to their needs as to result in the highest development of the race, in body, in mind, and in moral character. The so-called problems of the modern city are but the various phases of the one main question. How can the environment be most perfectly adapted to the welfare of urban populations? And science can meet and answer every one of these problems.

SHAW, George Bernard (1856-1950)

S78 — Take an opium eater's dream to Los Angeles, and they will realize it for you; the more it costs, the more they will believe in it. You can have a real Polar expedition, a real volcano, a reconstruction of the Roman Forum on the spot; anything you please, provided it is enormously costly.

S79 — The imagination cannot conceive a viler criminal than he who should build another London like the present one, nor a greater benefactor than he who should destroy it. *Maxims for Revolutionists*

SHAW, Irwin (1913-)

S80 — All cities, with the possible exception of Venice, have the right to change and, for good or ill, Paris has chosen to alter her face and figure in a thousand different ways. An American arriving in town these days, after a twenty-year absence, might feel that his memory had played him false as he searched for the Paris he had once known. And the writer who rereads his description of an earlier city must pay homage to today's truth in adding and subtracting for today's reader. *Paris, Paris*

S81 — Although statistically Paris has the least green space per citizen of any major city in Europe, there are so many trees that when they are in foliage and seen from above, much of the metropolis seems to be built in a giant park. *Ibid.*

S82 — If the awareness of city dwellers to what is going on in the world around them can be gauged by the number and variety of the newspapers that are available to them, the inhabitants of Paris must be among the best informed in the world. *Ibid.*

S83 — The least costly and perhaps the most satisfactory of Parisian amusements is merely to walk around the city. *Ibid.*

S84 — Paris in the wintertime is the city for misogynists, misanthropes, and pessimists, for students of history who believe that the whole thing is all one long downhill ride; for all lovers of the human race who are ready to shake their heads at man's ingratitude, to deplore the world's slack forgetfulness, and to weigh the vanity of mortal achievements. *Ibid.*

S85 — Paris is a beautiful woman, but so surpassingly so, so vital and self-renewing, that nothing — not the passage of years, not drink or drugs, not bad investments or unworthy loves, not neglect or debauchery — can ruin her. *Ibid.*

S86 — There is a cynical joke drivers repeat about the law of the road in Paris: 'To hit a pedestrian in the street — that is sport. But to hit him in the clous — that is sadism.' The clous is the crossing between curbs that is marked by iron buttons for the use of people on foot, and you have a feeling that thousands of Parisians have met their end in these deceptive sanctuaries. . . .On foot, the Parisian is as courteous as the citizen of any other city. But mounted, he is merciless. *Ibid.*

S87 — Travelers are always telling you their favorite times for seeing a city for the first time: Rome at Easter, London in June, New York in October, Pittsburgh at five o'clock in the morning. And you tell the girl to make sure to see Paris the next afternoon it is liberated. It is a city that takes gratefully to a mixture of riot, celebration, and bloodshed. *Ibid.*

SHECKLEY, Robert (1928-   )

S88 — The ability to live dramatically is the peculiar talent of our species. The city provides a frame for our endeavors, a platform for our thoughts, and a stage on which the tragi-comic actions of our lives are acted out. It is the basis for nearly all our culture. Without it, art and science could

not exist. History, too would be impossible without the continuity of city life. The city is our own unique product. It cannot properly be likened to anything else in nature. *Futuropolis*

S89 — What will Futuropolis be like? We may be able to put our city together and take it apart like a doll's house. Perhaps we will put it on wheels or rails, locate it under the sea or out in space. We might even dispense with any formal structure and carry individual sections of the city around with us, to plug in where we please. *Ibid.*

SHELDON, Sidney (1917-   )

S90 — Men mold some cities, some cities mold men. *The Other Side of Midnight*

SHELLEY, Percy Bysshe (1792-1822)

S91 — Go thou to Rome — at once the Paradise, / The grave, the city, and the wilderness. / *Adonais*

S92 — In the firm expectation that when London shall be a habitation of bitterns, when St. Paul's and Westminster Abbey shall stand shapeless and nameless ruins in the midst of an unpeopled marsh, when the piers of Waterloo Bridge shall become the nuclei of islets of reeds and osiers, and cast the jagged shadows of their broken arches on the solitary stream, some Transatlantic commentator will be weighing in the scales of some new and now unimagined system of criticism the respective merits of the Bells and the Fudges and their historians. *(Dedication to Peter Bell the Third)*

S93 — Another Athens shall arise, / And to remoter time / Bequeath, like sunset to the skies, / The splendour of its prime; / And leave, if nought so bright may live, / All earth can take or Heaven can give. / *Hellas*

S94 — Let there be light! said Liberty, / And like sunrise from the sea, / Athens arose! / *Ibid.*

S95 — London, that great sea, whose ebb and flow / At once is deaf and loud, and on the shore / Vomits its wrecks, and still howls on for more / *Letter to Maria Gisborne*

S96 — Sun-girt City, thou has been / Ocean's child, and then his queen / Now is come a darker day / And thou soon must be his prey / *Lines Written among the Euganean Hills*

S97 — Underneath Day's azure eyes / Ocean's nursling, Venice lies / A peopled Labyrinth of walls. / *Ibid.*

S98 — When o'er the Aegean main / Athens arose: a city such as vision / Builds from the purple crags and silver towers / Of battlemented cloud, as in derision / Of kingliest masonry: the ocean-floors / Pave it; the evening sky pavilions it; / Its portals are inhabited / By thunder-zoned winds. / *Ode to Liberty*

S99 — I stood within the City disinterred; / And heard the autumnal leaves like light footfalls / Of spirits passing through the streets; and heard / The Mountain's slumbrous voice at intervals / Thrill through those roofless halls. / [of Pompeii] *Ode to Naples*

S100 — Hell is a city much like London — a populous and a smoky city; There are all sorts of people undone, And there is little or no fun done; Small justice shown, and still less pity. *Peter Bell the Third*

S101 — Where Cicero and Antoninus lived, / A cowled and hypocritical monk / Prays, curses and deceives. / [of Rome] *Queen Mab*

S102 — The City's voice itself is soft like Solitude's. *Stanzas Written in Dejection, near Naples*

SHEPHERD, William G.

S103 — The Winded City. [of Chicago]

SHESHAN, Robert

S104 — It is highly improbable that Utica will ever become a metropolis, and it is doubtful if any one now living there wants to. . . . It's a pretty nice way of life, and of doing business, up Utica way. It is, one might say, the American way — without ulcers. *Fortune*

SIEGFRIED, Andre (1875-1959)

S105 — In the Montreal telephone directory, the Macs fill six pages. Tear them out, and Montreal is no longer a financial capital, but simply an immense French village with a little English garrison! *Quoted in Canada: An International Power*

SILVER, Nathan (1936-)

S106 — On my first visit to Los Angeles I was conventionally prepared for almost anything except for what it really looked like — a quite beautiful place. *New Statesman, March 28, 1969*

SIMINOV, Konstantin

S107 — Villages, villages, villages with graveyards, / As if all Russia converged on them. . . . / You must know after all that the Motherland / Is not the city where I lived festively, / But these hamlets in which our grandfathers strolled / With simple crosses on their Russian graves. / *Quoted in The Russians, by Hedrick Smith*

SIMMEL, Georg (1858-1918)

S108 — The feeling of isolation is rarely as decisive and intense when one actually finds oneself physically alone, as when one is a stranger, without relations, among many physically close persons, at a 'party,' on a train, or in the traffic of a large city.

S109 — The deepest problems of modern life flow from the attempt of the individual to maintain the independence and individuality of his existence against the sovereign powers of society, against the weight of the historical heritage and the external culture and technique of life. *The Metropolis and Mental Life*

S110 — The metropolis exacts from man as a discriminating creature a different amount of consciousness than does rural life. Here the rhythm of life and sensory mental imagery flows more slowly, more habitually, and more evenly. Precisely in this connection the sophisticated character of metropolitan psychic life becomes understandable — as over against small town life which rests more upon deeply felt and emotional relationships. *Ibid.*

S111 — If so many inner reactions were responses to the continuous external contacts with innumerable people as are those in the small town, where one knows almost everybody one meets and where one has a positive relation to almost everyone,

one would be completely atomized internally and come to an unimaginable psychic state. *The Sociology of George Simmel*

SIMON, Kate

S112 — Until, or unless, we reach the stage of a universal, classless society, all big cities will have their economic contrasts, easily available to anyone who cares to look. Like New York, London, Paris, Rome (even the fine museum which is Florence has its slum areas), Mexico [city] has its layers. Its special excitement is not so much in the carefully boxed-off contrasts one is accustomed to in other cities, but in the shiftings and blendings. *Mexico: Places and Pleasures*

S113 — Materialism, in its purest essence, is supposed to be the hallmark of the New Yorker. He is pictured as maimed in pursuit of the buck. But he is in reality a romantic — it isn't the buck, which he could have earned at home, in his safe small town, but the glitter of a mound of gold, like Spanish treasure, which lures him. To dream of being an actress is natural for any self-respecting little girl; to want it with fanaticism, to leave all safeties for it, is the drive of the romantic, as is a conviction that drawing a little isn't enough — a painter must live intensely with discomfort and

disorder in Greenwich Village in imitation of the Golden Age of Montmartre. Thus, the little dreams stay at home and the big ones come to New York. *New York: Places and Pleasures*

SIMONIDES of Ceos (556-469 B.C.)

S114 — The city is the teacher of the man. *Plutarch: Should Old Men Govern?*

SIMPSON, Louis (1923-   )

S115 — I wake and feel the city trembling. / Yes, there is something unsettled in the air / And the earth is uncertain. / [of San Francisco] *Lines Written Near San Francisco*

SIMS, George Robert (1847-1922)

S116 — O gleaming lamps of London, / That gem of the city's crown, / What fortunes be within you, / O Lights of London Town? / *The Lights of London Town*

SINCLAIR, (Sir) John (1754-1835)

S117 — Few more interesting objects can engage the attention of a humane, patriotic, and enlightened statesman, than the question, Whether the increase of population *in towns* be a full compensation for its diminution in the country? *Analysis of the Statistical Account of Scotland*

SITTE, Camillo (1843-1903)

S118 — The ancients did not conceive their city plans on drawing boards. Their buildings rose bit by bit in natura. Thus they were readily governed by that which struck the eye in reality. *The Art of Building Cities*

S119 — In modern cities irregularity in plan is unsuccessful because it has been created artificially with the straightedge. It most often takes the form of triangular public places — the fatal dregs of drawing board plotting. They nearly always have a bad effect. *Ibid.*

S120 — The notion of symmetry is propagating itself today like the spread of an epidemic. The least cultivated are familiar with it, and each one feels called upon to have his say about the involved artistic matters that concern the building of cities, for each thinks he has at his finger tips the single criterion — symmetry. *Ibid.*

S121 — We have three dominant systems for building cities, and a number of variations of them. They are: the rectangular system, the radial system, and the triangular system. Generally speaking, the variations are bastard offspring of these three. From an artistic point of view the whole tribe is worthless, having exhausted the last drop of art's blood from its veins. These systems accomplish nothing except a standardization of street pattern. They are purely mechanical in conception. They reduce the street system to a mere traffic utility, never serving the purposes of art. They make no appeal to the sense of perception, for we can see their features only on a map. *Ibid.*

S122 — Whoever studies a map of his own city can be convinced that violent irregularities, shown on the map, do not in the least seem to be striking irregularities when seen on the ground. *Ibid.*

SJOBERB, Gideon

S123 — The term 'city' has been utilized in varying fashions. We see it, in contrast to a town or village, as having greater size, density, and heterogeneity and including a wide range of non-agriculture specialists, most significant of whom are the literati. The information of the latter is . . . crucial for assigning a beginning date to city life. *The Preindustrial City*

SKLAR, Robert (1936-   )

S124 — In 1890, before his laboratory had perfected any motion-picture apparatus, Thomas A. Edison predicted that moving pictures and his phonograph would provide home entertainment for families of wealth. It turned out differently for one fundamental reason: movies developed during critical years of change in the social structure of American life when a new social order was emerging in the modern industrial city. The two decades from 1890 to 1910 span the gap from the beginning of motion pictures to their firm establishment as mass entertainment; they are also the years when the United States transformed itself into a predominantly urban industrial society. *Movie-Made America*

SLATER, Philip

S125 — 'Civilized' means, literally, 'citified,' and the state of the city is an accurate index of the condition of the culture as a whole. We behave toward our cities like an irrascible farmer who never feeds his cow and then kicks her when she fails to give enough milk.

SMITH, Adam (1723-1790)

S126 — There is no solitude so terrible and dreary as that felt in the very heart of a vast, unsympathizing city.

S127 — There are some sorts of industry, even of the lowest kind, which can be carried on nowhere but in a great town. *The Wealth of Nations*

SMITH, Alfred E. (1873-1944)

S128 — Any Mr. Smith in any part of the United States will prefer his own home place to any other part of America, for about him are his family and friends and associations of his adult life, if not of his childhood. These elements are what bind a man's affections to any particular area, and it will not matter if the place be one of the great centers of population or a remote and lonely corner of a wilderness, beautiful or bleak, north, south, east, or west. *American Magazine*

SMITH, C.W.

S129 — Los Angeles cannot be retarded in her development. She is and must be the center of everything in Southern California for all time to come.

SMITH, Daniel R.

S130 — For most Africans the move from the rural community to the city is the first step toward individual autonomy, a break from traditional tribal, clan, and familial bonds. In crowded urban areas it is virtually impossible for the extended family to survive. Thus, the modern nuclear family has become the basic social unity for industrialized Africa. Loyalty to the tribal group and to more distant relatives quickly vanishes in the diversified occupational pursuits and social activities of the city. *Cities in Africa*

SMITH, Goldwin (1912-   )

S131 — Ottawa is a sub-arctic lumber-village converted by royal mandate into a political cockpit.

SMITH, Richard Austin (1911-   )

S132 — Whatever glass and steel monuments may be built downtown, the essence of Los Angeles, its true identifying characteristic, is mobility. Freedom of movement has long given life a special flavour there, liberated the individual to enjoy the sun and space that his environment so abundantly offered, put the manifold advantages of a great metropolitan area within his grasp. *Fortune, March, 1965*

SMITH, Sydney (1771-1845)

S133 — I suspect the fifth act of life should be in great cities; it is there, in the long death of old age, that a man most forgets himself and his infirmities; receives the greatest consolation from the attention of friends, and the greatest diversion from external circumstances. *(Letter to an unidentified woman)*

S134 — I think every wife has a right to insist upon seeing Paris *(Letter to Countess Grey)*

S135 — Whenever I enter a village, straightway I find an ass.

SOCRATES (470?-399 B.C.)

S136 — They will take as their canvas a city and the characters of men, and they will, first of all, make their canvas clean. They will not start work on a city nor on an individual (nor will they draw up laws) unless they are given a clean canvas or have cleaned it themselves. *Quoted in The Exploding Cities*

S137 — I am not an Athenian nor a Greek, but a citizen of the world. [of being a cosmopolite] *Of Banishment, Plutarch*

SONDHEIM, Stephen (1930-   )

S138 — Dear kindly Sergeant Krupke, You gotta understand / It's just our bring' up-ke that gets us out of hand. / Our mothers all

are junkies, Our fathers all are drunks, / Golly Moses, natcherlly we're punks! / *Gee, Officer Krupke, from West Side Story*

SOPHOCLES (496?-406 B.C.)

S139 — The highest achievements of man are language and wind-swift thought, and city-dwelling habits. *Antigone*

SOUTH, (Rev.) Robert (1634-1716)

S140 — An Aristotle was but the rubbish of an Adam, and Athens but the rudiments of Paradise. *Sermons*

SOUTHEY, Robert (1774-1843)

S141 — Exeter is ancient and stinks!

S142 — The noise of Birmingham is beyond description; the hammers seem never to be at rest. The filth is sickening: filthy as some of our old towns may be, their dirt is offensive; ... But here it is active and moving, a living principle of mischief, which fills the whole atomosphere and penetrates everywhere, spotting and staining everything, and getting into the pores and nostrils. I feel as if my throat wanted sweeping like an English chimney. *Letters from England*

SPALDING, John Lancaster (1840-1916)

S143 — In a great city men jostle one another in the street who live in spheres of thought and feeling as widely apart as though they dwelt in separate planets. *Lectures and Discourses*

S144 — The agricultural life more than that of the city conduces to happiness and morality, and that it harmonizes better with the Christian ideal. *The Religious Mission of the Irish People and Catholic Colonization*

S145 — The air of the city, with the stir of the multitude and the whirl of business and pleasure, intoxicates, and men are drawn into the vortex by the craving for excitement, which is often so great that honor and all that is most precious are sacrificed to the indulgence of a fatal appetite. *Ibid.*

S146 — Christ, setting the supreme example to the conduct and thoughts of men, spent

nearly his whole life in the fields, looking with a tenderness almost akin to human love upon the grazing flocks, the whitening harvest, the budding trees, the lilies, and the birds, and the grass, which to-day is green and to-morrow is cast into the oven. He walks by the seashore, he goes up into the mountain, he withdraws into the desert but he will not so much as sleep within the wall of Jerusalem. *Ibid.*

S147 — The city . . ., is the paradise of adventurers and speculators, and there is the great matrimonial exchange which calls into play all the fine and subtle powers of woman. *Ibid.*

S148 — The country once abandoned is like a divorced wife. She will hardly be taken back, and if she is received again she will not be the mistress of the heart she once was. Those who have lived as servants in the houses of the rich will scorn the farmer's simple fare, and those who have labored in the factory will lack the energy to buffet the storm and breathe the crisp air of the open country. *Ibid.*

S149 — In other ages those who worked sang at their labor; and even in the South, in the days of slavery, the plaintive melodies of the Negro humanized his toil and helped to relieve the sadness of his heart; but here [in the city] man grows dumb, and works, like the horse and the ox, in silence. *Ibid.*

S150 — In the city old age and childhood are thrust out of sight, and the domestic morals and simple manners, which are above all price, cease to be handed down as sacred heirlooms. *Ibid.*

S151 — It is far from my thought to say that the city is wholly evil. It has a great and high social mission. It is the most complex and difficult work of civilized man, and its fascination is felt by all. It is full, and will be full, though all the world should speak ill of it. But if those I love were rich I should not wish them to live in the city; and if they were poor, and made it their dwelling-place, I should despair of them. *Ibid.*

SPARK, Muriel (1918-   )

S152 — New York, home of the vivisectors of the mind, and of the mentally vivisected still to be reassembled, of those who live intact, habitually wondering about their states of sanity, and home of those whose minds have been dead, bearing the scars of resurrection. *The Hothouse by the East River*

SPARROW, John

S153 — My impression is that in New York anything might happen at any moment. In England nothing could happen, ever. *The New Yorker, February 26, 1972*

SPECTORSKY, A.C. (1910-1972)

S154 — The exurbanite is a displaced New Yorker. He has moved from the city to the country. So, indeed, have hundreds of thousands of Americans, especially since the second World War; but for the exurbanite the case is different; for him the change is an exile. He will never quite completely permit himself to be absorbed into his new surroundings; he never will acclimate. He may join the Parent-Teacher Association in his new home, he may attend town meetings, he will almost surely try his hand at gardening or farming; but spiritually he will always be urban, an irreconcilable whose step, after walking a hundred country lanes, is still the steadiest when it returns to the familiar crowded cross-walks of Madison Avenue. *The Exurbanites*

S155 — The name of the subspecies, then, is Exurbanite; its habitat, the Exurbs. The exurb is generally further from New York than the suburb on the same railway line. Its houses are more widely spaced and generally more various and more expensive. The town center tends to quaintness and class, rather than modernity and glass, and the further one lives from the station the better. *Ibid.*

S156 — The word 'exurb' (and its derivatives 'exurban' and 'exurbanite') carries no connotation of something that has ceased to be, of something in the past; rather what is intended is a clarification of the something extra and special that has characterized the journey of the exurbanite, out and away from the city, in a wistful search for roots, for the realization of a dream, for a home. *Ibid.*

SPELLMAN, (Cardinal) Francis (1889-1967)

S157 — Father, a thousand tiny lights break through / The great grey darkness of the city night / And are as candles lit before Thy Shrine. / *What America Means to Me and Other Poems and Prayers*

SPENCER, Herbert (1820-1903)

S158 — 'The stones of Venice' did not produce in me so much enthusiasm as in many. Not that I failed to derive much pleasure; but the pleasure was less multitudinous in its sources than that which is felt, or is alleged to be felt, by the majority. *An Autobiography*

SPENDER, J.A. (1862-1942)

S159 — To most people the vision of a great city is that of streets, parks, rivers, bridges, and endless bustling crowds in the open under the sky. But the idea which most weighs on me as I sit here alone is that of a vast unexplored interior, with a million forms of hidden life. *The Comments of Bagshot*

SPENDER, Stephen (1909-)

S160 — Athens, Alexandria, Rome, Paris, Vienna — all echo through the work of poets. But ever since the industrial revolution, the poets, instead of regarding the cities as centers of civilization, have regarded them as destructive of the conditions out of which the supreme achievements of poetry in the past were created. The modern urban environment is ugly, overwhelming, materialistic. Its power is expressed in scientific, sociological vocabulary which is alien to the image-making vocabulary of past poetry. *Poetry and the Modern City*

SPENGLER, Oswald (1880-1936)

S161 — All effectual history begins with the primary classes, nobility and priesthood, forming themselves and elevating themselves above the peasantry as such. The opposition of greater and lesser nobility, between king and vassal, between wordly and spiritual power, is the basic form of all primitive politics, Homeric, Chinese, or Gothic, until with the coming of the City, the burgher, the Tiers Etat, history changes its style. But it is exclusively in these classes as such, in their class-consciousness, that the whole meaning of history inheres. The peasant is historyless. *The Decline of the West*

S162 — The city is intellect. The Megalopolis is 'free' intellect. *Ibid.*

S163 — Every springtime of a Culture is ipso facto the springtime of a new city-type and civism. *Ibid.*

S164 — Finally, there arises the monstrous symbol and vessel of the completely emancipated intellect, the world-city, the centre in which the course of a world-history ends by winding itself up. A handful of gigantic places in each Civilization disfranchises and disvalues the entire motherland of its own Culture under the contemptous name of 'the provinces.' The 'provinces' are now everything whatsoever — land, town, and city — except these two or three points. There are no longer noblesse and bourgeoisie, freemen and slaves, Hellenes and Barbarians, believers and unbelievers, but only cosmopolitans and provincials. All other contrasts pale before this one, which dominates all events, all habits of life, all views of the world. *Ibid.*

S165 — In all countries of all Late Cultures, the great parties, the revolutions, the Caesarisms, the democracies, the parliaments, are the form in which the spirit of the capital tells the country what it is expected to desire and, if called upon, to die for. The Classical forum, the Western press, are, essentially, intellectual engines of the ruling City. Any country-dweller who really understands the meaning of politics in such periods, and feels himself on their level, moves into the City, not perhaps in the body, but certainly in the spirit. *Ibid.*

S166 — It is the Forum of the City of Rome alone that is the scene of Classical history. Caesar might campaign in Gaul, his slayers in Macedonia, Antony in Egypt, but, whatever happened in these fields, it was from their relation to Rome that events acquired meaning. *Ibid.*

S167 — The man of the land and the man of the city are different essences. First of all they feel the difference, then they are dominated by it, and at last they cease to understand each other at all. To-day a Brandenburg peasant is closer to a Sicilian peasant than he is to a Berliner. From the moment of this specific attunement, the City comes into being, and it is this attunement which underlies, as something that goes without saying, the entire waking-consciousness of every Culture. *Ibid.*

S168 — The stone Colossus 'Cosmopolis' stands at the end of the life's course of every great Culture. The Culture-man whom the land has spiritually formed is seized and possessed by his own creation, the City, and is made into its creature, its executive organ, and finally its victim ... These final cities are wholly intellect. Their houses are no longer, as those of the Ionic and the Baroque were, derivatives of the old peasant's house, whence the Culture took its spring into history ... This city is a world, is the world. Only as a whole, as a human dwelling-place, has it meaning, the houses being merely the stones of which it is assembled. *Ibid.*

S169 — We cannot comprehend political and economic history at all unless we realize that the city, with its gradual detachment from and final bankrupting of the country, is the determinative form to which the course and sense of higher history generally conforms. World history is city history. *Ibid.*

SPENSER, Edmund (1552?-1599)

S170 — At length they all to merry London came, / To merry London, my most kindly nurse, / That to me gave this life's first native source: / Though from another place I take my name, / An house of ancient fame. / *Prothalamion*

SPILHAUS, Athelstan (1911-)

S171 — Cities grow unplanned; they just spread haphazardly. By planning now, the advantages of high-density living can be preserved without the ugliness, filth, congestion, and noise that presently accompany city living. The urban mess is due to unplanned growth — too many students for the schools, too much sludge for the sewers, too many cars for the highways, too many sick for the hospitals, too much crime for the police, too many commuters for the transport system, too many fumes for the atmosphere to bear, too many chemicals for the water to carry. *Daedalus*

S172 — The idea of experimental cities — where it is possible to start from scratch to conceive and execute a total urban enviroment — is currently enjoying a good deal of popularity. Having a new city arise out of a comprehensive planning process, instead of haphazardly, seems the only way to meet the problems that hold already established urban areas in an unremitting grip. *Inventing New Cities*

SPINOZA, Baruch (1632-1677)

S173 — In this flourishing republic, this city second to none, men of every nation and every sect live together in the utmost harmony; and all they bother to find out, before trusting their goods to anyone, is whether he is rich or poor and whether he is honest or a fraud. [of Amsterdam]

SPOONER, William Archibald (1844-1930)

S174 — You have deliberately tasted two worms and you can leave Oxford by the town drain. *Dismissing a Student*

SPREIREGEN, Paul (1931-)

S175 — Approach routes present cities to us. They must satisfy the visual requirement of presenting architecture and cities in their best light, while enabling us to find our destination readily. The two requirements go hand in hand. An approach route must both inform us and conduct us. *Urban Design*

S176 — The city's skyline is a physical representation of its facts of life. But a skyline is also a potential work of art. *Ibid.*

S177 — In colonial days the accents of skylines proclaimed a hierarchy of values. Characteristically, the skyline consisted of church steeples at a high point with a domed building, usually a seat of government, as the focus. Fire watch towers, shot towers, or signal towers had distinct profiles and did not add confusion — neither did a cluster of ships' masts in the harbor, for they were thin, almost lacelike. All of these secondary skyline features had secondary visual roles which complemented the one or two prime skyline accents. Our contemporary skylines cannot be read in such a simple way. *Ibid.*

STACKHOUSE, Max L. (1935-   )

S178 — The modern setting of man is an artifact. It is made, it was not given. It is invented, built, and contrived. It was not found or discovered. It is a product of human projects, even if the projects are made from the givens. Societies consist in the interplay of givens and projects. The city has tipped the balance: projects far outweigh the givens. *Ethics and the Urban Ethos*

STANESCU, Traian

S179 — The city is the social concept of life, it is the human culture, it is the love of the beautiful. The city represents investment on the long term, the respective vision of the future; the city is a synthesis of durabilities, a materialistic ideology, the history of a country, the philosophy of existence. [in general, and of Bucharest] *Bucharesti*

STANIHURST, Richard (1547-1618)

S180 — The seat of the citie is of all sides pleasant, comfortable, and wholesome. If you would traverse hills, they are not far off. If Champaign land, it lieth of all parts. If you would be delited with fresh water, the famous river called the Liffie, named of Ptolome Lybnium, runneth fast by. If you will take the view of the sea, it is at hand. [of Dublin]

STANLEY, Edward Henry

S181 — I will say that in these Lancashire towns — in these great industrial communities throughout that entire district which acknowledges Manchester as its centre — which may be almost regarded as one continuous town, and which, so regarded, exceeds in population and productive power London itself — there exists a more vigorous healthy life than among any other portion, be it what it may, of English society. *(Speech at Bolton)*

STARR, Kevin

S182 — Los Angeles is quintessentially California, a city of (A.D.) 2050, decades ahead of the rest of the country, a place where everything is naturally larger than life, from the kooks to the technology . . . I love Los Angeles because it is a city patterned after no model. It is unique, developed through its own energy and creativity. *The Los Angeles Times, May 22, 1973*

STARR, Roger (1918-   )

S183 — Living in a city is no longer regarded as a temporary necessity, perverting man's essentially rural nature; it is now generally accepted that our ancestors

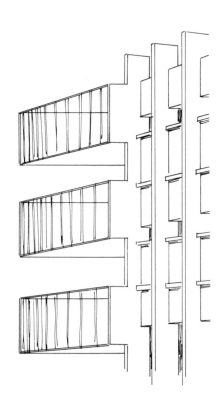

slid from the trees to stay, and that we had better reconcile ourselves to the pavements, or find a way to reconcile the pavements to us. *The Living End*

STATIUS, Publius Papinius (45?-96?)

S184 — Such, Marcellus, is the story I am singing on the Chalcidic strand, where Vesuvius hurls forth broken rage, outpouring fire that would rival Trinacrian flames. Marvellous, but true! Will future ages believe, when once more crops are growing, and these wastes are green again, that cities and people lie beneath, and that their ancestral lands have suffered a like fate? [of Pompeii, Herculaneum, Stabiae]

STEAD, William (1849-1912)

S185 — If a stranger's first impression of Chicago is that of the barbarous gridironed streets, his second is that of the multitude of mutilated people whom he meets on crutches. Excepting immediately after a great war, I have never seen so many mutilated fragments of humanity as one finds in Chicago. Dealers in artificial limbs and crutches ought to be able to do a better business in Chicago than in any other city I have ever visited. . . . The railroads which cross the city at the level in every direction, although limited by statute and ordinance as to speed, constantly mow down unoffending citizens at the crossings, and those legless, armless men and women whom you meet on the streets are merely the mangled remnant of the massacre that is constantly going on year in and year out. *If Christ Came to Chicago*

STEDMAN, E.C. (1833-1908)

S186 — Just where the Treasury's marble front / Looks over Wall Street's mingled nations, / Where Jews and Gentiles most are wont / To throng for trade and last quotations; / Where, hour, by hour, the rates of gold / Outrival, in the ears of people, / The quarter-chimes, serenely tolled / From Trinity's undaunted steeple. / [of New York City] *Pan in Wall Street*

STEELE, Marjorie

S187 — [A city composed of] people who get acquainted with their neighbors by meeting them in Miami. [of New York City]

STEFFENS, Lincoln (1866-1936)

S188 — Minneapolis is a New England town on the upper Mississippi. The metropolis of the Northwest, it is the metropolis also of Norway and Sweden in America. Indeed, it is the second largest Scandinavian city in the world. But Yankees, straight from Down East, settled the town, and their New England spirit predominates. *The Shame of the Cities*

S189 — Other American cities, no matter how bad their own condition may be, all point with scorn to Philadelphia as worse — 'the worst-governed city in the country.' St. Louis, Minneapolis, Pittsburgh submit with some patience to the jibes of any other community; the most friendly suggestion from Philadelphia is rejected with contempt. The Philadelphians are 'supine,' 'asleep'; hopelessly ring-ruled, they are 'complacent.' 'Politically benighted,' Philadelphia is supposed to have no light to throw upon a state of things that is almost universal. This is not fair. Philadelphia is, indeed, corrupt; but it is not without significance. *Ibid.*

S190 — St. Louis, the fourth city in size in the United States, is making two announcements to the world: one that it is the worst-governed city in the land; the other that it wishes all men to come there (for the World's Fair) and see it. It isn't our worst-governed city; Philadelphia is that. *Ibid.*

S191 — Yes, Chicago. First in violence, deepest in dirt; loud, lawless, unlovely, ill-smelling, irreverent, new; an overgrown gawk of a village, the 'tough' among cities, a spectacle for the nation; — I give Chicago no quarter and Chicago asks for none. *Ibid.*

STEIN, Clarence S. (1882-1975)

S192 — Most of us see the Great City as in a dream. It is the sum of all our possible aspirations. A picturesque skyline, massive towers, romantic beauty! Crowds swaying through the lighted streets in pursuit of pleasure; flashing lights, dancing feet, and delightful foods with the flavor of Rome, Paris, Vienna, Pekin or London. A far cry from the Ladies' Social of Gopher Prairie! Libraries of rare books, vast museums and universities, the grand opera and the concert hall — the city of culture! *The Survey Graphic, May 1, 1925*

STEIN, Gertrude (1874-1946)

S193 — When you get there, there isn't any there there. [of Oakland]

S194 — America is my country and Paris is my hometown. *An American in France*

STEINBECK, John (1902-1968)

S195 — I saw the city, and it horrified me. There was something monstrous about it. [of New York]

S196 — As I passed through or near the great hives of production — Youngstown, Cleveland, Akron, Toledo, Pontiac, Flint, and later South Bend and Gary — my eyes and mind were battered by the fantastic hugeness and energy of production, a complication that resembles chaos and cannot be. So might one look down on an ant hill and see no method or direction or purpose in the darting hurrying inhabitants. What was so wonderful was that I could come again to a quiet country road, tree-bordered, with fenced fields and cows, could pull up Rocinante beside a lake of clear, clean water and see high overhead the arrows of southing ducks and geese. *Travels with Charley*

S197 — I remembered Seattle as a town sitting on hills beside a matchless harborage — a little city of space and trees and gardens, its houses matched to such a background. It is no longer so. The tops of hills are shaved off to make level warrens for the rabbits of the present. The highways eight lanes wide cut like glaciers through the uneasy land. This Seattle had no relation to the one I remembered. *Ibid.*

S198 — In America I live in New York, or dip into Chicago or San Francisco. But New York is no more America than Paris is France or London is England. Thus I discovered that I did not know my own country. *Ibid.*

S199 — A long time ago I was in the ancient city of Prague and at the same time Joseph Alsop, the justly famous critic of places and events, was there . . . Joe and I flew home to

America in the same plane, and on the way he told me about Prague, and his Prague had no relation to the city I had seen and heard. It just wasn't the same place, and yet each of us was honest, neither one a liar, both pretty good observers by any standard, and we brought home two cities, two truths. *Ibid.*

S200 — When a city begins to grow and spread outward, from the edges, the center which was once its glory is in a sense abandoned to time. Then the buildings grow dark and a kind of decay sets in; poorer people move in as the rents fall, and small fringe businesses take the place of once flowering establishments. . . . Nearly every city I know has such a dying mother of violence and despair where at night the brightness of the street lamps is sucked away and policemen walk in pairs. And then one day perhaps the city returns and rips out the sore and builds a monument to its past. *Ibid.*

STEPHENSON, Ralph

S201 — This city's got the right name — New York. Nothing ever gets old around here. [worker at Penn Station at time of demolition] *The New York Times, October 29, 1963*

STERLING, George (1869-1926)

S202 — The winds of the Future wait / At the iron walls of her Gate, / And the western ocean breaks in thunder, / And the western stars go slowly under, / And her gaze is ever West / In the dream of her young unrest. / Her sea is a voice that calls, / And her star a voice above, / And her wind a voice on her walls — / My cool, grey city of love. / [of San Francisco]

STERNE, Laurence (1713-1768)

S203 — Whistled up to London, upon a Tom Fool's errand. *Tristram Shandy*

STERNLIEB, George (1928-   )

S204 — Our society has decided it's cheaper to turn our old cities over to the poor and buy them off with welfare. *U.S. News & World Report, April 7, 1975*

S205 — The size of the constituency which

lives outside the cities but still wants to preserve them at any cost grows smaller day by day. It is not exploitation that the core areas must fear. It is indifference and abandonment. *U.S. News & World Report, April 10, 1972*

STEVENS, Adlen

S206 — Washington the capital is a symbol of democracy and America. Washington the city is a symbol of almost everything that sincere and thoughtful men know is wrong with democracy and America. Washington the Capital is the hope of world freedom; Washington the city is overcrowded, badly housed, expensive, crime-ridden, intolerant, with inadequate transportation, schools, and health facilities. It staggers under a dilapidated and hopeless governmental organization, and its problems are rapidly getting worse. It is the most undemocratic city in America. *Washington – Blight on Democracy: Plain Talk about Our Capital City*

STEVENSON, Robert Louis (1850-1894)

S207 — As we drew near to New York I was at first amused and then somewhat staggered, by the cautious and the grisly tales that went the round. You would have thought we were to land upon a cannibal island. You must speak to no one in the streets, as they would not leave you till you were rooked and beaten. You must enter a hotel with military precautions; for the least you had to apprehend was to awake next morning without money or baggage, or necessary raiment, a lone forked radish in a bed; and if the worst befell, you would instantly and mysteriously disppear from the ranks of mankind. *The Amateur Emigrant: The Silverado Squatters*

STEWART, Cecil

S208 — That all roads lead to Rome is a cliche, and very misleading, for just as there must be two sides to an argument, there must be two ends to a road, unless it is a circular road. And the peculiar thing about Roman roads is that they were very straight, and led not to Rome, but away from it. The Romans were much more interested in where they were going than in where they had come from. *A Prospect of Cities*

STOKES, Carl B. (Mayor of Cleveland) (1927-)

S209 — You've got to rely on community good will. You've got to rely on hope that people are basically good.... Despite the litany of the sorrows of the city, we must believe in the ability of man to respond to the problems of his environment. *(at Yale University, April 2, 1969)*

STOPES, Marie Carmichael (1880-1958)

S210 — London, scarred mistress of proud Freedom's heart, / The love we bear you has no counterpart. / *London*

STOTHER, F.

S211 — A city inherited from the Middle Ages. [of Pittsburgh] *What Kind of Pittsburgh Is Detroit?*

STOUFFER, Samuel (1900-1960)

S212 — Rural people in every region are less likely to be tolerant of non-conformists than city people, even when we compare urban and rural people with the same amount of schooling. There is something about life in a small community that makes it less hospitable to divergent opinions than is the case in our urban centers. In the anonymity of city life it is much easier for deviant behavior to flourish than in the goldfish bowl of a small community. *Communism, Conformity, and Civil Liberties*

STOUT, Janis P.

S213 — American fiction of the early nineteenth century demonstrates that in the popular imagination the city aroused a strong distrust which, in grand contradiction, existed simultaneousy with the equally strong popular hopes for material advantages in urbanization. There is little ambivalence, however, in these fictional accounts of the blandishments of city life. It might be gay, diverting, even educational at times, and country people too might occasionally stray into sin, but the very terms of such concessions betray the writer's underlying assumptions: the city is a basically frivolous, hence morally insecure, place, and the countryside is the chief stronghold of sobriety and virtue. *Sodoms in Eden*

STOW, John (1525?-1605)

S214 — Men are congregated into cities and commonwealths for honesty and utility's sake, these shortly be the commodities that do come by cities, commonalities, and corportions. First, men by this nearness of conversation are withdrawn from barbarous fixity and force, to certain mildness of manners, and to humanity and justice.... Good behavior is yet called urbanitas because it is rather found in cities than elsewhere. In sum, by often hearing, men be better persuaded in religion, and for that they live in the eyes of others, they be by example the more easily trained to justice, and by shamefastness restrained from injury.

STRABO (63 B.C.?-24 A.D.?)

S215 — One may say that the earlier Romans cared little for the beauty of their city, since they were preoccupied with other, more utilitarian measure. But later generations — and especially those of the modern age and our own times — have by no means fallen short on this score, but have filled the city with many and splendid endowments of their munificence. *Geography*

STRAUSS, Anselm (1916-   )

S216 — The large American city, tending to be engrossed with economic expansion and having been faced with a continually unexpected increase of population, has never had much time to consolidate its past gains or leisure to take its attention off the alluringly expanding future. Unlike the large European cities, most of which developed into larger urban centers during the eighteenth and nineteenth centuries from smaller beginnings along established trade and water routes, American cities were plunked down in the middle of nowhere, in a hurry, and developed initially under conditions of intense and obvious competition.

S217 — Taken as a group, novelists have portrayed life in the city not only more dramatically — more humanly, if you wish — than their scholarly contemporaries, the sociologists, the geographers, the planners; but they have been less heir perhaps to inherited intellectual views which divert gaze and cramp vision. *Urban Perspectives: New York City*

STREET, Julian (1879-1947)

S218 — Call Chicago mighty, monstrous, multifarious, vital, lusty, stupendous, indomitable, intense, unnatural, aspiring, puissant, preposterous, transcendant — call it what you like — throw the dictionary at it!

STRONG, Josiah (1847-1916)

S219 — As a rule, our largest cities are the worst governed. It is natural, therefore, to infer that, as our cities grow larger and more dangerous, the government will become more corrupt, and control will pass more completely into the hands of those who themselves most need to be controlled. *Our Country*

S220 — As civilization increases, as society becomes more complex, as labor-saving machinery is multiplied and the division of labor becomes more minute, the individual becomes more fractional and dependent. Every savage possesses all the knowledge of his tribe. Throw him upon his own resources, and he is self-sufficient. A civilized man in like circumstances would perish. The savage is independent. Civilize him, and he becomes dependent; the more civilized, the more dependent. *Ibid.*

S221 — Because our cities are so largely foreign, Romanism finds in them its chief strength. *Ibid.*

S222 — The city has become a serious menace to our civilization, because in it, excepting Mormonism, each of the dangers we have discussed is enhanced, and all are focalized. *Ibid.*

S223 — It is the city where wealth is massed; and here are the tangible evidences of it piled many stories high. Here the sway of Mammon is widest, and his worship the most constant and eager. Here are luxuries gathered — everything that dazzles the eye, or tempts the appetite; here is the most extravagant expenditure. Here, also is the congestion of wealth the severest. *Ibid.*

S224 — Socialism centers in the city, and the materials of its growth are multiplied with the growth of the city. Here is heaped the social dynamite; here roughs, gamblers, thieves, robbers, lawless and desperate men of all sorts, congregate; men who are ready on any pretext to raise riots for the purpose of destruction and plunder; here gather foreigners and wage-workers who are especially susceptible to socialist arguments; here skepticism and irreligion abound; here inequality is the greatest and most obvious, and the contrast between opulence and penury the most striking; here is suffering the sorest. *Ibid.*

S225 — If we have not sufficient moral sense or common sense to prevent saloon-keepers, thieves, gamblers, jailbirds, and prize fighters from dominating our municipal politics, we have as good officials as we deserve.... Ignorance, vice, and wretchedness, combined, constitute social dynamite, of which the city slum is a magazine. *The Twentieth Century City*

STRUNSKY, Simeon (1879-1948)

S226 — New York has more hermits than will be found in all the forests, mountains and deserts of the United States. *No Mean City*

SUETONIUS, Gaius Tranquillus (75-160)

S227 — He [Caesar Augustus] found a city built of brick; he left it built of marble. [of Rome] *Caesar Augustus*

SULLIVAN, Frank (1892-1976)

S228 — A city of 7,000,000 so decadent that when I leave it I never dare look back lest I turn into salt and the conductor throw me over his shoulder for good luck. [of New York City]

SULLIVAN, Louis (1856-1924)

S229 — Architecture is not merely an art, more or less well or more or less badly done; it is a social manifestation. If we would know why certain things are as they are in our architecture, we must look to the people; for our buildings as a whole are an image of our people as a whole, although specifically they are the individual images of those to whom, as a class, the public has

delegated and entrusted its power to build. Therefore, by this light, the critical study of architecture becomes ... in reality, a study of the social conditions producing it.

SULLIVAN, Tim

S230 — Nobody ever writes about public housing from the point of view of the people who say, 'Things will be better when we get into the project.'

SUTCLIFFE, Anthony (1942-)

S231 — The visitor to London needs a guidebook to direct him to those corners of the City that can be described, without stretching the imagination too far, as Dickensian. But in central Paris most streets could still serve as a setting for a story by Balzac or Victor Hugo, and Maupassant would certainly be able to find his way unerringly there. *The Autumn of Central Paris*

SUTTON, Horace (1919-)

S232 — The pneumatic noisemaker is becoming the emblematic Sound of New York, the way the bells of Big Ben are the Sound of London. *Saturday Evening Post, March 11, 1961*

SUYIN, Han (1917-)

S233 — For centuries Lhasa was Jerusalem, Lourdes, Rome, Mecca, for believers in lamaism; the lodestone for millions of pilgrims from a vast area of Asia; from Mongolia in the north, from the five provinces of China where there are Tibetans, from Nepal, Kashmir, Bhutan and Kikkim; the Himalayan foothills on the Indian side, altogether far more numerous than the inhabitants of Tibet itself. Their fervour was uncompromising, their minds oriented towards future reincarnation. Suffering and misery in this one was but the retribution of past sinfulness, and a pilgrimage to Lhasa would guarantee rebirth to a better life. *Lhasa, The Open City*

SWIFT, Gustavus (1881-1943)

S234 — Chicago is the finest city for the moderate, natural, average man . . . in which to live. The New Yorker who says Chicago is a city of luxuries is probably one of the constantly growing number who are insatiable in their greed for the softer things of life. . . . I do not go in for luxuries myself.

SWINBURNE, Algernon Charles (1837-1909)

S235 — There's no good girl's lip out of Paris. *Ballad of the Women of Paris*

RENE KAMMELER

T

TACITUS, Cornelius (c. 55-120)

T1 — A town of the highest repute and a busy emporium for trade and traders . . . [of the City of London]

TALBERT, Robert (1909-)

T2 — Possibly since the beginning of urban life men have pointed with pride to their own town. Local pride and patriotism have been a common belief of urban dwellers from time immemorial, and many have agreed with Saint Paul in concluding, 'I am a citizen of no mean city.' *Cowtown – Metropolis*

TALESE, Gay (1932-)

T3 — I spent most of this year in southern California and pondered moving there, but it was never a serious thought. California has more space. I've got a suntan; I played tennis every day; I had a swimming pool — all the trappings of the good life. I returned to a New York brownstone on a dusty, dirty street with grim, angry people fighting for parking spaces — and I love it. New York is ugly; it's over-programmed, over-crowded, over-neurotic and over-skilled, but it's where I think I can do my best work. *(Interview, March, 1973)*

T4 — New York, where 250 people die each day, and where the living dash for empty apartments . . . Where on page 29 of this morning's newspaper are pictures of the dead; on page 31 are pictures of the engaged; on page 1 are pictures of those who

are running the world, enjoying the lush years before they land on page 29. *New York – A Serendipiter's Journey*

TALLEY, A.J.

T5 — The reason that American cities are so prosperous is that there is no place to sit down.

TALLMAN, Warren (1921-)

T6 — Cityside rigidity and unfreedom force severe limitations upon intelligence — the houses all look alike. *New American Story*

TALMADGE, Herman E. (Senator) (1913-)

T7 — Fun City isn't fun any more. Since the conclusion of World War II, we have been on a national joy ride that has produced the greatest migration of human beings in history. We have shoved untold millions of people into cities, because we failed to commit ourselves to the need for balanced growth. *(Television broadcast, June 25, 1972)*

TAMMEUS, William D. (1945-)

T8 — Hometowns seem to be loved most by people who *used* to live in them *Kansas City Star*

TANKEL, Stanley B. (1922?-1968)

T9 — I predict that more traditional urban values will reassert themselves after a lapse during the past generation and that we will increasingly appreciate the difference between city and country, knowing that you simply can't have both in the same location. We will renew our vital contact with Nature, and there may even be pedestrians again! *The Importance of Open Space in the Urban Pattern*

TARKINGTON, Booth (1869-1946)

T10 — The streets were thunderous; a vast energy heaved under the universal coating of dinginess. George walked through the begrimed crowds of hurrying strangers and saw no face that he remembered. Great numbers of the faces were even of a kind he did not remember ever to have seen; they were partly like the old type that his boyhood knew, and partly like types he knew abroad. He saw German eyes with American wrinkles at their corners; he saw Irish eyes and Neapolitan eyes, Roman eyes, Tuscan eyes, eyes of Lombardy, of Savoy, Hungarian eyes, Balkan eyes, Scandinavian eyes — all with a queer American look in them. *The Magnificent Ambersons*

TASSO, Torquato (1544-1595)

T11 — Jerusalem upon two hills is seen, / Of height unequal, and turned face to face; / A valley interposing sinks between / And marks them from each other by its trace. / *Gerusalemme Liberata*

TAWNEY, Richard Henry (1880-1962)

T12 — Industrialized communities neglect the very objects for which it is worthwhile to acquire riches in their feverish preoccupation with the means by which riches can be acquired. *The Acquisitive Society*

TAYLOR, Edward

T13 — Would God I in that Golden City were, / With Jaspers Walld, all garnisht, and made swash, / With Pretious Stones, whose Gates, are Pearles most cleare / And Streets Pure Gold, like to transparent Glass, / That my dull Soule might be inflamde to see / How Saints and Angells ravisht are in Glee.

TAYLOR, W. Cooke (1800-1849)

T14 — Now, is it at all a proved fact that a rural population is more virtuous, moral, and orderly than a town population? I know that such a notion is a very general prejudice — a remnant of the old infidel fallacy, started as a novelty, though it is as old as the hills, by Rousseau in the last century, that the life of the savage is more natural, and therefore more virtuous, than that of the civilised man. But our concern is with facts: those which best illustrate the subject . . . certainly give the balance of morality to the towns. *Notes of a Tour*

TEALE, Edwin Way (1899-1980)

T15 — The city man, in his neon-and-mazda glare, knows nothing of nature's midnight. His electric lamps surround him with

synthetic sunshine. They push back the dark. They defend him from the realities of the age-old night. *North with the Spring*

TEMKO, Allan

T16 — As long as people live under humiliating conditions, they are going to be bitter and brutal. Architecture is only part of the problem of cities. Conceivably we could have a great city of mediocre buildings. It might be a happy place in which to live. And you might have a beautiful city that is not a happy city. *The City*

TENNYSON, (Lord) Alfred (1809-1892)

T17 — The City is Built / To music, therefore never built at all, / And therefore built for ever. / *The Idylls of the King, The Coming of Arthur*

T18 — Is it well that while we range with Science, glorying the Time, / City children soak and blacken soul and sense in city slime? / There among the glooming alleys Progress halts on palsied feet, / Crime and hunger cast our maidens by the thousands on the street. / *Locksley Hall Sixty Years After*

T19 — I loathe the squares and streets, / And the faces that one meets. / *Maud*

T20 — Much have I seen and known; cities of men / And manners, climates, councils, governments, / Myself not least, but honour'd of them all; / And drunk delight of battle with my peers, / Far on the ringing plains of windy Troy. / *Ulysses*

TERKEL, Studs (1912-)

T21 — Chicago is a city of working people, who came to earn their daily bread in heavy industries — steel, packing, railroads, farm equipment. They came seeking more than bread though. There has always been, in this city, this cockeyed wonder of a town, a quest for beauty. *Quoted in Cities, John McGreevy*

T22 — Chicago is no one-dimensional town, nor are its people. No, signora, Chicago is more than that, much much more. And so up Jacob's ladder, one more rung upward towards the blue heaven of security. That is to own a two-flat, your piece of land but you're a landlord as well. On the first floor you and your family live, and up above your son-in-law and his family, or even a stranger. So you're getting rent. But always, if possible, a patch of green, a little garden, a flower or two — that quietly desperate search for just a small piece of beauty in everyday life. *Ibid.*

T23 — To some, Chicago with its lack of sophistication and its muscularity is comical, archaic in this cool era, somewhat like an old punch-drunk fighter, swinging wild roundhouse wallops to the laughter of the wisenheimers at the ringside. But when it connects — oh, baby! *Ibid.*

THACKERAY, William Makepeace (1811-1863)

T24 — A street there is in Paris famous, / For which no rhyme our language yields, / Rue Neuve des Petits Champs its name is — / The New Street of the Little Fields. / *The Ballad of Bouillabaisse*

THERNSTROM, Stephan (1934-)

T25 — One reason that a permanent proletariat along the lines envisaged by Marx did not develop in the course of American industrialization is perhaps that few Americans have stayed in one place, one workplace, or even one city long enough to discover a sense of common identity and common grievance. *Towards a New Past*

T26 — To be sure, immigration from abroad was extremely important in the building of America's cities down to World War I. But the most important source of population for the burgeoning cities was not the fields of Ireland and Austria, but those of Vermont and Iowa. The prime cause of population growth in nineteenth-century America, and the main source of urban growth, was simply the high fertility of natives living outside the city. *Ibid.*

THOMAS, Dylan (1914-1953)

T27 — I'm not going to London again for years; its intelligentsia is so hurried in the head that nothing stays there; its glamour smells of goat; there's no difference between good and bad. *Letters to Vernon Watkins*

THOMAS, Emile (1843-1923)

T28 — In no other literature do we find the two characters represented by the words *rusticus* and *urbanus* so violently contrasted with one another as in the Roman ... At no period of their history did the native Roman race attempt to conceal their contempt for the inhabitants of the city (urbani) ... The real Roman was a countryman ... *Roman Life under the Caesars*

T29 — It was Cicero more than anyone else who determined the respectable connotation of the word *urbane*, by constantly using it as an antonym of *rustic*. *Ibid.*

T30 — A spirit of contradiction, not without parallel in our own time, impelled the Romans when they wished to get away from Rome, to hasten off to places like Puteoli, Sorrento, or — favorite resort of all — Baiae, there to meet the whole of Roman society crowded into a still narrower circle. *Ibid.*

T31 — When Romans sought refuge in the country they had little appreciation of anything beyond its bracing air, which helped to restore their energies, its material comforts and pleasures, and the absolute repose it afforded to their minds ... At the great crises of their lives they could not endure the crowded city: their sole desire was for solitude.... Once the crisis had passed, however, the longing for the action soon took hold of them again. *Ibid.*

THOMAS, Wyndham (1924-)

T32 — The disadvantages of surburban life exist mainly in the minds of intellectual planners and social engineers. They apply their own criteria in judging the quality of life and conclude that, because they would not like it for themselves, it must be bad for everyone else. *New Towns Blues*

THOMSON, James (1700-1748)

T33 — The city swarms intense. The public haunt, / Full of each theme and warm with mixed discourse, / Hums indistinct. The sons of riot flow / Down the loose stream of false enchanted joy / To swift destruction. / *The Seasons*

T34 — Full are thy cities with the sons of art; / And trade and joy, in every busy street, / Mingling are heard; even Drudgery himself / As at the car he sweats, or dusty, hews / The palace stone, looks gay. / *Ibid.*

THOMSON, James (1834-1882)

T35 — The City is of Night, but not of Sleep; / There sweet sleep is not for the weary brain; / The pitiless hours like years and ages creep, / A night seems termless hell. / *The City of Dreadful Night*

T36 — The City is of Night; perchance of Death, / But certainly of Night. / *Ibid.*

T37 — That City's atmosphere is dark and dense, / Although not many exiles wander there, / With many a potent evil influence, / Each adding poison to the poisoned air; / Infections of unutterable sadness, / Infections of incalculable madness, / Infections of incurable despair. / *Ibid.*

T38 — The mighty City in vast silence slept, / Dreaming away its tumult, toil and strife; / But sleep, and sleep's rich dreams were not for me, / For me, accurst, whom terror and the pain / Of baffled longings, and starved misery ... / ... Drove forth as one possest. / *The Doom of a City*

T39 — Of the City's vast palatial pride / Of all the works of man on every side ... / ... Remained no vestige. / *Ibid.*

THOMPSON, Morton

T40 — A state of mind surrounded by Los Angeles. [of Hollywood]

THOREAU, Henry David (1817-1862)

T41 — City life: Millions of people being lonesome together.

T42 — The only room in Boston which I visit with alacrity is the Gentlemen's Room at the Fitchburg Depot, where I wait for cars sometimes for two hours, in order to get out of town.

T43 — Ye were the Grecian cities then, / Then Romes of modern birth, / Where the New England husbandmen / Have shown a Roman worth / [of Lexington and Concord]

T44 — As for these communities, I think I had rather keep bachelor's hall in hell than go to board in heaven. *Journal*

T45 — The mass of men lead lives of quiet desperation. What is called resignation is confirmed desperation. From the desperate city you go into the desperate country, and have to console yourself with the bravery of minks and muskrats. A stereotyped but unconscious despair is concealed even under what are called the games and amusements of mankind. There is no play in them, for this comes after work. But it is a characteristic of wisdom not to do desperate things. *Walden*

T46 — The whistle of the locomotive penetrates my woods summer and winter, sounding like the scream of a hawk sailing over some farmer's yard, informing me that many restless city merchants are arriving within the circle of the town, or adventurous country traders from the other side. As they come under one horizon, they shout their warning to get off the track to the other, heard sometimes through the circles of two towns. Here come your groceries, country; your rations, countrymen! Nor is there any man so independent on his farm that he can say them nay. And here's your pay for them! screams the countryman's whistle; timber like long battering rams going twenty miles an hour against the city's walls, and chairs enough to seat all the weary and heavy laden that dwell within them. With such

huge and lumbering civility the country
hands a chair to city. All the Indian
huckleberry hills are stripped, all the
cranberry meadows are raked into the
city. *Ibid.*

**THORNTON, Robert L. (Sr.) (Mayor of
Dallas) (?-1964)**

T47 — City-building is just a privilege of
citizenship. *The New York Times, February
16, 1964*

THORPE, Rose Hartwick (1850-1939)

T48 — Out she swung — far out; the city
seemed a speck of light below, / There 'twixt
heaven and earth suspended as the bell
swung to and fro. / *Curfew Must Not Ring
Tonight*

THUCYDIDES (471?-400? B.C.)

T49 — In such hurried fashion did the
Athenians build the walls of their city, to
this day the structure shows evidence of
haste. The foundations are made up of all
sorts of stones, in some places unwrought,
and laid just as each worker brought them;
there were many columns too, taken from
sepulchers, and many old stones already
cut, inserted in the work. The circuit of the
city was extended in every direction, and
the citizens, in their ardor to complete the
design, spared nothing.

T50 — Day by day fix your eyes upon the
greatness of Athens, until you become filled
with the love of her; and when you are
impressed by the spectacle of her glory,
reflect that this empire has been acquired
by men who knew their duty and had the
courage to do it. *Funeral Speech of Pericles*

T51 — It is men who make a city, not walls
or ships. *History*

TILLICH, Paul J. (1886-1965)

T52 — All forms of totalitarianism try to
avoid the strange, the problematic, the
critical, the rational. To do so, they must
deny the metropolitan spirit, equalize
everything in city and country, and retain a
center which is not the center of anything
because everything else is swallowed up by
it. Nothing strange — neither questions

criticism, nor competition — is left to the
spiritual life, and so it dies. *Quoted in The
Metropolis and Modern Life, E.M. Fisher, Ed.*

T53 — The centralized political power of the
metropolis can be accompanied, assisted, or
replaced by a centralized religious power.
The greatest example is the Roman Catholic
Church. Rome and the pope belong to each
other. The pope is in exile if he is not in the
metropolis. At the same time, his
sacramental power is real in every village
priest in the whole Catholic world. *Ibid.*

T54 — A metropolis, therefore, is a center
city. It is likewise an including city. It
includes everything of which it is the center,
and encompasses diversity and freedom of
individual creativity and competition. In
this connection, the term provincial is
revealing. So called provincial art has not
undergone the process of intense
competition which occurs in the metropolis.
It may be good art, but it cannot be great
art. To produce great art, the bearers of the
highest spiritual life must first undergo the
criticism and the competition provided by
the inclusive character of the
metropolis. *Ibid.*

T55 — There is no necessary conflict
between the metropolis and the
countryside. The metropolis is present in
the remotest hamlet as a focal point to
which rural life is partly directed. And the
reverse is also true, since the remotest
hamlet is present in the metropolis as an
element constituting its center. The power
of both is rooted in the mutual immanence
of the metropolis in the country and of the
country in the metropolis. *Ibid.*

TOCQUEVILLE, Alexis de (1805-1859)

T56 — America has no great capital city,
whose direct or indirect influence is felt over
the whole extent of the country; this I hold
to be one of the first causes of the
maintenance of republican institutions in
the United States. In cities men cannot be
prevented from concerting together and
awakening a mutual excitement that
prompts sudden and passionate resolutions.
Cities may be looked upon as large
assemblies, of which all the inhabitants are
members; their populace exercise a
prodigious influence upon the magistrates,

and frequently execute their own wishes without the intervention of public officers. *Democracy in America*

T57 — I look upon the size of certain American cities, and especially on the nature of their population, as a real danger which threatens the future security of the democratic republics of the New World; and I venture to predict that they will perish from this circumstance, unless the government succeeds in creating an armed force which, while it remains under the control of the majority of the nation, will be independent of the town population and able to repress its excesses. *Ibid.*

TOFFLER, Alvin (1928-   )

T58 — One way to grasp the meaning of [population growth today] . . . is to imagine what would happen if all existing cities, instead of expanding, retained their present size. If this were so, in order to accommodate the new urban millions we would have to build a duplicate city for each of the hundreds that already dot the globe. A new Tokyo, a new Hamburg, a new Rome and Rangoon — and all within eleven years. *Future Shock*

T59 — Already, within the main centers of change, in California and Cambridge, Mass., in New York and London and Tokyo, millions are living the life of the future. What makes them different? Certainly they are richer, better educated, more mobile. But what specifically marks them is the fact that they 'live faster.'

To survive in such communities, however, the individual must become infinitely more adaptable than ever before. Above all he must understand *transience*. Transience is the new 'temporariness' in everyday life. It can be defined as the rate at which our relationships — with things, places, people and information — turn over. *Quoted in Reader's Digest*

TOLMAN, W.H. (1861-c.1960), & W.I. HALL

T60 — There is one respect in which American cities are far behind those of the continent; it touches a matter which it would seem should only be mentioned in order that its need and usefulness should be universally admitted. I refer to the public conveniences of water closets and urinals which should be provided by the city for the free use of the entire civic population — men, women, and children. . . .

There are five public lavatories in this great metropolis.

Contrast these facts with those of English cities. Shall we be content that a saloon shall furnish what of right should be afforded by the city? . . . The time has come for civic manhood to assert itself in the behalf of humanity. [of New York] *Handbook of Sociological References for New York*

TOMLINSON, H.M. (1873-1958)

T61 — The sea is at its best at London, near midnight, when you are within the arms of a capacious chair, before a glowing fire, selecting phases of the voyages you will never make. *The Sea and the Jungle*

TOMPKINS, Kenneth O. (Mayor of Johnstown, Pa.)

T62 — The suburbanite should realize he is dependent on the city for a livelihood and should help to defray city expenses and not run to the woods every evening and leave the city to fend for itself. *(Interview, February, 1969)*

TORRIANO

T63 — If every one will sweep his own house, the City will be clean.

TOWNE, Charles Hanson (1877-1949)

T64 — To me, a skyscraper is as wonderful as a skylark; a human face, as magical as a tweet; a bridge, as beautiful as a tree. Such faith have I in great cities that I prefer to spend my days in them rather than on any hit-the-trail holiday that could possibly be arranged. *The American Magazine, March, 1920*

T65 — You can't tell me that civilization, the civilization of great cities, hasn't some distinct advantages. For one thing, I am used to cities. I know them, and I love them. I was born in one — in Louisville, to be exact; and I came to New York when I was four years old. I've lived there ever since, and I am not sorry. Everyone in America who can gravitates toward the metropolis sooner or later. Why? There must be a reason. There is. It is because Opportunity is writ large on the gateway of Manhattan; and a man isn't worth tinker's dam who doesn't want to embrace Opportunity. *Ibid.*

TOYNBEE, Arnold (1889-1975)

T66 — Before machinization generated expansion, the configuration of a typical city — a city, that is, with a central marketplace and a surrounding wall — was like that of the solid wooden wheel of a primitive ox-cart which centres on an axle and is held together compactly by an iron rim. The typical configuration is now coming to be, not a solid disc, but a hollow ring — the shape of an automobile tyre when it has been stripped off its wheel. *Cities on the Move*

T67 — A city is a human settlement whose inhabitants cannot produce, within the city-limits, all of the food that they need for keeping them alive. This feature is common to cities of all kinds. It is common to Jericho and Megalopolis, though superficially these two cities may look as different from each other as a poodle looks from a great dane or a domestic cat from a tiger. *Ibid.*

T68 — A city-state may be defined as a state in which there is only a single city or in which a single city is so superior in terms of population and power to any minor cities that may be included in its territory that this one city's paramountcy in the state is indisputable. *Ibid.*

T69 — A city's prestige has in some cases moved a government to retain it, or positively to select it, for serving as a capital, even if this city has nothing to recommend it on any other count and indeed if, on one or more counts, it is actually unsuitable for performing a capital's functions. *Ibid.*

T70 — Every city — or, it might be more accurate to say, every city before the present age of mechanization — has been, among other things, a holy city in some degree. . . . In the traditional city the most prominent public building was the principal place of worship of the prevalent religious community: a cathedral, mosque, church, or temple. It is only within the last two centuries that the principal architectural landmark in a typical city has ceased to be a minaret, or spire, or pagoda and has become a factory chimney, or a high-rise hotel or block of offices or flats. *Ibid.*

T71 — Everyone who makes money in the mechanized city uses the money that he makes there to escape, as far and as frequently as he can, from the inferno that is the source of his wealth. *Ibid.*

T72 — If the increase in the size of cities in the course of history is presented visually in the form of a curve, this curve will be found to have the same configuration as a curve presenting the increase in the potency of technology. *Ibid.*

T73 — In a city-state the city and the state are identical. A capital city, like a city that is a city-state, is a seat of government, but, unlike a city-state, a capital city is a seat of government merely; it is not a state as well. A state that is big enough to have a capital is governed from the capital, not by it. *Ibid.*

T74 — Mankind has committed itself to the World-City by the application of science to the technology of medicine and of agriculture. *Ibid.*

T75 — The megalopolises on all the continents are merging to form Ecumenopolis, a new type of city that can be represented by only one specimen, since Ecumenopolis is going, as its name proclaims, to encompass the land-surface of the globe with a single conurbation. The open question is not whether Ecumenopolis is going to come into existence; it is whether its maker, mankind, is going to be its master or to be its victim. *Ibid.*

T76 — Modern mechanized cities cannot feed themselves, even partially, as a few of the traditional walled cities once could. *Ibid.*

T77 — Rome was the highest point on the River Tiber that could be reached by sea-going ships, and, in the prerailway age, this was a commercially favourable location for a city. The reason why today Albany, not New York, is the capital of New York State is that Albany was the farthest point up the River Hudson that was accessible for seventeenth-century Dutch sea-going ships. *Ibid.*

T78 — The 'urban explosion,' like the population explosion with which it is bound up, is sensational and formidable, but it, too, is not an entirely new departure in human history. Like everything in life, it is an event in time, and therefore cannot be fully understood if it is not looked at in relation to the past. The mechanized city is the heir of the traditional city. The coming World-City, which is going to spread its tentacles round the globe, will be a human settlement of the same species as tiny Jericho and Ur and Weimar. *Ibid.*

TRENCH (Archbishop) (1807-1886)

T79 — The country man ... having gone for the first time to see some famous city, complained on his return home that he could not see the city for the houses. *Medieval Church History*

TREVELYAN, G.M. (1876-1962)

T80 — The agricultural labourer is now fast disappearing. He has suffered city change into something poor and strange. Rumours coming thick and fast from the great cities have destroyed for him the traditional piety and the honest customs of the countryside. He apes what he does not understand, — what indeed no one can understand, for it has no meaning, — the variegated, flaunting vulgarity of the modern town. *The Heart of the Empire*

T81 — The capability of the city-bred man, with his undoubtedly keen intellect and brain, ... to understand good literature and complex ideas when presented to him, is a fact insufficiently recognised by those who abuse the modern man instead of his surroundings. *Ibid.*

TROLLOPE, Anthony (1815-1882)

T82 — Speaking of New York as a traveler, I have two faults to find with it. In the first place, there is nothing to see; and, in the second place, there is no mode of getting about to see anything. *North America*

T83 — When success comes, when the happy hit has been made, and the ways of commerce have been truly foreseen with a cunning eye, then a great and prosperous city springs up, ready made as it were, from the earth. *Ibid.*

TROTSKY, Leon (1879-1940)

T84 — The fullest expression of our modern age. [of New York City]

TRUMPELDOR, Joseph (1880-1920)

T85 — [A place] of conventions and artificialities ... where the friends of today will fall upon one another tomorrow. [of the city]

TUCKER, George (1775-1861)

T86 — The love of civil liberty is, perhaps, both stronger and more constant in the country than the town; and if it is guarded in the cities by a keener vigilance and a more farsighted jealousy, yet law, order, and security, are also, in them, more exposed to danger, from the greater facility with which intrigue and ambition can there operate on ignorance and want. Whatever may be the good or evil tendencies of populous cities, they are the result to which all countries, that are at once fertile, free, and intelligent tend. *Progress of the United States in Population and Wealth*

TUNNARD, Christopher (1910-1979)

T87 — The city plan, being an art form, will never be an exact mirror of nature, in spite of the pseudobiological approach of the devotees of 'organic planning' although it may with virtue acknowledge the presence of nature and heighten our enjoyment of man-made environment by contrast. *The City of Man*

T88 — The classical image embraces all in its frame. It was this hated image, with the city at its center, that our false prophets and our Phaethons have abused, and they succeeded in destroying it by the time the forces of material expansion were in the land. Yet they believe that they can answer the problem with suggestions of merging city and country, of breaking up the metropolis into fragments of small cities and subsistence homesteads, a world so jejune that it would condemn us forever to the setting of soap operas. *Ibid.*

T89 — For all Jefferson's dislike of the city he was not afraid to build one; instinctively he saw it at the center of his dream and his reality. *Ibid.*

T90 — The gardens of a city should be many and various — like paintings on the wall of a living-room, their form and content may differ widely. *Ibid.*

T91 — It was a bold stroke of L'Enfant to turn to the most royal garden in Europe as model for the capital of a republic; Versailles gave shape to Washington, which was to become the Golden City, the cynosure of the world. [of Washington D.C.] *Ibid.*

T92 — The Renaissance city in its more advanced forms remains the truest expression of the power of man to create an esthetically satisfying environment. *Ibid.*

T93 — There are primitive communities in many parts of the world today in which tree worship is still practiced. There are also to be found in highly civilized communities certain advanced groups — mainly architects, planners and their disciples — who worship all forms of greenery indiscriminately. So great is the devotion of these latter-day hamadryads to the forms of nature that they wish to be surrounded by them at all times and in all places. *Ibid.*

TUPPER, M.F. (1810-1889)

T94 — Naples sitteth by the sea, keystone of an arch of azure. *Proverbial Philosophy*

TURGENEV, Ivan S. (1818-1883)

T95 — These empty, wide, gray streets, these gray-white yellow-gray, gray-pink peeling plaster houses with their deep-set windows — that is our northern Palmyra. Everything visible from all sides, everything frighteningly sharp and clear, and all sadly sleeping. [of St. Petersburg]

TURNER, Frederick Jackson (1861-1932)

T96 — The peculiarity of American institutions is the fact that they have been compelled to adapt themselves to the changes of an expanding people — to the changes involved in crossing a continent, in winning a wilderness, and in developing at each area of this progress out of the primitive economic and political conditions of the frontier into the complexity of city life. *The Significance of the Frontier in American History*

TURNER, John F.C. (1927-)

T97 — The city in the Third World is doomed to being a necropolis even before it becomes a metropolis or a megalopis. *Quoted in The Exploding Cities*

TURNER, Nancy Byrd (1880-c.1975)

T98 — When I go up to London / 'Twill be in April weather, / I'll have a riband on my rein / And flaunt a scarlet feather. / *Going up to London*

TWAIN, Mark (1835-1910)

T99 — The coldest Winter I ever spent was a Summer in San Francisco.

T100 — I suppose that London has always existed. One cannot easily imagine an England that had no London.

T101 — [London] is a collection of villages. When you live in one of them with its quiet back streets and its one street of stores and shops, little bits of stores and shops like those of any other village, it is not possible for you to realize that you are in the heart of the greatest city in the world.

T102 — It's a great place to live, but I wouldn't want to visit there. [of Los Angeles] *(letter)*

T103 — A state of mind. [of Boston]

T104 — The Vandal is bound for Venice! He has a long, weary ride of it, but just as the day is closing he hears someone shout 'Venice!' and puts his head out of the window, and sure enough, afloat on the placid sea, a league away, lies the great city with its towers and domes and steeples drowsing in a golden mist of sunset! Have you been to Venice — and seen the winding canals, and the stately edifices that border them all along, ornamented with the quaint devices and sculptures of a former age? *(Address: The American Vandal Abroad, November 17, 1868)*

T105 — We saw no energy in the capitals of Europe like the tremendous energy of New York, and we saw no place where intelligence and enterprise were so widely diffused as they are here in our country. *(Address, San Francisco, April 4, 1868)*

T106 — We take stock of a city like we take stock of a man. The clothes and appearance are the externals by which we judge. We next take stock of the mind, the intellect. These are the internals. The sum of both is the man or the city. New York has a great many details of the external sort which impress and inform the foreigner. Among these are the sky scrapers, and they are new to him. He hasn't seen their like since the Tower of Babel. The foreigner is shocked by them. I am not. *(Address: New York, December 6, 1900)*

T107 — Athens by moonlight! The prophet that thought the splendors of the New Jerusalem were revealed to him, surely saw this instead! It lay in the level plain right under our feet — all spread abroad like a picture — and we looked down upon it as we might have looked from a balloon. *Innocents Abroad*

T108 — Go back as far as you will into the vague past, there was always a Damascus. In the writings of every century for more than four thousand years, its name has been mentioned and its praises sung. To Damascus, years are only moments, decades are only flitting trifles of time. She measures time, not by days and months and years, but by the empires she has seen rise and prosper and crumble to ruin. She is a type of immortality. *Ibid.*

T109 — I cannot conceive of such a thing as Genoa in ruins. Such massive arches, such ponderous substructions as support these towering broad-winged edifices, we have seldom seen before; and surely the great blocks of stone of which these edifices are built can never decay. *Ibid.*

T110 — If you want dwarfs — I mean just a few dwarfs for a curiosity — go to Genoa. If you wish to buy them by the gross, for retail, go to Milan. There are plenty of dwarfs all over Italy, but it did seem to me that in Milan the crop was luxuriant. If you would see a fair average style of assorted cripples, go to Naples, or travel through the Roman states. But if you should see the very heart and home of cripples and human monsters, both, go straight to Constantinople. *Ibid.*

T111 — The most exquisite bronzes we have seen in Europe came from the exhumed cities of Herculaneum and Pompeii, and also the finest cameos and the most delicate engravings on precious stones; their pictures, eighteen or nineteen centuries old, are often much more pleasing than the celebrated rubbish of the old masters of three centuries ago. They were well up in art. *Ibid.*

T112 — Naples, with its immediate suburbs, contains six hundred and twenty-five thousand inhabitants, but I am satisfied it covers no more ground than an American city of one hundred and fifty thousand. It reaches up into the air infinitely higher than three American cities, though, and there is where the secret lies. *Ibid.*

T113 — Pompeii is no longer a buried city. It is a city of hundreds and hundreds of roofless houses, and a tangled maze of streets where one could easily get lost, without a guide, and have to sleep in some ghostly palace that had known no living tenant since that awful November night of eighteen centuries ago. *Ibid.*

T114 — Ruined Pompeii is in good condition compared to Sevastopol. Here, you may look in whatsoever direction you please, and your eye encounters scarcely anything but ruin, ruin, ruin! — fragments of houses, crumbled walls, torn and ragged hills, devastation everywhere! *Ibid.*

T115 — 'See Naples and die.' Well, I do not know that one would necessarily die after merely seeing it, but to attempt to live there might turn out a little differently. *Ibid.*

T116 — A street in Constantinople is a picture which one ought to see once — not oftener. *Ibid.*

T117 — The sun shines as brightly down on old Pompeii today as it did when Christ was born in Bethlehem, and its streets are cleaner a hundred times than ever Pompeiian saw them in her prime. *Ibid.*

T118 — The surest way to stop writing about Rome is to stop. I wished to write a real 'guide-book' chapter on this fascinating city, but I could not do it, because I have felt all the time like a boy in a candy-shop — there was everything to choose from, and yet no choice. I have drifted along hopelessly for a hundred pages of manuscript without knowing where to commence. I will not commence at all. *Ibid.*

T119 — There is a glorious city in the sea; / The sea is in the broad, the narrow streets, / Ebbing and flowing; and the salt seaweed / Clings to the marble of her palaces. [of Venice] *Ibid.*

T120 — They say the Sultan has eight hundred wives. This almost amounts to bigamy. It makes our cheeks burn with shame to see such a thing permitted here in Turkey. We do not mind it so much in Salt Lake, however. *Ibid.*

T121 — This Venice, which was a haughty, invincible, magnificent Republic for nearly fourteen hundred years; whose armies compelled the world's applause whenever and wherever they battled; whose navies well nigh held dominion of the seas, and whose merchant fleets whitened the remotest oceans with their sails and loaded these piers with the products of every clime, is fallen a prey to poverty, neglect and melancholy decay. *Ibid.*

T122 — What a funny old city this Queen of the Adriatic is! Narrow streets, vast, gloomy marble palaces, black with the corroding damps of centuries, and all partly submerged; no dry land visible anywhere, and no sidewalks worth mentioning; if you want to go to church, to the theater, or to the restaurant, you must call a gondola. It must be a paradise for cripples, for verily a man has no use for legs here. *Ibid.*

T123 — The first time I ever saw St. Louis I could have bought it for six million dollars, and it was the mistake of my life that I did not do it. *Life on the Mississippi*

T124 — This is the first time I was ever in a city where you couldn't throw a brick without breaking a church window. [of Montreal] *Quoted in Queen's Quarterly, Summer, 1935*

T125 — This poor little one-horse town. *The Undertaker's Story*

T126 — In Boston they ask, How much does he know? In New York, How much is he worth? In Philadelphia, Who were his parents? *What Paul Blouet Thinks of Us*

TYL, Josef Kajetan (1808-1856)

T127 — Once in his lifetime every Czech must see Prague, once he must make a pilgrimage there as a Moslem goes to Mecca. He who dies without having seen Prague didn't know the focus of our national history and the cradle of our future.

TYNAN, Kenneth (1927-1980)

T128 — Coming to New York from the muted mistiness of London, as I regularly do, is like traveling from a monochrome antique shop to a Technicolor bazaar. *Holiday Magazine, December, 1960*

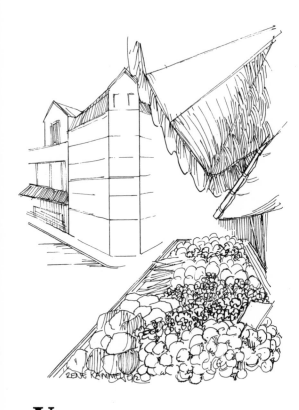

U

UDALL, Morris K. (1922-   )

U1 — We have got to save our cities, and we have to do whatever has to be done. New York is just the first. Detroit and Newark and Atlanta and St. Louis are going to be next. *(Meet the Press, April 4, 1976)*

UHLMAN, Wesley C. (Mayor of Seattle) (1935-   )

U2 — I am not wringing my hands. If Seattle is more desirable to singles and older people, or smaller households, or gays, that's not necessarily bad. Most Mayors wring their hands about the loss of the white middle class, but a city is like a living organism that changes every 20 or 30 years. *The New York Times, March 28, 1977*

UHLMANN, Fred (1901-   )

U3 — When night fell the view was as magic as looking down from Fiesole on Florence: thousands of lights, the air hot and fragrant with the smell of jasmine and lilac, and on all sides the voices, the singing and laughter of contented citizens, getting rather sleepy from too much food, or amorous from too much drink.... This town [Bologna] of less than half a million inhabitants had more opera, better theatre, finer museums, richer collections and a fuller life than Manchester or Birmingham, Bordeaux or Toulouse. *Reunion*

UNAMUNO, Miguel de (1864-1936)

U4 — In great cities culture is diffused but vulgarized.... In great cities proud natures become vain.... If you want to submerge your own 'I', better the streets of a great city than the solitudes of the wilderness. *Essays and Soliloquies*

UPDIKE, John (1932-   )

U5 — Clean straight streets. Cities whose cores are not blighted but innocently bustling. Anglo-Saxon face, British once removed, striding long-legged and unterrorized out of a dim thin past into a future as likely as any. Empty territories rich in minerals. Stately imperial government buildings. Parks where one need not fear being mugged. *Playboy, May, 1975*

U6 — The city overwhelmed our expectation. The Kiplingesque grandeur of Waterloo Station, the Eliotic despondency of the brick row in Chelsea ... the Dickensian nightmare of fog and sweating pavement and besmirched cornices ... We wheeled past mansions by Galsworthy and parks by A.A. Milne; we glimpsed a cobbled eighteenth century alley, complete with hanging tavern boards, where Dr. Johnson might have reeled and gasped the night he laughed so hard.... [of London] *The New Yorker, December 22, 1962*

USTINOV, Peter (1921-   )

U7 — City of Peter the Great, city of Lenin, and birthplace of the Russian Revolution. I wasn't born here, but my parents met and married here before moving to London, where I was born. I have it on the best authority that I was conceived here, and you can't get much closer emotionally to a city than that. *Quoted in Cities, John McGreevy*

V

VALERY, Paul (1871-1945)

V1 — There is no other place on earth where the great ensemble and the small detail are more beautifully blended. [of Prague]

V2 — To those of us who live and work amid the artificiality of city life there is something irresistibly attractive in the idea of being close to the heart of nature, wearing old clothes and living for a time the free and easy life which we like to imagine was lived before the call of the city became insistent. *Independent, June 6, 1912*

VAN DYKE, Henry (1852-1933)

V3 — Oh, London is a man's town, there's power in the air; / And Paris is a woman's town, with flowers in her hair. / *America for Me*

V4 — A little country town, with its inflexible social conditions, its petty sayings and jealousies, its obstinate mistrust of all that is strange and its crude gossip about all that it cannot comprehend ... may be as complicated and as hard to live in as great Babylon itself. *The School of Life*

VAN GROVE, Irwin

V5 — A collection of identical-looking houses containing commuting fathers, scurrying mothers, and socially-oriented children. [of suburbia]

V6 — Homes beside a freeway, a forest of television aerials, a church and synagogue, a shopping center, people of the same white, middle class standards, centered around their children's activities. This is suburbia.

VANBRUGH, John (1664-1726)

V7 — The worst place in the world for a good woman to grow better in. [of London]

VARRO, Marcus Terrentius (116-27 B.C.)

V8 — Life in the country preceded life in town by a tale of immemorial years. Nor is this to be wondered since 'God made the country and man made the town.' [divina natura dedit argos, ars humana aedificavit urbes] ... And, as life in the country is more ancient, so it is the better life ... *Rerum Rusticarum*

V9 — [I am] ... bewildered more by the hazard of human life than surprised that such a fate should be possible at Rome ... *Satire III*

VASILIADIS, C.G. (1930-)

V10 — Suburban America is often envied for many aspects of its life style, especially when compared to the environment of a large city. Lower crime rates, cleaner air, homogenous settings, home ownership, and good schools have drawn millions of Americans to this middle landscape. Howver, the arts were never part of the lure of suburbia. If there is one element in which cities feel clearly superior to their suburban neighbors, it is in the arts. The relative absence of culture in suburbia is one of the major reasons for its stereotyped image of blandness. In fact, for many, suburban culture is simply a contradiction in terms and is therefore dismissed or, worse, not even discussed. *The Arts and the Suburbs*

VAUGHAN, Henry (1622-1695)

V11 — O how I long to travel back, / And

tread again that ancient track! / That I might once more reach that plain, / Where first I left my glorious train; / From whence th' enlighten'd spirit sees / The shady City of palm-trees. / *Silex Scintillans: The Retreat*

VAUGHAN, Robert (1795-1868)

V12 — If any nation is to be lost or saved by the character of its great cities, our own is that nation. *The Age of Great Cities*

V13 — Our age is pre-eminently the age of great cities. Babylon and Thebes, Carthage and Rome, were great cities, but the world has never been so covered with cities as at the present time, and society generally has never been so leavened with the spirit natural to cities. *Ibid.*

V14 — The principles of self-government have ascended from the borough to the senate, from the councilmen of the city to the councilmen of the nation. Such is the natural course of things. The more the principles of self-government are acted upon in the parish, the town, the great city, and the district, the more will men be interested in the affairs of their country generally, the more competent will they be to judge of the manner in which the business of their country should be conducted,and the more probable will it be that statesmen will regulate their course . . . *Ibid.*

V15 — Regarding great cities in their relation to physical science, we may safely speak of this branch of intelligence as deriving all its higher culture, if not its existence, from the ingenuities which are natural to men in such associations. Cities are at once the great effect, and the great cause, of progress in this department of knowledge. *Ibid.*

V16 — When we look, moreover, on the distracting or absorbing effect of the ceaseless action pervading great cities, it must be remembered that the end of this action is accumulation, and that the effect of accumulation is not only to raise classes above the crowd, but to raise certain minds capable of excelling in abstract studies, and others capable of sympathizing with them, into positions favourable to the indulgence of their higher preferences. *Ibid.*

VAUGHAN, William

V17 — Where the developer bulldozes out the trees, then names the streets after them. [of suburbia]

V18 — A twofold national problem is how to preserve the wilderness in the country and get rid of the jungle in the cities. *Quoted in Reader's Digest*

VEBLEN, Thorstein (1857-1929)

V19 — The country town is one of the great American institutions; perhaps the greatest, in the sense that it has had . . . a greater part than any other in shaping public sentiment and giving character to American culture. *The Country Town*

V20 — Conspicuous consumption claims a relatively larger portion of the income of the urban than of the rural population, and the claim is also more imperative. . . . It is not that the city population is by nature much more eager for the peculiar complacency that comes of a conspicuous consumption, nor has the rural population less regard for pecuniary decency. But the provocation to this line of evidence, as well as its transient effectiveness, are more decided in the city . . . The standard of decency is higher, class for class, and this requirement of decent appearance must be lived up to on pain of losing caste. *The Theory of the Leisure Class*

VENDLER, Helen (1933-   )

V21 — The first difficulty for the lyric poet is the actual constitution of the city — large, heterogeneous, full of unknown people, political, landscaped, historical. Its largeness must be reduced to fit the brief scope of lyric; its heterogeneity must be preserved, at least symbolically; its inhabitants must be sorted out into populations (with risks of stereotyping); its politics must be made intelligible; its landscape given a shape and perspective; its history seen in its visible and invisible traces. *The Poet and the City: Robert Lowell*

VENKATARANGAIYA, M.

V22 — Many of the great cities of the world owe their development to the operation of only one or two factors like commerce or industry, defence or strategic advantage, administrative importance or education. In the case of Bombay and Calcutta all these factors have exercised their influence. *The Growth of Bombay and Calcutta*

VERGIL (70-19 B.C.)

V23 — Arms and the man I sing, the first who came, / Compelled by fate, an exile out of Troy / *Aeneid*

V24 — We have been Trojans; Troy was. *Ibid.*

V25 — The city, Meliboeus, which they call Rome, I, fool that I am, imagined to be like this town of ours. *Eclogues*

V26 — This city has reared her head as high among all other cities as cypresses oft do among the bending osiers. [of Rome] *Ibid.*

V27 — This was the life which once the ancient Sabines led, / And Remus and his brother; this made Etruria strong, / Through this, Rome became the fairest thing on earth. / *Georgics*

VERHAEREN, Emile (1855-1916)

V28 — These are the great dock-yards of madness / Full of dismantled barks / And broken spars / Beneath a sky of crucifixion / [of London] *La Morte*

VERNON, Raymond (1913-)

V29 — America's cities, like Topsy, just growed, accompanied by fires, epidemics, corruption, and crime. The disposition of America to let nature take its course in the cities was buttressed by the circumstance that, being largely a rural nation, it had other more pressing problems and other outlets for its energies. *The Myth and Reality of Our Urban Problems*

V30 — For contemporary America, the barefoot boy with cheek of tan is a nostalgic memory, the victim of hot asphalt roads and speeding auto traffic. Today, two out of three children in America are growing up in an urban setting. Raised in seedy brownstones, garden apartments, or trim suburban yards, they are strangers to the unpolluted swimming hole and the dusty country lane. *Ibid.*

V31 — If a major object of our existence were to create great cities of beauty and grace, there would be something to be said in favor of dictatorship. As a rule, the great cities of the past have been the cities of the powerful state — cities in which a dominant king or governing body has had the power and the will to impose its land-use strictures upon an obedient populace. Weak or divided local governments, responsive to the push and pressure of the heterogeneous interest groups which make up a city, have rarely managed to intervene enough to prevent the unpalatable kind of growth which typifies our larger America urban areas. *Ibid.*

V32 — Though every member of urban society has his problems, the tendency to define urban problems in terms of those which hit the well-to-do and the elite most starkly has been particularly strong. This tendency has prevented the public acceptance of proposed remedies, because the remedies have been addressed to difficulties with which only a small fraction of society identifies itself. *Ibid.*

VICUÑA-MacKENNA, Benjamin (1831-1886)

V33 — Nymph of idleness, asleep on the banks of the flowering Rimac, softly resting on the very spot that its masters first designated for it, surrounded by green fields, crowned with rustic diadems, lifting its voluptuous forehead to the caresses of a cloudless sky, she whose climate consists of light breezes without rainfall and a light that wears the impress of an eternal calm. [of Lima]

VIGNY, Alfred de (1797-1863)

V34 — Look from the height of our thoughts down on the servile cities, fatal rocks of human slavery. *La Maison du Berger*

VILLON, Francois (1430-1484)

V35 — There's no right speech out of Paris town. *Ballad of the Women of Paris*

VITRUVIUS POLLIO, Marcus (1st c. A.D.)

V36 — A city's public buildings serve three purposes: defense, religion, and convenience. To ward off hostile attack, we must defend the city with walls, towers, and gates. For the sake of religion, we plan shrines, and sacred temples to the immortal gods. For convenience, we arrange public sites for general use — harbors, open spaces, colonnades, theaters, promenades, baths, and all amenities for like purpose. All must be carried out with strength, utility, grace.

V37 — A divine intelligence placed the city of the Roman people in an excellent and temperate country, so that she might acquire the right to rule over the whole world.

VOGEL, Hans-Jochen (Mayor of Munich) (1926-)

V38 — A few years ago, I said Munich was not New York. But today, I'm no longer so sure . . . Cities can also die, or at least alter their character so that they are no longer places of peace, well-being, and fulfilled living, but concrete jungles dominated by hatreds, violence, decadence, and decline. *The Los Angeles Times, March 24, 1972*

VOLTAIRE (1694-1778)

V39 — In this sad town wherein I stay / Ignorance, Torpidity / And Boredom hold their lasting sway / With unconcerned Stupidity; / A land where old Obedience sits, / Well-filled with Faith, devoid of Wits. / [of Brussels]

V40 — The united magnificence of all the cities of Europe could but equal St. Petersburg.

V41 — Rival of Athens, London, blest indeed / That with they tyrants had the wit to chase / The prejudices civil factions breed. / Men speak their thoughts and worth can win its place / In London, who has talent, he is great. / *Verses on the Death of Adrienne Lecouvreur*

VON HOLTEI, Karl (1798-1880)

V42 — There's only one imperial city. / There's only one Vienna./ *Die Wiener in Berlin*

VON LAUE, Theodore H. (1916-)

V43 — There is no greater sight in all humanity than man's social labor throbbing in the life of a great metropolis, say New York or London or any of the sprawling metropoles of the West or even their counterparts throughout the world. At dawn the human beehive, laid out flat over plains and hills, spanning rivers and estuaries as far as the eye can see (on a rare clear day), stirs to send its millions to work. *The Global City*

VONDEL, Joost van den (1587-1679)

V44 — From old and new side of the town /

All foreign blood that afternoons collected here / Flowed in a single auricle / Fed by many veins / Giving life to the blood of the city. / [of the Amsterdam Stock Exchange]

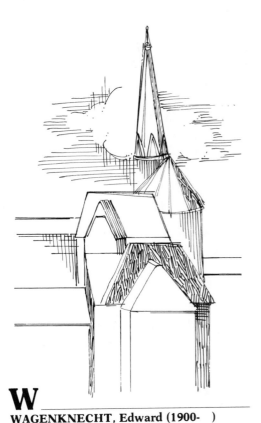

W

WAGENKNECHT, Edward (1900-   )

W1 — There is no use trying to be neutral about Chicago. *Chicago*

WAGNER, Philip L. (1921-   )

W2 — The urban environment is vastly different from the rural, for in it is always a concentration of services and varied goods. It is a meeting place and melting pot, both a refuge for people and ideas and also a reservoir of new ideas and venturesome populations. It feeds off the land, but nourishes the land with enlightenment and ingenious artifacts. In our world and time, it has begun virtually to absorb the countryside. *The Human Use of Earth*

WAGNER, Richard (1813-1883)

W3 — During the sixteen years that have passed since I last saw Vienna the whole city has been renewed: its half million inhabitants, all dressed in German colors, poured through the streets on Sunday as if in celebration — on the Saturday a wavering, incompetent Ministry had been forced out by the People's Committee! You should see the faces of these people: everything that disgusts you in the people of Dresden would appeal to you here.

W4 — Vienna, on which I first set my eyes again on a fine bright Sunday, enchanted me — I admit it! I found Paris again, only more beautiful, more gay and German.

W5 — As I was returning home late one night on the gloomy canal, the moon appeared suddenly and illuminated the marvellous palaces and the tall figure of my gondolier towering above the stern of the gondola, slowly moving his huge sweep. Suddenly he uttered a deep wail, not unlike the cry of an animal; the cry gradually gained in strength, and formed itself, after a long-drawn 'Oh!' into the simple musical exclamation 'Venezia!' *My Life*

WAGNER, Robert F. (1910-   )

W6 — Indeed, if I were asked to express in only one sentence the synthesis of my experience as Mayor of New York City, I would simply say we must act now, and make any sacrifices necessary to save our cities and the people in them, and the metropolitan environment of which the cities are the core. *Quoted in The Troubled Environment*

WALDO, Octavia (1929-   )

W7 — The rain fell like a cascade of pine needles over Rome. Rain — thirty days of it. It marked the interlude between winter and spring, and spring was late in coming. There was nothing to do about it but wait. There is nothing to do about most things that are late in Rome, whether it be an appointment, or a bus, or a promise. Or even hope. *Roman Spring*

WALKER, James J. (Mayor) (1881-1946)

W8 — The municipal government is the maternal, the intimate side of government; the side with a heart. The Federal Government doesn't have to look into suffering faces; it doesn't have to wander through darkened hallways of our hospitals, to witness the pain and suffering there. It doesn't have to stand on the bread lines, but the time has come when it must face the facts and its responsibility. *(Conference of Mayors, Detroit, June 1, 1932)*

WALKER, Stanley (1898-1962)

W9 — Well, there she sits, or squats, or sprawls, or festers, or blooms, depending upon how one looks at it. The city is quite vigorous, quite messy, and full of apparent contradictions. Not even its leading residents can agree on what is good about the place and what is wrong with it. And, paraphrasing the old line about New York, many a Texan says he likes to go to Houston to transact a little business, but he wouldn't want to live there if you gave him the place. [of Houston] *The New York Times Magazine, August 1, 1954*

WALLER, Edmund (1606-1687)

W10 — Rome, though her eagle through the world had flown, / Could never make this island all her own. / *Panegyric to My Lord Protector*

WALPOLE, Horace (1717-1797)

W11 — One hates writing descriptions that are to be found in every book of travels; but we have seen something today that I am sure you never read of, and perhaps never heard of. Have you ever heard of a subterraneous town? A whole Roman town, with all its edifices, remaining under ground? [of Pompeii] *to Richard West*

WALROND, Eric D. (1898-1966)

W12 — Her dark brown face / Is like a withered flower / On a broken stem. / Those kind come cheap in Harlem, / So they say. / *The Messenger*

WALTON, Clarence

W13 — The word 'city' once suggested 'civility' and those characteristics of culture and politeness which attend that term. In a generic sense, the 'City' referred to the financial and commercial district of greater London. In ways partially symbolic and partially real, the nexus between the cultural and commercial cores of the city remained in a healthy condition. Today, however, 'city' means crisis — a crisis occasioned by past neglect, present

indecisiveness, and bewilderment over future explosions of undetermined magnitudes in size, density, violence, and the like. *Concluding Note: Re-Creating the City of Man*

WARD, Barbara (1914-1981)

W14 — All the world over, often long in advance of effective industrialization, the unskilled poor are streaming away from subsistence agriculture to exchange the squalor of rural poverty for the even deeper miseries of the shanty-towns, *favelas, bidonvilles,* that year by year grow inexorably on the fringes of the developing cities. They are the core of local despair and disaffection — fuelling the *jeunesse* movements of the Congo, swelling the urban mobs of Rio, voting Communist in the ghastly alleys of Calcutta, everywhere undermining the all-too-frail structure of public order and thus retarding the economic development that can alone help their plight. Unchecked, disregarded, left to grow and fester, there is here enough explosive material to produce in the world at large the pattern of a bitter class conflict, finding to an increasing degree a racial bias, erupting in guerrilla warfare and threatening ultimately the security even of the comfortable West. *Quoted in The Exploding Cities*

W15 — The sudden expansion of city after city — Pittsburgh, Manchester, Dusseldorf, Milan — reflected the concentration of power and people in new *industrial* centres. But look at the developing continents; their vast cities — many of them already far beyond the million mark — are nearly all ports. This is the key. They grew up in the late eighteenth and nineteenth centuries to serve the commercial and imperial interests of Europe. They were the transmission belts for mines and plantations in a small modernized sector, transferring out the raw materials and bringing in Western manufactures for a small urban elite. *Ibid.*

W16 — Our first impression must surely be the degree to which the industrial city appears to have been not so much planned for human purposes as simply beaten into some sort of shape by repeated strokes from gigantic hammers — the hammer of techology and applied power, the overwhelming drive of national self-interest, the singleminded pursuit of economic gain. *The Home of Man*

W17 — How tragicomic it surely is to devote over $90-billion to an arms budget and then hang the title 'bankrupt' round the neck of the Statue of Liberty. The poor, the homeless, the huddled masses, the wretched refuse of the teeming shores, for whom it was once a beacon of hope, will see instead the image of a system indifferent to their problems and incapable of solving them. *The Washington Post, November 19, 1975*

WARNER, Charles Dudley (1829-1900)

W18 — The thing generally raised on city land is taxes. *My Summer in a Garden, Sixteenth Week*

W19 — New Orleans is the most cosmopolitan of provincial cities. Its comparative isolation has secured the development of provincial traits and manners, has preserved the individuality of the many races that give it color, morals, and character, while its close relations with France — an affiliation and sympathy which the late war has not altogether broken — and the constant influx of Northern men of business and affairs have given it the air of a metropolis. *New Orleans: The Foreign City*

WARNER, W. Lloyd (1898-1970)

W20 — The Jonesvilles, Smithtowns, Greenfields and all the other -villes, -towns and -fields of America are essentially alike.... No two American habitations are identical, but all of them, big or little, bear the strong family resemblance of the same parentage.... The lives of the ten thousand citizens of Jonesville express the basic values of 180,000,000 Americans. *Democracy in Jonesville*

WARREN, Earl (Chief Justice, U.S.) (1891-1974)

W21 — No rational person can look at our cities and say they're not deteriorating. What can we expect of our children and grandchildren unless we give very high priority to conditions in the cities, to the environment of our children, to their

education — all of which are worsening day by day? *(Interview, July 30, 1969)*

WATERHOUSE, Sylvester (1830-1902)

W22 — St. Louis is ordained by the decrees of physical nature to become the great inland metropolis of this continent. It cannot escape the magnificence of its destiny. Greatness is the necessity of its position. *Merchants' Magazine and Commercial Review*

WATTS-DUNTON, Theodore (1832-1914)

W23 — We looked o'er London, where men wither and choke, / Roofed in, poor souls, renouncing stars and skies. / *A Talk on Waterloo Bridge*

WAUGH, Alec (1898-1981)

W24 — It began with a quarrel about white elephants; at least that is what they believe on the banks of the Menam River.
In the middle of the fifteenth century the king of Burma asked the king of Siam to give him one of his white elephants. The king of Siam, although he had seven of his own, refused this neighborly request; that was the start of three hundred years of warfare. At the end of it, in 1767, Burmese forces captured and sacked the Siamese capital of Ayudhya. Which is why they say that but for a quarrel about white elephants, the city of Bangkok would not exist. *Bangkok, The Story of a City*

W25 — The most widely loved and admired people in Europe today are the Danes and the Thais have been called the Danes of Asia, not only because Bangkok is built as Copenhagen is — upon a series of canals — but because of their temperamental resemblances: their gaiety, their sunniness, their independence, their love of beauty, their frivolity. *Ibid.*

W26 — For nine-tenths of the year London life, with its noise and colour and animation, is like a story by Dostoieffsky. In August it's like a story by Turgenev, still and calm and deep. *On Doing What One Likes*

WAYS, Max (1905-)

W27 — An idea, a song, a discovery, an

invention, may be born anywhere. But if it is to be communicated, if it is to be tested and compared and appreciated, then someone has always carried it to the city. *(Speech to The Conference Board, November 28, 1967)*

WEAVER, Robert C. (1907-   )

W28 — I believe that the single most striking fact of the American city in 1965, and for some years to come, is that its fate is bound indivisibly to the fate of the American Negro. *Quoted in The Troubled Environment*

W29 — In all of the city's problems, the key element has been human beings. People conceived and developed cities. People have constantly threatened them. People, congregating into urban centers, made them the complex social organism we contemplate when the word city is used. It is human beings who, today, are shaping the vast metropolitan areas which house some two-thirds of the population in this Nation. Consequently, it is in terms of people that urban problems must be conceived and their solutions developed. *The Urban Complex*

WEBBER, Melvin M. (1920-   )

W30 — For the plain fact of the matter is that now, when the last rural threads of American society are being woven into the national urban fabric, the idea of city is becoming indistinguishable from the idea of society. *Order in Diversity: Community without Propinquity*

W31 — The popular notion among outsiders that Los Angeles is a cultural desert, is a myth whose basis lies in the ideology of metropolitan form. We have equated cultural wealth and urbanity with high-density cities; since Los Angeles is not spatially structured in the image of culturally rich cities we have known, some have therefore inferred that life there must be empty and deprived of opportunity. *Ibid.*

W32 — The spatial patterns of American urban settlements are going to be considerably more dispersed, varied, and space-consuming than they ever were in the past — whatever metropolitan planners or anyone else may try to do about it. *Ibid.*

WEBER, Adna F. (1870-c.1970)

W33 — In a new country, the rapid growth of cities is both natural and necessary, for no efficient industrial organization of a new settlement is possible without industrial centres to carry on the necessary work of assembling and distributing goods. A Mississippi Valley empire rising suddenly into being without its Chicago and its smaller centres of distribution is almost inconceivable to the nineteenth century economist. That America is the 'land of mushroom cities' is therefore not at all surprising. *The Growth of Cities in the Nineteenth Century*

W34 — The rise of the suburbs . . . furnishes the solid basis of a hope that the evils of city life . . . may in large part be removed. *Ibid.*

WEBER, Max (1864-1920)

W35 — Above all else, the [medieval] city sought to eliminate competition from the countryside brought under its domination. It attempted to suppress the rural pursuit of trade and to force the peasants to satisfy their needs in the city. It was in the interests of the city also to force the peasants to sell their products only in the city. *The City*

W36 — Christianity began its course as a doctrine of itinerant artisan journeymen. During all periods of its mighty external and internal development it has been a quite specifically urban, and above all a civic, religion. This was true during Antiquity, during the Middle Ages, and in puritanism. The city of the Occident, unique among all other cities of the world — and citizenship, in the sense in which it has emerged only in the Occident — has been a major theater for Christianity. *The Economic Ethic of World Religions*

W37 — From early historical writings the structure of the typical patrician city of antiquity may be discerned. It was fundamentally a coastal city. Until the time of Alexander and the Wars with the Samnites no polis was further removed than a day's journey from the sea. *Ibid.*

W38 — The many definitions of the city have only one element in common: namely that the city consists simply of a collection of one or more separate dwellings but is a relatively closed settlement. *Ibid.*

W39 — The medieval city knew nothing of such purely militarily conditioned philosophy. The victory of the popolo rested primarily on economic foundations. The medieval inland city was economic in character. The powers in the feudal Middle Ages were not primarily city kings or nobles. Unlike the nobles of antiquity they had no interests in peculiar military technical advantages offered only by the city. *Ibid.*

W40 — We wish to speak of a 'city' only in cases where the local inhabitants satisfy an economically substantial part of their daily wants in the local market, and to an essential extent by products which the local population and that of the immediate hinterland produced for sale in the market or acquired in other ways. In the meaning employed here the 'city' is a market place. *Ibid.*

W41 — Wherever it appeared the city was basically a resettlement of people previously alien to the place. Chinese, Mesopotamian, Egyptian, and occasionally

even Hellenistic war princes founded cities and transferred to them not only voluntary settlers but others kidnapped according to demand and possibility. *Ibid.*

W42 — While today we justly regard the typical 'urbanite' as a man who does not supply his own food need on his own land, originally the contrast was the case for the majority of typical ancient cities. *Ibid.*

WEBSTER, Daniel (1782-1852)

W43 — On this question of principle, while actual suffering was yet afar off, they (the Colonies) raised their flag against a power, to which, for purposes of foreign conquest and subjugation, Rome, in the height of her glory, is not to be compared; a power which has dotted over the surface of the whole globe with her possessions and military posts, whose morning drum-beat, following the sun, and keeping company with the hours, circles the earth with one continuous and unbroken strain of the martial airs of England. *(Speech in the Senate)*

WECHSBERG, Joseph (1907-)

W44 — Prague is called *Praha* in Czech, after *Prah*, 'the threshold.' The 'a' at the end of the word denotes a woman's name: Prague is a feminine city. Not a glamorous young woman, like Paris, but *maticka* (little mother) to her troubadours. *Prague, The Mystical City*

W45 — I heard the story (possibly apocryphal) about the old man who was born in St. Petersburg, went to school in Petrograd, was married in Leningrad, and if he had the choice, would like to live again in St. Petersburg. *The Two-Faced City*

WEIDMAN, Jerome (1913-)

W46 — Only by returning to life in the city does one rediscover the unbelievable complexity, excitement, and beauty of the human face. There are faces in the country, of course, but they are widely spaced like filling stations. *Back Talk*

WEINER, Howard R.

W47 — The motion picture appeared on the scene as the Western World groped toward a new urban consciousness. Cinematic images have thus become one of the great historic records of that effort. At the same time, the dissemination of films has played a role in the development of that very consciousness. *Journal of Popular Culture, Spring, 1970*

WELCH, Louis (Mayor of Houston) (1918-)

W48 — I think it is impossible to exaggerate the problems of the cities, because they are the problems of the people. *(Meet the Press, June 17, 1973)*

WELDING, J.M.

W49 — The general tendency, is, that whenever a country boy rises to eminence as a man, to add the fact of his country training to his frame. If one of equal eminence is known to have been city-bred, no comments are made as his success is considered as a matter of course. In cases where the early life of a distinguished man has been of a mixed town and country training it is usual to attribute the entire credit to his rural experience. *City Boy versus Country Boy*

WELLINGTON (Duke of) (1769-1852)

W50 — The most beautiful town [on earth]. [of St. Petersburg]

WELLS, H.G. (1866-1946)

W51 — Something inevitable and inhuman, as a blindly furious energy of growth that must go on.... New York's achievement is a threatening promise, growth going on under a pressure that increases, and amidst a hungry uproar of effort.

W52 — The thinnest sham of a community ... where a clerk or a working man will shift his sticks from one borough to another without ever discovering what he has done. [of suburbia]

W53 — And as for the world beyond our urban regions? The same line of reasoning that leads us to the expectation that the city will diffuse itself until it has taken up considerable areas and many of the characteristics, the greenness, the fresh air, of what is now country, leads us to suppose

also that the country will take to itself many of the qualities of the city. The old antithesis will indeed cease, the boundary lines will altogether disappear; it will become, indeed, merely a question of more or less populous. There will be horticulture and agriculture going on within the 'urban regions,' and 'urbanity' without them. *Anticipations of the Reactions of Mechanical and Scientific Progress*

W54 — Now, is this growth of large towns really ... a result of the development of railways in the world, or is it simply a change in human circumstances that happens to have arisen at the same time? ... the former is probably the true answer. *Ibid.*

W55 — We have heard so much of the 'problem of our great cities' ... the belief in the inevitableness of yet denser and more multitudinous agglomerations in the future is so widely diffused, that at first sight it will be thought that no other motive than a wish to startle can dictate the proposition that not only will many of these railway-begotten 'giant cities' reach their maximum in the commencing century, but that in all probability they ... are destined to such a process of dissection and diffusion as to amount almost to obliteration, so far, at least, as the blot on the map goes, within a measurable further space of years. *Ibid.*

W56 — He had a vision of city beyond city; cities on great plains, cities beside great rivers, vast cities along the sea margins, cities girdled by snowy mountains ... And everywhere now through the city-set earth, save in the administered 'black belt' territories of the tropics, the same cosmopolitan social organization prevailed, and everywhere from Pole to Equator his property and his responsibilities extended. The whole world was civilised; the whole world dwelt in cities; the whole world was his property. *The Sleeper Awakes*

W57 — Out of the dim south-west, glittering and strange, voluptuous, and in some way terrible, shone those Pleasure Cities ... Strange places reminiscent of the legendary Sybaris, cities of art and beauty, sterile wonderful cities of motion and music, whither repaired all who profited by the fierce, inglorious, economic struggle that

went on in the glaring labyrinth
below. *Ibid.*

W58 — The beginnings of civilization and
the appearance of temples are simultaneous
in history. The two things belong together.
The beginning of cities is the temple stage of
history. The city community arose round
the altar of the seed-time blood
sacrifice. *The Outline of History*

WEST, Jessamyn (1907-   )

W59 — Visitors to Los Angeles, then and
now, were put out because the residents of
Los Angeles had the inhospitable idea of
building a city comfortable to live in, rather
than a monument to astonish the eye of
jaded travelers. *Hide and Seek*

WEST, Rebecca (1892-   )

W60 — I am one of those who are so
enamoured of Rome that they will not
submit themselves to the magic of
Florence . . . *Ending in Earnest: A Literary
Log*

WHEELER, George Wellington

W61 — This is a frontier town and it's got to
go through its red blooded youth. A church
and a WCTU never growed a big town yet.
[of Chicago]

WHEELOCK, John Hall (1886-1978)

W62 — For the earth that breeds the trees /
Breeds cities too, and symphonies. / *Earth*

W63 — In the spring, on the pavements of
the city, / The little children play marbles,
and laugh and shout — / Their laughter is
drowned by the city all about; / But they
laugh back, regardless of the city, / And run,
and dance, and shout. / *New York: East Side*

WHITE, Andrew Dickson (1832-1918)

W64 — Without the slightest exaggeration
we may asert that, with very few exceptions,
the city governments of the United States
are the worst in Christendom — the most
expensive, the most inefficient, and the most
corrupt. No one who has any considerable
knowledge of our own country can deny
this. *The Government of American Cities*

WHITE, E.B. (1899-   )

W65 — For the urban population spring is
heralded by less celestial signs — not a
wedge of geese in the sky, but a span of new
plucked terriers on the Avenue, or a potted
hyacinth groomed for April. *Every Day Is
Saturday*

W66 — There is about Boston a certain
reminiscent and classical tone, suggesting
an authenticity and piety which few other
American cities possess. *Ibid.*

W67 — All dwellers in cities must live with
the stubborn fact of annihilation. . . . The
city at last perfectly illustrates both the
universal dilemma and the general solution,
this riddle in steel and stone is at once the
perfect target and the perfect demonstration
of nonviolence, of racial brotherhood, this
lofty target scraping the skies and meeting
the destroying planes halfway, home of all
people and all nations, capital of everything,
housing the deliberations by which the
planes are to be stayed and their errand
forestalled. *Here Is New York (Television
Program)*

W68 — You can see in pantomime the
puppets fumbling with their slips of paper
(but you don't hear the rustle), see them pick
up their phone (but you don't hear the ring),
see the noiseless, ceaseless moving about of
so many passers of pieces of paper: New
York, the capital of memoranda, in touch
with Calcutta, in touch with Reykjavik, and
always fooling with something. *Ibid.*

W69 — Commuters give the city its tidal
restlessness; natives give it solidity and
continuity; but the settlers give it
passion. *Quoted in Holiday*

W70 — New York is to the nation what the
white church spire is to the village — the
visible symbol of aspiration and faith, the
white plume saying the way is up! *Quoted
in Mental Health in the Metropolis*

WHITE, Edward E.

W71 — A mere roost where (the commuter)
comes at day's end to go to sleep. [of
suburbia]

WHITE, Kevin H. (Mayor of Boston) (1929-)

W72 — The real solution will only come when this country makes up its national mind what it wants to do about the cities — whether it wants to abandon them or whether it wants to tolerate them, which I think they do today, or whether they want to treat them as they are, real centers of our civilization. *(Meet the Press, July 6, 1975)*

WHITE, Morton (1917-) and Lucia

W73 — The fact that our most distinguished intellectuals have been on the whole sharply critical of urban life helps explain America's lethargy in confronting the massive problems of the contemporary city in a rational way. *The Intellectual versus the City*

W74 — The intellect, whose home is the city according to some sociologists, has produced the sharpest criticism of the American city. *Ibid.*

W75 — Too big, too noisy, too dusky, too dirty, too smelly, too commercial, too crowded, too full of immigrants, too full of Jews, too full of Irishman, Italians, Poles, too artificial, destructive of conversation, destructive of communication, too greedy, too capitalistic, too full of automobiles, too full of smog, too full of dust, too heartless, too intellectual, too scientific, insufficiently poetic, too lacking in manners, too mechanical, destructive of family, tribal and patriotic feeling. [of anti-urbanism] Ibid.

W76 — We have no persistent or pervasive tradition of romantic attachment to the city in our literature or in our philosophy, nothing like the Greek attachment to the polis or the French writer's affection for Paris. And this confirms the frequently advanced thesis that the American intellectual has been alienated from the society in which he has lived, that he has been typically in revolt against it. *Ibid.*

W77 — The wilderness, the isolated farm, the plantation, the self-contained New England town, the detached neighborhood are things of the American past. All the world's a city now and there is no escaping urbanization, not even in outer space. *Ibid.*

WHITMAN, Walt (1819-1892)

W78 — Once I pass'd through a populous city imprinting my brain for future use with its shows, architecture, customs, traditions, / Yet now of all that city I remember only a woman I casually met there who detain'd me for love of me. /

W79 — The splendour, the picturesqueness, and oceanic amplitude and rush of these great cities, the . . . lofty new buildings, facades of marble and iron, of original grandeur and elegance of masses, with the masses of gay color, the preponderance of white and blue, the flags flying, the endless ships, the tumultuous streets, Broadway, the heavy, low, musical roar, hardly ever interrupted, even at night; the jobbers' houses, the rich shops, the wharves, the great Central Park and the Brooklyn Park of hills . . . these, I say, and the like of these completely satisfy my senses of powerfulness, motion &c and give me, through such senses . . . a continued exaltation and absolute fulfillment. [of New York and Brooklyn]

W80 — When million-footed Manhattan, unpent, descends to its pavements; when the thunder-cracking guns arouse me with the proud roar I love; / When the round-mouth'd guns, out of the smoke and smell I love, spit their salutes; / When the fire-flashing guns have fully alerted me — when heaven-clouds canopy my city with a delicate thin haze; / When, gorgeous, the countless straight stems, the forests at the wharves, thicken with colors; / When every ship, richly drest, carries her flag at the peak; / When pennants trail, and street-festoons hang from the windows; . . . / I too, arising, answering, descend to the pavements, merge with the crowd, and gaze with them. / *A Broadway Pageant*

W81 — Ah, what can ever be more stately and admirable to me than mast-hemmed Manhattan? *Crossing Brooklyn Ferry*

W82 — I dream'd in a dream I saw a city invincible to the attacks of the whole of the rest of the earth, / I dream'd that was the new city of Friends. . . . / *Leaves of Grass*

W83 — My own Manhattan with spires, and / The sparkling and hurrying tides, and the ships. / *Ibid.*

W84 — City of hurried and sparkling waters! city of spires and masts! / City nested in bays! my city! [of New York]/ *Mannahatta*

W85 — Wait at Liverpool, Glasgow, Dublin, Marseilles, Lisbon, Naples, Hamburg, Bremen, Bordeaux, the Hague, Copenhagen, / Wait at Valparaiso, Rio Janeiro, Panama. . . . / I see the cities of the earth, and make myself at random a part of them, / I am a real Parisian, / I am a habitan of Vienna, St. Petersburg, Berlin, Constantinople, / I am of Adelaide, Sydney, Melbourne, / I am of London, Manchester, Bristol, Edinburg, Limerick, / I see Algiers, Tripoli, Derne, Mogadore, Timbuctoo, Monrovia, / I see the swarms of Pekin, Canton, Benares, Delhi, Calcutta, Yedo, / *Salut au Monde*

W86 — A great city is that which has the greatest men and women / If it has a few ragged huts it is still the greatest city in the world. / *Song of the Broad-Axe*

W87 — Where women walk in public processions in the streets the same as the men, / Where they enter the public assembly and take places the same as the men; / Where the city of the faithfullest friends stands, / Where the city of the cleanliness of the sexes stands, / Where the city of the healthiest fathers stands / Where the city of the best-bodied mothers stands / There the great city stands. / *Ibid.*

W88 — The human qualities of these vast cities, is to me comforting, even heroic, beyond statement. . . . In old age, lame and sick, pondering for years on many a doubt and danger for this republic of ours . . . I find in this visit to New York, and the daily contact and rapport with its myriad people, on the scale of the oceans and tides, the best, most effective medicine my soul has yet partaken — namely Manhattan island and Brooklyn, which the future shall join in one city — city of superb democracy, amid superb surroundings. *Walt Whitman Looks at New York*

WHITTIER, John Greenleaf (1807-1892)

W89 — Then life once more thy towers on high, / And fret with spires the western sky, / To tell that God is yet with us, / And love is

still miraculous. / [of Chicago fire of 1871] *Chicago*

WHYTE, William (1917-)

W90 — The city and specialization are inextricable. Most highly specialized activities, or services, flourish best at the center of things where they can draw on a huge area and still be near the center of its traffic. When we speak of 'urbanity,' we are often referring to the characteristic specialization of the city. *The Anti-City*

W91 — City life, almost because it has not changed much, has more and more become a mockery of the American dream. The norm of middle class aspiration is suburbia, and as our middle class has expanded the distance between city and the consensus of the good life has grown. *Ibid.*

W92 — Like war and the generals, city planning is too important to be left to the experts; a good planner needs a sophisticated and a critical audience, people who like cities. *Ibid.*

W93 — Look at the advertisements of happy families drinking beer, washing the car, or tinkering with hobbies; or take the *Saturday Evening Post* covers with their pictures of humorous incidents. Rarely is there a city in the background. In the pictorial representation of the American Dream the *mise en scene* is suburbia. Idealogically, as well as physically, no dialect jokes, no racial characteristics mar the picture. All that is behind us; it is the similarity that is celebrated, often with deliberate moral overtones. *Ibid.*

W94 — Sub-urban (what an apposite word) conveys to many people merely an extension of the city in an enlargement of its boundaries. When we speak of 'urbanization,' we tend to think of the city as sprawling, or oozing, over the landscape. But actually it is not the city that is spreading; it is suburbia. We would do well to keep the distinction in mind. There is a pitfall in the term 'urbanization,' for it implies the spread, not only of the city, but also of the city's values. *Ibid.*

W95 — The most frustrating part of U.S. cities is getting into them, or knowing when we have. Suburbia is behind us but the scene continues as before; used car lots, diners, borax furniture stores, gas stations, and gas stations, and gas stations. It is not just the blight but the interminability of it that is deadening, and this seems to be especially true of smaller cities, the approaches of which seem to stretch out in inverse ratio to the worth of what is being approached. Mile after mile they drag on, and the only indication that there is an entrance is the knot of signs saying where the Kiwanis and the Rotary meet. *The Last Landscape*

W96 — [Urban] sprawl is bad aesthetics; it is bad economics. Five acres are being made to do the work of one, and do it very poorly. This is bad for the farmers, it is bad for communities, it is bad for industry, it is bad for utilities, it is bad for the railroads, it is bad for recreation groups, it is even bad for developers. *Urban Sprawl*

WICKER, Tom (1926-   )

W97 — Here in Charlotte as elsewhere, mass transit facilities are minimal; in addition, this city has been built outward from its own center in long glittering strings of plastic, neon, glass and ersatz. Now, for miles before a motorist reaches what used to be the city, the shopping centers, the fast-food joints, the service stations, the apartment and housing developments, the glass office buildings and the ugly mobile home sales lots line the roads in endless tribute to an illusory prosperity. *The New York Times, December 4, 1973*

WIESEL, Elie (1928-   )

W98 — There is something strange about Jerusalem, something unique about it. When I visited the city for the first time, I had a feeling that it was not the first time, that I had been here many times before. But now each time I come back to Jerusalem, I have a feeling that it is my first time here. *Quoted in Cities, John McGreevy*

W99 — When Jews pray in other countries, they turn towards the Holy Land. When they pray within the Holy Land, they turn towards Jerusalem. No city is linked to so many customs, no city has inspired so many legends. Though afflicted and wounded, Jerusalem has outlived its enemies. *Ibid.*

W100 — Within the walls of Jerusalem, you are obsessed by history. No other city has such evocative power to bring the past back to life. Just walk, and listen. Someone is singing and you think of David. Someone is questioning and you think of Judah ha-Levi. Someone is conjuring the heavens in the name of hope and you think of Rabbi Akiba. Samuel and Isaiah, Elijah and Jeremiah. Hezekiah and his underground tunnels. The Herod Agrippas. Somehow they all invade your memory as it touches Jerusalem's. *Ibid.*

WILCOX, Delos F. (1873-1928)

W101 — The influence of cities upon the national life is quite out of proportion to their population. For the city is the distributing centre of intelligence as well as of goods. [It] tends to impose its ethical and social ideals upon the whole people. *The American City: A Problem in Democracy*

W102 — Under conditions as they exist, the great cities by the concentration of wealth resulting from the control of industry are seats of power of the privileged classes. *Great Cities in America*

WILDE, Oscar (1854-1900)

W103 — Flowers are as common in the country as people are in London.

W104 — I am on the side of the Trojans. They fought for a woman. *Picture of Dorian Gray*

W105 —   Mrs. Allonby: They say, Lady Hunstanton, that when good Americans die they go to Paris.
    Lady Hunstanton: Indeed? And when bad Americans die, where do they go to?
    Lord Illingworth: Oh, they go to America. *A Woman of No Importance*

WILES, Peter (1919-   )

W106 — China is to my knowledge the first country to have conceived *industrialisation without urbanisation*. In the USSR, on the other hand, the policy has always been *urbanisation on the cheap*. *The Political Economy of Communism*

WILHELM II (Emperor of Germany) (1859-1941)

W107 — Paris is the great whorehouse of the world; therein lies its attraction independent of any exhibition. There is nothing in Berlin that can captivate the foreigner, except a few museums, castles, and soldiers.

WILLIAMS, Charles

W108 — The main difference between the idea of the City and the idea of the Nation is that the first can involve the thought of choice. There is something fatal about the Nation, something in the blood. It is true that, historically, the City has often been as much a matter of birth as has the Nation. But the sense of deliberate action remains in our imagination; the speech of Pericles determined that, and the movement of Aeneas away from Dido to Italy. Bestowal of citizenship is not quite the same thing as the issue of naturalization papers. We can deliberately found the City; the nation can, at best, only appear. And even in patriotic national poetry it is often particular places which are named. *The Image of the City in English Verse*

WILLIAMS, Raymond (1921-   )

W109 — The lights of the city. I go out in the dark, before bed, and look at that glow in the sky: a look at the city while remembering Hardy's Jude, who stood and looked at the distant, attainable and unattainable, Christminster. *The Country and the City*

W110 — Out of the cities . . . came these two great and transforming modern ideas: myth, in its variable forms; revolution, in its variable forms. Each, under pressure, offers to convert the other to its own terms. But they are better seen as alternative responses, for in a thousand cities, if in confused forms, they are in sharp, direct necessary conflict. *Ibid.*

WILLIAMS, William Carlos (1883-1963)

W111 — Cities are full of light, fine clothes / delicacies for the table, variety, / novelty — fashion: all spent for this. / Never to be like that again: / the frame that was. / *A Morning Imagination of Russia*

W112 — I have watched / the city from a distance at night / and wondered why I wrote no poem. / Come! yes, / the city is ablaze for you / and you stand and look at it. / *Sour Grapes*

WILLIS, F. Roy (1930-   )

W113 — [Renaissance] city planners were fascinated by geometrical patterns, and they loved to work out abstractly all the variations possible in the planning of the city. In the simplest form, they worshipped the straight line, the search for the infinite, and from this they hit on the notion of the endless vista down a street of identical houses. *Western Civilization, An Urban Perspective*

W114 — In every period when civilization has achieved a kind of homogeneity, the city is the most revealing physical expression of the social and political realities of the age, or, to put it more bluntly, of the character and taste of the ruling classes. This was never more true than in the creation of the baroque city of the seventeenth and early eighteenth centuries. *Ibid.*

W115 — It can be argued that at the end of the Paleolithic Age humanity had already developed many of the social characteristics that were to be at the basis of city life, though in a very elementary form — respect for leadership, in obedience to the commands of the most skillful hunter; a sense of the supernatural or the religious, and provision and respect for the guardians of the secrets of the supernatural; a differentiation of occupation, accompanied by provision of part of the surplus for a class not actively engaged in the production of the group's economic livelihood; and recognition of the importance to the enrichment of life of non-material benefits of art. But the Paleolithic Age lacked that most essential urban characteristic — the determination to manipulate the natural environment. *Ibid.*

WILSHER, Peter & Rosemary RIGHTER

W116 — The 'urban squatter' — the man who arrives with nothing but a determination to make it in the big town, prepared to hole up in any filthy corner while he accumulates his initial stake — is a phenomenon as old as history. Excavations at Ur show that even 8,000 years ago the fringes of the city were befouled with shanties. But now, across the world, there are millions upon millions of such sub-minimal city-dwellers, with their own way of life, their own social stratifications, in many cases their own 'laws' and 'institutions,' and to an ever-increasing extent their own potentially formidable political strength. It is here, in the purulent enclaves and festering outskirts of Istanbul, Karachi, Rangoon and Rio de Janeiro, that the true city explosion is building up. *Quoted in The Exploding Cities*

W117 — When Paris still has its *bidonvilles*, and London, Tokyo and New York their deplorable slums, what hope have Calcutta, Kinshasa, Mexico City and the rest, with maybe one-tenth or less of the developed world's *per capita* income available to finance their multifarious tasks? *Ibid.*

WILSON, Charles E.

W118 — The mounting problems of America's large cities are steadily driving the already distracted members of the American community to the verge of insanity. *The White Problem of the Cities*

W119 — With their flight to the suburbs, the former city dwellers have come to adopt a new hostility toward the cities. Although many of their number still are dependent upon the city for their income, recreation, arts, and pleasures, they profess a disdain for the city, its taxes, its way of life. *Ibid.*

WILSON, Earl (1907-)

W120 — American city: A place where by the time you've finished paying for your home in the suburbs, the suburbs have moved 20 miles further out. *Quoted in Reader's Digest*

WILSON, Harry L.

W121 — A little strip of an island with a row of well-fed folks up and down the middle, and a lot of hungry folks on each side. [of New York]

WILSON, James Q.

W122 — If all Negroes were turned white tomorrow, they would still have serious problems. Whether these problems are more the result of a weak family structure, or of the impact of urbanization, or the past history of discrimination, or of a depressed economic position, is very hard to say. But I suspect that, whatever the cause, there are few aspects of this problem which will not be cured — will not cure themselves — in time . . . for the present, the urban Negro is, in a fundamental sense, *the* 'urban problem.' *The War on Cities*

W123 — What, indeed, is the 'urban problem'? The language of crisis with which this subject is normally discussed — 'sick cities,' 'the urban crisis,' 'spreading blight' — is singularly unilluminating. I doubt that most residents of most American cities would recognize in such terms a fair description of the conditions in their communities. Since such words are usually uttered or printed in Washington, D.C., or New York City, perhaps the most we can infer is that life is tough in these two places — though the staggering expense the authors of such words are willing to incur in order to live in the very center of these cities suggests that the 'crisis' is at least bearable. *Ibid.*

WILSON, Woodrow (1856-1924)

W124 — No single movement of reform in our government methods has been more significant than the rapid adoption of the so-called commission form of government in the cities of the country. The rapid spread of this reform has been extraordinary. In almost every State cities are now to be found which have been able to learn, the results have been admirable and the cities which have made the change have congratulated themselves upon it. *Commission Government (pamphlet)*

WINCHELL, Walter (1897-1972)

W125 — Broadway is the main artery of New York life — the hardened artery.

W126 — A town where they place you under contract instead of observation. [of Hollywood]

WINTER, Gibson (1916-   )

W127 — The metropolis has become an interdependent whole without adequate internal processes of communication to provide stability and direction. The most obvious symptom of this internal breakdown is the lack of political coherence in the metropolitan area — a void which has the most serious consequences for every aspect of metropolitan life, from park planning to police protection. *The Suburban Captivity of the Churches*

WINTHROP, John

W128 — Men shall say of succeeding plantacions: The Lord make it like that of New England: for we must Consider that wee shall be as a Citty upon a hill, the eies of all People are uppon us; . . .

WIRTH, Louis (1897-1952)

W129 — Ever since Aristotle's *Politics*, it has been recognized that increasing the number of inhabitants in a settlement beyond a certain limit will affect the relationships between them and the character of the city. Large numbers involve, as has been pointed out, a greater range of individual participation. Furthermore, the greater the number of individuals participating in a process of interaction, the greater is the potential differentiation between them. The personal traits, the occupations, the cultural life, and the ideas of the members of an urban community may, therefore, be

expected to range between more widely separated poles than those of rural inhabitants. *American Journal of Sociology*

W130 — The geographical frontier that in our national history has always lain to the West has suddenly disappeared; the new American frontier is in the city, for it is here that the significant changes in our life are being wrought and it is from there that they will reverberate throughout the land. It is not merely the people who actually live within the boundaries of the legally defined municipality, that have their mode of life determined for them by urban civilization, but those beyond the geographic limit of the city boundaries as well. The city has become the dominent influence upon national life. *New Horizons in Planning 1937 'The Urban Mode of Life'*

WITTGENSTEIN, Ludwig (1889-1951)

W131 — Our language can be seen as an ancient city: a maze of little streets and squares, of old and new houses, and of houses with additions from various periods; and this surrounded by a multitude of new boroughs with straight regular streets and uniform houses. *Philosophical Investigations*

WOHL, R. Richard (1921-1957)

W132 — In a very literal sense, the institutional structure of many American cities was jerry-built like many of its slums. *Urbanism, Urbanity, and the Historian*

W133 — In American cities the current of urban change has been rapid and urgent, and therefore the meaning and function of our cities for the people who live in them cannot be caught in a glance — whether by census, survey, or poll. Each city, large and small, is like a palimpsest, marked with hasty erasures, corrections, rebuilding, and redirection. Each city is the sum of its history. We become aware of this not primarily from any sense of sentimental tradition or local loyalty, but from the friction of daily urban life. *Ibid.*

W134 — It is one of the lasting ironies of American history that a people so eager and energetic in the creation and expansion of their cities — a nation which has so zestfully rushed into an urban existence — should support an elaborate network of ideologies condemning city life. *Ibid.*

W135 — It may well be that our tacit assumption that urban life, as opposed by implication to rural life, is already out of date. A thorough historical study of city life may reveal that the growth of the urban community and its expanding influence is creating and shaping a distinctive national American culture and civilizaton which blurs the line between town and country. *Ibid.*

WOLFE, Thomas (1900-1938)

W136 — For the first time his vision phrased it as it had never done before. It was a cruel city, but it was a lively one, a savage city, yet it had such tenderness; a bitter, harsh and violent catacomb of stone and steel and tunneled rock, slashed savagely with light, and roaring, fighting a constant ceaseless warfare of men and of machinery; and yet it was so sweetly and so delicately pulsed, as full of warmth, of passion and of love as it was full of hate. [of New York]

W137 — New York lays hand upon a man's bowels; he grows drunk with ecstacy; he grows young and full of glory; he feels that he can never die.

W138 — The place where men are constantly seeking to find their door and where they are doomed to wandering forever. [of the city]

W139 — [City people] endure their miserable existence because they 'don't know any better.' City people are an ignorant and conceited lot. They have no manners, no courtesy, no consideration for the rights of others, and no humanity. Everyone in the city is 'out for himself,' out to do you, out to get everything he can out of you. It is a selfish, treacherous, lonely self-seeking life. A man has friends as long as he has money in his pocket. Friends melt away from him like smoke when money goes. Moreover, all social pride and decency, the dignity of race, the authority of class is violated and destroyed in city life. *The Web and the Rock*

W140 — One belongs to New York instantly,

one belongs to it as much in five minutes as in five years. *Ibid.*

W141 — That enfabled rock, that ship of life, that swarming million-footed, tower-masted, and sky-soaring citadel that bears the magic name of the Island of Manhattan. *Ibid.*

W142 — In other times, when painters tried to paint a scene of awful desolation, they chose the desert or heath of barren rocks, and there would try to picture man in his great loneliness — the prophet in the desert . . . But for a modern painter, the most desolate scene would be a street in almost any one of our great cities on a Sunday afternoon . . . Nothing. Nothing at all. And this is what gives the scene its special quality of tragic loneliness, awful emptiness and utter desolation. Every modern city man is familiar with it. *You Can't Go Home Again*

WOLFE, Tom (1931-   )

W143 — There are men in New York who ride the subways but do not want it generally known. . . . The impulse is that the subways are for proles and the people of status travel only by cab, or perhaps once in a great while by bus. *The Kandy-Kolered Tangerine-Flake Streamline Baby*

WONDER, Stevie (1950-   )

W144 — His hair is long, his feet are hard and gritty / He spends his life walking the streets of New York City / He's almost dead from breathing in air pollution / He tried to vote but to him there's no solution / *Living for the City, Innervisions*

WOOD, Grant (1892-1942)

W145 — The artist no longer finds it necessary to migrate even to New York, or to seek any great metropolis. No longer is it necessary for him to suffer the confusing cosmopolitanism, the noise, the too intimate gregariousness of the large city. True, he may travel, he may observe, he may study in various environments, in order to develop his personality and achieve backgrounds and a perspective; but this need be little more than incidental to an educative process that centers in his own home region. *Revolt against the City*

W146 — But painting has declared its independence from Europe, and is retreating from the cities to the more American village and country life. Paris is no longer the Mecca of the American artist. *Ibid.*

W147 — Inevitable though it probably was, it seems nevertheless unfortunate that such art appreciation as developed in America in the nineteenth century had to be concentrated in the large cities. *Ibid.*

W148 — This urban growth [in the 1880's and 1890's], whose tremendous power was so effective upon the whole of American society, served, so far as art was concerned, to tighten the grip of traditional imitativeness, for the cities were far less typically American than the frontier areas whose power they usurped. Not only were they the seats of the colonial spirit, but they were inimical to whatever was new, original and alive in the truly American spirit. *Ibid.*

WOOD, Horatio

W149 — A dozen years ago, it was considered all desirable to discourage families of operatives from settling in the city; as, in times like these, the starvation

and riots of the manufacturing towns of the old world would be our inevitable lot. But the families would come and must come by a natural law. And the prophesied times have come without a thought of disturbance or a murmur of complaint; because of the influence of religion, the universality of school education, and the chances of life open to all.

WOOD, Robert C. (1923-)

W150 — A melting pot of executives, managers, white-collar workers, successful or unsuccessful, who may be distinguished only by the subtle variations of the cars they drive. [of suburbia]

W151 — Places in the country immediately outside a city (depending) upon the technological advances of the age: the automobile and rapid transit line, asphalt pavement, delivery trucks, septic tanks . . . and motor-driven pumps. [of suburbia]

W152 — A reasonable reconstruction of our heritage. [of suburbia]

W153 — The most fashionable definition of suburbia today is that it is a looking glass in which the character, behavior, and culture of middle class America is displayed. When we look at suburbanites we see ourselves. Suburbia, according to this interpretation, reflects with fidelity modern man, his way of living, his institutions and beliefs, his family, and his social associations. *Suburbia*

W154 — There is no economic reason for its existence and there is no technological basis for its support. There is only the stubborn conviction of the majority of suburbanites that it ought to exist, even though it plays havoc with both the life and government of our urban age. [of the suburb] *Ibid.*

WOODRUFF, A.M. (1912-)

W155 — For better or for worse, cities are among man's most durable artifacts. Their durability means that land, once committed to a particular use, will not be casually or capriciously recycled. An 'iron law' determines the process of recycling: property is not recycled until the land under a building is worth more without the building than the combined value of land and building for any purpose to which the building can be put. *Recycling Urban Land*

WOOLF, Virginia (1882-1941)

W156 — In people's eyes, in the swing, tramp, and trudge; in the bellow and uproar; the carriages, motor cars, omnibuses, vans, sandwich men shuffling and swinging; brass bands; barrel organs; in the triumph and the jingle and the strange high singing of some aeroplane overhead was what she loved; life; London; this moment in June. *Mrs. Dalloway*

WOOLLCOTT, Alexander (1887-1943)

W157 — A hick town is one where there is no place to go where you shouldn't go.

WORDSWORTH, William (1770-1850)

W158 — Once did She hold the gorgeous east in fee, / And was the safeguard of the West. . . . / Venice, the eldest child of liberty. / She was a maiden city, bright and free; / No guile seduced, no force could violate; / And, when she took unto herself a mate, / She must espouse the everlasting Sea. / *On the Extinction of the Venetian Republic*

W159 — Earth has not anything to show more fair: / Dull would he be of soul who could pass by / A sight so touching in its majesty: / This City now doth, like a garment, wear / The beauty of the morning; silent, bare, / Ships, towers, domes, theatres, and temples lie / Open unto the fields, and to the sky; / All bright and glittering in the smokeless air. / [of London] *The Prelude*

W160 — O Friend! one feeling was there which belonged / To this great city, by exclusive right; / How often, in the overflowing streets, / Have I gone forwards with the crowd, and said / Unto myself, 'The face of every one / That passes by me is a mystery!' / *Ibid.*

W161 — Oh, blank confusion! true epitome / Of what the mighty City is herself, / To thousands upon thousands of her sons, / Living amid the same perpetual whirl / Of trivial objects, melted and reduced / To one identity. / *Ibid.*

W162 — . . . what the mighty City is itself / To all except a straggler here and there, / To the whole swarm of its inhabitants; / An undistinguishable world to men, / The slaves unrespited of low pursuits, / Living amid the same perpetual flow / Of trivial objects, melted and reduced / To one identity, by differences / That have no law, no meaning and no end. / *Ibid.*

WRIGHT, Frank Lloyd (1869-1959)

W163 — I doubt if there is anything in the world uglier than a midwestern city. *(address in Evanston, Illinois)*

W164 — It is as if you tipped the United States up so all the commonplace people slid down here into Southern California. [of Los Angeles]

W165 — The outcome of the cities will depend on the race between the automobile and the elevator, and anyone who bets on the elevator is crazy. *The Chrome-Plated Nightmare (Television Program, May 27, 1974)*

W166 — Civilization always seemed to need the city. The city expressed, contained, and tried to conserve what the flower of the civilization that built it most cherished, although it was always infested with the worst elements of society as a wharf is infested with rats. So the city may be said to have served civilization. But the civilization that built the city invariably died with it. Did the civilizations themselves die *of* it? *The Future of Architecture*

W167 — Even the small town is too large. It will gradually merge into the general non-urban development. Ruralism as distinguished from urbanism is American, and truly democratic. *Ibid.*

W168 — Our modern civilization . . . may not only survive the city but may profit by it; probably the death of the city is to be the greatest service the machine will ultimately render the human being if, by means of it, man conquers. If the machine conquers, it is conceivable that man will again remain to perish with his city, because the city, like all minions of the machine has grown up in man's image — minus only the living impetus that is man. The city is itself only

man-the-machine — the deadly shadow of sentient man. *Ibid.*

W169 — The skyscraper is . . . the landlord's ruse to hold the profits not only of concentration but of superconcentration: in the skyscraper itself we see the commercial expedient that enables the landlord to exploit the city to the limit, and exploit it by ordinance. *Ibid.*

W170 — And when urban men of commerce themselves succeed, they become more than ever vicarious. Soon these very successful men sink into the sham luxury their city life so continually produces. But they create nothing! Spiritually impotent, a fixation has them where impotence wants them: fixation in a cliche. *The Living City*

W171 — Both landlord and tenant are the living apotheosis of rent. Rent! Always rent in some form is the city. If not quite yet

parasites — parasitic all. *Ibid.*

W172 — But life itself has become intolerably restless; a mere tenant of the big landlord: the 'big city.' Yes . . . above the belt, if he is properly citified, the citizen has long lost sight of the true aim of normal human existence. He has accepted not only substitute means but substitute aims and ends. *Ibid.*

W173 — The cave dweller became cliff dweller. He began to build cities. Establishment was his idea. His God was a malicious murderer. His own statue, made by himself more terrible than himself, was really his God; a God also hiding away. He erected this God into a mysterious covenant. When he could, he made his God of gold. He still does. *Ibid.*

W174 — The first and most important form of rent contributing to overgrowth of cities, resulting in poverty and unhappiness, is rent for land: land values created as improvements or by growth, held by some fortuitous fortune's accidental claim to some lucky piece of realty, private but protected by law. Profits from this adventitious form of fortune create a series of white-collarites — satellites of various other unearned increments, like real-estate traffic in more or less lucky land areas. The skyscraper as abused is also an instance of adventitious increment. The city the natural home of this form of 'fortune.' *Ibid.*

W175 — New York is the biggest mouth in the world. *Ibid.*

W176 — So it has already come true in our overgrown cities of today that the terms of feudal thinking are changing, if not by name, to terms of money and commercial diplomacy. But the old form of city, except as a market, has little or nothing substantial to give modern civilization above wagery, little or nothing above the belt — except degeneration. *Ibid.*

W177 — Were motor oil and castor oil to dry up, the great big city would soon cease to function: the citizens would promptly perish. *Ibid.*

W178 — Clear out eight hundred thousand people and preserve it as a museum piece.

[of Boston] *The New York Times, November 27, 1955*

W179 — New York: Prison towers and modern posters for soap and whisky. Pittsburgh: Abandon it. *Ibid.*

WURSTER, Catherine Bauer (1905-1964)

W180 — Traditionally, an urban community was a city, and the nature of a city was obvious. In a limited space it brought together a wide variety of people; it made them accessible to one another, provided them with communication with the outside world, and stimulated them to engage in many kinds of specialized but interdependent activity. The city had a government whose essential functions were to resolve the people's differences in the common interest and to provide their necessary services. The city was a little world and its tight-knit, articulated form reflected its structural unity. *The Form and Structure of the Future Urban Complex*

X

X, Malcolm (1925-1965)

X1 — Teen-agers in the ghetto see the hell caught by their parents struggling to get somewhere. They make up their own minds they would rather be like the hustlers whom they see dressed 'sharp' and flashing money. So the ghetto youth become attracted to the hustler worlds of dope, thievery, prostitution, general crime and immorality. *Autobiography of Malcolm X*

Y

YEATS, William Butler (1865-1939)

Y1 — What were all the world's alarms / To mighty Paris when he found / Sleep upon a golden bed / That first dawn in Helen's arms? / *Words for Music Perhaps*

YLVISAKER, Paul (1921-)

Y2 — The City has not just grown bigger than its boundaries — it has outgrown the concept and vocabulary of the city itself. The distinction, at least in this country, has been blotted out between agricultural and urban life; television, the automobile, and the agricultural revolution have taken care of that. Geographical distinctions are also fading; what we call the City today is to all intents and purposes the same as the nation. And in another generation or two — if we can survive the savagery of this latter-day and I think last-ditch stand of nationalism — urban society will dissolve into world society. *The Shape of the Future (address)*

Y3 — Crying the demise of the centralized city in the midst of a booming Manhattan may seem foolhardy; I still think the prediction is accurate. We will spill out onto the land for another generation at least.

Manhattan will survive longer than most; an exception, but a changing and misleading one. Already its downtown is an island of the old order in a flooding sea of the new; it is a Potemkin Village which obscures the view of the gray and green realities immediately beyond. *Ibid.*

YOUNG, Arthur (1741-1820)

Y4 — This great city appears to be in many respects the most ineligible and inconvenient for the residence of a person of small fortune of any that I have seen; and by far inferior to London. [of Paris] *Travels*

YOUNG, Coleman A. (Mayor of Detroit) (1918-)

Y5 — Downtown is an anchor and a radiator. Literally everything radiates from here. And if we have a rotten center, then we have a rotting city. *The Los Angeles Times, October 31, 1977*

Y6 — Detroit must diversify its industrial and commercial base if it is to escape the situation in which we now find ourselves. Every time — as the saying goes — the automobile industry catches a cold, Detroit catches pneumonia. *U.S. News & World Report, April 7, 1975*

YOUNGER, Evelle J. (Attorney General, California) (1918-)

Y7 — A city is like an apartment house. If it is filled, there should be no effort to bring in any more people. The concept that 'there's room for one more' just doesn't apply. *San Francisco Examiner, October 25, 1972*

Z

ZANGWILL, Israel (1864-1926)

Z1 — The great stone desert. [of New York City]

Z2 — Jerusalem, like Heaven, is more a state of mind than a place.

Z3 — There she lies, the great Melting Pot — listen! Can't you hear the roaring and the bubbling? There gapes her mouth — the harbour where a thousand mammoth feeders freight.... Celt and Latin, Slav and Teuton, Greek and Syrian, Jew and Gentile ... what is the glory of Rome and Jerusalem where all nations come to worship and look back, compared with the glory of America, where all races and nations come to labour and look forward! *The Melting Pot*

ZARUBIN, Madame

Z4 — Moscow wonderful, concerts wonderful, ballet wonderful, opera wonderful, Moscow big city — Ottawa nothing (*nichevo*) — cinema, cinema, cinema.

ZETTERLING, Mai (1925-)

Z5 — Stockholm is the city that provides

commuter tickets for dogs on trains and buses. It is probably the most law-abiding town in Western Europe, with laws and restrictions, reforms and protections against almost everything. A city with the architecture of seven centuries and in at least seventeen styles. Its god is a silent Lutheran God with little impact on society. Efforts have been made to disestablish the Lutheran Church. Most young people, indeed most people, are negative or indifferent to religion. *Quoted in Cities, John McGreevy*

Z6 — There are many Stockholms and the name means many things to many people, but for me it is the city of a thousand trades, the city of silent crowds, the city with no faces, the city of no dreams, the city with a million hidden people, the city with the greatest solitude, the city of prosperity, the city with its hard liquor zone. *Ibid.*

Z7 — This is a city poised between East and West that has the highest life expectancy in the world. And the highest standard of living in Europe. Everything is organized for its people, except sleep. [of Stockholm] *Ibid.*

ZICKERMAN, David (cab driver)

Z8 — Who the hell looks up in this town? Who has time? [of New York] *The New York Times*

ZIMBARDO, Philip G. (1933-   )

Z9 — Vandalism is rebellion with a cause. To prevent it, we must combat the cause itself — social indifference, apathy, the loss of community, neighborhood and family values. *Quoted in Reader's Digest*

ZINCKLE, F.B.

Z10 — The wheel within Massachusetts. Boston therefore is often called the 'hub of the world,' since it has been the source and fountain of the ideas that have reared and made America.

ZUCKMAYER, Carl (1896-1977)

Z11 — This city devoured talents and human energies with a ravenous appetite, grinding them small, digesting them or rapidly spitting them out again. It sucked into itself with hurricane force all the ambitious in Germany, the true and the false, the nonentities and the prize winners, and, after it had swallowed them, ignored them. [of Berlin in 1920] *A Piece of Myself*

ZUEBLIN, Charles (1866-1924)

Z12 — The future belongs not to the city, but to the suburb. *A Decade of Civic Development*

ZWEIG, Stefan (1881-1942)

Z13 — Nowhere did one experience the naive and yet wondrously wise freedom of existence more happily than in Paris, . . . *World of Yesterday*

Z14 — Since 1870, when Berlin had changed from the rather small, sober, and by no means rich capital of the Kingdom of Prussia into the seat of the German Emperor, the homely town on the Spree had taken a mighty upswing . . . The large concerns and the wealthy families moved to Berlin, and new wealth, paired with a strong sense of daring, opened to the theater and to architecture greater opportunities than in any other large German city . . . So it was natural that the young people of the entire Reich and even Austria thronged to Berlin, and results proved to the talented among them that they were right . . . *Ibid.*

ZWICKEY, Robert

Z15 — A nice city to visit but the suburbs thereabouts are better. [of San Francisco]

Cities
Index

CHICAGO A46, A47, A48, A49, A76, A77,
A89, A93, A178, A215, A219, B45,
B86, B159, B218, B224, B233, B242,
B253, B292, B306, B314, C22, C45,
C103, D22, D91, D92, D94, D95,
D97, E26, F3, F49, G20, G96, H34,
H44, H45, H62, H86, H126, H222,
J6, K5, K41, K43, L23, L68, L74,
L111, L112, L116, M37, M38, M71,
M126, M131, M137, M192, M250,
M272, N29, O6, O8, P51, P52, P53,
R6, R22, R35, R41, R54, R74, R91,
S7, S18, S21, S22, S24, S25, S29,
S50, S103, S185, S191, S198, S218,
S234, T21, T22, T23, W1, W33, W61,
W89
CHINON R4
CINCINNATI F66, H126
CLEVELAND B9, H124, J6, L96, S196
"COKETOWN" D35
COLOGNE C61, C106, P40, S13
CONCORD T43
CONSTANTINOPLE (See also ISTANBUL)
A62, C90, C128, C136, D67, F61, J9,
P104, T110, T116, W85
COPENHAGEN J4, W25, W85
CORDOBA E23
CORINTH A116, C171, H38, H47, H137
CORK H123
CUZCO M223
DALLAS B292, G150, K52, M37
DAMASCUS B292, M218, M221, T108
DANZIG G111
DARMSTADT S13
DELHI M249, P45, W85
DENVER D59, G95,
DERBY (England) H164
DERNE W85
DETROIT A85, B319, G54, G150, G161,
H103, L67, M37, S27, S35, S211,
U1, Y6
DEVON A118
"DIS" B292, M123
DONCASTER (England) H164
DOVER (England) P25
DRESDEN W3
DUBLIN A111, H123, H211, H212, J78,
M197, M224, S180, W85
DUBUQUE F17
DULUTH F44, K59
DUNMOW (England) H164
DUSSELDORF W15
EASTPORT (Maine) D112
EDINBURGH A183, B122, C47, C69, G20,
G113, H21, M254, W85
EDMONTON A89
EDOM B123
EPHESUS C171

EXETER S141
FERRARA B292
FIESOLE B256, U3
FLINT C178, P91, S196
FLORENCE A52, A107, B256, B278, C14,
C69, C134, D109, E25, E46, F52,
G52, G95, I8, L88, L124, M19, M57,
M176, P3, P83, S6, S112, U3, W60
FRANKFURT S13
GAUNT A173
GENEVA A3, K60, M225, M243, R70
GENOA H166, T109, T110
GETTYSBURG H163
GHENT M176
GLASGOW G20, L4, L5, O17, R41, R112,
W85
GOMORRAH B17, B96, B292, C31, D75,
K31, M193
"GOTHAM" A161, B220, I11
GREEN BAY B293
GROTON (Connecticut) B63
THE HAGUE W85
HAIFA M234
HALIFAX K48
HAMBURG J4, M221, S13, T58, W85
HAMPDEN (England) G115
HANGCHOW P84, S38
HARTFORD B202
HAVANA F10, J75
HELSINKI G109
HENOCH B95
HERCULANEUM S184, T111
HIROSHIMA M222
HOBOKEN H86, H124
HOLLYWOOD A54, B292, G54, L63, M28,
M311, P37, T40, W126
HONG KONG B287, C141, E11, E12, K44,
M239, M241
HOUSTON M37, W9
INDIANAPOLIS M162
ISFAHAN M215
ISTANBUL (See also CONSTANTINOPLE)
G148, M232, M245, W116
JERICHO B106, B107, T67, T78
JERUSALEM A43, A154, B79, B85, B99,
B100, B103, B105, B113, B114,
B116, B117, B119, B120, B124,
B126, B127, B128, B130, B144,
B147, B149, B150, B157, B168,
B169, B170, B209, B255, B292, C31,
C58, C61, C171, D50, D75, E25, F12,
F19, F60, F65, G150, K62, L26, M56,
M57, M58, M176, M234, N9, N21,
P20, R54, S68, S146, S233, T11,
T107, W98, W99, Z2, Z3
JOHANNESBURG M233
JUNEAU N12
KAIROUAN L39

KANSAS CITY C97, C98, C99, D1, K56,
    M37, M104
KARACHI M249, W116
KEOKUK (Iowa) H86
KEW N34
KIEV B80, F12
KINGSTON (Canada) D29
KINSHASA W117
KNOXVILLE S27
KYOTO A44, M248
LACEDAEMON M3
LA PAZ M221
LAS VEGAS A17, A21, B292, C129
LEEDS E68, G95
LEIPZIG H66
LEMSTER (England) H164
LENINGRAD (See also ST. PETERSBURG
    and PETROGRAD) A39, G107,
    G153, M103, M252, U7, W45
LEVITTOWN (Pennsylvania) A44, G6, G7
LEXINGTON T43
LHASA S233
LIMA A121, F10, V33, M61, M236, P60
LIMERICK H123, W85
LISBON W85
LIVERPOOL A44, W85
LONDON A3, A7, A12, A16, A52, A74, A75,
    A123, A124, A141, A146, A148,
    A183, A184, A212, A243, B40, B43,
    B52, B167, B171, B173, B187, B188,
    B200, B201, B204, B205, B213,
    B218, B256, B284, B297, B331,
    B332, C18, C23, C24, C25, C44, C50,
    C69, C70, C82, C112, C132, C134,
    C147, C149, C154, C157, C159,
    C166, D31, D32, D33, D47, D48,
    D49, D52, D53, D54, D55, D87, D89,
    D99, D101, D108, D109, D110, E15,
    E16, E25, E31, E38, E41, E67, E68,
    F6, F15, F34, F43, G14, G20, G27,
    G49, G55, G56, G57, G105, G114,
    G132, G141, G147, G148, G152, H5,
    H22, H26, H47, H49, H51, H55,
    H57, H66, H114, H150, H164, H186,
    H208, H210, I13, J1, J9, J21, J23,
    J26, J27, J28, J29, J32, J40, J66, J68,
    J69, J70, J71, J72, J73, K32, K46,
    K47, K62, L6, L7, L8, L21, L30, L33,
    L34, L40, L44, L46, L47, L88, L126,
    M10, M57, M86, M90, M92, M93,
    M97, M98, M123, M126, M135,
    M143, M144, M148, M168, M194,
    M211, M232, M235, M254, M256,
    M259, M260, N17, N34, O17, P30,
    P31, P45, P46, P58, P70, P81, P88,
    P90, P99, P102, R3, R54, R95, S47,
    S67, S69, S79, S87, S92, S95, S100,
    S112, S116, S170, S181, S192,

    S198, S203, S210, S231, S232, T1,
    T27, T59, T61, T98, T100, T101,
    T128, U6, U7, V3, V7, V28, V41,
    V43, W13, W23, W26, W85, W103,
    W117, W156, W159, Y4
LOS ALAMOS D71
LOS ANGELES A53, A59, A85, A112, A119,
    A126, B1, B9, B30, B31, B32, B33,
    B34, B35, B37, B38, C11, C51, C56,
    F5, F17, G70, G85, G129, G150,
    H213, J54, K5, K57, L72, L111,
    M23, M29, M63, M64, M106, M107,
    M177, M204, N29, O4, R11, R89,
    S26, S78, S106, S129, S132, S182,
    T40, T102, W31, W59, W164
LOUISVILLE (Kentucky) T65
LOURDES B292, S233
LUNA M6
MADRID B296, G150, M238, R85
MAINZ S13
MANCHESTER (England) A92, B297, C26,
    C46, D51, E64, E68, L30, S53, S181,
    U3, W15, W85
MANDALAY K46
MARRAKECH G148
MARSEILLES G96, M291, W85
MECCA B292, I3, J54, S233, T127, W146
MELBOURNE A164, W85,
MELIBOEUS V25
MEMPHIS (Egypt) A7, P44
MEMPHIS (Tennessee) A7, S27
MEXICO CITY F10, F12, W117
MIAMI A58, H67, H68, M268, S187
MIAMI BEACH B163
MILAN A107, T110, W15
MILETUS J83
MILWAUKEE B292, D10, L68, M35
MINNEAPOLIS F18, S27, S188, S189
MOGADORE W85
MONACO M60
MONMOUTH (England) H164
MONROVIA W85
MONTPAZIER L39
MONTREAL B70, B237, B317, D88, G128,
    M59, M226, S105, T124
MOSCOW A60, A80, B80, B292, B296, C35,
    C50, G96, G99, G145, G150, H15,
    K27, K78, L60, M244, M254, P2, Z4
MUNICH M221, V38
MUSSELBURGH C47
MYCENAE H47
NAGASAKI G96
NAPLES B179, G80, H34, K44, L120, M241,
    R41, S3, S102, T94, T112, T115,
    W85
NASHVILLE H78
NAZARETH B138
"NEPHELOCOCCYGIA" A80

M244, T58, T59, W117
TOLEDO (Ohio) B292, S196
TOLEDO (Spain) M146
TORONTO B234, B236, B297, C181, D28,
G106, G107, H133, J36, M195, P49,
U5
TORQUAY K44
TOULOUSE A192, P17, U3
TRIPOLI W85
TROY B330, B333, D97, F64, H47, H98,
H130, H181, L106, L127, M173,
O27, P42, S75, T20, V23, V24,
W104, Y1
TULSA D20
TUNIS C117
TUSCULUM M4
TYRE B93, B292, C27, M94
UR A132, A167, H48, T78, W116
URARTU J9
UTICA (New York) S104
VALPARAISO W85
VANCOUVER C10, C27, E17, M226
VATICAN CITY M60
VENICE A73, B81, B172, B286, B315, B326,
C19, C69, C134, D4, D15, D37, D109,
G17, G19, G79, G83, G110, G152,
H168, H173, J4, J9, J25, J30, L110,
M12, M46, M103, M147, M176,
M189, M219, M237, M241, P70, P95,
R87, R106, S43, S72, S80, S96, S97,
S158, T104, T119, T121, T122, W5,
W158
VERONA D37
VERSAILLES T91

VETULONIA J9
VICTORIA (Canada) K44
VIENNA A3, A134, B292, B303, B304, G148,
G150, G151, G153, G156, H18, H20,
H111, H112, H207, M57, M142,
M232, S45, S160, S192, V42, W3,
W4, W85
VIRGINIA CITY B247
WARSAW G150, G152, M221
WASHINGTON, D.C. B11, B246, B283, C8,
C166, D14, D98, E7, G96, G122,
G147, H147, H207, J56, L48, L56,
L87, M37, M39, M197, M228, P2,
Q4, R31, R53, R54, R64, R90, S48,
S206, T89, T91, W123
WAST J83
WATERLOO (Belgium) H163
WEIMAR T78
WELLINGTON M241
WHITTIER (California) N28
WICHITA S25
WILLIAMSBURG (Virginia) M25
WILLOW RUN D71
WINNIPEG K45, M226
"XANADU" B292
YEDO W85
YONKERS (New York) M193
YORK A183
YOUNGSTOWN S196
YPRES K56
ZANZIBAR K38
"ZENITH" M22
ZURICH I4, I5

Subject
Index